Buddhist Sutras:
Lesson Book

Buddhist Sutras: Lesson Book

Introduction to Rational Buddhism

IRV JACOB

authorHOUSE®

AuthorHouse™
1663 Liberty Drive
Bloomington, IN 47403
www.authorhouse.com
Phone: 1-800-839-8640

Published by AuthorHouse 12/06/2012

ISBN: 978-1-4772-9416-1 (sc)
ISBN: 978-1-4772-9417-8 (e)

Library of Congress Control Number: 2012922288

Contents

Introduction to Rational Buddhism

Read this book instead of eating chocolate, ice cream, cake or other comfort foods in the evenings. This is a systematic introductory study of the dharma of Buddhism, intended as a first book. It is organized for teachers and students alike. "Teaching and learning are said to be the real 'miracles' of Buddhism." (Inthisan, pg.15) This is a series of quotations, lesson plans, workbook pages, a glossary, bibliography, and there is a serious teaching about meditation practice in each lesson.

I have been acquainted with Buddhism and meditation for the last 45 years and in 2000 I went back to school and became a certified secondary teacher. Putting these two motivations together created a belief that studying and doing (practicing meditation, etc.) Buddhism in a thorough-going and active way is right for anyone who is serious about improving their lives. So preparing this lesson book that I could use repeatedly, seemed like a worthwhile and "skillful" effort for many different reasons, and now I want to share it.

The Beginning: I began this detailed study of Buddhism after a trip to Thailand (April 2007). In each of my (then) five trips to Thailand, I had significant and increasingly meaningful experiences with Buddhism, and finally I learned that these teachings reinforce my core values and that I can maintain my identity as an atheist and freethinker and still benefit from a Buddhist practice. In fact, it is probably a "Western" idea to juxtapose Buddhism with other religious teachings, since in "Eastern" culture, living Buddhism is almost always integrated with local religious teachings whether deistic or not. From the beginning as a tourist and guest at various shrines and ceremonies, I was intrigued. Subsequently as I wandered around visiting wats and studying the dharma I was impressed with the practical nature of Buddhist teaching, and even opened my mind to the mystical and esoteric nature of Buddhism. On other trips I visited Buddhist shrines and temples in Korea, Japan, throughout China (including Taiwan and Hong Kong) and most recently Singapore, and have always found these locations and the symbolism awe inspiring.

While in Thailand in 2007, I purchased a few books and two others were given to me by "Pa" my daughter-in-law's father who is a well-established member of the Thai Bar for attorneys, and an active, life-long Theravada Buddhist. I was inspired by both my Buddhist family and these books, but only indirectly. No one said "You should do this." Based on the Theravada Buddhist text (Wee), I estimated that it would take at a minimum of thirty consecutive lessons, given one each day possibly, for an instructor to adequately introduce these teachings. In this way a student can learn the basics of meditation, and more importantly, internalize the life style changes required to become a sincere novice Buddhist. I expected to learn as I progressed, to either become disenchanted or enamored with Buddhism, and was open to either outcome. I subsequently realized that the best kind of instruction is this progressive training, like learning how to dance practicing each move until eventually one becomes an accomplished amateur performer. (This format and series of lesson plans has proven very flexible and useful.)

Most of the mystery I found previously in Buddhism was apparently due to the foreign language issue, because the teachings generally are quite frank, practical and transparent. There are mysterious teachings in each of the most active traditions, but these can either be accepted or viewed as aesthetic expressions of our inherent human nature. The esoteric practices can be viewed as cosmological traditions grown up without the benefit of modern 20th century scientific discoveries (as with the development of Christianity). The art, the icons, the rituals and symbolism of Buddhism are most often devices to help devotees remember and incorporate the teachings into their lives. Buddhist sculpture (icons) and art in general can be viewed as a kind of language, when we know the meanings the mysterious nature usually disappears, and we see how these symbols and devices are important aspects of living in the "Eastern" traditions (where the majority of people have been illiterate for the 2,500 years during which Buddhism has evolved).

I now have a heightened appreciation for the spirituality of people in Southern Asia and their practice of the religion of Buddhism. I compare this enlightened sensitivity to the Western philosophic tradition. Spirituality in "Eastern" cultures is made more explicit by the presence of the icons and details of architecture (i.e. Spirit Houses and shrines along each street) that relate to Buddhist teachings. This points to the importance of an integrated kind of life rather than to a life as in the West that is more compartmentalized. The important teachings of mindfulness and awareness are fundamental elements not only of Buddhist training, but also of daily life. That makes this basic training important as a foundation for becoming an accomplished Buddhist.

The Lessons: The lesson format used here follows the general outline for lesson plans used in American public education, which is one of the features that makes this book unique. This does not represent a system of teaching; it is merely a guide and facilitation to help organize the information. Inside this structure I have added the famous instructional devises used by Siddhartha Buddha which follow three principal categories: sequence, technique and practice (this goes beyond the American "scope and sequence.")

The *sequence*: 1-a. after the appropriate preliminaries and review of each previous session, there are quotations for discussion about alms giving, receiving or compassion as it applies to the Training Objectives for each lesson (First Progressive), 1-b. this is followed by quotations dealing with moral principles and codes that arise from the daily material (Second Progressive), 1-c. then there are more quotations that explain the dharma (the teachings) that is pertinent (Third Progressive) and details about meditation and history.

2. The *technique* of "pointing out" means, each lesson consists almost entirely of quotations from various authors, with references and only brief commentaries, rather than a synthesis that I have re-written for which I might claim authorship. I use simple conventions for giving references; accumulate a bibliography of primary and secondary texts, and a lengthy glossary of terms. I

have included daily readings to prompt insight during meditation. The lessons can be used in a "silent retreat" or in a training that encourages discussion and the comparison of ideas, self-study, or sharing of questioning and inspirations.

3. The *practice* incorporated into each lesson is also assigned as personal meditation and intended to be **the most important part** of the learning process. Students are expected to enter the sala (classroom) in silence as with this description of Zen practice: "All usual social greetings and communications are suspended as we leave our social selves behind at the door [with our sandals]. We come to the [sala to learn and] to practice [Zen]. We do not come to make demands on anyone else . . . Communication with others develops differently as we sit in silence. It becomes deep, profound, and lasting. We speak and are spoken to in different ways [than outside the sala]." (Shoshanna, pp. 15-16) Each day there are several reviews, and the intention is to foster extensive discussion to "protect" students' understanding and correct any misconceptions. Assignments consist of meditation practices, insight questions relating to the daily readings, and an increasingly rigorous Sangha regimen. There is a *Workbook* page for each chapter to help each student review the day's lesson and engage in the particular step of meditation being suggested. It is appropriate to use the word "practice" because to learn Buddhism it is best to follow a "training" plan not intellectual arguments, theorizing or even extensive memorization.

The word "sutra" as used in the title means thread (or lesson), a metaphor to suggest a linking of thoughts and teachings. Thus it is appropriate and even traditional in Buddhism and other Indian teachings to suggest that this series of lessons is a sutra of connected teachings about Buddhism. As suggested, the lessons present excerpts tersely in the manner suggested elsewhere as "pointing-out", and participants are to hear these quotations, make notes and develop and share their own interpretations. After meditation and after having received insights, students can share what they choose of their inspirations and spontaneous journaling. The meditations and "*protecting*" is part of the essential work that converts the lessons from intellectual exercise to spiritual practice.

These lessons emphasize ". . . the essential spiritual orientation of Buddhism, its core teachings and its openness to the whole

Buddhist tradition . . . [this is a] flexible and exploratory approach to understanding what Buddhism should look like in the modern world." (Vishvapani, pg. 27) The goal of Buddhist dharma—Teachings—as well as the *Buddhist Sutras,* is to make a transformation in the mind of the participants and thus have a significant and positive impact on each person's life. "There is, of course, an enormous diversity within Buddhism and no fixed standard of orthodoxy. Nevertheless, even differing conceptions of the authentic tradition—and each school has some notion of orthodoxy—reveal a common ground of discussion." (de Bary, pg. i) These lessons are intended to facilitate individual study and stimulate interest, clarify and combine intellectual effort with practice. Thinking about this activity as parallel to learning to dance, however, rather than learning about history, literature or science, is a useful perspective.

It is important to repeat and emphasize that the practice beyond the lessons is the essential ingredient of a rational Buddhist training. "There are both direct and indirect ways of transforming the mind. Meditation is the most direct method, because in meditation the mind changes itself. But many other activities can have a positive, even transforming, effect through less direct means: friendship, Right Livelihood, and [participation in] the arts can all be seen as practices in this sense . . ." (Vishvapani, pg. 45) Furthermore it is possible to rigorously test one's self-discipline, growth in awareness and equanimity when one engages in meaningful, daily activities with family and friends.

"Practice (which means meditating, discussion and studying) needs to be regular and systematic. Some people are attracted to Buddhism from a desire for spiritual or psychic attainments. But genuine and lasting change means getting to grips with the whole of one's experience . . . people coming to Buddhism may start by feeling attracted to advanced practices, but eventually they need to follow the 'path of regular steps,' starting with the most basic elements of Buddhist practice, and building up from there [paradoxically to emptiness.]" (Vishvapani, pg. 45) Furthermore, ". . . The mind is always moving, always processing new ideas, new perceptions, and new sensations. That's its job. Meditation is about learning to work with the mind as it is, not about trying to force it into some sort of Buddhist straitjacket." (Mingyur, pg. 196)

"Buddha:" in these lessons when capitalized refers to Siddhartha Gautama Buddha, also referred to as Shakyamuni. When not capitalized "buddha" refers to the title in general, or buddhahood inherent in each person that can blossom into "enlightenment." Those who follow the entire course of lessons will be initiated progressively, and informally from being "Student" to "Practitioner" to "Stream Enterer" to "Samahito" (concentrated mind) to being "Arahant." The purpose for doing this is to acknowledge the training that has been accomplished and the growth each person has achieved, and to again "protect" the insights that arise from individual practice and meditation. Other terms (and spellings) could be chosen to designate these levels of knowledge and practice, but these are identifiers often found in Buddhist literature that give skillful recognition to the effort and progress made by each student.

Buddha is thought to have been born toward the end of the sixth century B.C. There are many intriguing myths associated with his birth and youth up to the time, at age 29 or so, he left his sheltering home to become an ascetic yogi. His early life was near Kapilavastu to the north of what is now India, at the foot of the Himalaya Mountains near the present frontier of Nepal. "The life of Sakya is divided by the Buddhist theologians into twelve 'acts' . . ." (Getty, pg. xvii) and this has become a liturgy for memorization by many young aspirants to the clergy of Buddhism in many locations. Much of Buddha's life story, and the history of his innovation **"The Middle Way",** to the extent that it is known, will unfold with the sequence of these lessons. It is significant to note that he repudiated his original act of leaving his family to pursue asceticism, and along with his enlightenment came a reintegration with his family and community. In fact many of his family members joined his Sangha as lay members and some became teachers and monks themselves.

Modern Teaching: It may be a doctrine unique among religions that "Buddhists are taught to compare an opinion with teachings, reason, and actuality to determine whether it is true." (Mizuno, pg. 183) Consequently, these lessons are not dogmatic and do not rely substantially on the mystic nor mythological (nor Tantric) traditions that have evolved in many Hindu, Yoga and even some Buddhist sects. I have not relied on the hyperbole that makes up many of the sutras from ancient sources, but these poetic writings can inspire and guide those who choose to use them as part of their practice. This kind of critical thinking has been the pattern of my life since I was a teenager, and as it turns out, is a key feature of Buddhism that, once discovered, opened the door to my expanded interest and now to this immersion.

In fact the more I progressed in preparing these lessons the further apart I came from any of the esoteric or even mildly mystical teachings, and the closer I came to the rational teachings attributed to Buddha. "After having made a thorough investigation of the doctrines of the religions and philosophies of his time in order to determine which were correct and perfect, he compiled the distinctive teachings like the Law of Causation [which anticipates modern day scientific inquire, including physics and psychology] that distinguish Buddhism from other religions. Consequently, Buddhism has a rational foundation enabling it to withstand any criticism on the theoretical plane. Its rationalism is not concerned solely with abstract truth for its own sake but is a basis for actual practice or religious faith. This means that Buddhist faith is not merely unfounded enthusiasm but a practical faith with a firm rational and ethical basis." (Mizuno, pg. 159)

"The turn of the 21st century presents both opportunities and dangers for Theravada in the West: Will the Buddha's teachings be patiently studied and put into practice, and allowed to establish deep roots in Western soil, for the benefit of many generations to come? Will the current popular Western climate of 'openness' and cross-fertilization between spiritual traditions lead to the emergence of a strong new form of Buddhist practice unique to the modern era, or will it simply lead to confusion and the dilution of these priceless teachings? These are open questions; only time will tell." (Bullitt, internet) To further confirm the relevance of Buddhism, ". . . modern Hindus do not regard the Buddha as an outsider . . . he is considered a manifestation of the great god Vishnu, one of the Hindu trinity, who descends into the world in various forms at particularly difficult times to help set things right. The Hindu system derived much from Buddha's teaching, and Buddhism, during the more than fifteen hundred years it was part of the Indian spiritual scene, also derived much from Hinduism" (Snelling, pg. 29) Many traditions incorporate nature and mystical teachings, but it is left up to the individual to incorporate "super-natural" (i.e. Christian), esoteric or intuitive (call it what you may) teachings into his/her belief and practice.

We suspend our rational thinking long enough and in the same way we might when reading, feeling or writing poetry with the intention of being inspired and moved emotionally. And likewise, each time I have used these lessons they have been improved, since everything is impermanent! For example, during my visit to Thailand in April 2008 I came across the teachings of the famous monk Buddhadasa Bhikkhu. After I attended a retreat a year later, I made adjustments to *Buddhist Sutras: Lesson Book* accordingly.

Sequential Format for Lessons

Lesson Title: **The topic of each Lesson**

Lesson Number: **Preface (Each lesson proceeds based on this format.)**

Rationale: This section contains a brief description of why a lesson topic was chosen. Siddhartha Buddha was considered a master teacher during his 45 years of traveling and preaching. His success is often attributed to the way he could simplify a lesson and create a sequential, discursive development in the unfolding of the truths he wished to communicate. Quite apart from the unique information that he taught—his innovative concept of The Middle Way—his teaching methods are an inspirational model and even a paradigm of how lessons concerning difficult and often very personal subjects might be presented. The people who come to these lessons are self-selected and presumably experienced at least in a cursory way with Buddhism, Yoga or some other "new-age teaching." Practitioners are expected to be receptive and positive toward Buddhism, and there is no need nor attempt to proselytize, argue or convince anyone to be involved actively in this course of training.

Discussion of Prior Lesson: As the previous assignments are reviewed and shared, students are invited to "protect" personal inspirations and experiences since the previous lesson. It is this experiencing of the dharma that ought to be the most sought after result of

Buddhist meditation and teaching (in contrast to intellectual development). Students are encouraged to keep their discussion in the "present" and on topic to protect their new understanding of the dharma. There will be other opportunities to share and discuss previous learning gains and life experiences.

Training Objective: The teacher offers a brief summary of the goals and dharma that are covered by this Lesson, previewing the most important information to be learned. There is to be a round of discussion relating to what is read after each topic, and frequently during each lesson. Ask often: What do you want to learn about this Topic? These lessons are intended for 30 consecutive days, but could be used as a night class option, or with three to five meetings each week (or one per week for thirty weeks with changes.) The lessons incorporate the best rational teachings offered by Siddhartha Buddha and his principal successors, and it is important to remind participants that this is a training experience not unlike learning to dance.

Materials Required: Lessons usually have different requirements, but both the lesson period (usually early in the morning) and the afterward period of self-study will require the use of a notebook as a journal or diary, thick enough to contain students' individual comments and writings for the entire thirty lesson sequence. Students attending a retreat do not receive a copy of the Lesson Book (they get a Workbook), but hopefully create their own record that can map their growth for future reference.

Motivational Statement: This is concerned with making connections to students' Prior Knowledge—Often this will be augmented with a poem or short quote relating to the Training Objective which may originate from a student. Students are invited to describe their own understanding of the current Lesson Title, predicting what is ahead. Since students will come with different preparations and from different backgrounds this initial, brief sharing will be both an assessment for the instructor (analogous to a pre-test), and a way for students to connect personally to the group (Sangha) and to the dharma. Adept instructors can use students' personal comments to "connect" the content in a meaningful and relevant way to each student during the progress of the session.

First Progressive: Alms-giving or receiving—Compassion. Siddhartha Buddha had the technique of beginning his lectures with a discussion of charity and making merit as the first topic. "Benefactions" or altruism as it relates to each lesson is to be discussed at the end of each reading. In our modern Western society donating time and money are often substituted for the practice of alms collecting or giving, but developing compassion, empathy, and making a sincere effort to pass on the dharma to our neighbors, society and humanity is also what is addressed during discussions in this section. Political concerns—global issues—might be topics of discussion here.

Second Progressive: The virtue of abiding by moral principles and the discussion of ethical requirements of Buddhism were traditionally the second part of Buddha's lesson, and are emphasized here. Moral Conduct and rules of the Sangha are outlined and discussed at the end of each reading. One central purpose of any religion is to improve the lives of the adherents by influencing and being a catalyst for change. This is often considered the essence of Buddhism (at least for Theravada Buddhism) and as we will see, this is an essential step toward enlightenment. So much of "official teaching" sounds like it is sloganeering and buzzwords; in *Buddhist Sutras* we try to use concrete examples and useful explanations to get into the meaning of the slogans.

Third Progressive: The intellectual teachings and principles of Buddhism are the third component of Buddha's lessons. At the conclusion of the reading the Sangha discusses how the content relates to "cause and effect," part of what is described by the law of karma and the Law of Causation. Buddha proved in his own lifetime how we can each develop our thinking minds to concentrate and gain insight and wisdom. Beyond that, the lesson encourages students to discuss how Buddhist teachings relate to other religions, philosophical concepts and schools of thought. This is where information for the development of knowledge and understanding (leading to the growth of wisdom) about Buddhism is presented and exchanged. Discussion of mysticism and esoteric teachings, for the sake of completeness, is presented here, and belief or acceptance is left up to each student. A meditation training is part of this, but described separately.

Quotations are used throughout these lessons, and these are taken from commentators, basic scriptures and major writings of Buddhist thinkers who are representative of their sects and at the mainstream of Buddhist thought and practice. The diversity within Buddhism creates an eclectic source of myth and allegory that offers a convincing message when organized both topically and structurally. Being a Buddhist and studying the traditions is like living in a poem, you get to both read it and do it. These lessons are not as much about Buddhism, as they are in fact Buddhist. Sharing conceptions from so many authentic traditions, from Western philosophy and religions, reveals a common ground of discussion and hopefully fertilizes the challenging mind each student brings to the sala.

Meditation Practicum: There are many ways to meditate. A different tradition, prompt or practice is introduced in each lesson. The lessons invite students to use these progressive practices in a systematic and conscientious way, like an expanding spiral students are expected to return to repeat the practices introduced in earlier lessons as well. These *Buddhist Sutras* are more than a step by step meditation manual, however, since the lessons involve a pointing-out style of instruction, incorporate diverse meditation techniques (including a good deal of sharing) and describe practices from several cultural origins (including Yoga.) The focus of the meditation training is to use Anapanasati (vipassana) techniques, using in-and-out breathing as a basis for insight.

Biographical Sketch: Another frequent way of teaching in the Buddhist tradition is to share stories about the life experiences of accomplished bodhisattvas, and show how these individuals exemplified aspects of the Training Objective. Or, acknowledgment will be given to existing Orders, contemporary Buddhist sects and the legends of Siddhartha Buddha. This is where I share some of my own personal experiences, and acknowledge how many of my previous ordinary life experiences were not so ordinary after all.

Students may begin to get impatient and wish to have the content of all thirty lessons open to their view at once. This is unwise because a) it is not possible to absorb so much at once, and b) again—Training requires moving slowly and progressively through the teachings allowing plenty of time for meditation and repetition of each aspect of what is being presented. The goal is to become skillful and learn how to practice.

Reading for the Day: Many Buddhist traditions use selected readings as the primary lesson content, and likewise in this curriculum inspirational readings are used throughout and especially at the end of each lesson to be fresh on the mind of each practitioner before they begin to practice the assigned meditation. There are also chants that will be used during some of the lessons. The central theme is—sharing insights from the work and practice students do after the lesson—this is the most important aspect of the dharma. Students may read their own inspirational poems or prayers, but it is not appropriate for students to try to teach or preach to others; it is enough for them to apply the lessons they learn to their own lives.

Key Vocabulary: (for each Lesson) dharma (dhamma), karma, Siddhartha, The Middle Way, pointing-out, sala, chants

Protecting: This is the place for a ceremony or recognition of achievement relating to the teachings. A brief period for clarification and questioning follows, i.e. "This is what I heard." "Protecting signifies a review period, though a particular kind of review . . . the practitioner goes back over the unit of practices, paying particular attention to the ***view of the mind*** inherent in those practices. First, the practitioner tries to nurture this view in order to bring it more into direct experience in the unfolding mental continuum [make the Lesson personally relevant]. Second, the practitioner tries to protect the practice from going astray or becoming defective by comparing immediate experience of the unfolding mental continuum to the view imparted by the teachings [i.e. not jumping ahead]." (Brown, pp. 145-146)

Another kind of protecting is to develop and/or accept norms of behavior or rules of operation for the class of instruction or retreat.

Develop Norms: rules of conduct

speaking:
rising—and going to sleep
lesson times
No phones, no tv, no DVDs
Music times
Books or reading
food

Developing a convenient, simple routine that minimizes distractions is skillful.

Assignment: Questions for thinking about the dharma and a minimum length of meditation practice relating to the content of the Reading for the Day and Training Objectives. Each assignment and the vocabulary words are also printed in a separate Workbook provided for each student. Journaling is recommended.

In each lesson: Define each of the Key Vocabulary in your own words after each Lesson. This is a recurring assignment and helps students take ownership of the special vocabulary of Buddhism.

Additional Teaching:

There are some optional quotes for discussion. These lessons may be used by an experienced teacher in a retreat setting, or as a self-study "virtual retreat," and the student will likely have very different experiences in either case. But this simple fact does not invalidate the "virtual" experience, because if one person were to attend three different retreats, especially if these were offered by three different traditions, the novice can expect three very different outcomes. The information in *Buddhist Sutras* is gathered from authentic, authoritative sources (with an expanded Bibliography and Glossary) and is largely intended as a substitute for or beginning Training for people who have not grown up from youth in a Buddhist culture. A companion volume, *Bodhicitta, Higher Truth,* has subsequently been prepared as an extension and follow-up text.

The last activity of the lesson is to *share merit* and compassion with each other and the world! Sharing Merit: is most often done as a group chanting or oral mantra.

Table of Meditations for *Buddhist Sutras*

One	Essence of Buddhism	Natural Awareness/ The Open Mind
Two	To have Faith	Object Meditation / Shinay
Three	Four Noble Truths/ Suffering	Dealing with unpleasant thoughts.
Four	Cause and Effect	Visualize your Teacher
Five	Cessation of Suffering	Using Physical Senses (Practitioner)
Six	Right view (understanding)	Awareness of Pain—Chasing
Seven	Right thought	On Cleansing—Long Breaths
Eight	Right speech	Short Breaths/Standing/On Sound
Nine	Right action	Clarity /Seven Points/ Conditioning
Ten	Right livelihood	Contemplation/Directing/ Calming
Eleven	Right effort	Mantra meditation—Intensifying
Twelve	Right mindfulness	Pliancy / Walking—Piti
Thirteen	Right concentration	Sukha—Awareness (Stream Enterer)
Fourteen	Kinds of People	Protecting Images/ Dynamic

Buddhist Sutra

Lesson Title: Essence of Buddhism—Three Jewels

Lesson Number: One

Rationale:

This lesson (indeed all thirty lessons) offers a general introduction to what might be considered the most essential elements of Rational Buddhism for people during the 21st century in Western culture. Buddhism is a religion that has evolved over a period of 2500 years, it has been adopted in many nations, adapted by leaders in these different cultures to respond to the needs of the people and influenced by their pre-existing beliefs and mythical systems. We will learn how the core beliefs and practices of Buddhism (i.e. Taking Refuge in the Triple Gem) are still relevant to modern, technologically savvy people (wealthy and poor alike) because these are based on fundamental principles that derive from human nature and Buddhism (in spite of its many sects) seeks to unfold human capacities and support each individual's growth in a way that no other religion has attempted (The Middle Way).

Training Objective:

Compare Buddhism to other religions/ philosophies familiar to students. Point to (and share) the essential elements of Buddhist teaching, and identify how essential meditation practice is for each student. Recognize the role of *Interest*. Going for *refuge* to the Sangha. Natural awareness and calm abiding. Letting go of craving.

Materials Required: Loose fitting, modest clothing (no elastic to create discomfort.) Notebook and pen for journaling. Drinking water (for each lesson). *Workbook*

Motivational Statement:

Make connections to Prior Knowledge—Students are to describe their prior experiences with Buddhism (and Yoga or other meditation training,) and analyze their personal commitment to this training (or spiritual practice).

Siddhartha Buddha wanted to lead his listeners and followers to the all-important task: solving life's problems and living a life which brings happiness to common people as well as to monks. The essence of the Teachings is to help all those who are sincere in heart to follow a path of ethical (the Buddhist moral code) living to eliminate suffering.

This series of thirty lessons ". . . represent only the first stage of the path toward realization of your full potential, your buddha nature. On their own, these exercises about learning to calm your mind, becoming familiar with it [the mental continuum], and developing a sense of loving-kindness and compassion can effect undreamed-of changes in your life. Who wouldn't want to feel confident and calm in the face of difficulties, reduce or eliminate their sense of isolation, or contribute, however indirectly, to the happiness and well-being of others, promoting thereby an environment in which we ourselves, those we love and care for, and generations as yet unborn can flourish? All it takes to accomplish these marvels is a little patience, a little diligence, a little willingness to let go of conditioned ideas (cultural stories) about yourself and the world around you. All it takes is a bit of practice in waking up in the middle of the dream-scape of your life and recognizing that there is no difference between the experience of the dream and the mind of the dreamer." (Mingyur, pg. 245) This ought to be the student's perspective—"patience . . . diligence, etc."—toward the practice of Buddhism, quite apart from any consideration of the value or persuasiveness of these lessons. (Pause long enough for students to reflect and discuss before each new section.)

First Progressive:

As suggested, it was a tradition with the preaching and teachings of Buddha to begin each lesson with a discussion of giving and (for monks) receiving alms and other benefactions. In Thailand and many other Asian countries, it is common to see monks and aspirants roaming the streets shortly after daybreak with a bag over their right shoulders and carrying an alms bowl. Sabbai is the practice for the lay person of rising early on special days and meeting these holy people and *giving prepared offerings(dana)*. This is a form of religious practice, and the donor receives a blessing from the monk who is not wandering around just to provide for his own sustenance. He or she is actually performing a religious ritual, making it possible for Buddhists to fulfill their sacred obligation to be charitable and to make merit (or perform cleansing) both for themselves and for their departed loved ones. Each of these points will be developed later. To understand and appreciate this institution is to understand and appreciate that Buddhism is not just a philosophy, and that Buddhists do have important, useful and powerful beliefs.

This priority for charity (and growth of compassion) is often overlooked by those who say that Buddhism is "just a philosophy." When *we gain the compassion for ourselves and others* as taught by the Buddha we ". . . develop some sense of understanding of the other person's feelings—an understanding that, just like ourselves, everyone shares the same basic desire to be happy and to avoid unhappiness." (Mingyur, pg. 230) The further we progress in Buddhist education, the more we understand and develop the role of our Hearts in leading our lives, (not completely but to a great extent) this simple fundamental activity solves what might seem like contradictions and mysteries of Buddhist teachings. If we say or believe that Buddhism is mostly a philosophy, we underestimate the dhamma and role of compassion, and minimize the benefits that are available from an active intellectual and spiritual life based on Buddhist teachings.

Second Progressive:

The purpose of the extensive and detailed teachings about meditation, and the insistence on practicing, is to foster development of the mind to enable each person to live a better life, meaning both ethically and with happiness. "To practice the Teachings means to practice [and train] oneself to develop both external wholesomeness through body and speech and internal wholesomeness which is mental wholesomeness by 1) giving, 2) observing precepts and 3) mind development. Especially mind development is considered the most important." (Wee, pg. 60) This comes from the Theravada tradition but is a consistent element in all the schools and traditions of Buddhist teachings. By training our mind we gain the self-discipline from minute to minute to follow the moral code taught by Buddhism. Such issues as "right speech" (one of the steps of the Eight-Fold Path) require changing the way our personality reacts to that of other people and improving our conversations in each moment. It is taught that even the intention to change will lead to better consequences and a cycle of improvements (making merit) in our lives because of the law of cause and effect.

Hopefully these lessons will only be the first step in our Buddhist practice. One goal is to inspire each student to seek out a lama, yogi or monk who agrees to be a teacher for an advanced student. This person is often a paradigm of good behavior, and will be someone who follows a strict and exemplary moral code. When we meet this teacher ". . . The result of such a meeting is called the certainty that generates belief by Tashi Namgyel, and—generating an open, interested mind through listening by Kunga Tendzin. The meeting produces a definitive effect; something is generated within the mental continuum of the listener. For a beginner, **interest** ('dun pa) is generated; for a more clever listener, interest develops into belief (yid ches pa).

In the beginning we naturally want to listen, read and progress, thus "*Interest* is a very important mental factor among the approximately fifty mental factors that comprise ordinary consciousness . . . Interest is defined as a mental factor that gets involved with an object so as to highlight its particular qualities. It sets the foundation for further exploration of the object." (Brown, pg. 45) Consider viewing two different paintings, both attractive scenes, one is painted by a very famous artist while the other by an accomplished amateur. Notice if you have a higher level of interest in the more famous artist's painting?

Thus having humility to find and accept a teacher, having ***interest*** to study the Teachings, having receptivity to learn and train one's mind in a new direction—are aspects of ethical living that ought to characterize the behavior of the beginning student. This kind of attitude leads to the realization of the importance of and eventual acceptance of the most fundamental teaching of Buddha: The Four Noble Truths. This ". . . may be more accurately described as 'Four Pure Insights into the Way Things Are'—summarized as follows:

1. Ordinary life is conditioned by suffering [of many different kinds.]
2. Suffering results from causes [i.e. cravings—The Law of Causation.]
3. The causes of suffering can be extinguished [Cessation of Suffering.]
4. There is a simple path through which the causes of suffering can be extinguished." (Mingyur, pg. 70) This is the Eight-fold Path.

Each of these elements becomes a Learning Objective for Lessons Three-Thirteen. And since there are numerous sources for suffering, this central theme of Buddhism is revisited and discussed in many lessons in *Buddhist Sutras* (e.g. mid-life crisis, angst, stress, unease, fatigue, sorrows, family strife, depression—are just a few common words for suffering.)

Third Progressive:

"When we, who practice the Teachings, know the main objective of Buddhism, it is beneficial for us—because we can study and understand what Buddhism teaches, what the essence is. When we practice to develop mind, we will certainly understand how to practice fruitfully and correctly, we will not lose our way. When we start practicing, we will gain results quickly." (Wee, pg. 65) I like to think that Buddhism fosters 99% positive activity, not the negative space of dwelling on suffering, though this is acknowledged, identified and targeted for cessation. Developing the mind in order to live a better life, helping others and having Interest (beyond mere curiosity) is all about being in a positive and optimistic mental space more and more with each passing day.

As we learn more about the teachings of Buddhism we learn an elaborate and even complex intellectual explanation of why our lives are the way they are. But there is a simple truth that can set us free, so to speak. "In a way, letting ourselves be controlled by our mental afflictions is an 'inside job.' The pain we feel when we lose something we're attached to, or when we confront something we'd rather avoid, is a direct result of not knowing everything we could or should know about our own mind. We're caught by our own ignorance, and trying to free ourselves through some sort of external means—which are simply reflections of the dualistic ignorance that got us into trouble in the first place—only makes our [psychological and emotional] prisons close around us more tightly and securely."

"Everything I've learned about the biological processes of thought and perception indicates that the only way to break free from the prison of pain is by performing the same type of activity that imprisoned us in the first place. As long as we don't recognize the peace that exists naturally within our own minds, we can never find lasting satisfaction in external objects or activities."

"In other words, happiness and unhappiness are 'inside jobs'." (Mingyur, pg. 221)

Through the use of meditation we can experience the painful situations that confront us in our relationships for example, in a safe and private way, and rise above these and free ourselves from the restraints imposed on ourselves by our own mental habits—by employing the Teachings of Buddhism. We can prevent these painful situations from having the same deleterious effects on our lives as in the past, even if the events happen again or occur repeatedly. This may seem like a tall order, and it isn't a benefit of studying Buddhism as much as a result of recurring *practice and meditating*.

"The beginner starts to entertain the possibility that he or she, too, might become such a perfected spiritual being, [like a lama] and even thinks like such a perfected spiritual being, and even thinks that such a thing might be accomplished in this lifetime. Entertaining this proposition at first may seem unlikely, if not preposterous, in light of the beginner's entrenched worldview and lifestyle. Ordinary resistance to change [even positive change] attests to the difficulty of cultivating faith. Nevertheless to even consider the possibility [having Interest] of spiritual development at all is the first sign (rtags pa) of faith." (Brown, pg. 59) What are your goals? Your expectations?

"Our wish to pursue the Buddha's way is therefore founded on *informed confidence* in the soundness of the teachings rather than on blind faith or misguided attraction to its superficial aspects." (Snelling, pg. 47) This is a preview of the teachings discussed in Lesson Six. But even so, Buddhism is still a religion ". . . a system of practice based on morality, concentration, and insight, and culminating in liberating insight; a system which when practiced to completion enables one to break free from suffering. This is Buddhism as Religion." (Buddhadasa, 2005, pg. 20)

Meditation Practicum:

Most people are familiar with the sitting, legs crossed posture of meditation; this seven point posture is described in detail in Lesson Nine. "Thus, we have to know well about meditation so that we can practice [and develop] our mind correctly." (Wee, pg. 34) But the way we sit is not as important as the way we think and the effort we make day after day. Since most students will have had some exposure to meditation, whether they know it or not, it is important to offer this following item of good advice, more even than offering a specific training regimen: "The most important lesson I learned was to avoid becoming attached to my positive experience if it was peaceful. As with every mental experience, bliss, clarity, and non-conceptuality spontaneously come and go. You didn't create them, you didn't cause them, and you can't control [or force] them. They are simply natural qualities of your mind. I was taught that when such very positive experiences occur to stop right there, before the sensations dissipate. Contrary to my expectations, when I stopped practicing as soon as bliss, clarity, or some other wonderful experience occurred, the effects actually lasted much longer than when I tried to hang on to them. I also found that I was much more eager to meditate the next time I was supposed to practice."

When we learn new techniques or activities we can expect to begin, if not with baby steps, at least with halting, deliberate steps. "Even more important, I discovered that ending my meditation practice at the point at which I experienced something of bliss, clarity or non-conceptuality. [A quiet mind] was a great exercise in learning to let go of the habit of dzinpa, or grasping. *Grasping or clinging* too tightly to a wonderful experience is the *one real danger of meditation*, because it's so easy to think that this wonderful experience is a sign of realization. But in most cases it's just a passing phase, a glimpse of the true nature of the mind, as easily obscured as when clouds obscure Sun. Once that brief moment of pure awareness has passed, you have to deal with the ordinary conditions of dullness, distraction, or agitation that confront the mind. And you gain greater strength and progress through working with these conditions than by trying to cling to experiences of bliss, clarity, or non-conceptuality." (Mingyur, pg. 219) Letting go of "grasping" is a real challenge because it is such a subtle, insidious characteristic of our Western Culture invested in each of us. Starting with charity and generosity is a good beginning, and this is one way to practice letting go.

A simple meditation to follow is what is called "Natural Awareness" or simply sitting in your own real nature and being aware of your thoughts. "This spontaneous awareness is known in Buddhist terms as clarity—the clear light of mind. It's the cognizant aspect of the mind that allows us to recognize and distinguish the infinite variety of thoughts, feelings, sensations, and appearances that perpetually emerge out of emptiness . . . self-illuminating—like the flame of a candle, which is both a source of illumination and illumination itself . . . simply notice the fact that you're aware. The challenge, of course, is that clarity, or natural awareness, is so much a part of everyday experience that it's hard to recognize. It's like trying to see your eyelashes without using a mirror." (This is the foundation of mindfulness.)

"So how do you go about recognizing it?"

"According to the Buddha, you meditate—though not necessarily in the way most people understand it."

"The kind of meditation involved here is . . . a type of 'non-meditation.' There's no need to focus on or visualize anything . . . sit up straight, breathe normally, and gradually allow your mind to relax . . . just allow yourself to become aware of all the thoughts, feelings, and sensations passing through it. And as you watch them pass, simply ask yourself, 'Is there a difference between the mind and the thoughts that pass through it? Is there any difference between the thinker and thoughts perceived by the thinker?' Continue watching your thoughts with these questions in mind for about [five] minutes or so, then stop." (Mingyur, pp. 94-95)

When we record our thoughts in our diary, we are in essence involved in a form of natural meditation, focusing on our thoughts and trying to take them from our mind into a coherent pattern of speech (called writing). This is a form of meditation that seeks to rest and calm the mind. "In Sanskrit, the non-analytical approach is known as shamata. In Tibetan, it is called shinay . . . simply allowing the mind to rest calmly as it is. It's a basic kind of practice through which we rest the mind naturally in a state of relaxed awareness in order to allow the nature of mind to reveal itself." (Mingyur, pg. 138)

> (shinay—shi = peace or tranquility nay = to abide or stay—Calm Abiding.)

Biographical Sketch:

Many of us have experienced some moment of ecstasy or ecstatic experience, an epiphany perhaps; a moment of rapture or serene peace. I had one experience that I think about occasionally, when I thought I was conscious of consciousness—and have tried to get back to that place using meditation as a tool. Maybe we have only had one such huge memorable experience and we have been disappointed with subsequent meditation. If we could just get there each time we meditate, or even half way there, that would be a strong motivation to meditate more often and—with this worthwhile purpose in mind something important might happen. But when we don't return to that magical moment, or enlightened mental space, we can become disappointed or disenchanted. I see now that I experienced grasping, dzinpa, relating to this experience. I haven't had that same sensation again but many others that were almost like that. Possibly it is my own perception and interpretation that has given me the illusion that my notable experience was so exceptional and thus I devalue my subsequent experiences? I acknowledge I need to work on this issue during insight meditation.

But meditation isn't just about experiencing "bliss, clarity or non-conceptuality," it is also about doing some work to develop our minds and changing and improving our thinking—in Western terms it is partially about expanding our capacity to "meta-cognate"—think about our thinking, although a better description is watching the mind from the inside. As a pre-service teacher I was taught to help students think about their thinking, but at the time I didn't connect this with the practice of meditation. This is also a concept that is taught to teachers—to be "reflective" and do a self evaluation of their daily experience to improve their practice. Otherwise introspection and being sensitive to others are first steps toward a meditation practice. We have all learned to crawl, so to speak, now we need to walk and accept help to develop our meditation skills beyond these prosaic everyday tools. As we look back over our lives it is likely that we will identify many cases where we engaged in meditation, i.e. praying, even though we did not call it that or think about doing it explicitly. We are not strangers to mindfulness.

"The purpose of all Buddhist schools [and traditions] is to teach a path to Enlightenment that will enable practitioners to become like the Buddha. What makes someone a Buddhist is their commitment to this endeavor, and all the doctrines, practices, institutions, and schools of Buddhism are useful to the extent that they help people to follow the Buddhist path. The traditional way in which Buddhists of all schools express this commitment is to say that they 'go for Refuge to the Buddha, Dharma, and Sangha' (the Three Jewels). Sangharakshita emphasizes that the Buddhist tradition is united by the defining act of Going for Refuge to the Three Jewels. This is the key to being a Buddhist . . . Going for Refuge to the Three Jewels is the central principle of orientation of the FWBO (Friends of the Western Buddhist Order), and all its activities are understood in relation to it." (Vishvapani, pg. 24) This Buddhist organization was founded by an Englishman named Sangharakshita, born Dennis Lingwood in South London in 1925. It is one of the significant Western traditions where Buddhism has been interpreted and adapted to fit the needs and life style of not only people of Great Britain but many others in Western cultures. The history of this organization is a good example of how one can obtain support from the Teachings and learn from experience.

"When I read Diamond Sutra I knew that I was a Buddhist [age 16] . . . I had known it and believed it and realized it ages before and the reading of the Sutra as it were awoke me to the existence of something I had forgotten . . . Whenever I read the text I would be thrown into a kind of ecstasy . . . At about the same period I had for the first time experiences of the type which are generally known as psychic . . . Without any warning a whole series of future events would suddenly unroll themselves like a cinematograph before me . . . I saw not with the physical eyes but with what the Buddhist tradition terms the 'divine eye' . . . While such powers undoubtedly can be developed by anybody who is prepared to submit to the proper training and discipline, Buddhist tradition is unanimous in maintaining that the better course is to direct all one's energies to the attainment of Enlightenment and to allow psychic powers to come, it they do come, of their own accord." (Sangharakshita, pp. 80-81) There's no grasping or craving for para-normal experiences, thus another training of letting go.

Those who are attracted to and *interested* in Buddhism are likely those who are looking for some more profound experience in their lives, to fill their lives with additional meaning much like that described above. There need no longer be restless nights, sleeplessness is just another opportunity for meditation as is any moment of peace and quiet during the day. There is no such thing as boredom (nor insomnia) in a sincere Rational Buddhist's life, because at any time we have a moment to spare, we will want to meditate. "Meditation is not an activity conducted while sitting on the pillow but a way of being, a way of living with complete awareness . . . art, poetry, and cooking are wonderful media to express meditation experience." (Brown, pg. xxi)

Reading for the Day:

"Those who are interested in the Dhamma and want to study and understand clearly Buddhism, have to study thoroughly the Four Noble Truths. It is because they are the truths that the Lord Buddha has discovered, attained and [these are] propagated until now."

"The essential substance [distinctive teaching] is suffering and cessation of suffering. It is the major part to study in order to [gain] fundamental knowledge [to be knowledgeable] for interested people [and] to practice [in order] to develop mind to higher levels." (Wee, pp. 16-17)

Because the basic teachings of Buddhism are so simple to grasp—and Buddha intended it to be that way—and put into practice, progress to change one's life at first can be very quick. There is even the promise for a few that enlightenment can be achieved very quickly depending on one's prior training, karma (actions—will), and receptivity to the Teachings. I believe this goal can be obtained by someone during this series of thirty lessons. The first step is having ***Interest***, then comes faith and confidence in Buddhism, that the Teachings and practices espoused are essential and contain sufficient truth to guide each serious student.

"These instructions are for those whose minds have become very tired of ***samara***'s misery; for those who have the willingness to renounce [ordinary activities] so that perfection of buddhahood can quickly come; for those who become purified on the path, empowered by an understanding lama; and for those intent upon the way the realized mind stays; that is, it is for those who are content because they have had occasion to believe."

"Tashi Namgyel [the author of that advice] is raising the problem of certain truth (nges don), and also the problem of its acquisition. One purpose of the lama's advice is to confront the listener's ignorance and ordinary ways of thinking. The beginner is told to give up thinking in favor of direct experience. Jampel Pawo, another important commentator on the mahamudra [Tibetan tradition] says, 'This discourse is difficult to understand for those who [only] have ears for reason.' The earliest mahamudra songs state that people actually run away in fear when they hear such advice." (Brown, pg. 41)

Protecting:

"This is what I heard," both from students and teacher.

Ceremony: "Making anjali . . . In making this gesture of respect, the hands—palm to palm with the fingers extended—are brought together in front of the chest, then raised to the forehead whilst the head is slightly brought forward. It is as if one is symbolically making the gesture to point the hands towards the head—the highest part of the body, home of the wisdom faculty . . . a gesture to convey greetings, a taking one's leave, a request to speak . . ." (Cittaviveka, pg. 11) Each time be careful and aware of what you are doing.

"We put our hands together many times during Zen practice [as well as with any Buddhist practice.] In doing this we bring all parts of ourselves together—left and right, good and bad, masculine and feminine . . . Putting our hands together also contributes to our focus [and to being one-pointed;] most important, it is a way to express our thanks and acknowledgment, to stop and say 'thank you' to everything—to the room for being here, to the cushions and bells, to others who have come to offer their presence and support . . . When we carry this mindfulness and gratitude throughout our day, everything appears different." (Shoshanna, pg. 24) We can say "Namaste" as a blessing to each other, or "Sawatdee" Thai for welcome and hello, or use any other language that is known.

Additional Teachings:

Refrain: "In this way, in regard to the mind he abides contemplating the mind internally . . . externally . . . internally and externally. He abides contemplating the nature of arising . . . of passing away . . . of arising and passing away in regard to the mind. Mindfulness that 'there is a mind' is established in him to the extent necessary for bare knowledge and continuous mindfulness. And he abides independent, not clinging to anything in the world. That is how in regard to the mind he abides contemplating the mind."

Satipatthana Sutta (Analayo, pg. 8) This is part of what is regarded as "The Direct Path to Realization." This teaching is taken up in detail in *Bodhicitta: Higher Truth.*

Preview—Lesson Twenty-six: "If we recall that nirvana is a point of view as well as a way of living, we can see that it is obtainable, it is not a mystical connection of constant or even frequent bliss—it is the mind's intrinsic nature."

"In reality, as we said before, this thing called Nibbana is voidness, the epitome of purity, enlightenment, and peace, because it is the absence of all mental defilements, of all mental suffering." (Buddhadasa, 1999, pg. 82)

Rejoicing In Others' Merit (Saying Sadhu)

Buddhists usually share their merits with others whenever they have performed meritorious deeds [which is thought to include studying dharma and meditating.] "Sharing one's merit with others is called "Pattidana kusala" and "Rejoicing in others' merits" is known as "Pattanumodana kusala" in Pali.

In Tirokutta Sutta, it is stated by the Buddha that: "if the deceased relatives are reborn as petas who can rejoice in others' merit, one should perform meritorious deeds for the sake of them, and share merit with them. If the petas can say "Sadhu", they will be free from the miserable existences and they can receive celestial clothings, celestial mansions, celestial gardens and celestial utensils." In the Peta Vatthu also, it is mentioned that if a peta can rejoice in others' merits by saying "Sadhu", he will be immediately transformed into a deva. (ukonline)

Buddhist Sutra

Lesson Title: Essence of Buddhism—Three Jewels

Lesson Number: One

Key Vocabulary: dzinpa, grasping, dreamscape, bliss, clarity, nonconceptuality, Theravada, Mahamudra, samara, enlightenment, Sangha, meta-cognate, 'purified on the path', Sawatdee, Namaste, Sabbai, dharma (dhamma), karma, Siddhartha, The Middle Way, pointing-out, sala, object, Interest, dualistic ignorance, anjali, conditioned ideas, letting go

Assignment: "The beginner is told to give up thinking in favor of direct experience." What does this statement mean to you?

Define each of the Key Vocabulary in your own words.
What is peculiar about this approach to religion that makes it so special?

Does Buddhism require one to surrender rational thought to follow a charismatic leader?

Compare what you know about Buddhism with religions/ philosophies with which you are well acquainted.

Point out (and share) the elemental teachings of Buddhism, and identify how essential this practice is or might be for yourself.

Meditate using "Natural Awareness" ten times during the remaining day for about 5 minutes at a time and record any significant experiences or memories in your journal.

"Is there a difference between the mind and the thoughts that pass through it?"

What is your level of Interest in Buddhism? What are your goals? . . . your interests?

"Is there any difference between the thinker and thoughts perceived by the thinker?"

Memorize: The Four Noble Truths:

1. Life is made up of Suffering (dukkha): ". . . that is woe, mental discomfort, physical discomfort i.e. birth, old age, sickness and death.
2. The cause of suffering (samudaya): cravings and desires [leading to defilements.]
3. The noble truth of the extinction of suffering or the cessation of suffering (nirodha): resulting from practicing the Teachings. The extinction of total suffering comprising greed, aversion and ignorance is the Final Goal, the Supreme Goal of Buddhism (nirvana).
4. The Noble Truth of the Path Leading to the Extinction of Cessation of Suffering: this path is the Noble Eight-fold Path . . . The Four Noble Truths are the superb truth. No other truth is as important as these truths of our life . . ." (Wee, pg 12)

Compare karma to the concept and teaching of "original sin" in Catholicism.

Materials for Next Lesson: meditation notes, drinking water, Buddha icon, two candles.

Buddhist Sutra

Lesson Title: **Essence: To have Faith**

Lesson Number: **Two**

Rationale:

The changes that must occur in one's life to bring about the cessation of suffering and benefits of Buddhism begin when students have faith in the efficacy of the teachings. "There's been very little disagreement between Buddhists and modern scientists that a person's state of mind [i.e. optimism] has some effect on the body . . . Science [and medicine have mostly] focused on looking at what goes wrong with the mind and body rather than at what goes right." (Mingyur, pg. 237) Having faith in this Buddhist practice is the beginning of seeing "what goes right" in our lives.

Discussion of Prior Lesson:

Answer: nothing is to be taken for granted, and every teaching can be challenged and tried on for size. So to "give up thinking" is not about surrendering or living a life without logic, scientific inquiry or rational thought, it is about in addition to having these, developing an active spiritual practice that involves meditating and expanding the mind's ability to understand the capabilities of human nature.

(To what extent does Buddhism interest you?)
(A few thoughts by students after the first lesson?)

Training Objective:

The importance of faith, a result of Admiration. "How, then, are we to recognize the value of Buddhist teachings? How do we make the decision to begin [or expand] a ***spiritual practice***?" (Brown, pg. 37) What is Awakening? Object meditation.

Materials Required: meditation notes, drinking water, Buddha icon, two candles.

Motivational Statement:

Buddha was asked many questions which are still being asked today such as: Is there a God? Who created the world? Is there life after death? Where is heaven and hell? The classic answer given by Buddha was silence. He refused to answer these questions purposely because "these profit not, nor have they anything to do with the fundamentals of the religious life, nor do they lead to Supreme Wisdom, the Bliss of Nirvana."

Even if answers were given, he said, ". . . there still remain the problems of birth, old age, death, sorrow, lamentation, misery, grief, and despair—all the grim facts of life—and it is for their extinction that I prescribe my teachings." The essential religious nature of Buddhism is to lead sincere adherents into having their own experiences that become life changing. No amount of academic or intellectual activity (developing *concepts* or philosophizing) can replace the experience that comes from diligent and repeated meditation along with sharing with other members of the Sangha. Many people have found it possible to continue in their religious traditions and still embrace Buddhism.

Furthermore: "Buddhism picks up where successful therapy leaves off, addressing ordinary unhappiness and how to overcome it." (Brown, pg. 6) This practice is considered sub-clinical, not intended to cure serious behavioral or psychological problems.

Once we begin to seriously practice and go beyond Interest ". . . The first change you'll notice is a greater degree of openness, confidence, and self-honesty, and an ability to recognize the thoughts and motivations of other people around you more quickly . . . it's the beginning of wisdom." (Mingyur, pg. 243) It is the beginning of love toward the buddha within, and its about getting the bigger picture. (Each student is to describe their experience and state of mind as a baseline before they begin to get the bigger picture.)

First Progressive:

(Alms-giving or receiving) "The Principal Teachings are the teachings for the practice to attain wholesomeness—if we study them [we will] understand them best [in the necessary way]." This is how we gain control of our personalities.

"There are other ways to perform *wholesome deeds* such as three of the meritorious actions namely:

1) benefactions [compassion and external actions]
2) moral conduct [external actions]
3) mental development" [internal actions]

"These three aspects cover all [preliminary choices of] how to perform wholesome actions according to Buddhist Teachings."(Wee, pg. 18) And this is the progressive sequence incorporated into each of the thirty lessons. *Giving alms and being charitable* is an expression of faith that leads to making merit. Making merit is the opposite of performing karma or action that develops into suffering. The worthy actions we perform are sure to manifest as blessings and success in our lives. (If there is a monastery or retreat center nearby, begin to support and participate in charitable activities. If not, actively look for other opportunities (i.e. food banks, hospice, and shopping at thrift shops.)

During the time students are preparing their lives to be more actively involved in Buddhism as a way of life—many changes well occur in their lives. There are many choices or paths to take to follow the "Buddhist Teachings." Being more charitable is an obvious choice, but being more involved in humanitarian, political and altruistic activities are essential aspects of a worthwhile spiritual practice as well. Once we begin to seriously practice and go beyond interest or curiosity, we will feel a love toward Buddhism as we might for a brother or a wise teacher, and to our Sangha members, we will soon find a stronger connection to humanity in general, and we will quickly begin to notice how the teachings influence the choices we make.

Second Progressive:

(Unfolding the Moral Code of Buddhism)

"In Buddhism, the wholesome action that is considered best virtue is the one in[volving the] mind by concentrating mind [during meditation] to be one-pointed and develop ***wisdom (Panna)*** to get rid of all ***defilements*** completely. It is called mind development." This is how we gain control of our futures. This is, however, a very succinct statement of what we are to do, but there is very little information there about how we are to go about it. These *Buddhist Sutras* flesh out these terse statements.

"In order to be able to practice the Teachings to scrape off and extinguish all defilements, to make merit by various means till the achievement of the ultimate goal in Buddhism, we have to prepare ourselves with ***confidence.*** We are to acquire knowledge and clear understanding of the Teaching so that we can practice by ourselves in a correct way and fruitfully. The teachings that we should follow are: Firstly, we have to know that according to the Buddhist Teachings we obtain wholesomeness and happiness as results from wholesome deeds [having faith.] Thus, we have to know which actions are wholesome and which ones are not. In the Principal Teaching, the Lord Buddha taught all Buddhists 1) to refrain from all wrong actions 2) to perform wholesome actions only and 3) to purify one's own mind to be free from all defilements."

"To refrain from wrong actions—to perform wholesome actions only—

Wholesome actions through body:
. no killing
. no stealing
. no sexual misconduct

Wholesome actions through speech
. no lies
. no harsh speech
. no idle speech

Wholesome actions through mind
. no greed for what belongs to others
. no vindictiveness
. taking right for righteousness (not being self-righteous)

"In order to do internal wholesome deeds, we need to have knowledge on religious essence which provides right practices through body and mind . . . we should know about the truth of our life. The truth of life is characterized according to the Four Noble Truths. It depends on mindfulness and wisdom of each person to consider the truth accordingly. Thus, when we start studying Buddhism, we should study the Four Noble Truths [which includes the Noble Eight-fold Path]." (Wee, pp. 22-23) Beginning in Chapter Three. Mindfulness training should play a key role in our early meditation training. But mindfulness is only one of the steps along the Eight-fold Path, so we have to learn about the others as well.

1. Right view, understanding (beginning in Chapter Six)
2. Right thought
3. Right speech
4. Right action
5. Right livelihood
6. Right effort
7. Right mindfulness
8. Right Concentration (from the Theravada tradition)

So the next eleven lessons are devoted to these topics in particular detail.

Third Progressive:

Recall the Four Noble Truths—"The Lord Buddha discovered that our lives are [made up of] two kinds of suffering which are 1) physical and mental discomfort and 2) the Three Characteristics comprising 1] ***impermanence*** (changing), 2] state of being [in] suffering [unsatisfactoriness] 3] and state of being non-self [***soul-lessness***]. All lives whoever they are, of whatever race, or whatever caste, encounter the same suffering." These three characteristics of karma (action) and the world, will be identified repeatedly during these lessons.

"That is why we have to study and understand the Buddhist Teaching in the Section of suffering of lives to verify if it is true as the Buddha taught. [Know for yourself.] We have to ponder with mindfulness and wisdom over the reason why lives are suffering according to the Buddhist Teachings. We have to think over the concerned [relevant] Teachings so carefully that we accept that it is true according to what the Buddha taught [i.e. develop faith.] Then we will be able to understand them clearly." (Wee, pg. 66) This is a key principle of Rational Buddhism.

How do we know? "Like scientists, Buddhists recognize the five senses of sight, hearing, smell, taste, and touch . . . the five sense faculties are known as the ***doors of perception*** . . . Buddhist science adds a sixth sense, the mental consciousness. There's nothing mysterious or occult about the sixth—consciousness. It has nothing to do with extrasensory perception or being able to talk to spirits. It's simply the capacity of mind to know and discern what we see, smell, hear, taste, or touch." This is related to our capacity to imagine, intuit and to be creative. The fact of this sixth sense is what makes meditation so important, consider it as important as using your eyes for a sighted person, or as touch for a blind person, etc . . .

We are not expected to have blind faith, but we learn to rely on the results of meditation in the same way we learn to rely on our hearing and smell, etc . . . "Although 'saddha' is translated as 'faith,' it refers more to a heartfelt sense of 'rightness'—an instinctive awareness that 'this is Right.' When our saddha is unshakably rooted (Taking Refuge) in the Buddha, Dhamma and Sangha, they, in their turn, evoke a sense of zest and enthusiasm to continue . . ."

(Cittaviveka, pg. 7-8) There is an all pervading sense that beneath the superficial turmoil and struggle of life, all is well; there is something beyond our limited vision worthy of exploration, worthy of intense effort. Obviously we don't know what is in store for us in the next 28 lessons, but we come to believe very quickly that what is being taught here is vital for our lives.

Meditation Practicum:

"One problem that is deemed a very important hindrance for practicing the Teachings is lack of knowledge and understanding in the Buddhist Teachings or in short still—lack of *confidence in Buddhism*."

"In this regard, confidence in Buddhism is very important for practicing the Teachings because if one does not have confidence in Buddhism, he[/she] will not believe in the Buddhist Teachings and will not practice to develop mind to reduce defilements, desire and ***attachment*** which pile up in mind and [are residual] inborn traits. If one does not practice, [meditate] one will not understand the profound essence of the Buddhist Teachings. In this connection, whoever has mindfulness and wisdom to know and understand the Buddhist Teachings will have good confidence in Buddhism and will understand the profound Teachings of the Lord Buddha." (Wee, pg. 3) Initially this may seem like a dogmatic assertion, or is it just good coaching to anticipate the goal? Effort to meditate breeds success, which breeds faith, which breeds study and understanding, which creates enthusiasm for learning more, which overcomes attachments, and a positive cycle begins.

A popular, yet hypothetical analogy for the normal, untrained mind follows: "Now suppose someone sets a monkey loose in this building [that has five doors or windows]. The monkey represents the mental consciousness. Suddenly set free in a big house, the monkey would naturally go crazy jumping around from opening to opening to check things out, looking for something new, something different, something interesting. Depending on what it finds, this crazy monkey decides whether an object it perceives is pleasurable or painful, good or bad, or in some cases simply boring. Anyone passing by the house and seeing a monkey at every opening might think there are five monkeys loose in the house [having possibly different characteristics]. Really, though, there's only one: the restless, untrained mental consciousness [also referred to as the ***mental continuum***]." There is only one "sixth sense" that we use to think and mentally visualize and when we gain control and harness this sense, we can use it like an artist or a great chef.

"But like every other sentient being, all a crazy monkey really wants is to be happy and avoid pain. So it's possible to teach the crazy monkey in your own mind to calm down by deliberately focusing its attention on one or another of the senses." (Mingyur, pg. 143) It is this combination of different kinds of mental activity—the autonomic functioning, the subconscious, the intuitive and creative minds and the ordinary thinking mind, the *mental continuum*—that we try to develop and train during Buddhist meditation. It is useful also to read scientific literature about the brain, so much more is known now than 2,500 years ago, but it's uncanny how prescient Buddha was.

Object Meditation: "... We inevitably experience a sense of futility if we attempt to disengage completely from our senses or block the information we receive through them ... The more practical approach is to make friends with our senses, and to utilize the information we receive through our sensory organs as a means of calming the mind [shinay]—self-antidote—using the source of distraction itself as the means to attain freedom from distraction . . . In object meditation practice, we use our senses as a means of stabilizing the mind. We can use the faculty of sight to meditate on form and color; the faculty of hearing to meditate on sound; the faculty of smell to meditate on odors; the faculty of taste to meditate on flavors; and the faculty of touch to meditate on physical sensations. Instead of distractions, the information we receive through our senses can become great assets to our practice." Light three incense sticks to represent the Triple Gem and notice the pleasant aspect (smell).

One immediate improvement could be our capacity to reduce our negative responses to others. "A corollary to this is to use the conscious mind to meditate on our emotional experiences . . . Just through learning how to rest my attention very lightly on the sensory information I was receiving, and disengaging from the emotional or intellectual content normally associated with the *sounds* (i.e. harsh language) . . . and by being able to listen to [the speaker] non-defensively, I found myself open enough to respond in a way that defused his apparent anger without diminishing my own integrity." (Mingyur, pp. 144-145) Using this approach, the student is to look at an icon of Buddha and understand the visual and emotional reactions involved in *perception*. This is a neutral source, one that is present in the moment rather than imported from various past experiences. Use a mala to focus your mind on *touch* as you handle each bead. Later it will be useful to meditate on whatever objects or experiences that have caused joy or suffering, and essentially unload or discharge the negative emotional effects. Drink some water or tea and notice the *taste* and texture.

"In order to achieve realization, the important thing is to allow your practice to evolve gradually, beginning with very short periods, several times a day. The incremental experiences of calmness, serenity, and clarity you experience during these short periods will inspire you, very naturally, to extend your practice for longer periods. Don't force yourself to meditate when you're too tired or too distracted. Don't avoid practice when the small, still voice inside your mind tells you it's time to focus." (Mingyur, pg. 218)

"Many feel uneasy as they start to practice, wondering if they are doing it correctly. But if you follow the simple instructions, you cannot make a mistake. You can do nothing wrong. Whatever happens during that particular sitting is perfect, just as it is. All you need to do is experience it. There is no way you can fail . . ." (Shoshanna, pg. 25)

Biographical Sketch:

To a follower who insisted on knowing, "Is there a God?" Buddha replied with the parable of the poison arrow: "If you were shot by a poison arrow, and a doctor was summoned to extract it, what would you do? Would you ask such questions as who shot the arrow, from which tribe did he come, who made the arrow, who made the poison, etc., or would you have the doctor immediately pull out the arrow?"

"Of course," replied the man, "I would have the arrow pulled out as quickly as possible." Buddha concluded, "That is wise O disciple, for the task before us is the solving of life's problems; when that is done, you may still ask the questions you put before me, if you so desire."

"Buddha taught hundreds, probably thousands, of ordinary people—how to direct their minds in ways that would create the kinds of subtle changes in their physiology that would allow them to override their biological and environmental conditioning and achieve a lasting state of happiness. If what he'd taught hadn't been effective, no one would know his name, there would be no tradition known as Buddhism, and you wouldn't be holding this book in your hands." (Mingyur, pg. 223) Why has Buddhism persisted? Certainly one explanation for the permanence of Buddhism is the flexibility and potential for helping people that it entails.

"We practice the Teachings in order to sense the truth of life that is 'suffering' [which we take up in Lesson Three.] It is real suffering because our body is 1] not permanent. It is transient, 2] involved in suffering and 3] soullessness. [We will compare this to Yoga concepts as well.] These are the truths. We have to practice the Teachings to attain insight into the state of compounded things . . ." (Wee, pp. 73-74) These three causes of suffering occur throughout our lives in so many different ways. I used to think I was the same person I was fifty years ago, now I know that I have not only grown older, I am a completely different person who has suffered from some of the changes in my life, and I still suffer in a lot of different ways, and my identity and self-concept has changed as well. (Students are encouraged to begin listing their most obvious sources of suffering in their journals.)

"Any bhagavan who takes even a single step toward the cause [of spiritual development], by listening to the Dharma or its explanation, or even takes in or gives out a single breath [of its message], will [eventually] completely grasp the holy Dharma, because this is the proper thing to do. So it is said." (Kagyu, pp. 18-21 in Brown, pg. 46) This is essentially a mystical explanation for the longevity of Buddha's teaching, in that they are being aided by the very esoteric forces they describe. (Light the two candles.)

Reading for the Day:

"The ***awakened*** mind of the Buddha manifests as **infinite wisdom** and **inexhaustible compassion**. Thus while early Buddhism emphasizes the eradication of negative qualities, Mahayana [Tibetan] enlightenment entails the full manifestation of all positive qualities of mind, the quintessence of our human potential." (Brown, pg. 7) We begin our awakening when we first begin to feel receptive to Buddhism.

"Interest is said to ripen into ***admiration*** (mos pa) . . . intensified interest . . . Admiration requires sufficient attention [during meditation] to examine the perceptual object in greater detail, that is, to fix the object as a mental representation (dmigs pa). It also requires sufficient concentration so as not to be taken away from the object easily. The object has become so interesting that the perceiver is able to sustain attention on it. Furthermore, admiration implies that the perceptual object has had sufficient impact on the observer to require further involvement with it . . . Therefore admiration is one of the five factors that make an object certain (yul nges) . . . the object is taken as precious (gnyes) . . . 'admiration' is meant to [have the following effects]

1. intensified interest;
2. making an impact;
3. distinguishing the features of the object;
4. having all the features become clear; and finally,
5. taking the object as precious . . ."

"This same semantic field for the term mos pa applies whether it pertains to an encounter with a mundane object of perception (ma dag pa) or to an encounter with a sacred holy being (dab pa) [such as an enlightened lama or even an icon or statue of Buddha] . . . Admiration is something 'generated deep in the heart' . . . the listener grasps the full impact of the teaching and thereby becomes amazed at its potential benefit (phan yon) . . ." (Brown, pp. 46-47) We can still maintain an objective position, just as we can to evaluate the accomplishments and honesty of our children or siblings.

"Once you commit yourself to developing an awareness [also mindfulness,] of your Buddha nature, you'll inevitably start to see changes in your day-to-day experience. Things that used to trouble you gradually lose their power to upset you. You'll become intuitively wiser, more relaxed, and more openhearted. You'll begin to recognize obstacles as opportunities for further growth. And as your illusory sense of limitation and vulnerability gradually fades away, you'll discover deep within yourself the true grandeur of who and what you are." A timid person can become strong, an introvert can become powerful, a shy person can become accomplished.

"Best of all, as you start to see your own potential, you'll also begin to recognize it in everyone around you. Buddha nature is not a special quality available to a privileged few. The true mark of recognizing your Buddha nature is to realize how ordinary it really is—the ability to see that every living creature shares it, though not everyone recognizes it in themselves." (Mingyur, pg. 248) There is so much of our etiquette, manners, courtesies and customs that we practice every day and often take for granted, but these show our good dispositions and "Buddha nature" that can blossom. This is not about having a passive/aggressive nature, it is about taking control of our lives.

Protecting:

"This is what I heard," both from students and teacher.

"When you have faith, you have a lot of energy. When you believe in something really good, true, and beautiful, you are very alive." (Hanh, pg. 241) This is a promise to each person that we can grow out of the confines of our own circumstances that tend to restrict our growth. In Chapter One we learned about the elements of Taking Refuge which is arguably the most significant ritual of Buddhism. We kneel, we form our hands into Anjali, we repeat "I take refuge in the Buddha, . . . Dharma, . . . Sangha." Gradually we learn the significance of Taking Refuge for ourselves.

"Tibetans do a full-length prostration; the Japanese bow from the waist; in Thailand and South-East Asia one sees the kneeling bow, and in Sri Lanka, people offering respect may squat down on the haunches and lower the head . . . In the ***five-point prostration***, a kneeling posture is assumed, the hands are placed in the anjali posture before the heart, then raised towards the forehead as the head is tilted forward a little to meet them. The body is then bent from the waist so that each forearm can be placed full-length on the ground, with the head touching the ground between the hands; thus head, forearms and palms of the hands complete the five points of contact . . . This gesture is then repeated three times—once each for the Buddha, the Dhamma, and the Sangha—and after the last repetition, the head is slightly tilted forward to complete the whole movement . . . the gesture should convey a sense of calm composure . . ." (Cittaviveka, pg. 12) Initially this kind of bowing is easy to do with mindfulness because it is so deliberate. Even after it becomes habituated it must be accomplished with composure and sincerity, whether in privacy or in the middle of the temple floor.

Additional Teachings:

"The only proper and unerring way to venerate the Triple Gem—or go to them for refuge . . . is by zealously committing oneself to the Dhamma practice. This is certainly the most concrete and meaningful way to be a refuge unto oneself too. One way to practice the Dhamma is also to support the Sangha so that the Dhamma will be further preserved and promoted for the welfare and benefit of the world." (Plamintr, 2007, pg. 13)

"Fundamentally, there are three advantages derived from an act of Buddhist worship . . . the practice helps to inspire virtues and inculcates the noble qualities associated with the Triple Gem into the mind. Wholesome qualities such as wisdom, compassion and mental purity are essential in all spiritual efforts. Second, the act of worship has a deep purifying effect on the devotees' consciousness and the power to remove impurities [cleansing] from their minds. Often a sense of serenity and peace is produced. Third, Buddhist worship can be performed as a meditative exercise for developing concentration and wisdom. Prayer for material gains and success is, therefore, never part of true Buddhist worship . . . Like all other actions it should be based on wisdom and understanding." (Plamintr, 2007, pg. 36) Boil this down to developing the Heart.

Even though it may be difficult to expect a person just newly come to the study of Buddhism to have faith, perhaps it is enough to simply understand how important faith is in some traditions, especially in Pure Land Buddhism of Japan. "Rather than material benefits from faith, Shiran's teaching offers us realistic self-understanding which is the greatest benefit of all . . . Religious devotion and commitment are expressed in the recitation of Amida Buddha's Name, Namu-amida-butsu, understood as an act of gratitude and spiritually as the call of Amida to our hearts . . . As the bright light sharpens the shadows, Amida's compassion and wisdom illuminate the inner recesses of our consciousness and empower and transform us within the process of our daily living. Shinran indicates that in trusting faith the true mind of Amida works within our lives to bring the Buddha's wisdom and compassion to bear on our daily activities and our relations to others." (Bloom, pg. 8) This can be thought of as the Grace of Buddhism.

Sharing Merit:

I share all of my merits with all sentient beings. [maitri]

I share all my merits with my parents, teachers, relatives[, my guardian deva, the guardian deva of my home, the guardian deva of my village, the guardian deva of my town, the guardian deva of my country, the guardian deva of the earth, the king of death. the king of men. the king of devas. all devas and all petas.]

May they all gain the merits of my meritorious deed as much as I do and may they all be happy and free from enmity.

[May I call upon the guardian deva of the earth to bear witness.]

May they all hear my words and rejoice in my meritorious deed!

Sadhu _ Sadhu _ Sadhu

Well-done, Well-done, Well-done (ukonline)

Buddhist Sutra

Lesson Title: **Essence: To have Faith**

Lesson Number: **Two**

Key Vocabulary: concepts, doors of perception, impermanence, soul-lessness, compounded things, semantic field, Admiration, confidence in Buddhism, mental continuum, nirvana, object meditation, spiritual practice, one-pointed, wisdom (panna), attachment, defilements, awakening, saddha (faith)

Assignment: Using the image of Buddha, and "Object Meditation" practice, alternate between looking at Buddha and closing your eyes in shinay meditation and only seeing, not thinking, to visualize the image. Do this for short periods, between five and ten minutes—ten times during the day.

How does your belief (or disbelief) in a god influence your expectations about Buddhist practice?

Define each of the Key Vocabulary in your own words.

Do you believe that you have or will have a "Buddha nature?"

For what else in your life do you feel "admiration?" Light two candles, one for **infinite wisdom,** and one for **inexhaustible compassion**.

Keep notes on the meditation with respect to your relationship (see and name the emotions) to the image of Buddha.

Can you achieve enlightenment within a thirty day session of concentrated practice?

Recall from Lesson One: What does it mean to have "patience and diligence?"
What was your reaction or impression of Taking Refuge?

How do you go about letting go "of conditioned ideas about yourself?" Can you do that? Students are encouraged to begin listing their most obvious sources of suffering.

Is the teaching about "confidence" a dogmatic assertion or just good coaching?

Materials for the next lesson: one remembrance (i.e. credit card), journal, water to drink, small mirror.

Buddhist Sutra

Lesson Title: **Suffering—The Four Noble Truths**

Lesson Number: **Three**

Rationale:

This is the first concept introduced by Siddhartha Buddha as his fundamental point of view toward the world that confronts each human born into each challenging and often harsh society. Even though we are nurtured hopefully by loving parents and possibly by siblings, we, from the very beginning of our lives, crave mother's milk—a metaphor for the craving in which we engage throughout our lives. Buddha required that his students see the world from this point of view, not in a pessimistic way, but in a hopeful way because he offered at the same time the necessary perspective and skills training to overcome the causes of suffering.

Discussion of Prior Lesson:

During your practice of "object meditation" what relationship did you feel toward the image of Buddha? Even a tranquil, neutral state is quite an achievement, since this is the most desirable stage of meditation. "If there is a distinction between true love and the kind of love that can only engender suffering and despair, the same can be said of faith. There is a kind of faith that sustains us and continues to give us strength and joy. Then there is the kind of faith that may disappear one morning or one evening and leave us completely lonely and lost." (Hanh, pg. 243)

"The Kalama Sutta requires us to have wisdom before having faith. If one wants to have faith come first, then let it be the faith which begins with wisdom, not faith which comes from ignorance. The same holds true in the principle of the Noble Eightfold Path: take wisdom or right understanding as the starting point, then let faith grow out of that wisdom or right understanding. That is the only safe approach. We ought never to believe blindly immediately upon hearing something, nor should we be forced to believe out of fear, bribery, and the like." (Buddhadasa, 1999, pg. 6) This suggests the virtue of studying the Buddhist teachings well, before expecting to become an accomplished meditator.

Training Objective:

Introduce The Four Noble Truths and identify what "suffering" means and how it has been a part of students' lives. How is this teaching the "middle way?" Why is this an important perspective? Temporary nature of pleasure; dealing with unpleasant thoughts.

Materials Required: one remembrance (i.e. credit card), journal, water, small mirror

Motivational Statement:

"According to the meaning of 'suffering' in the First Noble Truth, we have to accept that when we are born to be a human being, we have to know and understand that it is a life of suffering. We have to certainly encounter physical and mental discomfort daily. This is the truth which is the Teaching, the real truth that the Lord Buddha has discovered and propagated to all teachable persons to know and understand that all lives are really born suffering. They are not happy lives as almost all people on the earth misunderstand."

(Wee, pg. 66) How does the object of remembrance relate to any suffering that has occurred in your life?

"Suffering follows a negative thought as the wheels of a cart follow the oxen that draw it." The Dhammapada (Mingyur, pg. 115) "Buddhism is sometimes naïvely criticized as a 'negative' or 'pessimistic' religion and philosophy. Surely life is not all misery and disappointment: it offers many kinds of happiness and sublime joy. Why then this dreary Buddhist obsession with suffering?"

"No one can argue . . . [that] Dukkha lurks behind even the highest forms of worldly pleasure and joy, for, sooner or later, as surely as night follows day, that happiness must come to an end. [No one takes pleasure in these losses.] Were the Buddha's teachings to stop there, we might indeed regard them as pessimistic and life as utterly hopeless. But, like a doctor who prescribes a remedy for an illness, the Buddha offers both a hope (the third Noble Truth) and a cure (the fourth). The Buddha's teachings *thus give cause for unparalleled optimism and joy*. The teachings offer as their reward the noblest, truest kind of happiness, and give profound value and meaning to an otherwise grim existence. One modern teacher summed it up well: 'Buddhism is the serious pursuit of happiness'." (Bullitt) It can also be a Rational pursuit. (Discuss together.)

First Progressive:

The development of compassion and empathy—Before Siddhartha left his father's household permanently he made four trips outside the protected and sheltering compound. "The trips through the four gates symbolize the state of mind about which Shakyamuni later spoke in the following way: Though I was young and was living a life of luxury, I was often obsessed with the thought that many people pay no heed to the aging, illness, and death of others. They consider the affairs of outsiders none of their business and, failing to *apply the experiences of others to themselves*, refuse to realize that they too must grow old, fall ill, and die. But I did relate the aging, illness, and death of others to myself, and this caused me to suffer and be ashamed and to abandon pride in vigorous youth, health, and life." (Mizuno, pg. 17) Buddha challenges us to be aware not only of our own suffering but of the plight of other people in society, to have empathy.

Buddhism grew in part because of the inspired gifts of property given by important nobles of the day for the purpose of supporting the Sangha. "These generous bequests demonstrate how, from the very start, the Sangha was supported by a sympathetic lay community. In return the Buddha gave discourses to lay people and, the general monastic bias of early Buddhism notwithstanding, certainly encouraged them to practice to as great an extent as they were able. His qualified bhikkhus of course gave teachings too. This reciprocal relationship, which so clearly illustrates the Buddhist virtue of dana or giving, survives in many Buddhist countries to this day. Besides food and shelter, the laity may donate cloth for robes, medicines, and other requisites to the Sangha." (Snelling, pg. 27) This practice is still active in Thailand, and seems a little naive to visitors, but makes up an important component of the spiritual life of average people who are sincere about their beliefs. This is a way to make merit (or boon) and becomes a central part of their religious practice.

Second Progressive:

"To live is to act, [karma] and our actions can have consequences that are either harmful or beneficial to others and ourselves. Buddhist ethics means acting with an awareness of this truth—seeing that our actions have consequences, and learning the skill of acting for the best. The Buddha did not lay down sets of rules governing how we should act in every instance. Instead, he emphasized the importance of considering what drives us to act in particular ways, and purifying our hearts and minds through practices such as meditation. For Buddhists, ethics is less about doing good than being good." (Vishvapani, pg. 46) The importance of ethics (and motivation) in the spiritual life is stressed in *Buddhist Sutras*, but this must actually lead to changes in the way we operate on a day to day basis. This "value" of positive change is not obtained by asceticism or isolating oneself from the real world. It is not realized by indulging in hedonistic pleasures of the world—being an avid TV sports fan, for example; nor from avoiding the duties implied by one's work, family and friends. Real change begins a cycle of improvements and leads to a better, more holistic life. This is the "middle way."

"When we study the Four Noble Truths and understand that [our] lives regardless of race, religion, language, class and caste are all suffering, we will find that the Lord Buddha also rendered the ways for us to lead our lives to attain salvation and eradicate suffering. That is Nirodhagamini, the Noble Truth or Path leading to the cessation of suffering or the Noble Eight-fold Path [the moral code.] The Lord Buddha mentioned in the Three Baskets (Tipitaka):

1. Right view, understanding (Sammadithi)
2. Right thought (Sammasankappa)
3. Right speech (Sammavaca)
4. Right action (Sammakammanta)
5. Right livelihood (Sammavayama)
6. Right effort (Sammavayama)
7. Right mindfulness (Sammasati)
8. Right concentration (Sammasamadhi)" (Wee, pg. 27)

"The Yoga Sutras say that Nature is the great teacher of the Self. Nature provides us with experiences that we decide are 'good' or 'bad', and it is through these experiences, particularly the ones that provide us with pain and loss, that we learn about ourselves. This school of hard knocks is the great teacher. [Although it is certainly possible to learn from others' experiences as well as from dharma.] It is only when we have been disappointed and defeated that we realize the need to change our attitudes and responses to life, and through coping with experiences of failure are able to grow and extend ourselves into something greater and finer." (Forstater, pg. 70)

By following Buddhism and engaging in training the mind, we can essentially short-circuit the necessity to learn in the school of hard knocks. When we realize the Three Characteristics: ". . . that all things are impermanent we mean that all things change perpetually, there being no entity or self that remains unchanged for even an instant. That all things are unsatisfactory means that all things have inherent in themselves the property of conducing to suffering and torment. They are inherently [or eventually] unlikable and disenchanting. That they are not selves [not mine or me] is to say that in nothing whatsoever is there any entity which we might have a right to regard as its 'self' (myself) or to call 'its own' (mine.) If we grasp at things and cling to things, the result is bound to be suffering." (Buddhadasa, 2005, pg. 33) Discuss—***Impermanent, unsatisfactory and not-self,*** because these are repeatedly pointed to as the sources of suffering.

Third Progressive:

"The first of the Four Noble Truths (the Truth of Suffering) states that all existence is suffering. The nature of the state of suffering must be accurately understood. No matter whether the individual diagnoses his own suffering or that of others, suffering itself must be clearly seen for what it is. It is wrong to interpret as a normal state something that is actually suffering or to suffer when there is no cause to do so. In other words, the first requirement is to see things accurately and completely—neither in a distorted way, as through colored glasses,—nor partially, as through clouded glasses. In order to allow people to see things correctly, before teaching the Four Noble Truths, Shakyamuni employed the gradual teaching method . . . This method enables his followers to accept the Law of Causation and to understand causation correctly." (Mizuno, pg. 45)

"The Buddhist world-view therefore comprises a mind-boggling range of possible literal and psychological states, most of them fraught with more or less terrible forms of suffering, in a universe of equally mind-boggling spatial and temporal dimensions. All is in a constant state of flux and every now and then undergoes more or less catastrophic convulsions. Merely to be born in this system is very bad news, for the beings that are embroiled in it cannot escape, not even into Keats' 'easeful death,' for they are subject to continual rebirth through beginning-less and endless time. If the bones of all the bodies that a person's consciousness-continuum has inhabited during one age alone were piled up, they would form a cairn higher than Vulture Peak Mountain, where the Buddha taught. All the tears of sorrow that have been shed during the long journey would exceed the waters of the four oceans; and the same might be said of all the mothers' milk that has been drunk. In Buddhist terminology, this is samsara, the churning sea of cyclic existence in which beings are ceaselessly thrown about like tide-wrack." (Snelling, pg. 40) This is the concept of life (described in hyperbole) that an enlightened person overcomes, by coming to the knowledge that they are not bound in this life of suffering, nor are they in any way destined to be reborn into a continuing existence of suffering.

"Good things do come to us in the course of events and should be accepted and enjoyed while they last, but we tend to want only the good and, resisting all else, pursue it exclusively and cling to it desperately if we do get it . . . So the beginning of the road to wisdom begins with a realistic (not pessimistic) recognition of the fact of duhkha (suffering). Life usually has to have bitten us quite deeply, and often many times over, before we reach this stage. But when we do reach it, we have in a very real sense come of age as human beings, for an immature, butterfly existence in pursuit of mere happiness is unsatisfying in the final analysis. When we face up to the dark side of life, on the other hand, *we begin to appreciate the full grandeur and challenge of human existence*. Now too we can start to do something about changing our lives and putting them [the sense of grandeur and challenge of life] on a deeper, more authentic footing." (Snelling, pg. 44) It is relatively easy to acknowledge the physical suffering caused by a disease, most people feel stress from work or have the occasional argument at home, and these examples begin to teach us what suffering is and that we are in this respect united with all mankind.

Meditation Practicum:

"When we, who practice the Teachings, know the main objective of Buddhism, it is beneficial for us because we can study and understand what Buddhism teaches, what the essence is. When we practice to develop mind, we will certainly understand how to practice fruitfully and correctly, we will not lose our way. When we start practicing [meditating,] we will gain results quickly." (Wee, pg. 65)

Dealing with unpleasant thoughts: ". . . It can be very difficult to observe thoughts related to unpleasant experiences—particularly those aligned with strong emotions such as jealousy, anger, fear or envy—with bare attention. Such unpleasant thoughts can be so strong and persistent that it's easy to get caught up in following after them . . . The best way to work with these kinds of thoughts is to step back and rest your mind in objectless shinay for a minute, and then bring your attention to each thought and the ideas that revolve around it, observing both directly for a few minutes, just as you would observe the shape or color of a form. Allow yourself to alternate between resting your mind in objectless meditation and bringing your attention back to the same thoughts."

"When you work with negative thoughts in this way, two things happen. First, as you rest in awareness, your mind begins to settle. Second, you'll find that your attention to particular thoughts or stories comes and goes, just the way it does when working with forms, sounds, and other sensory supports. And as the thought or story is interrupted by other issues—like folding the laundry, buying groceries, or preparing for a meeting—the unpleasant ideas gradually lose their grip on your mind. You begin to realize that they're not as solid or powerful as they first appeared. It's more like a busy signal on the telephone—annoying, perhaps, but nothing you can't deal with."

More importantly: "When you work with unpleasant thoughts in this way, they become assets to mental stability rather than liabilities—like adding weight to the bar when you're exercising in a gym. You're developing psychological muscles to cope with greater and greater levels of stress." (Mingyur, pp. 166-167)

Of all the forms of meditation students will practice, this practicum of dealing with unpleasant thoughts may be the one which gets the most air time, and is likely to be the most useful. In a way being at a retreat and taking lessons on Buddhism is an isolation from the real world, and how can you be sure the effort you expend will have some practical use when you are subsequently confronted with difficult situations when you return to your work and families? Using this meditation to deal with negative thoughts, one by one, instead of avoiding them as you might try to dismiss a nightmare, may be the most beneficial and practical advantage of following this course of study. "If you're distracted by strong emotions, you can try focusing . . . on the mind that experiences the emotion. Or you might try switching to ***tonglen*** practice, using whatever you're feeling—anger, sadness, jealousy, desire—as the basis for the practice." (Mingyur, pg. 211)"

"***Tonglen***, which may be translated into English as 'sending and taking' . . . a simple coordination of imagination and breathing. The first step is simply to recognize that as much as you want to achieve happiness and avoid suffering, other beings also feel the same way. There is no need to visualize specific beings, although you may start out with a specific visualization if you find it helpful. Eventually, however, the practice of taking and sending extends beyond those you can imagine to include all sentient beings—including animals, insects, and inhabitants of dimensions you don't possess the knowledge or capacity to see." (Mingyur, pg. 187)" We practice this in Lesson Twenty-two.

"When people begin to observe themselves they are often shocked and complain that Buddhist practice is actually making them worse human beings. Actually they were that bad all along, only they never paused to look! We tend to select data and construct an idealized self-image [failing to take ownership.] Unpleasant characteristics are suppressed because they don't harmonize with this pretty fiction. Once awareness is brought to play, however, the dark, unconfronted side of ourselves has to be faced and that is invariably painful. Mindfulness also brings us squarely up against the world as it is rather than as we would like it to be."(Snelling, pg. 56)

Biographical Sketch:

For each of us, society imposes duties, whether to country, to family, to friends, and to ourselves certainly. So it was in the time of Buddha: "The birth of his son Rahula made it easier for him to leave. In the India (Nepal) of his day, providing an heir to carry on the family line was a major duty toward one's ancestors. To abandon home, even for the sake of pursuing enlightenment, without furnishing an heir was considered undutiful. Though natural affection may have hindered him, the birth of his son provided the occasion for Shakyamuni's departure, since he had fulfilled his duty to his father and his wife. There is a tradition that he left his father's home at the age of nineteen, but the oldest and most reliable documents give twenty-nine as his age at the time." (Mizuno, pg. 18) How do the duties we carry illustrate the Buddhist teaching of suffering?

Shortly after leaving home Siddhartha was to have said: "O King, I have left my family and do not have any earthly desires. They are too often binding. In escape from them is peace. I am turned in the direction of abstinence and purification for the sake of finding the way. This is my goal. I wish for nothing else." (Mizuno, pg. 22) This was the naïve Siddhartha speaking, and it took seven more years of difficult work for him to discover enlightenment and take a different approach, to come back into the world and teach, lead and interact with the family he had left behind.

The Buddha achieved Enlightenment at Uravela (presently Bodh Gaya) . . . [after several months failing to find other worthy students] he set off on foot for Sarnath, the deer park at Varanasi, about one hundred forty-two miles away, where the five [former friends and fellow practitioners of ascetic life for six years] bhikkhus were, [but] they decided they would ignore him and not [show] him honor. However, when the Buddha came near they lost their resolve because they were so impressed by the glory and serenity of his countenance . . . The Buddha told the five ascetics that he was the fully Enlightened One and that he would teach them the truth of the Dhamma. He said that if they practiced the Dhamma, as instructed by him, they would achieve Nibbana, Enlightenment [Buddha has made the same promise to us all] . . . So at Sarnath . . . Buddha delivered to the Pancavaggiya his first discourse, 'Setting in Motion the ***Wheel of the Dhamma***.' The first discourse was concerned with the Middle Way and the Four Noble Truths . . . the way leading to Enlightenment-which lies between the extremes of sensual gratification, on the one hand, and of the self-mortification of the ascetic life, on the other."

"Sarnath, also previously known as Mrigadava, Rishipattana, and Isipatana, located about six miles from Varnasi (Benares, India) is the 'deer park' where the Buddha delivered the first discourse, set in motion the wheel of the Dhamma, and founded the Sangha . . . By the seventh century AD (about 1,000 years later) when the

Chinese traveler Hsuan Tsang visited Sarnath, there were thirty monasteries and three thousand monks there. The site became an important center for one of the Theravada schools [Teaching of the Elders.] . . . Sarnath was rediscovered about 1800, and excavations began . . . Sarnath is the site of many important Buddhist monuments, the most notable being the Dhammarajika stupa, the Dhamek stupa, the Mulagandhakuti (the main shrine), the Asokan pillar and lion capital, and the preaching Buddha statue."

". . . The Dhammacakka mudra . . . the preaching posture . . . is very naturalistic . . . His seat is magnificently carved . . . and contains the 'wheel of the law,' the halo around the Buddha's head is intricately [golden floral] designed . . . an image of a deer appears on either side of the Buddha. The positioning of the hands has come to symbolize the turning of the wheel of the law. The middle finger of the right hand touching the middle finger of the left suggests The Middle Way. Between the two front legs of the seat appear figures of the Pancavaggiya, as well as those of a woman and child, Yasa and his mother." (Inthisan, pp. 43-46)

Reading for the Day:

The truth of life Buddha discovered and attained is "the Four Noble Truths"—

1) "The truth that life is full of suffering (***Dukkha***): that is woe, mental discomfort, physical discomfort, birth and re-birth, old age, sickness and painful death . . .
2) The truth regarding the causes of suffering (***Samudaya***): the cause of suffering is cravings which mean desires, kharma [based on] inheritance, defilements and mistaken efforts to overcome suffering—[this creates a] spiral of pain and agony.
3) The truth that it is possible to extinguish suffering—thus the Cessation of Suffering (***Nirodha***): resulting from practicing the teachings, cleansing, meditating to expand the mental capacity and following the moral codes. The extinction of total suffering comprising greed, aversion and ignorance is

the Final Goal, the Supreme Goal of Buddhism (Nibbana or Nirvana).

4) The truth about the path leading to the extinction or cessation of suffering: this path is ***the Noble Eight-fold Path*** (for purposes of this lesson those taken from the Theravada tradition) consisting of right understanding, right thought, right speech, right action, right livelihood, right effort, right mindfulness and right concentration." (Wee, pp. 12-13)

"Ordinary life is filled with suffering, and this suffering is the result of attachments and passions. Such attachments obscure (sgrib pa) understanding. Our belief systems and view of reality are inevitably limited, so ordinary beings are not capable of judging which beliefs are false and which hold certain truth (nges don). The Buddha's teachings, the Dharma (chos), are said to be valuable precisely because they directly (mngon du) pertain to the condition of everyday life. Yet, blinded by ignorance, sentient beings fail to realize even the first noble truth about their lives and the world around them; namely, that the condition of everyday life and of the entire phenomenal realm—samsara ('khor ba)—is one of misery. Sentient beings are often so blind that they fail to grasp even the 'smallest particle' of the world's misery, let alone the extent of their own suffering." (Brown, pg. 37) Therefore Taking Refuge makes supreme sense.

Protecting:

"This is what I heard," both from students and teacher.

Additional Teachings:

"The Legend of Suffering:

1) On Delusion depend the (life-affirming) Activities (***sankhara***).
2) On the Activities depends Consciousness (***vinnana***): (rebirth consciousness in womb?)

3) On consciousness depends the Psycho-physical Combination (nama-rupa).
4) On the psycho-physical combination depends the Sixfold Sense-activity (chal-ayatana).
5) On the sixfold sense-activity depends the Sensorial Impressions (phassa).
6) On the sensorial impression depends Feeling (vedana).
7) On feeling depends Craving (tanha).
8) On craving depends Clinging to Existence (upadana).
9) On clinging to existence depends the Process of Becoming (kamma-bhava, action process).
10) On the process of becoming depends Rebirth (jati).
11) On rebirth depends Decay and Death (jara-marana), sorrow, lamentation, pain, grief and despair.
12) Thus arises this whole mass of suffering. This is called the noble truth of the origin of suffering.") (Goddard, pg. 40)

"There are six qualities attributed to the Dhamma in the Pali scriptures . . . in the meditation technique known as Recollection of the Dhamma.

1) comprehensive exposition . . . good in the beginning, good in the middle and good in the end . . .
2) realizable through the practitioners' own efforts . . . no need to blindly believe [nor to have an intermediary.]
3) akalika: which is 'timeless' or 'yielding immediate results.'
4) ehipassika: 'come and see.' completely open to investigation and verification.
5) leads to higher knowledge and the realization of Nibbana.
6) paccattam: directly known through intuitive insight and is thus a matter of personal knowledge . . . and requires direct experience." (Plamintr, 2007, pp. 65-67)

"The Dhamma is nourishment for the mind; it cleanses the mind, and makes the mind pleasant and beautiful . . . a mind starved of Dhamma is also weak and becomes a source of problems. Crime, corruption, violence and immoral behavior are some of the symptoms of a mind which uncared for, uncleansed, and unbeautified by the

Dhamma. It is therefore important to train the mind, and the best way to do this is through meditation." (Plamintr, 2007, pp. 80-81)

Sharing Merit:

I share all of my merits with all sentient beings. [maitri]

I share all my merits with my parents, teachers, relatives[, my guardian deva, the guardian deva of my home, the guardian deva of my village, the guardian deva of my town, the guardian deva of my country, the guardian deva of the earth, the king of death. the king of men. the king of devas. all devas and all petas.] May they all gain the merits of my meritorious deed as much as I do and may they all be happy and free from enmity.

[May I call upon the guardian deva of the earth to bear witness.]

May they all hear my words and rejoice in my meritorious deed!

Sadhu _ Sadhu _ Sadhu Well-done,
Well-done, Well-done (ukonline)

Buddhist Sutra

Lesson Title: **Suffering—The Four Noble Truths**

Lesson Number: **Three**

Key Vocabulary: shinay, awareness, Dukkha, metaphor, re-birth, suffering, Tipitaka, Law of Causation, Tonglen practice, defilements, empathy, The Wheel of the Dhamma, Samudaya, niroda

Assignment:
Both during casual times and during formal meditation pay attention to your unpleasant thoughts and add to your list of Sufferings those you have experienced, especially during the last two years in terms of Buddhist Teachings.

Define each of the Key Vocabulary in your own words.

How does our inheritance of DNA and our genetic code affect suffering in our lives?

How is suffering a part of everyone's life? How does that unite us?
How do the duties we carry illustrate the Buddhist teaching of suffering?
Consider the lives of people born into a 'third world' life.

"Yoga is a good method for freeing the spirit . . ." How does this compare to Buddhist teachings?

How is this teaching the "middle way" so unique?
Why is it such an important perspective?
Answer these four questions for yourself:

1. Is there a God?
2. Who created the world?
3. Is there life after death?
4. Where is heaven and hell?

Sharing Merit:

I share all of my merits with all sentient beings. [maitri]
I share all my merits with my parents, teachers, relatives
May they all gain the merits of my meritorious deed as much as I do and may they all be happy and free from enmity.
May they all hear my words and rejoice in my meritorious deed!
Sadhu _ Sadhu _ Sadhu
Well-done, Well-done, Well-done

http://web.ukonline.co.uk/buddhism/merits.htm

Materials for fourth lesson: journal entries relating to suffering, a brief genealogy, drinking water

Buddhist Sutra

Lesson Title: **Cause and Effect**

Lesson Number: **Four**

Rationale:

The Law of Causation is viewed by Buddhists as a scientific truth. It should be intuitively obvious to any casual observer of human nature that the comments we make and the ethical choices we follow have both immediate and long term consequences for our lives. The truth regarding the causes of suffering is the concern of the second of the Four Noble Truths. Many Buddhists (and Hindus before) go beyond this and postulate that the inheritance from kharma of previous lives may influence the kind and duration of suffering we experience in this life, and this even pre-disposes those who have arrived at this point in *Buddhist Sutras* to be receptive to the dharma. Buddhism is not fatalistic, however, because it teaches us how to eliminate and prevent any negative consequences from any source, and how to avoid creating new causes of suffering. There are also many ways to make merit to improve and perfect our lives to create happiness.

Discussion of Prior Lesson:

We must think carefully before we accept greater duty that might create more suffering, and even challenge in ourselves the desire to embark on the path to enlightenment. These examinations can sustain the growth of wisdom. Suffering occurs in both direct and indirect ways. Consider the philosophical study of Existentialism and the concept of "***angst.***" (To be revisited in Lesson Twenty-seven)

"When you're done [meditating], ask yourself what the experience was like for you. Did you have a lot of [distractions]? Were you able to see your [former negative] thoughts very clearly? Or were they hazy and indistinct? Or did they just vanish into thin air as soon as you tried to look at them?" Did they dominate and oppress your mind?

"Now I'm going to let you in on a big secret: There is no secret! Both extremes that people describe—and anything in between—are experiences of meditation. If you're afraid of your thoughts, you're giving them power over you, because they seem so solid and real, so true. And the more afraid of them you are, the more powerful they appear to be. But when you start to observe your thoughts, the power you give to them begins to fade." (Mingyur, pp. 64-65)

Training Objective:

How does our inheritance (DNA, nature vs. nurture) affect the decisions we make each day? How do these factors create, influence or demonstrate kharma? How do we make the decision to begin a spiritual practice? The scientific nature of the law of cause and effect. Bowing.

Materials Required: journal entries relating to suffering, a brief genealogy, drinking water

Motivational Statement:

". . . Most sentient beings, due to their ignorance and past karma (las in Tibet) are not likely to believe in the Dharma teachings enough to undertake spiritual practice of their own accord [and persist in doing so] . . . most will lose interest in the discipline and revert to previous bad habits . . . Therefore in the Mahayana

Buddhist tradition, where the role of a teacher as spiritual friend is central, [persisting] in a lasting way [occurs] mainly through direct intervention by a teacher . . . He is the embodiment of realized truth and is capable of directly transmitting this truth to others . . ."

". . . To understand spiritual practice [it is necessary to make reference] to ***the doctrine of cause and effect***, for it provides the rationale for why meditative practice works as a solution to suffering . . . The effects become manifest in our experience in the form of signs that appear first as mental events that arise in our stream of consciousness and then later in our observable behavior." (Brown, pp. 37-39) (Identify each important teaching here and in each section, and discuss together.)

First Progressive:

"Since the ***Law of Causation*** is difficult to understand, ***Shakyamuni*** suspected that people blinded by desires and pleasures would not comprehend it even if he taught it . . . and his efforts [immediately after he achieved enlightenment] would be wasted . . . According to ancient writings, at this time, ***Brahma,*** the highest of the Hindu gods, appeared to Shakyamuni and said that if he, the World-honored One, failed to teach his truth, the world would become even more degraded and dark than it already was. If he would devise a method of teaching, however, in spite of the difficulty of his message, some people would understand. Brahma pleaded with Shakyamuni to *condescend to carry his truth and salvation to the world.* This story, which has come to be known as the Pleading of Brahma, is, like the stories of demons assailing Shakyamuni before and after his enlightenment, a *narrative representation* of the hesitations, doubts, and complex feelings that he must have experienced . . ." rather than literal truth. "Narrative representation" suggests that this legend as with others is food for thought, not history.

"As an outcome of the Pleading of Brahma, Shakyamuni decided to teach the truth to which he had been enlightened. And when he had arrived at a method of making his message as easy to understand as possible, he concluded his weeks of meditation and began his teaching." (Mizuno, pg. 30) The decision to share the teachings of Buddhism with others is an important decision and often goes against the innate shyness, introversion and lack of self-confidence most people feel, especially when it comes to such a personal issue as deeply held religious convictions. Contrast this kind of compassion to charity.

"There is also a great but subtle power in receiving guidance from a teacher trained in an established ***lineage tradition***: the power of interdependence . . . When you work with a teacher trained in a lineage, you become part of the 'family' of that lineage . . . you will gain priceless lessons just through observing and interacting with a true ***lineage teacher*** . . . a qualified teacher *must also demonstrate compassion* and, through his or her actions, subtly make clear his or her own realization without ever mentioning it. Avoid teachers who talk about their own accomplishments—because that kind of talk or boasting is a sure sign that they have not achieved realization at all." (Mingyur, pp. 247-248) We always learn more from the examples of our parents and teachers than from their words alone. (Discuss each section before moving ahead.)

Second Progressive:

"When we know and understand how suffering is, the next step is to know the cause of suffering which are cravings. It is the current of desires and thrusts. They are cause of suffering (***samudaya***) which is the second Noble Truth." If "cravings" are the river that propels our lives, the current is "desires and thrusts." Can we change our river into a calmly flowing, flat and placid stream? How can meditation help us? Why is engaging in a full-time spiritual practice so important?

"When we know and understand suffering, Buddhism then teaches how to put an end to the causes of suffering. That is to cease cravings in one's own mind by training the mind to be pure and free from all defilements by means of Concentration Meditation and Insight Meditation. In this regard, we have to know cessation of suffering and how to do so." (Wee, pg. 68) Many of the unethical actions people take are attempts to relieve suffering, for example over-indulgence (a ***defilement***) in alcohol (and alcoholism) or use of dangerous narcotics is often identified as an attempt to escape from suffering. This presumptive escape often creates more serious consequences and complications until the individual "bottoms out" and is forced to rely on a "higher power" to control his or her life. It is easy to recognize theft of money as a craving, or attempt to overcome the suffering of not having sufficient funds, and so this wrong thinking can be described as a ***defilement***. An addiction to gambling is a craving and an example of how wanting to obtain something for the least possible effort or none at all, can lead to serious consequences.

"From the Four Noble Truths, we will know how our life is. If we can reflect ourselves to understand them, we will know that every single life encounters suffering. [If] we cannot understand well the Four Noble Truths [it is] because we lack thorough reflection upon them. We suffer due to three cravings:

1. Sensual cravings: desire for 5 sensual pleasures consisting of visible object, sound, smell, taste, touch and desire for sexual intercourse.
2. Cravings for rebirth: desire for existence, for process of becoming.
3. Cravings for self-annihilation: desire for non-existence.

According to the Four Noble Truths, the real state of our life is the state of suffering. It is the supreme truth in accordance with the Three Characteristics namely, impermanence, suffering and soullessness." (Wee, pp. 25-26)

The essence of Buddhism is to follow a path inspired by ethical training. "In short, the real essence of Buddhism is to release mind from all defilements." (Wee, pg. 56) But is this enough to eliminate suffering? "But though a person may be thoroughly moral, he may still be far from free from the suffering attendant on birth, aging, pain, and death, still not free from oppression by the mental defilements [Lesson Twenty-one.] Morality stops well short of the elimination of craving, aversion, and delusion, so cannot do away with suffering. Religion, particularly Buddhism, goes much further than this. It aims directly at the complete elimination of the defilements, that is, it aims at extinguishing the various kinds of suffering . . . This indicates how religion differs from mere morality, and how much further Buddhism goes than the moral systems of the world in general." (Buddhadasa, 2005, pg. 27)

Another source of suffering is associated with the temptation to look for ***essences*** and to theorize even about Buddhist teachings. This is in part what gives rise to the concept of emptiness, because such theoretical answers and generalizations are never adequate explanations of what Buddhism is about, for example, thus they are empty. We look for absolute meaning when it would be better to explain the language game. More on this later.

Third Progressive:

"The second of the Four Noble Truths (the Truth of Cause) [or law of cause and effect] postulates that illusion and desire [craving] are the causes of suffering. Since there is no suffering without a cause, it is essential to determine whether that cause is the outcome of internal or external elements or a combination of both. If the cause is understood, by eliminating it one eliminates the suffering itself." (Mizuno, pg. 45)

". . . Duhkha has an identifiable cause. This is ***trishna*** (Pali: tanha) which is literally translated as 'thirst,' but in fact possesses the same kind of spectrum of connotations [semantic map] as ***duhkha***. There are gross forms of trishna, like obsessive lust for money and sensual pleasures; and there are exceedingly subtle forms, like a desire to do good, [to obsessively follow rules] or to know the truth. And of course there is a whole gamut of middling connotations in between."

"Basically trishna can be reduced to a fundamental ache that is implanted in everything that exists: a gnawing dissatisfaction with what is and a concomitant reaching out for something else. So we can never be at rest but are always grasping for something outside ourselves." (Snelling, pg. 44) It is easy to be in denial or ignore this kind of sensation, yet it looms large in the subconscious and influences the ways we conduct our relationships. How can we know the influence of these subtle messages? Can we engage in a thorough, objective introspection to identify when in our lives we see cause and effect in some kind of alignment, or floating on the surface like debris?

"Scientific investigation adopts a two-stage method. In the **first stage**, laws are formulated about the operations of the phenomena under investigation [hypothesis] . . . the first step in scientific investigation is discovering the Law of Causation in the world of phenomena [and human activity]. This is identical with the Buddhist method of acquiring a correct view of the world and of human life as operations of the Law of Causation. Understanding the actual world as suffering arising from desires and attachments in the terms of the Four Noble Truths—corresponds with the first stage of scientific investigation."

"The **second stage** is the application [or testing] of the Law of Causation. Creation of conditions and states of affairs that human beings consider ideal is a matter of applied research. All the conveniences of civilization and the products of culture have resulted from the application of scientific laws. Putting to use laws of phenomena in spiritual culture, politics, and economics for the sake of improvement of humanity would probably result in the creation of an ideal culture and society. Viewed in this light, the . . . Law of Causation . . . is in line not only with medical science but also with all of the other sciences. It is amazing that Shakyamuni evolved these teachings, which distinguish Buddhism from all other religions and philosophies, as long as two thousand five hundred years ago. The teachings prove the universal applicability, truth, and *rational nature* of the doctrinal theories of Buddhism." (Mizuno, pp. 46-47) Thus each of the doctrines of Rational Buddhism can undergo the same kind of scrutiny by students; such esoteric beliefs as: reincarnation, histories of previous lives, influences of gods, charisma of a teacher, suspension of natural laws—the super-natural—all these are subject to scientific scrutiny, and belief or disbelief is left up to the student without diminishing the basic tenants and usefulness of the practice of Buddhism. Looking for evidence that satisfies the hypothesis can involve bias; is the supporting evidence an outlier, or how else can suffering happen? and do all bad deeds have obvious consequences? Do white lies, and cheating on income taxes always create negative consequences?

Understanding how the law of cause and effect works in our lives requires a serious focus on and even ***admiration*** of past events as objects of appraisal (recall from the Reading of Lesson Two)—how we got to be where we are. This results in taking our mental object as precious. ". . . The object [or events in our lives] become so interesting that the perceiver is able to sustain attention on it. Furthermore, admiration implies that the perceptual object has had sufficient impact on the observer to require further involvement with it . . . The perceiver is able more carefully to distinguish the specific features [of an event in their lives when] . . . all of the features of the object should become clear . . . Another feature of admiration is that the object is taken as precious . . . it is meant to capture the entire fabric of meaning: 1. intensified interest; 2. making an impact; 3. distinguishing the features of the object; 4. having all the features become clear; and 5. finally, taking the object as precious." Imagine examining an event in your life as if it were a jewel and notice the form, color, shape, clarity and other characteristics that influence your judgment then and now about the event (or friendship)—thus scrutinize with dispassion in order to understand and learn from the past.

This would be the same kind of examination that ought to be applied ". . . whether it pertains to an encounter with a mundane object of perception [i.e. an inspiring musical score] or to an encounter with a sacred holy being [or teacher]." (Brown, pp. 46-47) We will gradually come to understand that even followers of Rational Buddhism can be inspired by "holy" objects or charismatic teachers—as if we were living inside a poem.

Meditation Practicum:

"There are at least three areas where Buddhist meditation teachings in their indigenous form are not ideally matched to Western students. First, traditional meditation development includes a set of preparatory practices, which are designed to make the body and mind fit for meditation, and make progress with meditation more likely . . . five to ten years . . . Many Westerners balk at these preparatory practices because the form of presentation is quite foreign to us . . . [we prefer to] begin immediately with formal meditation. [Westerners] are likely to recreate many of the bad habits of everyday living on the meditation pillow and never progress as a result. Other practitioners readily embrace these preparatory practices in a mindless way and spend years making prostrations, reciting prayers without knowing their meaning, offering various acts of devotion, and blindly imitating or idealizing a teacher in such a way that not only fails to make the body and mind fit for meditation, but also undermines self-confidence, further hindering their development."

"Second, we need to see [and adopt] what methods have been most effective for Westerners in bringing about real inner change . . . various schools of psychotherapy currently exist as the West's great tradition of growth and development . . . [in which] A fundamental feature of most psychotherapy is the primacy of the therapeutic relationship . . . factors like empathy, acceptance, encouragement . . . the therapist providing an emotionally corrective relationship for the patient . . . a relationship-based method of teaching meditation is best matched to this culture . . . psychotherapy alone fails to accomplish the broad range of skills cultivated by the preparatory practices of the great contemplative traditions."

"Third . . . A unique contribution of the cognitive-behavioral literature is the targeting of specific behaviors, detailed step-by-step instructions for change, and clear benchmarks of progress . . . For Western practitioners, Eastern meditation traditions that present clearly defined meditation stages [with transparent goals] are perhaps most helpful, especially those that describe the main techniques, intended results, and benchmarks of progress, and carefully delineate common problems and how to remedy them." (Brown, pp. xvi-xvii) Not all Buddhist training is of this sort, but the *Buddhist Sutras* have endeavored to incorporate this advice by advocating and presenting one specific Sixteen Step practice that is developed gradually along with other related lessons.

These *Buddhist Sutras* can be a self-help prompt, pointing-out the dharma, describing Rational Buddhism, but it is not intended to substitute for counseling processes or psychotherapy. It is assumed that those who pursue these Lessons are emotionally and temperamentally in control of their own minds and reasonably well adjusted to society. The assumption that we all need a little counseling with friends or professionals, and training in our lives is accepted explicitly here. What kind of counseling, is left up to each person's conscience, influenced carefully by family members and friends that are in our social support groups.

As a useful and immediate preparatory practice, it is customary for Buddhists to bow and show respect to shrines and important teachers. As part of devotional practice, offering candles, incense and flowers is a long standing tradition as well. Chanting is a frequently practiced support to prepare the mind for meditation. Bowing is likewise a practice that helps create a focus immediately before meditation, to help prevent the mind from being distracted by those commonplace manifestations of the ego which we all carry during the day ". . . our wanting something, our hoping to 'get somewhere', or the longing to achieve, acquire and possess some self-oriented goal. Instead, we should be seeking the very opposite motivation—to give up 'doing' anything; to cease the constant wanting, and to practice humility and relinquishment." (Cittaviveka, pg.2) When entering the sala it is important to carry as little mental baggage as possible, to be open and receptive.

Biographical Sketch:

Whenever I bow, even in private, I have a self-conscious sense of being watched, or of watching myself, and each time this nervousness makes the event significant. Possibly if I had been taught from youth to do this, I would take it for granted, but would it be better for all that?

Imagine in a month, or year from now: "By this point in the developing process, the teacher has made some impact . . . the listener grasps the full impact of the teaching and thereby becomes amazed at its potential benefit. Just as a mundane perceptual object may compel its observer to pay closer attention, the teacher, as an object of interest, invites the beginner to listen closely so as to perceive the benefit directly." (Brown, pg. 47) The important message here is that it is inevitable that we reason "ad hominem," that is, the teacher is part of the message and influential toward students' ability to understand and sustain interest in meditation and dharma. For that reason, all great teachers admonish restraint, and approach their vocation with humility.

"The Law of Causation, which is perfectly sound from the rational, ethical, and religious viewpoints and which has a universal validity enabling it to withstand any criticism, was formulated as a result of examination and criticism of all the other imperfect and irrational systems in India in Shakyamuni's time. The Law of Causation teaches both the theoretical and practical application of the idea that there is no immortal, immutable self or soul."

"The Law had never been taught in India before. It is the characteristic that sets Buddhism apart from other philosophies and religions. But though he discovered it, Shakyamuni did not create it. This Law is an absolute truth—recognizable as true by all peoples, in all places, and at all times—existing eternally independent of the appearance in the world of a ***Tathagata*** (a term for a Buddha . . . one who has come the full Way, who has reached the truth and come to declare it). Shakyamuni merely discovered and taught the Law." (Mizuno, pp. 29-30) Whether this is historically valid or not is questionable.

"On the ninth level [described in the Lotus Sutra] are the ***bodhisattvas*** . . . who out of compassion postpone their entry into Buddhahood and remain in the saha, world, to alleviate the sufferings of others. On the tenth and highest level are the buddhas or the state of Buddhahood. It is this level, according to ***Mahayana*** doctrine, that all living beings should seek to attain, and which, it insists, they can in time attain if they will not content themselves with lesser goals but have faith in the Buddha and his teachings as these are embodied in the sacred scriptures."(Watson, pg. xiv) "This great emphasis upon the role of the bodhisattva is one of the main characteristics that distinguish Mahayana thought from that of earlier [Theravada] Buddhism." (Watson, pg. xiii) These personages are thought to be (or have been) the greatest recognized teachers. And thus these teachers are used as models for crafting The Buddha icons in many Asian countries.

Selecting a teacher (or Lama, Guru or Monk) ". . . has three components: 1) meeting, 2) giving advice, and 3) hearing the advice . . . The entire event, though seemingly mundane, is in fact an extraordinary event . . . Why, then, is meeting a lama and hearing his advice so profoundly transformative? The answer resides in the person who gives the advice. He is a Holy being. He is the embodiment of realized truth and is capable of directly transmitting this truth to others." (Brown, pp. 38-39) The Dalai Lama is such a teacher for many even in the West where most people have never met him.

Visualize yourself with different teachers. Who will be transformative in your life? Have you already met this person? Will there be more than one? Can you see your first meeting or feel the thrill of first recognition? Must this teacher still be alive? How does meditation practice prepare us to meet an inspirational teacher?

Reading for the Day:

". . . A reader unfamiliar with Buddhism may not fully grasp the meaning of [a] passage, but he or she may still perceive enough value in the distinction being made to be able to admire what is offered. Listening to and seeing the benefit does not require that the listener understand [everything.] As the passage indicates, the essential function of listening is to act at the level of the ***propensities.*** According to the doctrine of cause and effect, propensities, good or bad, eventually ripen into actions. The virtuous actions of listening and seeing the benefit, even when not fully comprehended, may ripen into resultant action of becoming a Buddha. The groundwork has now been laid for the eventual realization of buddhahood." How predictable and consistent are you? and Why are you so disciplined and responsible?

". . . The beginner must give up disrespect and build respect with the actions of his body, speech and mind. Genuine respect is free from the extremes of over-dependence and rebellion. Genuine respect [including self-respect] is reflected in subtle ways... someone who sits quietly composed and 'listens undistracted as if he were in a deep meditative state' is said to manifest bodily respect . . . Likewise, a beginner who disputes the Dharma, [i.e. uses sarcasm or ridicule] forgets it, or ignores it has not taken it seriously or listened carefully. In contrast, 'repeating the teachings over and over to oneself as if continuously singing a song' is an example of speech-respect . . . mental respect requires that a beginner orient his mind toward the lama's presence [and Buddha's image] and teachings 'as if looking into a mirror' . . . The beginner monitors the ongoing events exactly as they occur in his own mental continuum while simultaneously observing the behavior of and listening to the lama. This special mode of attention is called ***putting in order*** one's own mental continuum. The verb to put in order is a technical term with a very specific usage. It refers to the act of looking at seemingly external appearances introspectively, such that one's perspective is transformed or rearranged . . . an inner transformation takes place by which one's own mental continuum begins to 'mirror' the virtuous qualities of the lama." (Brown, pp. 52-54)

It is possible to extrapolate from the Teachings that since there is Buddhahood in each one of us, when we look at the image of Buddha in whatever configuration, we are looking, at least figuratively, at a mirror showing our own potential. Thus 'worship' in front of a Buddha icon in Rational Buddhism is like sitting in front of a mirror and feeling love for oneself. We celebrate our own rectitude that comes from our internal strength when we follow the Path of The Buddha.

Protecting:

"This is what I heard," both from students and teacher.

"Admiration means that the object is taken as precious . . . it is meant to capture the entire fabric of meaning:

1. intensified interest; (use the kneeling posture)
2. making an impact;
3. distinguishing the features of the object;
4. having all the features become clear;
   and
5. finally, taking the object as precious." (Brown, pp. 46-47)

Additional Teachings:

Key to understanding Rational Buddhism is being aware of the special language used in both the archaic and many modern teachings. "In everyday language, the word 'birth' refers to physically coming into the world from the mother's womb. A person is born physically only once. Having been born, one lives in the world until one dies . . . In Dhamma language, the word 'birth' refers to the birth of the idea 'I' or 'ego' that arises in the mind throughout each day. In this sense, the ordinary person is born very often, time and time again; a more developed person is born less frequently; a person well advanced in practice . . . ultimately ceases being born altogether. Each arising in the mind of the idea of 'I' in one form or another is called a 'birth' [or rebirth.] . . . The word 'birth' is very common in the Buddha's discourses . . . when discussing conditioned arising he used the word 'birth' [the idea of 'I' or 'me'] . . . he wasn't talking about physical birth [or rebirth.] He was talking about the birth of attachment to the ideas of 'me' and mine,' 'myself' and 'my own'." (Buddhadasa, 1999, pg. 29) During the oral traditions of Buddhist teachings, the concept of reincarnation which is still taught by Hindu sects and Yogis was confused with this particular use of the word 'birth,' and thus many Buddhist traditions have conflicting teachings about transmigration or reincarnation. These are not to be taken literally as this concept is used in ordinary language.

Repeat frequently:

"I take refuge in the Buddha.

I take refuge in the Dhamma.

I take refuge in the Sangha." (Buddhadasa, 1999, pg. 76) To see any Buddha icon completely, is to extend and broaden the meaning of an image and connect all three of these aspects. This is one way of putting in order the influence of these teachings.

The Final Salutation to the Triple Gems

(1) Imaya dhammanu dhammapatipattiya Buddham pujemi
(2) Imaya dhammanu dhammapatipattiya Dhammam pujemi
(3) Imaya dhammanu dhammapatipattiya Samgham pujemi

Meaning: (can be recited in English)

(1) I pay homage to the Buddha by the practice of charity, morality, and meditation in conformity with the Nine Supramundane Dhammas.
(2) I pay homage to the Dhamma by the practice of charity, morality, and meditation in conformity with the Nine Supramundane Dhammas.
(3) I pay homage to the Samgha by the practice of charity, morality, and meditation in conformity with the Nine Supramundane Dhammas. (ukonline)

Sharing Merit:

Rejoicing In Others' Merit (Saying Sadhu)

Buddhist Sutra

Lesson Title: **Cause and Effect**

Lesson Number: **Four**

Key Vocabulary: Mahayana, Buddhahood, put in order, Shakyamuni, "no immortal, Tathagata, immutable self or soul," bodhisattvas, five-point prostration, impermanence, narrative representation, icon (vs. idol), admiration, lineage tradition, propensities, Brahma, tishna

Assignment: Practice using past events in your life as objects of meditation. Immediately before each meditation perform the five-point prostration three times.

Identify the five stages of admiration.
Identify ways in which the law of cause and effect influences your life.
How will wholesome deeds result in happiness and satisfaction?

Define each of the Key Vocabulary in your own words.

How does our inheritance (DNA, nature vs. nurture) effect the decisions we make each day, compared to our upbringing?

How do we create and demonstrate kharma?
Compare the compassion of teaching to charity?
How did you make the decision to begin a spiritual practice?

Visualize and imagine a Teacher and your experience with that person. Do this at least three times for at least ten minutes each. Practice using previous meditation assignments.

Visualize yourself with different teachers. Who will be transformative in your life?

Have you already met this person? Will there be more than one?
Can you see your first meeting or feel the thrill of first recognition?

How does meditation practice prepare us to meet an inspirational teacher? Must this teacher be alive?

How predictable and consistent are you?
Why are you so disciplined and responsible (or have this propensity)?

Why are the three characteristics of being human (impermanence, suffering—unsatisfactoriness, and soul-less-ness) so important?

Materials for next lesson: photograph of someone you love, (polished stone)

Buddhist Sutra

Lesson Title: Cessation of Suffering

Lesson Number: Five

Rationale:

This is the goal of Buddha's teachings, the mission of his life, to bring all people to an understanding of how to enjoy their lives which otherwise are encumbered by many different kinds of suffering stemming from disease, deaths, hunger, exploitation, anger, addictions, abuse and social discord; just to name a few. There is a way for this to happen and that is central to the mystic and expertise of Rational Buddhism.

Discussion of Prior Lesson:

Based on my memory of my educational psychology class in college, it is a scientific conclusion that as much as 80% of our personalities are determined by our genetic inheritance. I certainly notice traits in my two sons that correspond to my father's personality, whom they never knew. Certainly some of the crap we encounter in life we have earned for ourselves based on the Law of Causation, and the idea of a spiritual practice is to change the direction of our lives to avoid making these same old mistakes, but are there somethings that we can't change?

Review from Lesson One: "... What makes someone a Buddhist is their commitment to this endeavour, and all the doctrines, practices, institutions, and schools of Buddhism are useful to the extent that they help people to follow the Buddhist path. The traditional way in which Buddhists of all schools express this commitment is to say that they 'go for Refuge to the Buddha, Dharma, and Sangha' (the Three Jewels) . . . the Buddhist tradition is united by the defining act of Going for Refuge to the Three Jewels . . ." (Vishvapani, pg. 24) Eventually we may come to anticipate this act with a sense of affection.

Training Objective:

How is happiness connected to the Law of Causation? Can we achieve perfection of character and enlightenment in this lifetime? Protecting learning gains. Cognitive Restructuring. Every complaint we express is a voice of suffering. Breathing meditation.

Materials Required: photograph of someone you love, (polished stone)

Motivational Statement:

According to this author from a Japanese tradition: "No matter how eager and assiduous a person is in religious training, achieving enlightenment depends on primary and secondary causes from previous existences. For people with the right causes, the opportunity for enlightenment will come readily; for people without them, the opportunity will probably not develop. Although it is true that the Buddha-nature is inherent in all sentient beings, the speed with which enlightenment is reached depends on the causes from previous existences and causes in the present life." (Mizuno, pg. 117) This belief (Mahayana) is innocent enough, but like all Buddhist teachings it can be challenged by the rational mind. It is possible that people will use this teaching in the wrong way, to excuse or enable inappropriate behavior (defilements) that lead to suffering that can otherwise easily be prevented. If you are here, ready for enlightenment, what does that imply about your level of preparation?

First Progressive:

"There are two kinds of happiness: temporary and permanent. Temporary happiness is like aspirin for the mind, providing a few hours of relief from emotional pain. Permanent happiness comes from treating the underlying causes of suffering . . . Genetically, it appears that human beings are programmed to seek temporary states of happiness rather than lasting traits. Eating, drinking, making love, [laughing] and other activities release hormones that produce physical and psychological sensations of well-being . . . ensuring we survive . . . the pleasure we feel in such activities [even in helping others] is transitory by genetic design. If eating, drinking, making love, and so on were able to produce permanent sensations of happiness, we'd do these things once and then sit back and enjoy ourselves while others took over the tasks involved in perpetuating the species. In strictly biological terms, the drive to survive propels us more strongly [craving] toward unhappiness than toward happiness . . . we can actually train ourselves to recognize, accept, and rest in a more lasting experience of peace and contentment. This 'quirk' [in the structure of our brains] is actually the highly developed ***neocortex,*** the area of the brain that deals with reasoning, logic, and conceptualization." (Mingyur, pg. 222)

When we give coins from our pocket to a street urchin, we may feel pleasure or possibly satisfaction; we may have the illusion that we have accomplished our duty. When we think about the old proverb about the difference between giving a hungry person fish, and teaching them how to fish, we realize that we have only given temporary pleasure. However, when we develop a pattern of charity, we can combine all these events in our mind into a lasting experience of peace and contentment; we ***make merit*** for ourselves *by finding ways to give appropriately and effectively based on our means*. Compassion becomes part of our character and we can derive recurring happiness (and "make merit") by making this a routine part of our lives.

Look at the photograph of your loved one. Identify the compassion you feel towards this person. Look at the photograph of another person's loved one unknown to you, and note the difference in your recognition and compassion.

The epitome of compassion is to travel on the Bodhisattva path where ". . . we commit ourselves to work not just toward self-improvement but toward transcending the whole notion of self and selfishness. This endeavor goes against the grain of every self-help program our culture has conditioned us to seek . . . [this means] letting go of these desires as we turn our focus instead in the opposite direction and concentrate on what we can do for the genuine benefit of all out of a felt sense of universal responsibility . . . A sublime beauty results from this kind of training. In releasing us from the petty and recurrently painful narrowness of more selfish goals, it allows us to live far more expansively, joyfully, and productively. But if we set out on the path with the objective of attaining this wonderful new life only for ourselves, [the arahant] we're aiming in the wrong direction, hobbling our best selves, and defeating ourselves from the start."

". . . The traditional Bodhisattva Vow. As the first step along the Bodhisattva path for formal practitioners of Mahayana Buddhism:

Sentient beings are numberless: I vow to liberate them.

Delusions are inexhaustible: I vow to transcend them.

Dharma teachings are boundless: I vow to master them.

The Buddha's enlightened way is unsurpasable: I vow to embody it.

The vows help their upholders ensure that their intentions are clear, pure, altruistic, and un-muddied by self-serving motives." (Surya Das, pg. 11) Our suffering is lifted as we help others reduce the suffering in their lives.

Second Progressive:

". . . Training in eight aspects of human behavior is provided in the Eight-fold Noble Path. The system inherent in this path is intended not only to eliminate temporary suffering but also to create a perfectly healthy character in which suffering will not arise under any circumstances. Buddhist training and enlightenment employ present suffering as the occasion to institute a course leading ultimately to the *perfection of the character*." (Mizuno, pg. 30) Each of the "Eight-fold" steps is given careful and measured consideration in this and the next seven lessons, but before that, students must make a commitment to strive to develop a virtuous character, and Buddhists do that by the formal recitation the Three Refuges (as above) and in addition they "take the oath" by repeating the ***Five Precepts***:

1) To refrain from killing living creatures.
2) To refrain from taking what is not given.
3) To refrain from sexual misconduct.
4) to refrain from harsh and false speech.
5) To refrain from taking intoxicating liquor and drugs.

"There is a universal need to give them [the Refuges and Precepts] a particular place in the heart, and it is the role of religious ceremonies and rituals to do just that."

"By so doing, our practice becomes more alive and tuned to those particular occasions, *imbuing them with a special kind of auspiciousness*; a greater attention to the occasion in all its detail serves to convey the quality of that occasion more deeply. Furthermore, such ceremonies as *taking the Three Refuges and Five Precepts* have a valuable role in group situations where there might be a number of people with no special affinity to one another, yet who feel united and bound in a common initiative, realizing, in their collective devotions, a wider, all-embracing sense of fellowship and community." (Cittaviveka, pp. 3-4) Each time we are involved in this kind of character molding ceremony, we move closer to developing the mental strength to accept enlightenment.

This commitment is not necessarily the first step to the elimination of suffering, but a necessary and important step eventually. "Inside every one of us is a garden, and every practitioner has to go back to their garden and take care of it. Maybe in the past, you left it untended for a long time. You should know exactly what is going on in your garden, and try to put everything in order. Restore the beauty; restore the harmony in your garden. If it is well tended, many people will enjoy your garden." (Hanh, pg. 93)

Third Progressive:

"The third of the Four Noble Truths (the ***Truth of Extinction***) deals with the ideal condition in which suffering has been totally extinguished. This is the standard against which to judge suffering and non-suffering. Although only a person who has reached this state can understand it completely, correct awareness of ideals and even scant familiarity with the Four Noble Truths gives a certain amount of knowledge about it. Without such knowledge, it is impossible to recognize suffering as suffering, to know that elimination of the cause of suffering removes the suffering itself, or to put into practice the means of achieving such an elimination." (Mizuno, pp. 45-46) This is how wisdom emerges.

"Trishna [thirst or craving] is not an aberration. It is entirely natural. But if we want to get off the Wheel of Life and thereby liberate ourselves from duhkha, we must do something about it. This brings us to the third noble truth. This tells us that there is a method: a way or path that can be traveled to ultimate freedom." This knowledge was a huge relief for me when I finally understood this.

"Freedom from trishna is known in Pali as nibbana, the Sanskrit equivalent of which, ***nirvana*** 1. That which has a *residual basis* (The first [life-long nirvana] arose in Shakyamuni Buddha as he sat beneath the bodhi tree at Bodh Gaya on the fateful night of the full moon of May) . . . or 2. That which has *no residual basis* (when he finally passed away at Kushinagara—when there was complete extinction Parinirvana: nothing tangible remained behind)." (Snelling, pg. 44)

It is helpful to examine each of the following ten factors (fetters) that might *prevent* students from alleviating the many different kinds of suffering they encounter ". . . that bind individuals to samsaric existence:

1. Belief in personality [the "I" "mine" egoism]
2. Skepticism—lack of certainty about the Buddha's teaching
3. Attachment to rules and rituals—[strict vegetarianism, ***celibacy***]
4. Sensuous craving—[inappropriate sexual conduct or stalking]
5. Ill will—[vengeance and hatred]

6. Craving for material existence—[luxury consumption]
7. Craving for non-material existence [afterlife in a heaven]
8. Conceit [you already know what is good for you]
9. Restlessness
10. Ignorance—[laziness toward studying dharma]

These 'mind-forged manacles' must be broken if development is to take place and freedom be won. Even the dharma must be laid aside once its purpose is served. The Buddha himself likened it to a raft that can be used for crossing the river of samsara to the further bank of enlightenment. Just as a traveler, once he has crossed a river, will not hoist the boat onto his back and go carrying it, so a person who has achieved the goal will lay the dharma aside. The person of the way travels light and lets no opportunity to further lighten his luggage slip by." (Snelling, pp. 66-67) This discussion of "fetters" is taken up again in subsequent lessons. Until then we should read this list everyday to see what aspects of this list we can own.

Meditation Practicum:

"The term *skyong ba* means 'to protect, guard, or defend,' as if defending a fort. The same term also means 'to care for, attend to, nurture.' Protecting is a practice typically utilized at the formal conclusion of any unit of meditation practiced, that is, at the end of *1) preliminaries, 2) concentration, 3) special insight, or 4) extraordinary meditations*, respectively. The introduction of protecting practice at this point signifies the conclusion of the preliminary practices." (Brown, pg. 145) This protection, as with the review during each lesson, is intended to solidify and clarify the learning gains being made. Recognition of each Student's effort and dedication by their becoming a Practitioner identifies and "protects" their knowledge and recognizes the diligence they manifest in their spiritual practice.

As we understand the technique and significance of protecting, and we engage in this practice, this turns a casual spiritual practice into a skillful activity. It is a key to relieving suffering and is the schema for the Sixteen Step meditation which we are approaching, elaborated by Buddhadasa Bhikkhu of Thailand. It is interesting how these same teachings are explained, summarized or offered differently in the various Buddhist traditions, i.e. the four foundations of meditation.

The virtue that comes into ones life from meditation must be obtained by **'barter'** with the actuality of making changes in ones own life. This was an insight that came to me while editing this lesson the first time; since I was educated as an economist, this analogy of a necessary exchange seems useful. Meditation is not just for pleasure or to create a momentary feeling of relaxation, euphoria or happiness, it is to internalize changes in one's life that will generate positive effects and reduce suffering according to the law of cause and effect. ". . . A given action proliferates in its effects. The act of stilling the body eventually manifests its effect as mental calm. The ultimate design of the exercises [we will be learning and practicing] is to re-order the body and mind so as to become a suitable vessel for the nectar of wisdom received by oral advice. The commentary illustrates the interrelationship between settling the body and settling the mind . . ." (Brown, pg. 160) Each Practitioner is committed to this barter, **an exchange of personal effort to be a better person, for the reward of mental development**.

It may come as a relief or encouragement to seriously rational students that there is a measurable change in their minds as suffering disappears. Scientific inquiry has been done to identify the effects of meditation on the mind. ". . . Preliminary examinations of the pilot study indicated shifts between large sets of neuronal circuits in the monk's brain that at least suggest a correspondence between the changes in his brain activity and the meditation techniques he was asked to practice. By contrast, similar scans performed on subjects who'd had no meditation training indicated a somewhat more limited ability to direct the activity of their brains voluntarily while performing a specific mental task." This does not describe the level of suffering in each of the subjects, but one presumes the "changes in his brain" lead to positive changes in his/her life.

". . . A test performed by scientists at University College London using magnetic resonance imaging (MRI) technology had shown that London taxicab drivers—who must undergo a two- to four-year training, known as 'the Knowledge,' through which they learn to navigate the complicated network of streets in that city—have shown a significant growth in the hippo-campus region of the brain, the area associated most typically with spatial memory. In very simple terms, this study begins to confirm that repeated experience can actually change the structure and function of the brain." (Mingyur, pp. 225-226) Complete faith in Rational Buddhism is possible because there is nothing at stake, any new scientific discovery and all the old ones, can be accepted. There is no need to believe in miracles or esoteric teachings, rational judgment is not suspended, there is nothing to lose and everything to gain.

We will sit now for a brief guided meditation which we will do together, and you can repeat this anytime for yourself. (read slowly out-loud)

"Meditating on Physical Sensations:

One of the easiest ways to begin object-based shinay practice is to rest your attention gently on simple, physical sensations. Just focus your attention on a particular area—for example, your forehead." Close your eyes.

"Start by straightening your spine and relaxing your body . . . It doesn't matter whether you keep your eyes open or closed as you practice. In fact, some people find it more helpful to keep their eyes closed . . ."

"Let your mind rest for a few moments, just as it is . . ."

"Now slowly bring your awareness to your forehead . . ."

"You might feel a sort of tingling there, or maybe a sensation of warmth. You might even feel some sort of itchiness or pressure. Whatever you feel, just allow yourself to be aware of it for a minute or two . . ." [it is okay to wrinkle your muscles to prompt your attention in the beginning.]

"Just notice it . . ."

"Just gently rest your attention on the sensation . . ." [possibly there is a breeze or a fly? You might see a point of light?] Before you open your eyes, prepare yourself to look ahead and down at one single point.

"Then let go of your attention and let your mind rest as it is. You can open your eyes as suggested."

"How was that?" [use introspection.]

"After you've spent a little time resting your awareness on the sensations in one part of the body, you can extend the technique by gently drawing your attention throughout your entire body. [Notice any aches or constriction,] I sometimes refer to this extended approach to physical sensations as 'scanning practice." (Mingyur, pp. 145-146) This is great to repeat as a skillful technique to relieve stress, something we can each do to eliminate suffering caused by each day's frustrations.

The breath is extensively used in Buddhist meditation, it is life giving energy and ". . . we can master [the flesh-body] by using the breath. If we act in a certain way toward the breath-body, there will also be a specific effect upon the flesh-body. This is why we take the breath as the object of our training. Supervising the breath, to whatever degree, is equivalent to regulating the flesh-body to the same degree. This point will be more clearly understood when we have trained up to that particular stage of ***anapana'sati*** . . . [accent on a'.] Every kind of breath is noted and analyzed. Long breaths, short breaths, calm breaths, violent breaths, fast breaths, slow breaths—we learn to know them all. We examine the nature, characteristics, and functions of each kind of breath that arises." (Buddhadasa, 1988, pp. 7-8) Some effects are subtle, calming, some are more noticeable and easier to describe. Identify as many as possible during your next meditation practice.

Biographical Sketch:

Can we also learn to relieve suffering by following the good examples of others? "Then Shakyamuni preached a sermon for Sudatta [a wealthy and generous merchant.] As was his custom, he moved gradually from the triple doctrine of alms-giving to the poor—and to holy people abiding by the moral precepts, and the assurance that good acts are rewarded by rebirth in a blessed state, to the Four Noble Truths of suffering [dharma], its cause, the elimination of the cause, and the way to that elimination. As a result of this sermon, Sudatta attained the Eye of the Law and came to embrace the Buddhist interpretation of the world and human life. He then took refuge in the Buddha, the Law, and the Order and vowed to be a Buddhist believer for the rest of his life." Sudatta insisted on serving a meal on the following day, and "requested that the Buddha and his followers come to Savatthi, his city, and remain there throughout the rainy season." (Mizuno, pg. 137) There are many such incidences in Buddha's life that can be inspirational.

When we know that we are part of a compassionate and rational world, that should give us assurance that our suffering can be relieved. "The story of Kisa Gautami . . . illustrates the Buddha's sensitivity as a teacher [and the issue of Cessation of Suffering]. She turned up one day with a dead child in her arms and begged the Buddha for medicine to bring him back to life. The Buddha saw at once that she simply could not accept her child's death, so he told her, 'Yes, I can help you. First you must bring me a mustard seed, but it must come from a house in which death has never taken place.' Of course, Kisa Gautami searched all day but could not find such a house, so in the evening when she came back to the Buddha she learned a deep lesson. 'I know now,' she told him, 'that I am not alone in my grief. Death is common to all people'." (Snelling, pg. 31) This may turn suffering into pain, but a pain we may expect to feel throughout our lives.

However, the search for relief can lead us to an enticing illusion. "Contentment and tranquility are the Holy Grail of the spiritual path [according to Yoga teachings.] We can achieve this state of calm and stillness when we manage to let go of our limited selfish desires and instead find a healthier relationship with the world, one in which we discover our true Self and identify with others. To do this, we need to place our trust in something greater than ourselves, and rely on that unknown something to provide us with the sustenance we require." (Forstater, pp. 68-69) This is quite a different teaching than what is found in most Buddhist dharma generally and Rational Buddhism in particular. It is seductive, but it leads to becoming dependent on an external source to give us happiness, and therefore it eventually fails and becomes weak, ineffective and always becomes unsatisfactory.

Reading for the Day:

What gives each of us the resolve to keep going? Are we motivated by different factors? "In essence, the Buddhist path offers a choice between familiarity and practicality. There is, without question, a certain comfort and stability in maintaining familiar patterns of thought and behavior. Stepping outside that zone of comfort [changing from a mere Student to being a Practitioner] and familiarity necessarily involves moving into a realm of unfamiliar experience that may seem really scary—an uncomfortable in-between realm . . . You don't know whether to go back to what was familiar but frightening [or insufferable] or to forge ahead toward what may be frightening simply because it's unfamiliar . . ." These may be unconscious impulses, so in spite of the declarations of support and the promises we receive from our Sangha and teachers, we can get derailed. People tell us their truth but it takes a good deal of personal effort, reaching and stretching out of our old patterns, to have an impact on our negative habits.

"Ultimately, happiness comes down to choosing between the discomfort of becoming aware of your mental afflictions and the discomfort of being ruled by them. I can't promise you that it will always be pleasant to simply rest in the awareness of your thoughts, feelings and perceptions, and to recognize them as interactive creations between your own mind and body. In fact, I can pretty much guarantee that looking at yourself this way will be, at times, extremely unpleasant. But the same can be said about beginning anything new, whether it's going to the gym, starting a job, or beginning a diet . . . Meditation works the same way . . . The body says, 'I can't,' while the mind says, 'I should.' . . . Buddhism is often referred to as the "middle way' because it offers a third option . . ." (Mingyur, pp. 249-251) This activity is self-determined, self-help, and not achieved by any repeated threats, nor under duress. You might notice after a while, that you have fewer causes for complaining.

Remember from Chapter Four we studied `putting in order`. Here is another explanation to show the realistic possibility of eliminating suffering. We must allow ourselves to shift our ". . . mental perception about being hot and sweaty [as being distasteful for example,] . . . just phenomena to which [we've] assigned different meanings . . . Psychologists often refer to this sort of transformation as '***cognitive restructuring***.' Through applying *intention as well as attention* to an experience, a person is able to shift the meaning of an experience from a painful or intolerable context to one that is tolerable or pleasant [or at least instructive]. Over time, *cognitive restructuring* establishes new neuronal pathways in the brain, particularly in the limbic region, where most sensations of pain and pleasure are recognized and processed . . . What happens when you begin to recognize your experiences as your own projections? What happens when you begin to lose your fear of the people around you and conditions you used to dread?" (Mingyur, pg. 103) This is more like voluntarily joining a sports team and actively exercising on a regular basis. Is "cognitive restructuring" brainwashing? Not if it is self-determined, self-willed, self-help and not based on intimidation, repeated threats from an outside source, or subject to any kind of duress. This is like a flower blooming.

One last clarification as a reminder: "The term **karma means action;** specifically it refers to willed actions of body, speech and mind. All such actions, barring alone those of a buddha or arahat, produce subtle seeds which in time will spawn further consequences. These will be wholesome, unwholesome, or neutral according to the nature of the original action . . . wholesome actions like giving alms to a beggar [or monk] or upholding the truth will produce pleasant ones. As the very first verse of the Dhammapada puts it: 'if a person speaks or acts with unwholesome mind, pain pursues him, even as the wheel follows the hoof of the ox that draws the cart'." (Snelling, pg. 57) It works in positive ways as well.

Protecting:

This is a special day for those who wish to profess their faith in the Teachings of Buddha. "This kind of faith demands decisiveness toward the object of faith and, moreover, determination to persist over and against episodes of intense doubt . . . faith is a way of letting go . . . The Abhidharma literature uses the example of a water-purifying gem, which when placed in murky water makes it instantly calm and clear. [***Practitioners*** are those] 'whose nature is *incapable* of being obscured by any bad karma' . . . In order to take up the teachings, the beginner must overcome fear (dogs pa), the emotional counterpart of doubt . . . Likewise, a single moment of decisive action cuts through all the un-virtuous mental factors that might otherwise inhibit spontaneous, proper action, much like a flash of lightening or a water-purifying gem . . . The [Practitioner] who acts decisively toward the teachings quickly sees the value of such acts . . . to have this kind of faith is to yearn for something. The image of the wish-granting gem exemplifies this dimension of faith . . . you purify the path in which you want only one thing, buddhahood. 'You [begin to] improve by virtue of its greatness'." (Brown, pp. 61-62)

May this gem help you gain insight through meditation and by leading a dedicated, morally upright life? You need only make that promise to yourself—that you will endeavor to seek the understanding of enlightenment. Nothing more is required than you accept this jewel as a remembrance, an amulet of faith.

"This is what I heard," review by both Practitioners and teacher.

Additional Teachings:

Remember—for all the good we might do—our suffering will be diminished. A good deed is its own reward. "Mahatma Gandhi, himself an exemplar of generosity for giving his life to the cause of social justice and freedom in India,[and South Africa] had a similar understanding of the cosmically reciprocal effect of generosity. When a reporter asked him, "Why do you give so much to others? he replied, "I don't give to anyone. I do it all for myself." By "myself," he was not referring to the egotistic or social persona that might expect a specific this-for-that reward. He was referring to the inner self, which is not attached to any concept of reward but is the pure spirit of generosity that must give to live. He was echoing the old adage that virtue is its own reward, and doing the right thing is the best thing to do, personally as well as more generally."(Surya Das, pg. 35) This is self-satisfaction of the most humble kind.

Buddhist Sutra

Lesson Title: Cessation of Suffering

Lesson Number: Five

Key Vocabulary: Practitioner, mental afflictions, making merit, perfection, trishna, Wheel of Life, Bodhi tree, Bodh Gaya, Kushinagara, barter, Yoga, scanning practice, cognitive restructuring, residual basis nirvana, Parinirvana, neocortex, Five Precepts, Anapanasati, extinction

Assignment: Hold onto the "wish-granting gem" while you engage in shinay meditation, watching your mind examine the changes that need to be made in your life to move further along the path of the Teachings of Buddhism.

Define each of the Key Vocabulary in your own words.

Focus on the in and out of different kinds of breath as an empirical experiment and identify what effects if any you feel. While doing this use object-based shinay practice to rest your attention gently on simple, physical sensations. (Such as touching and feeling the gem.) Just focus your attention on a particular body part—for example, your forehead.

Extend the time of your meditation to at least twenty minutes for six to ten times during the next twenty-four hours.

Distinguish between residual—and non-residual basis nirvana.
How is happiness connected to the Law of Causation?

If "cravings" are the river that propels our lives, the current is "desires and thrusts." Can we change our river into a calmly flowing, flat and placid stream? by engaging in a full-time spiritual practice?
Memorize the Five Precepts.

Light a candle and identify the ways you can be compassionate.
Can you achieve perfection of the character and enlightenment in this lifetime?

How has your spiritual practice changed during your life?

"The traditional way in which Buddhists of all schools express this commitment is to say that they 'go for Refuge to the Buddha . . . Dharma . . . and Sangha' (the Three Jewels)." (Vishvapani, pg. 24) And repeat to yourself the ***Five Precepts.***

What signs have you experienced during meditation?
Are there certain thoughts or kinds of thoughts that recur for you?
Is it true that each time we complain (out loud or silently) we are signaling our suffering?

Materials for next lesson: Utilitarianism, light two candles, drinking water

Buddhist Sutra

Lesson Title: **The Eight-fold Path—Right View (understanding)**

Lesson Number: **Six**

Rationale:

This is most often found as the first stage along the Eight-fold Path, although since it relates to Wisdom, it might be better held to the last of the list. "In the Principal Teaching, the Lord Buddha advised us to stop all wrong actions first and then perform only right actions. This is the fundamental [meaning] of wholesome deeds. [The Right View is] performing wholesome deeds in mind . . . developing mind by concentrating mind to be one-pointed and cultivate ***wisdom (panna)*** to eradicate all defilements because all defilements in mind are the causes of all suffering . . . It is called mind development." (Wee, pg. 21) Of course the question arises—How do we get there from where we are? The way we think is the way we act.

Discussion of Prior Lesson:

At the level of Practitioner there is no longer a question about one's conviction, it remains only to improve self-discipline that will help us do what we know is best for our lives. "A beginner who acts in faith no longer requires the presence of the spiritual being but acts independently." (Brown, pg. 58)

"As we become more deeply attentive to what we feel, we begin to recognize feelings that aren't necessarily related to tactile contact, feelings that are referred to as 'subtle physical sensations'." (Mingyur, pg. 146) If these feelings occur during meditation you should "protect" them and understand them. "We need to see clearly the great effect that the breath has on the physical body . . . until it becomes clear that the two . . . are interconnected and inseparable." (Buddhadasa, 1988, pg. 8)

Training Objective:

To see things as they are—is Buddhism similar or different than Utilitarianism? How do we go about gaining clear understanding? We learn the techniques for reducing defilements by eliminating ignorance, attachments and aversions. Develop the Basis of practice and the basis of Enlightenment. Anapanasati and sixteen steps.

Materials Required: Utilitarianism, light two candles, water for drinking

Motivational Statement:

"Imagine spending your life in a little room with only one locked window so dirty it barely admits any light . . . suppose one day you spill some water on the window . . . and you use a rag . . . to dry it off. And as you do that, a little of the dirt . . . comes away. Suddenly a small patch of light comes through the glass. Curious, you might rub a little harder, and as more dirt comes away, more light streams in. Maybe, you think, the world isn't so dark and dreary after all, maybe it's the window." (Mingyur, pg. 105)

As the window becomes transparent we see the ***external life*** outside our minds clearly, with integrity and accurately. We don't immediately become clever, sly or inventive, but growth of wisdom does follow our effort. "When we study Buddhism and gain knowledge, the next important step is to understand. If we acquire knowledge but lack understanding, we will not be able to practice correctly. Therefore, we are to study and understand the Scriptures so that we can practice for our advantages. The essence of Buddhism we should know and understand is 'suffering and cessation of suffering' which are included in ***the Four Noble Truths***." (Wee, pg. 65) Thus we are being exhorted to study the Dharma as well as practice, which confirms the relevance of *Buddhist Sutras*. Then eventually we get the bigger picture, a perspective of how important Buddhism is.

First Progressive:

Light a candle for compassion to the world and read the following: "In a sense, the uncertainty surrounding the choice to recognize [and strive to fulfill] your full potential is similar . . . [to] ending an abusive relationship: There's a certain reluctance or sense of failure associated with letting go of the relationship [self-criticism or dissonance.] The primary difference between severing an abusive relationship and entering the path of Buddhist practice is: . . . [by entering] the path of Buddhist practice you're ending an abusive relationship with yourself. When you choose to recognize your true potential, you gradually begin to find yourself belittling yourself less frequently, your opinion of yourself becomes more positive and wholesome, and your sense of confidence and sheer joy of being alive increases! At the same time, you begin to recognize that *everyone around you has the same potential,* whether they know it or not [you are developing compassion.] Instead of dealing with them as threats or adversaries, you'll find yourself able to recognize and *empathize* with their fear and unhappiness and spontaneously respond to them in ways that emphasize solutions rather than problems." (Mingyur, pg. 250)

As we have learned: "The proper way for a Buddhist to live and behave is not only to seek the attainment of this ideal state [nirvana] for himself but also to strive to help other people and all of society to attain it too." (Mizuno, pg. 51) "*Wisdom and compassion* are aspects of the same non-dual realization. Therefore the experience of certainty about the mind's real nature necessarily leads to compassionate desire that others find this same truth . . . The 'lofty ideal' [as for a Bodhisattva] is to desire to realize truth for the sake of all others." (Brown, pg. 149)

One way to achieve this is to be generous. "Being generous according to the Buddhist concept of *dana* calls for the same kind of dynamic shift in consciousness [i.e. focusing on the ten perfections.] . . . We learn to welcome occasions for generosity as golden opportunities to express our noble Bodhicitta and, in doing so, realize the wealth and abundance of our innate goodness. In giving, we too receive. Through being generous, we erase the troublesome, dualistic distinction between giver and receiver. Buddha said, 'Generosity brings happiness at every stage: in framing the intention, in the act of giving, and in rejoicing afterward'." (Surya Das, pg. 22)

Second Progressive:

"Thus . . . enlightenment is both liberation and also a manifestation of omniscience—the awakened wisdom of the Buddha. The awakened mind of the Buddha manifests as 1) infinite wisdom (the first candle) and 2) inexhaustible compassion (the second candle). Thus while early Buddhism emphasizes the eradication of negative qualities, Mahayana enlightenment entails the full *manifestation of all positive qualities of mind*, the quintessence of our human potential." (Brown, pg. 7) We light the second candle in the same way we light up our minds—for ourselves and those with whom we share Rational Buddhism. We come to know that we are not in the business of self-improvement just to gain a shallow happiness, but to strengthen the Sangha and reach beyond to concern ourselves about others.

This can be called, keeping our lives in perspective. "In order to live our lives according to [the last] of the Four Noble Truths which is called the Noble Eight-fold Path. We have to understand clearly how to behave to live our lives accordingly. The Right Understanding [the Right View, refers to] the right [knowledge] of what the Buddha has attained: [the knowledge that] life is suffering." (Wee, pg. 28)

Why should we act virtuously according to any ethical or moral code? What creates moral authority? One of the original discussions in Western philosophy for the motivation, "ought," and rationale for virtuous action (ethical imperative), centered on the concept of ***Utilitarianism.*** This is the ethical (being determined by reason instead of a moral code determined by a religion) doctrine that the moral worth of an action is determined solely by its contribution to overall utility or greater good. Often this is abbreviated by the slogan: "The greatest good for the greatest number." This is classified as a form of consequentialism, meaning that the moral worth of an action is determined by its outcome not only for the individual but for society.

Likewise in Buddhism the consequences of action (or karma) based on individual choices are the *effects* (as well as the motivation) created by each action, and these are the measure of the worthiness or merit of an action. Karma is equivalent to the philosophical concept of "Will" because will isn't created until intention is acted upon. If we don't do something, we haven't exercised our will. "Utility" is a generalized benefit from our conduct and social decisions—the good to be maximized—has been defined in the simplest terms by various Western thinkers (i.e. Jeremy Bentham and John Stuart Mill) as happiness or pleasure. (Yet what holds true for the whole of society [if indeed it is true] does not necessarily hold true for each or any one individual.) This philosophizing was an outgrowth of the Reformation Era of Western culture in Europe and helped usher in the period that is called the Enlightenment.

This kind of theory building based on vague terminology is a tempting and sometimes entertaining pastime for those with a philosophical bent. However, looking at ethics based on generalized outcomes, rather than based on the specific details associated with the Law of Causation, are two quite different perspectives. The concept of Utilitarianism ignores the many other causes of action, the strong component of compassion and altruism as influencing factors for making our conscious choices and decisions. "The ***conditioning factors*** are often referred to in Buddhist terms as 'mental afflictions,' or sometimes 'poisons.' Although the texts of Buddhist psychology examine a wide range of conditioning factors, all of them agree in identifying three primary afflictions that form the basis of all other factors that inhibit our ability to see things as they really are: ***ignorance, attachment, and aversion***." (Mingyur, pp. 116-122)

These 'poisons' offer one explanation of the causes of our inability to follow a sacred moral code from week to week, there are other factors of course. Understanding these, being objective about ourselves (taking ownership) and the way we interact with others, is at the very core of Rational Buddhism. "If understanding is not there, no matter how hard you try [even during meditation,] you cannot love. If you say, 'I have to try to love him,' this is nonsense. You have to understand him[/her as well as the dharma,] and through understanding, you will be able to love him[/her.]" (Hanh, pg. 267) So Buddhism is also a great source for marriage and personal counseling and advice.

Buddhist teachings explain how those three primary factors prevent us from following a moral code. "***Ignorance*** is a fundamental inability to recognize the infinite potential, clarity, and power of our own minds, as if we were looking at the world through colored glass . . . On the most essential level, ignorance distorts the basically open experience of awareness into ***dualistic distinctions*** between inherently existing categories of 'self' and 'other' . . . as we become accustomed to distinguishing between 'self' and 'other,' we lock ourselves into a dualistic mode of perception, [or bias] drawing conceptual boundaries between our 'self' and the rest of the world 'out there' . . . We begin looking at other people, material objects, and so on as potential sources of happiness and unhappiness, and life becomes a struggle to get what we need in order to be happy before somebody else grabs it . . . This struggle [suffering caused by craving] is known in Sanskrit as samsara, which literally means 'wheel' or 'circle.' . . . Samsara is best understood as a point of view."

"***Attachment*** . . . when we generalize biologically essential things into areas that have nothing to do with basic survival . . . like ignorance, can be seen as having a purely neurological basis [thus it can be changed.] Attachment is in many ways comparable to addiction, a compulsive dependency on external objects or experiences to manufacture an illusion of wholeness. Unfortunately, like other addictions, attachment becomes more intense over time. Whatever satisfaction we might experience when we attain something or someone we desire doesn't last [we need a progressively greater amount to create satisfaction.] . . . The Buddha compared attachment to drinking salt water from an ocean. The more we drink, the thirstier we get . . . we also reinforce the neuronal patterns that condition us to rely on an external source to give us happiness" (as we see with Yoga.) Some people hold to their religious beliefs as a result of discipline, irrational faith, based on a kind of disciplined sacrifice of reason. This is a form of attachment (clinging.)

"***Aversion*** . . . Every strong attachment generates an equally powerful [a dialectic] fear that we'll either fail to get what we want or lose whatever we've already gained . . . a resistance to the inevitable changes that occur as a consequence of the impermanent nature of relative reality . . . When we've achieved some condition that makes us feel whole and complete, we want everything to stay exactly as it is . . . the deeper our attachment . . . the greater our fear of losing it . . . *Aversion* reinforces neuronal patterns that generate a mental construct of yourself as limited, weak, and incomplete . . . all these sensations are symptoms of stress . . . [which] can cause a huge variety of problems, including depression, sleeping disorders, digestive problems, rashes, thyroid and kidney malfunctions, high blood pressure, and even high cholesterol . . . On a purely emotional level, aversion tends to manifest as anger and even hatred [related to the possibility of losing someone's love, in the same way we might fear losing employment.] Instead of recognizing that whatever unhappiness you feel is based on a mentally constructed image [these are expectations or conditioning factors,] you find it only 'natural' to blame other people, external objects, or situations for your pain. When people behave in a way that appears to prevent you from obtaining what you desire, you begin to think of them as untrustworthy or mean, and you'll go out of your way either to avoid them or strike back at them. In the grip of anger, you see everyone and everything as enemies. As a result, your inner and outer worlds become smaller and smaller. You lose faith in yourself, and reinforce specific neuronal patterns that generate feelings of fear and vulnerability." (Mingyur, pp. 116-122) Be mindful of these three conditions and come back and review them in your notes.

Third Progressive:

"The fourth of the Four Noble Truths (the Truth of the Eight-fold Noble Path) sets forth the means of eliminating suffering step by step . . . prescribes indirect and direct methods. Either the desires and attachments causing suffering are directly eliminated, or a state or environment in which such desires and attachments and the suffering they entail do not occur is produced. ***The Eight-fold Noble Path*** contains all the direct and indirect methods needed to remove suffering and to build a perfect personality in physical and spiritual terms. Developing such a personality—that of a Buddha or an arhat—resembles physical therapy aiming both to cure the present sickness and to create a sound, healthy body in which sickness does not occur. The comparison with the healing principle shows how *rationally organized* the doctrine of the Four Noble Truths is. It further shows the identity between these Truths and the research attitude of such fields of learning as modern natural science." (Mizuno, pg. 46.) The conclusion of studying many explanations of Right View, is to recognize the need to study Dharma from both original sources and from inspired commentators.

As we have seen, Buddhist science adds a sixth sense, the mental consciousness. This is the capacity to process input from the other five senses and discern and interpret what we see, smell, hear, taste, or touch; as well as the ability to create wholly new and original images. It is the development of this sixth sense, the filter of wisdom, as part of the mental continuum, which is primary focus of the Eight-fold Path. "The wisdom element features in right understanding, which implies the obvious, but perhaps often missed, point that in order to practice we need to have heard (or read) the Buddha's teachings, notably that of the four noble truths, and have not merely understood them theoretically but have actively penetrated their truth by testing them against experience [i.e. protecting.] Our wish to pursue the Buddha's way is therefore founded on *informed confidence* in the soundness of the teachings rather than on blind faith or misguided attraction to its superficial aspects." (Snelling, pg. 47) This is a significant justification for studying and practicing all thirty of the lessons in *Buddhist Sutras*.

"The essence of Buddha's teachings, however, can be reduced to a single point: The mind is the source of all experience, and by changing the direction of the mind, we can change the quality of everything we experience . . . [Recall cognitive restructuring.] If you put on a pair of green glasses, everything you see is green . . . ***Clarity***, in this sense, may be understood as the creative aspect of mind. Everything you perceive, you perceive through the power of your awareness. There are truly no limits to the creative ability of our minds. *This creative aspect is the natural consequence of the union of emptiness and clarity* . . . To the extent that you can acknowledge the true power of your mind, you can begin to exercise more control over your experience. Pain, sadness, fear, anxiety, and all other forms of suffering no longer disrupt your life as forcefully as they used to. Experiences that once seemed to be obstacles become opportunities for deepening your understanding of the mind's unimpeded nature." (Mingyur, pg. 102) As long as we don't become attached to these outcomes.

An example of *aversion* is to hide oneself in the thrill of drug use, intoxicants and other pleasures of the flesh. "In the time of Shakyamuni, there were people who believed that hedonistic pursuit of the pleasure of the moment was the greatest human happiness and their highest human ideal. Shakyamuni . . . had seen that a life of sensual pleasure does not lead to holiness and is useless in the attainment of ideal human aims. This is part of the Buddha's teaching that extremes of sensuality and physical mortification must be avoided for the sake of the Middle Path leading to the ideal." (Mizuno, pg. 30)

Ignorance manifests itself in subtle ways as well. ". . . The greatest of all obstacles—[heresies] is for a person who holds such heretical views [rejecting the law of karma] would under no circumstances desire to be admitted to the Buddhist following. In the wider sense, heresies—the opposites of right view—include mistaken views: failure to realize that all things are impermanent and that nothing has an ego [the Yoga Self that does not exist] and the resultant belief in a real individuality and the things belonging to it; holding extreme views, such as the all-encompassing belief that all is immutable [fatalism] or the nihilistic belief that nothing exists; being attached to practices and observances that are irrational and superstitious and that, while admitting the law of cause and effect, misinterpret the relations between the two or that advocate incorrect training methods as correct ones. As long as these kinds of heresies persist, it is impossible to eliminate ignorance and lust." (Mizuno, pp. 54-55) The *Buddhist Sutras* is just a beginning at removing ignorance, meditating using Anapanasati and Satipatthana as we will learn later, are the best ways to remove ignorance and create wisdom.

Meditation Practicum:

Fundamental to the practice of Buddhist meditation is the allegory of developing our Hearts. This attribute and capacity of our being becomes the most elastic during our practice, and is the seat of most of our change and development. "In the context of actual meditation practice, the presence of right view finds its expression in a growing degree of detachment and disenchantment with conditioned phenomena, owing to a deepening realization of the truth of dukkha, its cause, its cessation, and the way leading to its cessation. Such detachment is also reflected in the absence of 'desires and discontent' . . . [and] in the instruction to avoid 'clinging to anything in the world'." (Analayo, pp. 163-164) This metamorphosis is achieved in our Hearts.

Another explanation of this follows: "When I first began to practice this sort of shinay technique, I discovered that when I tried to avoid a particular sensation, it increased. But when I learned to just look at it, whatever discomfort I felt became more tolerable. Being a curious child, of course, I had to know why this shift occurred. Only after watching the process for a while did I realize that when I simply allowed myself to observe a sensation, I was actively participating in what was occurring right then, at that moment. I saw part of my mind resisting a painful sensation and part of my mind urging me to just look at it objectively. When I looked at these conflicting impulses simultaneously, I was able to see my whole mind engaged in the process of dealing with avoidance and acceptance, and the process of observing the workings of my mind became more interesting than either avoidance [aversion] or acceptance. Just watching my mind work was fascinating in itself. This, I think is the most practical definition of ***clarity*** I can offer: the capacity to see the mind working simultaneously on many levels." How is this clarity the same or different from meta-cognition?

"Because pain and discomfort are such direct sensations, they're actually very effective objects of meditative focus. Most of us regard pain as a threat . . . when we worry or allow ourselves to become preoccupied by this threat, the pain itself almost always increases. On the other hand, if we consider pain or discomfort as an object of meditation, we can use such sensations to increase our capacity for clarity, simply through watching the mind deal with various solutions . . . If I feel some pain in my legs or lower back while sitting in formal meditation or even while just sitting in a car or an airplane, instead of stretching, getting up, or moving around, I've learned to look [first] at the mental experience of pain. It's the mental consciousness, [the sixth sense] after all, that actually recognizes and registers sensations. When I bring my attention to the mind that is registering pain, rather than focusing on a particular area of pain, the pain doesn't necessarily disappear, but it becomes a point of actively engaging with whatever I'm experiencing here and now, rather than trying to avoid it . . . Even while taking prescribed or over-the-counter medications recommended by a doctor, you may experience some pain, in which case you can try working with the physical sensation of pain as a support for meditation." (Mingyur, pp.146-148) Right View is often circular, in that it refers back to the first three steps of the Four Noble Truths, where we deal with suffering, causes and cessation of suffering.

During the course of Buddhist Sutras each Practitioner will become acquainted with different meditation techniques. The most important of these is a sequence of sixteen steps that have been identified by the great Theravada teacher Buddhadasa Bhikkhu, of Suan Mokkh, Thailand, about whom we will learn more later. "This sixteen-step form of ***anapanasati*** may seem long and detailed, as is fitting for anything complete . . . but for those who want to study and train thoroughly, it is just right . . . This is required by nature." (Buddhadasa, 1988, pg. 18)

Follow this guided meditation as a brief practice and set of instructions:

Breathe normally. "If you are serious about what you are doing and have a sufficiently strong mind, it is not difficult to practice with the eyes left open. Begin with the eyes open . . ." Gaze at the tip of the nose without crossing your eyes which causes fatigue. "Meditating with the eyes open will help us to stay awake and will keep the eyes cool and comfortable . . . (pg. 27) We must develop ***sati (mindfulness or reflective awareness)*** by being mindful of each in-breath and out-breath. We train in sati by noting that we are about to breathe in or breathe out . . . How are we breathing in? What is the out-breath like? Use sati to note the ordinary breath . . . and train sati by using a technique called 'following,' or 'chasing.' We imagine the in-breath starting from the tip of the nose and ending at the navel . . . contemplate the breath as if chasing it, without ever losing it . . . (pg. 29) Do not allow empty spaces where the mind might wander but keep the mind constantly focused on the breathing in and out . . . This is the first lesson to learn, the foundation for all the rest . . . we contemplate the different kinds of breath [as well]: long and short, coarse and fine, easy and uneasy. Begin to observe the various kinds by experiencing them with sati . . . (pg. 30) We must learn to know [our own individual] reactions to these various properties of the breath . . . we must learn to know when these qualities influence our awareness, our sensitivity, our mind . . ." (pg. 31) Breathe with long breaths [counting to yourself to ten slowly] without holding, fill the lungs completely. Continue until you have a well developed fluency with long breaths.

"It is also important for us to note the effect or flavor of each kind of breath. The flavors that arise as different kinds of feeling are: happiness, dukkha, annoyance, and contentment . . ." Evaluate that for yourself. Now breathe short breaths but softly [by counting in your mind to five quickly.] "Find out [for yourself] why they have different flavors . . . Finally, we can discover the various causes that render our breathing either long or short. We gradually learn this by [observing] ourselves . . . What kind of mood makes the breath long? What kind of mood makes it short?" (Buddhadasa, 1988, pg. 32) Study this more on your own, because it will be the basis of most of our future concern about meditation. Following the breath "chasing" is the key to developing jhana meditation and continued levels of spiritual development and personality change.

Biographical Sketch:

As a visitor to many Buddhist ***wats*** in Thailand, I observed ceremonies often without knowing the significance. I tried to simply be open to making an emotional connection, but failing that just remembering the details, like listening to an opera in a foreign language. It is common practice to place flowers (especially ***lotus buds***) and to light candles and incense before a shrine with a Buddha-image as the central feature—or some other symbol of the presence of the Buddha. Monks ***chant*** together and the lay family offers a prayer. The flowers, beautiful one moment and wilted the next, are to remind offerers of the impermanence of life; the odor of the incense (usually three sticks) calls to mind the sweet scent of moral virtue that emanates from those who are devout; the candle-flame symbolizes enlightenment. These are possible interpretations, but each of these gestures (action, kamma) is also intended to make merit for the lay practitioner. Once these rituals have been joined, I find that the experience never leaves my mind and I can relive it and re-experience it during meditation even after several years. And as I learn and understand more, that original ritual takes on more significance than I gave it at the time of the actual event.

"According to the Theravada tradition, the long journey to Awakening begins in earnest with the first tentative stirrings of right view—the discernment by which one recognizes the validity of the four Noble Truths and the principle of kamma. One begins to see that one's future well-being is neither predestined by fate, nor left to the whims of a divine being or random chance. The responsibility for one's happiness rests squarely on one's own shoulders. Seeing this, one's spiritual aims become suddenly clear: to relinquish the habitual ***unskillful tendencies*** of the mind in favor of ***skillful*** ones. As this right resolve grows stronger, so does the heartfelt desire to live a morally upright life, to choose one's actions with care." (Bullitt)

Reading for the Day:

Recall from Lesson Five: "According to the law of cause and effect, a given action proliferates in its effects. The act of stilling the body eventually manifests its effect as mental calm. The ultimate design of the exercises is to 're-order the body and mind so as to become a suitable vessel for the nectar of wisdom received by oral advice . . .' The Ancient Ones call it taming the artifice of the body when desiring the mind to stay. You must rearrange the interconnected processes in the body, and by that, understanding arises in the mind." (Brown, pg. 160) Each time we meditate our "right view" will expand as we become a more ". . . suitable vessel" each time a little more.

The practitioner has advanced from the stage of just having faith ". . . abandoning higher cognitive operations such as reasoning and reflection [during meditation in favor of practice.] During the next stage, called faithful recognition, however, cognitive processes play an important role. A beginner who has faith is said to be capable of intellectually understanding the truth . . . Intellectual operations, in addition to reflection, are harnesses in the service of spiritual transformation . . . The [Practitioner] is now ready to receive advice as to the *basis of practice*. The word ***basis*** refers to a condensed version of the right view expressed by the perfectly enlightened mind. Direct transmission of this view, the ***basis of enlightenment***, constitutes a fundamental shift in the beginner's perspective, though it is a shift that manifests only over time as it ripens in the beginner's mental continuum. Intellectual understanding—an event that occurs directly within the mental continuum—is considered to be the first type of direct experience of the truth." (Brown, pg. 65) "Basis" is like the roots of a tree; not obviously these often mirror the top in function and growth with opposite scope and purpose. Come back to this explanation after having studied all the lessons.

Protecting:

"This is what I heard," review by both practitioners and teacher.

"Reflection is a cognitive process, and therefore subject to possible error . . . the 'five faults of not grasping the basis' . . .

1) not grasping the words,
2) not grasping their meaning,

3) not grasping their subsequent explanation,
4) grasping the meaning incorrectly,
5) and grasping only part of the meaning.

These errors must be guarded against, and abandoned when discovered . . . The [Practitioner] has, however successfully completed the very first stage of spiritual development. By opening to the possibility that something 'precious' has transpired, the novice has succeeded in *cultivating the seeds of* trust . . . A positive momentum begins to develop as more of the beginner's mental factors are enlisted in the process of spiritual transformation." (Brown, pg. 57) We begin here and then come back to review our progress from time to time.

Additional Teachings:

"Mental freedom must come from the most profound knowledge of the 'what is what.' [The Right View] As long as one lacks this knowledge, one is bound to go on mindlessly liking or disliking things in one way or another. As long as one cannot remain unmoved by things, one can hardly be called free. Basically we human beings are subject to just two kinds of emotional states: liking and disliking . . . We fall slaves to our moods and have no real freedom simply because we don't know the true nature of moods . . . Liking has the characteristic of seizing on things and taking them over; disliking has the characteristic of pushing things away and getting rid of them . . . For this very reason, this highest teaching of Buddhism condemns grasping and clinging to things attractive and repulsive, ultimately condemning even attachment to good and evil. When the mind has been purified of these two emotional reactions, it will become independent of things." (Buddhadasa, 2005, pg. 35)

Sharing Merit:

Rejoicing In Others' Merit (Saying Sadhu)

Buddhist Sutra

Lesson Title: **The Eight-fold Path—Right View (understanding)**

Lesson Number: **Six**

Key Vocabulary: clarity, external life, chant, Utilitarianism, lotus buds, wat, Yoga, basis of enlightenment, wisdom, panna, samsara, ignorance, attachment, aversion, sati, conditioning factors, chasing, informed confidence, dualistic distinctions, skillful tendencies, dana, basis of practice, seeds of trust

Assignment: Allow yourself to stay in the same meditation position long enough to experience pain, and use that as a focus or object of meditation. Continue your study of breathing short and long breaths by "chasing." No brake between the breaths.

Define each of the Key Vocabulary in your own words.

How is Wisdom connected to the idea of seeing things as they are?
What creates moral authority?
How do we go about gaining clear understanding?
How is clarity the same or different from meta-cognition?
What can we do to internalize the techniques of reducing defilements?

What other factors affect our ability to follow a sacred moral code from week to week?

How do "ignorance, attachments and aversion" factor into our lives?

What is symbolized by each offering?

The flowers, beautiful one moment and wilted the next . . .
The odor of the incense calls to mind . . .
The candle-flame symbolizes . . .
(Two candles: 1)infinite wisdom and 2) inexhaustible compassion.)

Review the ten factors that prevent people from relieving suffering. (fetters)

1. Belief in personality [egoism, conceit, I, mine, etc.]
2. Skepticism—lack of certainty about the Buddha's teaching
3. Attachment to rules and rituals—[strict vegetarianism, celibacy]
4. Sensuous craving—[inappropriate sexual conduct or stalking]
5. Ill will—[vengeance and hatred]
6. Craving for material existence—[luxury consumption]
7. Craving for non-material existence [afterlife in a heaven]
8. Conceit
9. Restlessness
10. Ignorance—[laziness toward studying dharma

Which is most significant for you?
Compare these to "conditioning factors."

Materials for the next lesson: water ceremony, Teleology, tea service

Buddhist Sutra

Lesson Title: **The Eight-fold Path—Right Thought**

Lesson Number: **Seven**

Rationale:

This is the second stage of development on the Eight-fold Path to Enlightenment. Each of the eight stages must be accepted by Practitioners sequentially, then repeatedly revisited and developed simultaneously as well; like an expanding spiral. It is essential to know the contribution each stage can make in our lives and how each topic is to fit into the greater whole of one's spiritual practice—this is how wisdom develops.

Discussion of Prior Lesson:

"Actually the essence of meditation practice is to let go of all your expectations about meditation. All the qualities of your natural mind—peace, openness, relaxation, and clarity—are present in your mind just as it is. You don't have to do anything different. You don't have to shift or change your awareness. All you have to do while observing your mind is to recognize the qualities it already has." (Mingyur, pg. 98)

The flowers, beautiful one moment and wilted the next, are to remind offerers of the impermanence of life; the odor of the incense calls to mind the sweet scent of moral virtue that emanates from those who are devout; the candle-flame symbolizes enlightenment.

Training Objective:

How we eliminate guilt and boredom to increase happiness. The sequence: precepts, concentration and wisdom. The meaning of: Where your mind goes you follow. Identify your own motivation—your true intentions. *Kayanupassana.* Study long breaths.

Materials Required: water ceremony, Teleology, tea service

Motivational Statement:

"Buddhism defines everyday unhappiness in terms of an habitual dysfunction in the way we process our experience . . . it can be identified and corrected, and the root of everyday unhappiness can be eradicated." (Brown, pg. 6) "When we have right understanding of Buddha's teaching we have to seek ways to annihilate suffering; that is the second aspect—Right Thought which is right mental conduct consisting of: 1. no greed for others' belongings; 2. no vindictiveness; 3. taking right for righteousness [not being self-righteous.]" (Wee, pg. 28)

"Our wish to pursue the Buddha's way is therefore founded on **informed confidence** in the soundness of the teachings rather than on blind faith or misguided attraction to esoteric or superficial aspects . . . The wisdom element . . . implies that in order to practice we need to have heard (or read) the Buddha's teachings." (Snelling, pg. 47) (see pg. 61) Just as we have control of our own minds—although we may not understand that yet—we have control of our own ***happiness***—as a matter of choice.

First Progressive:

Bhikkhus: Literally translated from the Pali means beggars, as "used by Theravada Buddhists. The Sanskrit form is bhiksu. Here the word is generally translated 'monk'." In my own mind monks who wear habits (raps) seem to show externally their Buddha nature, and thus I feel inclined to show them respect. ". . . your innermost being, what the Buddha called your Buddha nature, the aspect of you that is most intimately interconnected with the entire universe . . . what we seek is within us . . . Buddha nature pervades the entire universe, and we are each challenged to do our part in embodying and expressing it." (Surya Das, pg. xvii) Knowing this is the highest perfection of wisdom, pranja paramita.

"The legends which were told about [Buddha] in later times are mostly unreliable, though they may contain a grain of historical truth here and there. Moreover many of the sermons and other pronouncements attributed to Buddha are not his, but the work of teachers in later times and there is considerable doubt as to the exact nature of his original message. However, the historicity of the Buddha is certain . . . The band of yellow-robed bhikkhus which the Buddha left behind him to continue his work probably remained for some two hundred years [as] one small group among the many heterodox sects of India, perhaps fewer in numbers and less influential than the rival sects of Jains and Ajivikas. Though by Western standards its rule was rigid, involving continuous movement from place to place for eight months of the year and the consumption of only *one meal a day, which was to be obtained by begging,* it was light in comparison with the discipline of most other orders, and the members of which were often compelled to take vows of total nudity, were not permitted to wash, and had to undergo painful penances . . . It is evident that between the death of the Buddha and the advent of ***Ashoka,*** the first great Buddhist emperor, over two hundred years later, there was considerable development of doctrine." (de Bary, pp. 6-7) There are many ways to give and to ask for donations, do fund raising and accept alms rather than just walking barefoot along the streets in the early hours of the day. What is the best way to share our own abundance?

Much of our thinking involves memories, reminiscences, ideas about recent events in our lives; how much of our thinking involves compassion in one form or another? If we only remember the "good times" does that make us healthier, or are we just being naive? How do we expand this mental health?

Second Progressive:

It is useful to examine the underling principles that influence our ability to create happiness for ourselves and follow an ethical moral code? "People living in societies characterized by technological and material achievements were just as likely to feel pain, anxiety, loneliness, isolation, and despair as people who lived in comparatively less-developed areas . . . when the pace of external or material progress exceeded the development of inner knowledge, people seemed to suffer deep emotional conflicts without any internal method of dealing with them . . . eventually the excitement dies down; the new sensations, new friends, or new responsibilities become commonplace . . . The trouble with all these solutions [i.e. trying each new form of recreation] is that they are, by nature, temporary. All phenomena are the results of the coming together of causes and conditions, and therefore inevitably undergo some type of change. When the underlying causes that produced and perpetuated an experience of happiness change, most people end up blaming either external conditions (other people, politicians, work obligations, a place, the weather, etc.) or themselves . . . However, because it reflects a loss of confidence in oneself, or in the things we're taught to believe should bring us happiness, blame only makes the search for happiness more difficult." (Mingyur) Happiness is not just a trick we play on our minds, but an assumption that we make which we are capable of achieving.

We can create the environment and physical health to make happiness easier. "Our bodies play a much bigger role in generation of emotions than most of us recognize. The process begins with perception . . . Most of us would assume, quite naturally, that once the object [or event] is perceived and recognized, an emotional response is produced, which in turn generates some sort of physical reaction . . . In fact, the opposite occurs. At the same time that the thalamus sends its messages higher up to the analytical regions of the brain, it sends a simultaneous 'red alert' message to the amygdale, the limbic region which governs emotional responses, particularly fear and anger . . . Upon receiving it [the stimulus], the amygdale immediately sets in motion a series of physical responses that activate the heart; the lungs; major muscles . . . and the organs responsible for producing hormones like ***adrenaline***. Only after the body responds does the analytical part of the brain interpret the physical reactions in terms of a specific emotion [and sometimes we engage the mind to calm our emotions and manage our image] . . . You see something scary, start to run (as the heart pounds and adrenaline surges through your body), and then interpret the body's reaction as fear. In most cases, though, once the rest of your brain has caught up with your body, which takes only a few milliseconds, you're able to assess your reactions and determine whether they're appropriate, as well as adjust your behavior to fit the particular situation . . . our ability to evaluate our reactions is inhibited, and we find ourselves responding to a situation without thinking . . . Such a powerful 'emergency response' mechanism undoubtedly has important survival benefits . . . But because the ***neuronal patterns*** stored in the amygdale can be triggered easily by events that bear even a slight resemblance to an earlier incident, they can distort our perception of present-moment events." (Mingyur, pp. 111-114) We don't control our emotions, we control our intellectual response to these emotions—or we don't. Moral codes require us in most cases to change the way we might otherwise act if our personalities were left untutored according to our primitive instincts. This civilizing process need never end as we learn to eliminate suffering, as we learn how to control the features of our physical lives and learn how to make our lives less complicated thus avoiding new suffering and egoism.

Third Progressive:

Why do events happen the way they do, car accidents, disease epidemics, landslides? Is any portion of our lives dictated by fate—destiny? Teleology is the study of why things happen, or at least the study of what people believe the reasons are behind events, such as religious "truth" and rationalizations, and deciding on virtue and justice based on preconceived absolute goals or dogma, i.e. merit. In Buddhism we learn to not make supernatural suppositions, and we learn to work with reality as we meet it.

The Buddhist Law of Causation is part of this greater field of ***Teleology.*** How much can we know about the results of our own karma, about cause and effect? and how much of our attempt to attach reasons, such as previous karma to current events, is based on belief, coincidence, superstition or simply conjecture? Can we recognize the difference? "Although these theories of good producing a good effect [i.e. making merit,] and evil producing an evil effect are not necessarily those of Buddhism alone, understanding them is a prerequisite to understanding and accepting the Buddhist faith. A person who fails to comprehend the law of karma or who rejects the law of cause and effect cannot possibly accept the correct doctrines of Buddhism." (Mizuno, pg. 37)

"Within the past several years, a number of projects have demonstrated very strong links between positive mental states and a reduction in the risk or intensity of various physical illnesses [i.e. the history of spiritual healing in the USA beginning even before Mary Baker Eddy.] The subjects [in a Harvard medical study] were primarily military veterans . . . the study . . . focused on specific manifestations of these emotions: namely, ***optimism and pessimism*** . . . that equates optimism with the belief that your future will be satisfying because you can exercise some control over the outcome of important events [vs.] pessimism with the belief that whatever problems you're experiencing are unavoidable because you have no control over your destiny."

"At the end of the study, Dr. Kubzansky found that after statistically adjusting for factors including age, gender, socioeconomic status, exercise, alcohol intake, and smoking, the incidence of some forms of heart disease among subjects identified as optimists was nearly 50 percent less than that of subjects identified as pessimists." One wonders if the optimists in the study held such a mental perspective only prior to the time they were inflicted by the heart disease, etc., and did the others maintain their optimism after the progress of their illness?

"Another research study . . . Duke University . . . looked at the physical effects of two other positive emotions associated with ***happiness***: **hopefulness and curiosity**. Nearly 1,050 patients of a multi-practice clinic agreed to participate by responding to a questionnaire about their emotional states, physical behaviors, and other information such as income and educational level . . . over the course of two years . . . higher levels of hope and curiosity were associated with a lower likelihood of either having or developing diabetes, high blood pressure, and respiratory tract infections . . . 'positive emotions may play a protective role [against] the development of disease'." (Mingyur, pp. 238-239) We can use Teleology both retrospectively and prospectively.

"Right thinking: In the Buddhist and the secular senses, this means thinking without desire [craving,] anger, or will to harm. In other words, it is thinking removed from covetousness, wrath, and foolishness. When, as a result of right view, the mind is correctly oriented, thinking in all instances is free of egoism and the emotions characterizing it. Right view [Lesson six] produces the will and determination to think right [thus these are connected.] This will and determination manifest themselves in right speech, right action, and right living [all of a piece]." (Mizuno, pg. 55) The Buddhist teachings of ***impermanence, unsuitability and soul-lessness***, suggest that we are not the same person today as we were five or fifty years ago. There is nothing in us that is permanent much less eternal. We can love that person of yesterday, but we are not restrained by whom we were, nor by what we did or believed. Is this a kind of schizophrenia? As long as we don't live contemporaneously with more than one mind, possibly we are not clinically schizophrenic? Buddhist training is in large part about unifying our mind, incorporating optimism, hopefulness and creativity; having integrity in our personality from day to day with an optimistic mind single-pointed toward enlightenment.

Searching for explanations is where superstitions begin, i.e. what is an omen? Even karma becomes an explanation based on cause and effect, and looking forward, trying to avoid further ego gratification and self-aggrandizement and suffering is a strong "why" that can become a source for self-motivation. "Because we cannot bear very much [negative] reality we often escape to illusions to soothe ourselves, a process that can cause enormous disappointment and pain. However, [positive] reality is the medicine. The facts of our lives when we are able to know them, will free us from the torment we are in. When we can bear [all] reality thoroughly, suffering is over. Pain may exist, but it is only pain. *Suffering is what we add to pain*. It is the refusal to experience life as it is, [like packing our luggage and carrying it with us for years] moment by moment. It is the many layers of fabrications—meanings and interpretations—we add to whatever we come up against."

"We can imagine all kinds of explanations [for the circumstance and complications of our lives,] but the deepest truth is, we don't know. Explanations bring superficial consolation. A don't-know mind is different. It is able to take life as it is given, and no matter what happens, to dare to get up and live. A don't know mind is humble and supple. It does not impose itself upon the facts of life. It eliminates catastrophic expectations. It learns to simply accept and go on." (Shoshanna, pg. 13) This is the opposite of what Teleology is about—explanations. How much talk about "karma," from past lives and the ***super natural*** teachings of Tantra can we really accept as fact? What superstitions are useful and beneficial in our practice? Or are they always wrong as an abuse of reason and wisdom? Think clearly and discuss each event in your life with those you trust; keeping an open mind is a prescription to develop right thinking. (see page 48)

The ultimate of Right Mindedness [Thought] is keeping an open mind: ". . . Whatsoever there is of thinking, considering, reasoning, thought, ratiocination, application—the mind being holy, being turned away from the world and *conjoined with the path, the holy path being pursued*:—these Verbal Operations of the mind are called the Ultramundane Right Mindedness, which is not of the world, but is ultramundane and conjoined with the paths. Majjhima-Nikaya" (Goddard, pg. 42) Part of what we call creativity, intuition and inspiration are related to and perhaps derived from this "Ultramundane Right Mindedness." Asking for alms may be an example of this, as disconnected as this might seem, and is done as a sacred ceremony that permits the donor to gain merit. Right Thought (Intention) is the inside game, what we practice and the way we learn from our minds and inspiration, as well as the integrity of our personality.

Meditation Practicum:

Meditation is concerned with ". . . observing your mind [and] recognizing the qualities it already has . . . But that doesn't mean you have to be a slave to whatever your mind produces. When you don't understand the nature and origin of your thoughts, your thoughts use you. When the Buddha recognized the nature of his mind, he reversed the process. He showed us how we can ***use our thoughts*** instead of being used by them . . . And once you begin to work with these thoughts and emotions, you'll begin to discover a whole new dimension of freedom from ancient, survival-based patterns. You begin the process by questioning whether every thought you think, every feeling you feel, is a fact or a habit." (Mingyur, pg. 98) Writing in a journal or writing poetry are parallel activities to meditation. As we have a thought, wrestle to explain it and then write it down; we are viewing and watching our thoughts. Eventually we have the thoughts we want to have, get clarity, and even writing becomes pleasant, organized and easier.

Occasionally meditate on your childhood and adolescence, and identify the suffering you experienced. Identify the causes of that suffering, both external and internal, and determine what influence that has on your life now. How does this carry over to your personality—onto your family and friends? Identify the mistakes you made, but don't get stuck there, don't obsess about these nor become preoccupied with these thoughts to the exclusion of positive, forward looking thoughts. Can you find a way to forgive yourself for those mistakes, or celebrate again your achievements? "There are three types of learning that embrace all Buddhist doctrines and practices . . . *precepts, concentration, and wisdom.*"

1. Precepts (or morality) are for the sake of correctly training mind and body and establishing correct physical and mental habits.

2. Concentration, or meditation, is for the sake of spiritual unification after the mind and body have been properly trained. It produces a state in which the mind is as clear as a mirror and as still as the surface of an undisturbed body of water.
3. Correct wisdom, reached when this kind of spiritual unification has been attained, makes possible correct judgments and suitable actions.

In the light of this progression, the order for training and attainment in the three types of learning is this: precepts, concentration, and wisdom." (Mizuno, pg. 53) When we apply these three types of learning as feedback based on the experiences of our own lives, it is like reading a textbook of how to live properly. This is how we enlarge our frame of reference as well. The Eight-fold Path is often organized into these three categories.

"To meditate means to be invited on a journey of looking deeply in order to touch our true nature and to recognize that nothing is lost." (Hanh, pg. 225) This is what makes Rational Buddhism useful for even the most staunch religious participants of whatever persuasion, because Buddhism is about improving our realities. "The ability to experience and understand truth depends a great deal upon the quality of the unfolding mental continuum; [based on each person's development and education.] In the protecting exercise, the practitioner discerns some similarity between the truth represented by the teachings and the qualities of his or her own mental continuum. Typically the practitioner's first attempts to protect only serve as a reminder of how far the emerging activity of the mental continuum has gone astray from any approximation of realized truth . . . ***Protecting*** [like active reflection] entails a comparison of immediate experience and the teachings given . . . The profound changes in lifestyle and view of the mind that constitute the preliminary practices help to generate meditation, and open the way to the essential meditations that follow." (Brown, pp. 147-151) Freethinkers are using the capacities they inherited and have developed to evaluate the experiences they have, to weigh the truth they encounter. As we meditate about our youth and earlier life, we learn and internalize the valuable lessons we have gained.

The simple exercise of chasing our breath is an important technique which will be emphasized in several succeeding lessons. Remembering and identifying our sensations for different breaths is also a practice involving protecting. This chasing is also called "following" and is much more significant than it may originally seem, and will eventually lead to the development of jhana/absorption as we will learn later. There are many Buddhist retreats that teach this practice in association with Mindfulness training.

Now we can do slow, deep breathing together. "To control the breath [Sanskrit: prana, Pali: ***pana***] is to control life . . . These trainings are called Pranayama . . . breath control . . . When the prana enters the body, it is called ana and when it leaves it is called apana . . . combined become anapana . . . [remember anapanasati, sati is mindfulness] To control the prana is to control that which enters to preserve life. Then we live a life that is fresh and cheerful, ready and fit for training and practice . . . This system of *kayanupassana* (contemplation on the body) takes up the Pranayama of the Indian yogas and improves upon them in appropriateness and practicability . . . Since we cannot regulate the flesh-body directly [quite apart from eating and hygiene], we regulate it indirectly [with the prana-body.]"

"The first lesson is the contemplation of the long breath [in more detail.] . . . its properties, qualities, influence, and flavor.

> When a breath is long, how pleasant is it?
> Is it natural and ordinary?
> What kinds of calmness and happiness arise?
> In what ways is it different from a short breath?

Observe how the body works in relation to long breaths. Place a hand on your abdomen.

> How does the body move when there is a long inhalation?
> In what places does the body expand?
> Where does it contract?
> With the deepest possible long breath, does the chest expand or contract?

Does the abdomen expand or contract? [continue slow, deep breathing]

(The chest expands with long breaths.) In order to know the nature of the long breath, we study all the secrets and attributes of the long breath. We are able to contemplate its long duration, learning to protect and maintain it. In fact, we become experts in all matters concerned with the long breath. Practicing with the ***long breath is lesson one*** . . . We learn in a deeper way, through personal experience rather than through thinking, that the breath is intimately associated with the body." (Buddhadasa, 1988, pp. 35-39) We gain experience by frequent and repeated application of chasing; we test long breaths the full length and pathway of the airflow, from abdomen to the exit at the nostrils until we are at ease with this technique with both the in and out breaths. This is like learning to ride a bike and involves a similar delicacy of balance and movement.

Biographical Sketch:

During May of 2007, we (my wife and I) visited Guatemala for a brief vacation to familiarize ourselves with a culture and people we had never met. The hotel, where we chose to stay for four days, offered a hike and a tour near Lake Atitlan. One feature of the guided hike was a visit with a Maya shaman who gave us a cleansing ceremony. The ceremony was an amalgam of Maya tradition and Catholic beliefs. At a sacred, natural, well used rock altar, a site atop Cerro d'Oro a parasitic volcanic outcrop rising from the shore of the lake, the shaman built a fire with corn pellets and herbs surrounded by a ring of sugar, he prayed, blessed us and doused us with sprinkles of water and smoke. From this cleansing we felt we were better prepared for a new and happier life.

In Theravada Buddhism, the monks use water to transfer merit to the laity; the laity pour water (and cool the Buddha) to share this merit with their ancestors. This is a cleansing. In another way water is poured on a Buddha icon as a reminder of the coolness of Nirvana as a goal. Many religions use water in special rituals.

"Yoga was conceived by the ancient Indian ***rishis [mystics]*** as a practical method for the complete physical, mental and spiritual transformation of the individual. We are often told, 'To change your life you only need to change your mind. If you change your mind, the way you see the world, you and your world will automatically change.' As the Buddha said, "All that we are is the result of what we have thought. We are made of our thoughts' . . . it is not only very difficult to change the way you see the world, but even harder to maintain a new vision, and not backslide into old and habitual conditioning, losing the very gains you have made." (Forstater, pg. 27) A key to taking advantage of our thoughts is being honest with ourselves as a first step. Occasionally you may have to make a new beginning (and be "reborn.")

"Not lying, truthfulness, means to be true to your inner Self [your core values] and to express your heart's truth openly and freely in speech and action. When thoughts, words and deeds are all one, we live an integrated life and are part of the unity that we feel all around us. The truth has a power that we are able to use consciously and unconsciously to further everything we do." (Forstater, pp. 64-65) Expressing the truth about oneself is one thing, and expressing negative emotions that arise and essentially belong to someone else, is quite another issue. Learning to separate the two is a step toward wisdom. How does telling the truth or falsehood change your breath? What does the idiom mean to "Breathe a sigh of relief?"

Reading for the Day:

"Right thought, must include correct motivation [which we can supply for ourselves.] We need to realize that we are practicing [meditation,] not to acquire greater powers and more possessions for ourselves, but rather to move away from the basic egocentric orientation to a new, wider, more selfless one. In short: there is in the final analysis no pay-off for 'me' in practicing Buddhism [because the force of our egos is reduced not expanded.] That having been said, it has to be admitted that none of us have perfect understanding and motivation at the start. As we continue, however, practice will tend to uncover all sorts of blind spots and subtle forms of self-centeredness. The Buddha's way is an ever-deepening learning process."

"An actual change in our thinking process must begin to take place too. The unreformed mind, [***selfish, craving, greedy***] like a mill in perpetual motion, is constantly devising plans, plots, and strategies for advancing its own cause, outflanking rivals [initiating complications] and undoing enemies. Or else it indulges itself in egoistic or hedonistic fantasies. Right thought is about switching over to other-directed mental modes: ones that are more altruistic and benign. We should also become increasingly concerned to act responsibly towards the environment. We think too of religious questions with a view, not to promoting ourselves as gurus or pundits, but in order to be of better service to the world." (Snelling, pg. 47)

Protecting:

"This is what I heard," review by both practitioners and teacher.

After the review, the teacher will use the water and sprinkle each student with a blessing—*that they will retain their development and the mental perspectives they have gained;—that their wisdom will grow to benefit themselves and others; and—that their life will be changed in positive ways. (Reminder: Suffering is what we add to pain.)*

> (Prayer for ***Enlightenment***: Forever am I liberated,
> This is the last time that I'm born, No new existence waits for me.
> This verily, is the highest, holiest wisdom:
> To know that all suffering has passed away.
> This, verily is the highest, holiest plead: Appeasement of greed, hatred and delusion.
> 'I am' is a vain thought; 'I am not' is a vain thought;
> 'I shall be' is a vain thought; 'I shall not be' is a vain thought.
> Vain thoughts are a sickness, an ulcer, a thorn.
> But after overcoming all vain thoughts one is called a silent thinker.
> And the thinker, the silent One, does no more arise,
> No more pass away, no more tremble, no more desire.

For there is nothing in him(her) that should arise again.
And as these arise no more, how should they grow old again?
And as we grow no more old, how should we die again?
And as we die no more, how should we tremble?
And as we tremble no more, how should we have desire?
Hence, the purpose of the Holy Life does not consist in acquiring alms,
Honor, or fame, nor in gaining morality, concentration, or the eye of knowledge.
That unshakable **deliverance of the heart:**
That, verily, is the object of the Holy Life, that is the essence, that is its goal.)

Majjhima-Nikaya (Goddard, pp. 59-60)

Sharing Merit:

Rejoicing In Others' Merit (Saying Sadhu)

Buddhist Sutra

Lesson Title: The Eight-fold Path—Right Thought

Lesson Number: Seven

Key Vocabulary: teleology, bhikkhus, happiness, Ashoka, technology, neuronal pattern, adrenaline, emotional response, intentions, precepts, wisdom, kayanupassana, reborn, Heart, citta, pranayama

Assignment: Meditate on your childhood, adolescence and experiences of your life—identify the suffering you experienced and the lessons you learned, the changes you have achieved.
Repeat the guided meditation and study long breathing repeatedly in serious detail.

> When a breath is long, how pleasant is it?
> Is it natural and ordinary?
> What kinds of calmness and happiness arise?
> When you chase your breath what happens to your concentration?

"If I have a cruel thought or if my words carry hatred in them, then those thoughts and words will be reborn. It will be difficult to catch them and pull them back. They are like a runaway horse." (Hanh, pg. 137) How does this quote fit into your life?

How much of your suffering is mental: i.e. shyness, paranoia, insecurities, self-doubt?
Identify at least one cause of suffering and determine what influence that has on your life.

How does this carry over to your personality—and influence the relationships you have with family and friends?
Identify one mistake you made . . . Can you forgive yourself for that mistake?

Define each of the Key Vocabulary in your own words.

How do we really eliminate guilt from our lives?

What is boredom, and how can these periods of emptiness (as a blessing) be used to increase happiness?

What does it mean to say: "Where your mind goes you follow?"
What does it mean to be a free thinker?
What superstitions are useful and beneficial in our practice? if any.
How do other religions use water in special ways?
How much can we know about "karma," about cause and effect? and how much of our attempt to attach reasons to events is based on belief, coincidence, superstition and simply conjecture? Can we recognize the difference?

Material for next lesson: Deontology, drinking water, (candle of wisdom)

Buddhist Sutra

Lesson Title: The Eight-fold Path—Right Speech

Lesson Number: Eight

Rationale:

There is a good deal to learn about how our speech portrays who we are, how what we say can create effects, both positive and negative. For some people, following the Buddhist path will be extremely difficult because it requires them to think before they speak and change their entire way of relating to other people in society—thus we experience rebirth.

Discussion of Prior Lesson:

"All things whatsoever have the property of changing incessantly; they are unstable. All things whatsoever have the characteristic of unsatisfactoriness; seeing them evokes disillusionment and disenchantment in anyone having clear insight into their nature. Nothing whatsoever is such that we are justified in regarding it as "mine." To our normally imperfect vision, things appear as selves; but as soon as our vision becomes clear, unobscured, and accurate, we realize that there is no self-entity present in any of them." (Buddhadasa, 2005, pg. 41)

"Intellectual operations . . . [Right Thought] are harnesses in the service of spiritual transformation . . . Intellectual understanding . . . [Right View] is considered to be the first type of direct experience of the truth." (Brown, pg. 65)

Training Objective:

Speech patterns and habits portray who we are. What we say (and do, karma) displays our compassion and can create causes and effects, both positive and negative. Buddhist Etiquette. Standing meditation, and short breathing. The sacred breath.

Materials Required: Deontology, water, candle of wisdom

Motivational Statement:

Does morality exist prior to human action, (***deontological***) such as might be called an absolute truth of right and wrong, good and bad. Are there '***universal values***' to which all well-intentioned people subscribe? To suggest a special code of ethics that is on the face of it clearly best, is to make a well-educated claim that is influenced by that very education, thus ***ethnocentric***.

"First of all, we should know about the truth of our life. The truth of life is characterized according to the Four Noble Truths. It depends on mindfulness and wisdom of each person to consider the truth accordingly . . . to know how our life is. If we can reflect [within] ourselves [we can begin] to understand [The Four Noble Truths,] we will know that every single life encounters suffering [in the same way we do.] We cannot understand well the Four Noble Truths [if] we lack thorough reflection upon them." (Wee, pg. 25)

"Whatever you do or say in a state of anger will only cause more damage in the relationship. Instead, try not to do anything or say anything when you are angry." (Hanh, pg. 109)

First Progressive:

Most modern Buddhists like to examine scientific evidence. "Two distinct but related functions of the limbic system are involved in the development of loving-kindness and compassion. The first is what neuroscientists have identified as ***limbic resonance***—a kind of brain-to-brain capacity to recognize the emotional states of others through facial expression, pheromones, [***empathy***] and body or muscular position . . . In most cases, if we haven't trained ourselves to pay bare attention to the shifts and changes in observing our minds, the process of *limbic resonance* occurs unconsciously . . . The second function is referred to as ***limbic revision,*** which in simple terms means the capacity to change or *revise the neuronal circuitry of the limbic region*, either through direct experience with a person like a lama or a therapist, or through direct interaction and a set of instructions . . . It would seem that *meditation—particularly on compassion*—creates new neuronal pathways [i.e. modifying your first impressions] that increase communication between different areas of the brain, leading to what I've heard some scientists refer to as '*whole brain functioning'*."

"From a Buddhist perspective, however, I can say that meditation on compassion fosters a broadening of insight into the nature of experience that stems from unchaining the habitual tendency of mind to distinguish between self and other, subject and object—a unification of the analytical and intuitive aspects of consciousness that is both extremely pleasurable and tremendously liberating." (Mingyur, pp. 226-227) We can learn, partly through training in meditation, to say the right thing, offer condolences, compliments, sympathy, affirmations and blessings at the right time as if speaking to ourselves, and this is enabled by whole brain functioning.

"Nothing can heal anger except compassion." (Hanh, pg. 151) Compassion is the capacity in the mind that makes our thoughts and speech turn toward tenderness and genuine concern (also for ourselves.) Since our speech uses the same pathway as our breath, it is particularly important that we develop patterns of speech that do not essentially contaminate our breath passage. And obviously the history of our speech is a picture of the state of our minds, our morality and our consciousness (in the same way that our accent, grammar, inflection and diction), and these are tell-tale signs of our erudition, sincerity and compassion. We are taught that more than 90% of communication is other than speech, so we must think of "body language" and our facial expressions as part of our language pattern that comes under the tutelage of Right Speech. We can take encouragement that it is possible to expect beneficial changes from limbic revision by virtue of our meditation practice.

Second Progressive:

"The third aspect is Right Speech . . . which means wholesome and correct speech which does not cause any annoyance and trouble to others, nor make others misunderstand. Right speech is called ***Vacisucarita*** (good conduct in speech) comprising: 1. no false speech; 2. no ***harsh speech***; 3. no malicious speech; 4. no idle speech. All the above are called moral conducts (***Sila***) which means to keep body and speech wholesome." (Wee, pg. 28) When we put ourselves under the influence of a healthy Sangha, we grow based on limbic resonance. We simply learn how to act and speak by following the examples of others.

"Right speech . . . is about not telling lies, slandering and backbiting, swearing and using 'harsh' language, wasting one's own and other peoples' time with frivolous chatter, and generally not using one's speech faculties in harmful or unproductive ways. It is also about being truthful. This is in fact very important, especially as our modern Western culture has debased truth, and facts are wantonly suppressed or twisted to suit self-interest [e.g. political spin and marketing hype] or in order to generate sensation." (Snelling, pg. 48) For ancient yogis even before the Buddha, telling the truth was a way to sanctify the breath and was thought as a path to holiness, to replace the Branan/Vedic reituals. (Armstrong)

Each culture has certain words that are offensive, vulgar (being uneducated) or obscene when spoken in normal public discourse, i.e. 'fuck.' References to scatological issues, i.e. 'shit,' are nearly universally considered impolite or 'swear words.' The word 'bloody' for the English is a cuss word, while in the US it sounds innocent, albeit strange, to hear that word used; it is not loaded in the same way. It is clear that words have emotional power from the most mundane utilitarian pronoun to the highest form of praise or the 'name of God'. It makes sense to learn and practice acceptable speech etiquette in whatever language one converses. Polite speech and soft pleasant speech are virtues of Buddhism and an important part of etiquette for a Rational Buddhist, and included as part of the Five Precepts. In this way we hallow our breath.

"The ***law of cause and effect*** pertains to the operations of all phenomena in the universe—not just to good and evil. It is taught in relation to what is called ***the Law of Causation***, but there is a difference between the two. The law of cause and effect *deals with the individual* in terms of a temporal chain extending from past into present and then into the future. The Law of Causation, however, deals not merely with the individual but also with spatial and temporal relations among individuals and everything in their environment: family, local society, school, regional society, national society, [fiscal complications,] international society, the natural environment, politics, economy, culture, spiritual fields, natural phenomena, and so on. An accurate interpretation of the world and of human life, this law [causation] is extremely extensive. It is the basis on which Buddhism teaches the impossibility of true happiness for an individual without development in the direction of happiness for all the other people in that individual's environment." (Snelling, pg. 96) Paraphrase this for yourself.

Third Progressive:

"Right speech means refraining from lying, malice, a double tongue, careless language, and fruitless chatter. In practical terms, all of these kinds of speech impede efficiency; in Buddhist terms, they stand in the way of training along the Path. Avoiding them and telling only the truth, praising and encouraging others properly, speaking to arbitrate for the sake of accord, and talking in a way that serves in the attainment of the ideal are what is meant by right speech. As I have said, right speech derives from well-intentioned, right thinking. It generates reserve energy giving rise to good habits. All actions leave a reserve of energy that become habits for further action. Accumulation of such habits forms the personality. Both habit and personality play an immense role in everyday life. Because it includes the element of correct speech habits, this aspect of the Eightfold Noble Path belongs in the *precepts* category of Buddhist learning. The same thing is true of right action and right living." (Mizuno, pp. 55-56)

There are many books in the popular, self-help genre in the marketplace that teach the importance of "right speech" as it relates to marriage and family relationships. "One way to express love emotionally is to use words that build up. Solomon, author of the ancient Hebrew wisdom literature, wrote, 'The tongue has the power of life and death.' Many couples have never learned the tremendous power of verbally affirming each other." (Chapman, pg. 39) Consider this new and useful vogue with the understanding that Buddha taught the same idea in the Dharma 2,500 years ago. It's never too late to share feelings and encouragement (as well as to receive these humbly and politely) as well as words of love.

Meditation Practicum:

"Meditating on sound is very similar to meditating on form, except that now you're engaging the faculty of hearing. Start by just allowing your mind to rest for a few moments in a relaxed state, and then gradually allow yourself to become aware of the things you hear close to your ear, such as your heartbeat or your breath, or sounds that occur naturally in your immediate surroundings. Some people find it helpful to play a recording of natural sounds or pleasant music. There's no need to try to identify these sounds, nor is it necessary to focus on a specific sound. In fact, it's easier to let yourself be aware of everything you hear. The point is to cultivate a simple, **bare awareness** of sound as it strikes your ear."

"As with form and color meditation, you'll probably find that you can focus on the sounds around you for only a few seconds at a time before your mind wanders off. That's okay. When you find your mind wandering, just bring yourself back to a relaxed state of mind and then bring your awareness back to the sound once again. Allow yourself to alternate between resting your attention on sounds and allowing your mind simply to rest in a relaxed state of open meditation." (Mingyur, pp. 151-152)

". . . Buddha's early followers . . . came up with a way to organize the various meditation practices the Buddha taught into two basic categories: ***analytical methods*** [insight meditation] and non-analytical methods [concentration.] The non-analytical methods are usually taught first, because they provide the means for calming the mind . . . [shinay—calm abiding] to simply be aware of various thoughts, feelings, and sensations without getting caught up in them. The analytical practices involve *looking directly at the mind in the midst of experience*, and are usually taught after someone has had some practice in learning how to rest the mind simply as it is . . . and can provoke a lot of questions . . . Shinay . . . is a basic kind of practice through which we rest the mind naturally in a state of relaxed awareness in order to allow the nature of mind to reveal itself."

"That's how to rest the mind in objectless shinay meditation: as though you've just finished a long day of work. Just let go and relax [be aware of everything you hear—bare awareness of sound.] You don't have to block whatever thoughts, emotions, or sensations arise, but neither do you have to follow them. Just rest in the open present, simply allowing whatever happens to occur." (Mingyur, pp. 137-138)

"Standing Meditation. We practice by standing upright with no bending back, heels next to each other, in a collected posture with two eyes closed, left palm on the surface of the belly and the right one on the former. Stand in a comfortable manner, not stiffly, stand still, do not sway nor fidget. Standing in a collected manner, we begin to practice mind to be aware of inhalation and exhalation by directing the mind at the tip of the nose only." (Wee, pg. 128)

Meditation, as discussed before, can be practiced in many different circumstances and formally in four different postures: sitting, lying, walking and standing. "In the beginning, most of us aren't able to rest our minds in bare awareness for a very long time at all. If you can rest for only a very short time, that's fine. Just follow the instruction given earlier to repeat that short period of relaxation many times over in any given session. Even resting the mind for the time it takes you to breathe in and breathe out [or on a single sound] is enormously useful. Just do that again and again and again.

Conditions are always changing, and real peace lies in the ability to adapt to the changes." (Mingyur, pg. 210)

Experiment as in the previous lesson with short breaths by counting to five quickly during a silent breath drawn through the nose in and out, following these breaths from beginning to end. You will be asked to answer the same questions as identified for long breaths. Practice with short, shallow breathing for only a few minutes to learn about it, not for any mystical purpose, the same as with long breaths. With each in-breath recite or think Bud—dho with each out-breath; this is an acknowledgement of our natural buddhahood, and hallows our breath in a different way.

Biographical Sketch:

Some monks refuse to speak to members of the opposite sex, and some men in Thailand use fans to shield their eyes so they will not see the faces of women. Such extreme precautions are a symptom of 'objectification,' where their culture has taught them to treat women as visual objects of sexual attraction, thus they fear being distracted into a state of mental impurity and defilement. How much better is it to speak politely and evenly to both men and women, and regard them as rational humans irrespective of their gender, sexual preference and physical appearance? Even where nudity is concerned, the human body need not be considered an overt sexual attractor. "On the subject of monastic life Bikkhu Soma's views were even less conventional. Discussing an incident that had occurred during the voyage (an attempt, it seemed, had been made to seduce him), he declared that the true monk should rise above temptation rather than run away from it and that he should, if necessary, be able to look at a naked woman without desire." (Sangharakshita, pg. 138) We do this with respect to children, and men and women can learn this kind of neutrality toward each other as a form of etiquette.

Another aspect of Buddhist etiquette is: when entering a Buddhist wat or significant shrine, it is required that each visitor take off their shoes and remain silent as in a library. Most Buddhists genuflect to the shrines (and touch their finger tips in ***anjali*, *namaste)***, light candles and/or incense and meditate or pray in front of the shrines as part of their regular religious practice. It is useful to think about this as showing respect to the abstract concept of buddhahood that is present in each of us. We can obtain the same enlightenment and nirvana for which we offer this demonstration and sense of respect.

At some of the shrines in Thailand there are fortune telling sticks: shake a package of sticks until one stick falls out; read the numbered fortune that corresponds to your stick. You can purchase gold foil, lotus buds, plastic necklaces and prayer beads, all part of the religious practice. These can be thought of as ways of teaching us to remember who we are and that we are sacred.

Theravada Buddhists celebrate the birth, enlightenment, and death of the Buddha on the same day the full moon of May, called Vaisakha. In Sri Lanka, it is a festival of lights, when houses, gardens and streets are decorated with lanterns. It is not a major festival in other Theravada countries, but, occurring on an Observance Day, it is at least an occasion for special food offerings to the monks and more than the usual devotion to keeping the moral precepts. These are special days for cleansing and renewal.

Japanese Buddhist celebrate the Buddha's birth, death, and enlightenment on different days of the year: the birth on April 8, the enlightenment on December 8, and the death on February 15. The birth celebration, Hanamatsuri, is a flower festival and time for ritually bathing images of the Buddha. Enlightenment Day (Bodhi) and Death Day (Nehan [Nirvana]), are simply occasions for social worship.

Reading for the Day:

"The ability to experience and understand truth depends a great deal upon the quality of the unfolding mental continuum [the grace you received at birth and capabilities you have developed through conscientious education.] In the ***protecting*** [after each meditation] exercise, the practitioner discerns some similarity between the truth represented by the teachings and the qualities of his or her own mental continuum. Typically the practitioner's first attempts to protect only serve as a reminder of how far the emerging activity of the mental continuum has gone astray from any approximation of realized truth . . . the mind can be described from two perspectives: 1. from the perspective of the mind that observes these events,—non-analytical; 2. from the perspective of the observable events in the unfolding stream of experience [from the outside looking in] . . . From the perspective of the mind that observes . . . it easily becomes distracted. Awareness of the unfolding stream of experience is discontinuous."

"From the perspective of the unfolding events within the mental continuum, the very structure of the ordinary mind is disorganized. A mind that gets distracted from its intended object of awareness and gets lost in the construction of more and more mental content is said to become elaborated [i.e. listening vs. hearing.] Continuous elaboration is called 'wandering' [losing track of the meditation process.]" (Brown, pp. 151-152) This same kind of wandering can happen when we tell stories or offer elaborate explanations for our actions. This may be worthwhile for intimate social conversations, but for practice in the Sangha, when describing orally the results of meditation as a form of protecting, *brevity and succinctness are virtues*.

Protecting:

"This is what I heard," review by both practitioners and teacher.

Additional Teachings:

"The breath alone is well worth knowing, even if only in terms of health. If we know how to breathe properly [naturally,] we will have good health. Thus, the body and everything associated with the body—the breath, the emotions, our health—is considered to be a very important subject. [Thus] get the fullest benefits from this stage of anapanasati." (Buddhadasa, 2005, pg. 96)

"There can be a variety of offerings [at a Buddhist altar,] but the most common in the Theravada tradition consist of the three items . . . incense sticks, candles and flowers. They bear symbolic significance representing the virtues of the Triple Gem."

"As a rule, three incense sticks are used. They reflect the ***three virtues*** of the Buddha, namely,

1) universal compassion,
2) perfect purity and
3) supreme wisdom . . . [also the sequence of Buddha's teaching method]

Mahayana and Vajrayana traditions also hold that lighting incense . . . helps ***purify*** the atmosphere [with esoteric significance] making the site (a shrine, for example) ready for devotional service that will follow . . . By reflecting on what the three incense sticks represent, devotees will be inspired to follow in the footsteps of the Buddha."

"The two candles represent the two aspects of the Buddha's teaching, namely the ***Doctrine and the Discipline*** . . . when we study and accept (Dhamma-Vinaya) in our hearts—the darkness of ignorance and delusion will be eliminated from our minds. Lighting of the candles therefore symbolizes our sincere effort to practice the Buddha's teaching." The doctrine and discipline are united in the same way that Speech is united with our physical mechanism of in-and-out breathing that is essentially a sacred aspect of our Buddhist practice because it is not only a frequently used object of meditation, but subtly behind the success of all meditation.

"Flowers represent the ***Sangha or community*** of monks or enlightened disciples of the Buddha. (Plamintr, 2007, pp.184-185)

Sharing Merit:

Rejoicing In Others' Merit (Saying Sadhu)

Buddhist Sutra

Lesson Title: **The Eight-fold Path—Right Speech**

Lesson Number: **Eight**

Key Vocabulary: objectification, Vaisakha, Sri Lanka, Vacisucarita, intention, harsh words, blurting, universal values, limbic resonance, empathy, analytical methods, elaborated, protecting, affirmation, ethnocentric, deontological, limbic revision, Law of Causation, bare awareness, three virtues

Assignment:
Meditate on sound for five periods of about twenty minutes each (at least one time in the dark out of doors.) Use both seated and standing postures.

Study short breaths.

When a breath is short, how pleasant is it?
Is it natural and ordinary?
What kinds of excitement, energy or happiness arise?
When you chase your breath what happens to your concentration?

"Speech patterns and habits portray who we are." Do you agree? and What is the significance of this?

Give examples—what we say creates causes and effects, both positive and negative.

Describe Buddhist Etiquette. Describe the three virtues of the Buddha.

". . . Buddhism teaches the impossibility of true happiness for an individual without development in the direction of happiness for all the other people in that individual's environment." Paraphrase and discuss.

Define each of the Key Vocabulary in your own words.

Meditate at least once on compassion—look at when you have received the benefit of someone else's compassion . . .
. . . and when you have given based on compassion
. . . and compare your different emotional experiences.

Give an example of each of these:

Precepts
Concentration
Wisdom

As these relate to a growth experience you have had.

Materials for next lesson: Ontological, Tea Ceremony

Buddhist Sutra

Lesson Title: **The Eight-fold Path—Right Action**

Lesson Number: **Nine**

Rationale:

This is a broad category that goes beyond personal considerations. How should we relate to our neighborhood, community, state, nation and the world? "If we live with the understanding of impermanence, we will cultivate and nurture our love. Only then will it last." (Hanh, pg. 269). "The real practice of Buddhism is based on purification of conduct by way of body and speech, [actions] followed by purification of the mind, which in its turn leads to insight and right understanding." (Buddhadasa, 2005, pg. 19)

Discussion of Prior Lesson:

"One of the great benefits of meditation on sound is that it gradually teaches you to detach from assigning meaning to the various sounds you hear. You learn to listen to what you hear without necessarily responding emotionally to the content. As you grow accustomed to giving bare attention to sound simply as sound, you'll find yourself able to listen to criticism without becoming angry or defensive and able to listen to praise without becoming overly proud or excited." (Mingyur, pg. 152)

". . . We observe and feel immediately that the long breath brings ease and comfort while the short breath leads to abnormality, that is, uneasiness, agitation, and discomfort. Thus through our ability to regulate the breath, we know how to make the body either comfortable or uncomfortable." (Buddhadasa, 1988, pg. 39)

Discuss: Universal compassion, perfect purity, and supreme wisdom.

Training Objective:

The meaning of 'right action' in Buddhism and having discipline. How does *clarity* become important in meditation? Seven point sitting position. The role of celibacy and vegetarianism. Introduction to anatta.

Materials Required: Ontological, Tea Ceremony

Motivational Statement:

"A student sought out a great Zen Master to discover the secrets of this universe and what his life truly meant. He traveled far and wide and finally located a Master living simply in a hut on top of a mountain . . . the master motioned for him to sit down on a mat on the floor and went to boil water for tea. The student had to wait for the tea to be ready."

"The water boiled slowly. The student grew restless, eager to get the preliminaries over with, ask his question, and get his answer to the true meaning of the universe . . . The more restless he grew, the more slowly the water boiled . . . Finally the tea was ready. The Master gave the student a teacup and the student trembled excitedly. His mind and body were not stable. In fact he began to have more and more thoughts of additional questions he could ask after the Master answered this one."

"The Master began to pour the tea, up to the very top of the cup . . . the Master kept pouring . . . the hot tea spilled over the edges and onto the student's trembling hands."

"'What are you doing?' the student cried out."

"'What are you doing?' the Master replied. 'Just like this teacup you are full of yourself, full of opinions, desires, questions, imagination. How can you receive anything from me when your cup is so full? In order to receive any teaching, first you must empty your cup." (Shoshanna, pg. 53) The Practitioner must be receptive to guidance, learn the proper ways to act, then have the discipline to make changes in their lives. (The tea should be steeped by now and shared as with guests in a home, during the course of this lesson and subsequent lessons.)

First Progressive:

"The Buddhist understanding of *compassion* is, in some ways, a bit different from the ordinary sense of the word. For Buddhists, compassion doesn't simply mean feeling sorry for other people. The Tibetan term—***nying-jay***—implies an utterly direct expansion of the heart. Probably the closest English translation . . . is 'love'—but a type of love without attachment or any expectation of getting anything in return. Compassion, in Tibetan terms, is *a spontaneous feeling of connection with all living things*. What you feel, I feel; what I feel, you feel. There's no difference between us . . . along with our tendency toward aggression [in society], our survival instinct has provided us with 'an even stronger biological bias for kindness, compassion, love, and nurture'." (Mingyur, pg. 105) How do we teach each new generation to share this broader vision? How do we cultivate this (Can we train our minds to be more compassionate?) and exercise our compassion for humanity while we are still learning to love our own family well?

"General Shiha . . . was a highly influential ***Jainist*** in the capital [Vesali] . . . who heard all of this [the growing influence of Buddha] . . . thought to himself . . . 'I think I will go to meet Gotama and investigate this myself.' He then went to Nataputta [Jainist leader] and explained his wish. But Nataputta dissuaded him [twice] . . . [later on the significant third impulse] he took five hundred carts and went to the Great Forest Monastery, where Shakyamuni was staying. During the ensuing discussion, karma was a subject. From Shakyamuni, General Shiha heard many detailed teachings that were totally new to him. He was greatly moved and entrusted himself to the Buddhist faith."

"But Shakyamuni reproved him by saying, 'A person of your importance and position must not change his religious faith lightly.' The general replied, 'I am not being rash. I have made this decision after mature consideration. And the fact that the World-honored One gives me such advice only strengthens my resolve. If some other religion had converted a person of my authority and fame, its believers would have rejoiced wildly and would have announced it throughout the streets of Vesali with great waving of flags. But instead of this you urge me to consider my step carefully. This makes me more determined than ever to entrust myself to the Buddha, the Law, and the Order'."

"Then Shakyamuni said, 'Believer, for a long time you have been a fount of all kinds of offerings, fulfilling all of the wishes of the followers of Nigantha [Jainist]. Even after you become a Buddhist, you must continue to make offerings to them cordially'." (Mizuno, pp. 128-129) Is this not the compassionate way to live? This provides continuity in our lives.

Second Progressive:

"[Buddhist] precepts control body and speech to be in the stream of wholesomeness. When speech is controlled by precepts, there are doctrines to guide body to lead a wholesome life. They are the forth aspect 'Right Action' . . . The action according to these two doctrines is called 'bodily good conducts' comprising three conducts: 1. no killing; 2. no stealing; 3. no sexual misconduct." (Wee, pp. 28-29) When we follow these precepts we minimize future suffering and complications in our lives.

Since most of our actions are determined by our mind, our physical state and motivation come into major prominence in this topic of right action. "Most brain activity seems due to a very special class of cells called ***neurons.*** Neurons are very social cells: They love to gossip . . . the secret conversations between neurons are mainly about sensations, movement, solving problems, creating memories, and producing thoughts and emotions . . . They pass their messages to one another across tiny gaps between the closest branches. These gaps are called ***synapses.*** The actual messages that flow across these gaps are carried in the form of chemical molecules called ***neurotransmitters***, which create electrical signals that can be measured by an EEG. Some of these neurotransmitters are pretty well known . . . ***serotonin,*** which is influential in depression; dopamine, a chemical associated with sensations of pleasure; and ***epinephrine,*** more commonly known as adrenaline, a chemical often produced in response to stress, anxiety, and fear, but also critical for attention and vigilance. The scientific term for the transmission of an electrochemical signal from one neuron to another is ***action potential*** . . . When neurons connect, they form a bond very much like old friendships. They get into a habit of passing the same sorts of messages back and forth, the way old friends tend to reinforce each other's judgments about people, events, and experiences. This bonding is the biological basis for many of what we call mental habits, the kind of 'knee-jerk' reactions we have to certain types of people, places, and things [and most spur-of-the-moment actions.]"

". . . The capacity to replace old neuronal connections with new ones is referred to as neuronal plasticity [pliability. This] . . . repeated experience can change the way the brain works. This is the why behind the how of the Buddhist teachings that deal with eliminating mental habits conducive to unhappiness." (Mingyur, pp. 34-35) Learning new, positive habits (as with learning to have Compassion) takes time, practice or some serious form of shock. But it is possible to succeed!

"Stealing of any kind is obviously a potent form of harm and violence, and if at the same time we deny the reality of our actions to ourselves, we add lying to the mix." (Forstater, pg. 66) If our theft is an acting out against perceived suffering, it will be self defeating and likely bring on more suffering based on the Law of Causation.

"Right action is about decent behavior generally. A lay person may, as a token of their commitment to the Buddha's way, subscribe to Five Precepts—Pancha Shila—and accordingly undertake to train him/herself to:

1. Refrain from taking life. (taking away another's breath)
2. Refrain from taking that which is not given.
3. Refrain from misuse of the senses.
4. Refrain from telling lies.
5. Refrain from self-intoxication with drink and drugs . . ."

"Not taking life . . . inevitably raises the question of whether meat-eating is permissible or not in Buddhism. The members of the original Sangha were mendicants and as such were supposed to accept whatever food they were given. Thus it was technically permissible for them to eat meat, but only if they knew that an animal, bird, or fish had not been killed specially to provide them with food . . . Later, when the Mahayana developed, strong calls for total vegetarianism were put out."

"Misuse of the senses embraces a spectrum of vices. There is over-indulgence in food, which not only causes the rich and powerful to gorge themselves at the expense of the underprivileged—in its global aspect, this results in the appalling malnutrition suffered in the third world—but also leads to disease and torpor . . . Strictly observant Theravada Buddhist monks eat only one meal a day and that before noon."

"The mind is a sense organ in the Buddhist view, one can overindulge in intellectual pastimes—also glutting the eye with beautiful sights and the ear with beautiful sounds—with similar negative results. And one can abuse the body [risk taking recreation] both one's own and others', for selfish pleasure."

"***Celibacy*** has become highly unpopular [in general Western society, but] . . . misguided indulgence and overindulgence in sex are as likely to lead to psychological problems [and huge emotional issues and complications] as non-indulgence . . . Lay people are not expected to be strictly celibate, but still their sexual activity should be contained within reasonable constraints . . . we should firstly try not to hurt others; and secondly we should try to be moderate, [communicate forthrightly] for immoderate indulgence of sexual desire will only serve to feed the fires of passion and attachment, which cuts completely contrary to the direction and spirit of the Buddha's way." (Snelling, pp. 48-49) In our modern, enlightened society where gender rights are to be equalized, it is especially important to refrain from treating others [of either gender] as sexual ***objects*** (de-humanizing, objectification) for merely the pleasure of sight or merely for recreational orgasms. This is a category mistake, mistaking such pleasures for love that can inspire. Natural bonding promotes unification of the whole integrated personality, thus love that is rooted in and creates compassion can be a completion of not detraction from spiritual practice.

"Therefore, Ananda, [spoke Buddha] a man who tries to practice dhyana without first attaining control of his mind is like a man trying to bake bread out of a dough made of sand; bake it as long as he will, it will only be sand made a little hot. It is the same with sentient beings, Ananda. They can not hope to attain Buddhahood by means of an indecent body. How can they hope to attain the wonderful experience of Samadhi out of bawdiness? . . . Sexual lust leads to multiplicity; control of mind and Samadhi leads to enlightenment and the unitive life of Buddhahood. Multiplicity leads to strife and suffering; control of mind and dhyana leads to the blissful peace of Samadhi and buddhahood." The Surangama Sutra (Goddard, pg. 263) If our sexuality is based on trying to assuage a low self-esteem, then we should find other ways to empower our personalities during mediation. Whatever we choose, we need to show honesty and consideration for others. Sexuality is under the consideration of ethics and morals in every culture that I am aware of, but for Buddhism it is pragmatic, not wishing to create complications and future suffering.

Third Progressive:

"Right Action means abstaining from deliberate killing, from stealing, and from wrong sexual activities. In other words, right action entails love and protection for living things, generous almsgiving, expounding the Law, and proper marital relations. They too are the outcome of will and determination produced by right thinking and include the reserve energy for the creation of habitual right actions." (Mizuno, pg. 56) The first reason for right action is the reciprocal—respect that we get back in kind—this is a good source for enhancing self-esteem.

"The Yogis, like the ***Taoists***, believe that sexual energy is a potent form of life energy, and that ejaculation [what about female orgasm?] drains away this life force. To conserve this energy we need to be sexually moderate." (This is a superstition from the yoga tradition.) What, if any, is the medical or scientific basis for this teaching? Sexual energy can be a source of bonding for two mature adults, and this results from non-reproductive sex and is possibly (or infrequent reproductive sex) the most emphasized use for our sexuality.

"For people who reject celibacy and believe that sexuality should be another form of spirituality, sexual moderation means acting without exploitation of others, not using other people's bodies for one's own gratification [avoid ***objectification***.] In a sexual relationship, we interchange our deepest creative energies with another person, and join our two selves in a physical and spiritual unity. This mingling of two selves, two sexual energies, if treated lovingly, openly and reverentially, can regenerate our spirituality and deepen our commitment. This is much more than just the friction of two bodies to release built-up [chemical] tension." (Forstater, pg. 66) What is numinous about sexuality?

There is another practical reason for right action in Buddhism. "Buddhism has its own version of learning theory. We could call it karma theory. Just as learning theory emphasizes behaviors [comprehension and retention], karma theory addresses actions—both observable and mental. But whereas learning theory stresses that strengthening associations [i.e. scaffolding, Constructionists] reinforces learning, karma theory simply asserts that: 1. actions have predictable consequences, 2. repeated actions increase the force or weight of any action, and 3. discontinuing the action diminishes the consequences. The main emphasis of karma theory is that all actions have consequences. The consequences of any given action are said to ripen (smin ba) over time, first as mental events and later as behaviors. A cumulative consequence of habitual negative actions is obscuration of the ordinary mind [e.g. ennui, or losing ones scruples or conscience.] Conversely, an accumulation of positive actions over time decreases negative mind-states, and increases positive states [i.e. making merit] that make the mind fit for higher spiritual realizations and enlightenment." This is a simple message that bears repeating; the more sophisticated message follows.

Buddhists are taught to have patience. "The gradual path involves progressive learning. According to karma theory the skillful practitioner gradually refines the ordinary mind and its dysfunction so that the subtle and very subtle minds become manifest. Sometimes this process is likened to refining crude ore into a precious metal." (Brown, pp. 11-12) How can we recognize these different levels of the mind?

Ontology in philosophy comes up often in discussions about the existence of god, for example, in Western philosophy. "Something than which nothing greater can be conceived . . ." is often a statement of a logical necessity for the existence of a Creator. This is the kind of discussion, Buddha thought, was unnecessary to address. There is no question about our existence, and theorizing about the origin of god or the universe takes one chasing his/her tail toward an infinite continuum. Man exists ontologically, not because "I think, therefore I am." But I am, and therefore I find myself sitting here thinking (Which is the solipsism?) and my very human nature and existence are beyond questioning, and implicit in the fact that I can think, and to say so is merely a redundancy. Is thinking our only level of mental activity? 2500 tyears ago Buddha explained that he was Tathagata, thusness, and we are just the same.

Thus Buddhism is not an atheist religion, but it allows each practitioner to draw their own conclusions, so it is a religion of many atheists. And along with this "freedom" is the obligation each practitioner has to find meaning in life for themselves, and share this with their loved ones and Sangha members. The teachings (and poetry) of ***Nagarjuna*** is famous in Buddhist circles for elaborating on these issues:

> "Neither from itself nor from another,
> Nor from both,
> Nor without a cause,
> Does anything whatever, anywhere arise."
> (Garfield, pg. 3)

Advanced Arahants may choose to entertain and meditate on some of these philosophical discussions (verbal paradoxes, koans) once they have understood well the basics of Buddhism. Nagarjuna dedicated an entire section to "Examination of the Agent and Action" (Garfield, pp. 23-25) which is largely unintelligible, or at least readily susceptible to misunderstanding without some serious commentary.

Meditation Practicum:

The sitting position (***seven points***) (half or full lotus position) is the most commonly used and most widely recognized posture for meditation. (Sitting in a straight backed chair is certainly acceptable.) "The Buddha taught that the body is the physical support for the mind. The relationship between them is like the relationship between a glass and the water it contains . . . If you set a glass on a flat, stable surface, the water in it will remain perfectly still . . . aligning the body in a balanced way allows the mind to remain relaxed and alert at the same time . . . Over the years, this physical alignment has become known as the seven-point posture of ***Vairochana***, an aspect of the Buddha that represents enlightened form."

1) "The first point of the posture is to create a stable basis for the body . . . if possible, crossing your legs so that each foot rests on the opposite thigh. If you can't do this, you can just cross one foot on top of the opposite thigh, resting the other beneath the opposite thigh. If either position is uncomfortable, you can simply cross your legs. You can even sit comfortably in a chair, with your feet resting evenly on the floor. The goal is to create a physical foundation that is simultaneously comfortable and stable." There are many options to allow Practitioners to avoid pain at the beginning of meditation.
2) "The second point is to rest your hands in your lap just below your navel, with the back of one hand resting in the palm of the other. It doesn't matter which hand is placed on top of the

other, and you can switch their positions at any time during your practice . . . or palm down over your knees."

3) "The third point is to allow a bit of a space between your upper arms and your torso. The classic Buddhist texts call this 'holding your arms like a vulture,' which can easily be mistaken for stretching out your shoulder blades as if you were some sort of predatory bird . . . enough to make sure that your chest is open and relaxed, so you can breathe nice and freely . . . find a balance between your shoulders so that one is not dipping below the other . . ."
4) "The fourth point of the physical posture is to keep your spine as straight as possible—as the classic texts say, 'like an arrow.' But here, again, it is important to find a balance."
5) "The fifth point involves letting the weight of your head rest evenly on your neck, so that you're not crushing your windpipe or straining so far backward that you compress the cervical vertebrae, the seven little bones at the top of your spinal cord, which is vital in transmitting neuronal signals from the lower parts of your body to your brain . . . you'll probably notice that your chin is tilting just slightly more toward your throat than it ordinarily does . . ."
6) "The sixth point concerns the mouth, which should be allowed to rest naturally so that your teeth and lips are very slightly parted [take a few breaths orally to test this.] If possible, you can allow the tip of your tongue to gently touch the upper palate just behind the teeth. Don't force the tongue to touch your palate; just allow it to rest there gently . . . the most important thing is to allow the tongue to rest naturally."
7) "The seventh point of the meditation posture involves the eyes. Most people who are new to meditation feel more comfortable keeping their eyes closed. They find it easier that way to allow the mind to rest and to experience a sense of peace and tranquility. This is fine at the beginning. One of the things I learned early on, however, is that keeping the eyes closed makes it easier to become attached to an artificial sense of tranquility. So, eventually, after a few days of practice, it's better to keep *your eyes open when you meditate, so that you can stay alert, clear, and mindful.* This doesn't

> mean glaring straight ahead without blinking, but simply leaving your eyes open as they normally are throughout the day . . . Vairochana is really a set of guidelines . . . everyone is different. The most important thing is to find for yourself the appropriate balance between tension and relaxation." (Mingyur, pp. 132-136) There are many actions that can be taken to improve posture like stretching and yoga exercises. Likewise, over eating, accumulating extra fat and useless muscles, will interfere with comfortable sitting meditation postures.

Close your eyes and follow this next discussion and use this opportunity for an objective self-evaluation. Choose a single object like the sky with no clouds, for your focus initially. "Objectless shinay meditation doesn't mean just letting your mind wander aimlessly among fantasies, memories, or daydreams. There's still some presence of mind that may be loosely described as a center of awareness . . . you're still aware, still present to what's happening in the here and now [like peripheral vision.] . . . When we meditate in this objectless state, we're actually resting the mind in its natural clarity, entirely indifferent to the passage of thoughts and emotions. This natural clarity—which is beyond any dualistic grasping of subject and object—is always present [as is consciousness of dreams] for us in the same way that space is always present. Objectless meditation is like accepting whatever clouds and mist might obscure the sky while recognizing that the sky itself remains unchanged even when it is obscured . . . [your] Buddha nature is always open and clear even when thoughts and emotions obscure it. Though it may seem very ordinary, all the qualities of clarity, emptiness, and compassion are contained within that state . . . All you need to do is rest within the awareness of your mind . . . The most effective process is to rest the mind for very short periods many times a day. Otherwise, you run the risk of growing bored or becoming disappointed with your progress and eventually give up trying altogether . . . Practicing like this, '*one drip at a time,*' you'll find yourself gradually becoming free of the mental and emotional limitations that are the source of fatigue, disappointment, anger, and despair, and discover within yourself an unlimited source of clarity, wisdom, diligence, peace, and compassion." (Mingyur, pp.139-141) As passive as this approach to meditation seems, it involves discipline and is the key to changing the way we perceive sensory information; thus to the way we act.

"Discipline also means the willingness to give up something of ourselves, an act of self-sacrifice that provides a control over sensual desires, rather than always being a victim of those desires. We need to accept that we can't get everything we want or do everything we desire, and so discipline means . . . we become open to a larger view of life. This expansion of consciousness enables us to make better decisions about things, learning to discriminate between the essential [action] and the superfluous. To do this shows a certain maturity and means that we are able to grow beyond our childhood illusions." (Forstater, pp. 69-70) Growth from meditation requires discipline especially in the beginning stages until meditation becomes an habitual practice.

After using long breaths and short breaths we notice ". . . that it is possible to regulate, control, limit, and *manage the emotions by using the breath.* We can make the emotions correct, useful, and beneficial through the breath . . . our practice is not complete until we can see this clearly." (Buddhadasa, 1988, pg. 40) This becomes the focus of steps 5-8.

"In step three, the aim is to experience all kaya, all bodies [in addition to the breath-body.] . . . While practicing the [long and short breaths] . . . we investigate this fact [that the breath conditions our flesh-and-blood body.] . . . We contemplate in a deeper way that there are two kaya (bodies). We should continuously observe this while breathing in and breathing out . . . We should analyze this experience to see clearly that there are two groups and that they condition each other. Contemplate this thoroughly until it becomes obvious . . . [What is our breath made of?] The specific aim of this third step is to come to understand (1) that there are two groups and (2) that one group conditions, nourishes, and supports the other group. The breath-body group nourishes the flesh-body group. [This is known as kaya-sankhara (body-conditioner).] . . . See them arise together, fall together, coarsen together, become fine together, grow comfortable together, and become uncomfortable together . . . This is valuable for seeing truth more extensively, even for realizing anatta . . . [this] is a natural process of conditioning. There is no atta, no self, no soul involved. Although it is beyond the specific objective of this step, such an understanding can have the highest benefit. For now, however, our purpose in understanding this conditioning is to be able to calm the flesh-body by regulating the breath-body." (Buddhadasa, 1988, pp. 43-44) What seems a trivial process of knowing that breathing conditions and nurtures the body, instead becomes a serious consideration (a way of describing *clarity*) connected to the understanding that there is no living-eternal "Soul" inside the body somewhere, but that the breath is what enters the body to sustain life and influence emotions. (Can we use this process to increase self healing?)

Biographical Sketch:

Thich Nhat Hanh is a popular author in the US among Buddhist students, and there are numerous meditation centers around the country which devote their practice to his teachings. "Thich Nhat Hanh has been a Buddhist monk since the age of sixteen. He has survived three wars, religious and political persecution, and more than thirty years of exile. He is the master of a temple in Vietnam whose lineage goes back to the Buddha himself. The author of more than one hundred books of poetry, fiction, and philosophy, including the national bestsellers *Anger* and *Living Buddha, Living Christ*. Hanh lives in France and Vermont." (Hanh, cover leaf) Many of his teachings and aphorisms are included among these Buddhist Sutras and can be used as mental nutrition for Practitioners and a source of spiritual guidance. Hanh's newest book about "Awakening of the Heart" is perhaps the first book that any new Buddhist student should acquire.

The pre-Buddhist tradition regarding the breath was largely incorporated into the Buddha's teaching about meditation and the human condition. "The atman was not what we in the West would call a soul, because it was not wholly spiritual. In the early stages of this speculation some of the Bramins believed that the self was physical, the trunk of the body, as opposed to the limbs. Others began to look deeper. Sound was such a powerfully sacred reality that perhaps a man's atman resided in his speech? Others thought that breath, without which life is impossible, must constitute the essential core of the human being, and a strong case could also be made for the heat (tapas) that welled up within the sacrificer while he sweated beside the sacred fire and that filled him with divine energy . . . once the inner fire—the atman—had been created within the sacrificer, it became his permanent and inalienable possession . . . therefore the sacrificer was equal to the gods and did not need to worship them anymore . . . He no longer had to service his atman by continually participating in the external ceremonies of the liturgy, because his inner fire did not need fuel. All that was necessary for the self-sacrificer was to speak the truth at all times, the special virtue of devas and warriors alike. By acting and speaking in accordance with truth and reality, he would be imbued with the power and energy of the Brahman." (Armstrong, pg. 84) The speech (the truth) and the breath continued being regarded as sacred.

My childhood guidance was from traditional, limited Western sources. As a child walking to and from school, I was for a time very self-conscious about how I walked to the point, while focusing on the movement of my legs, I could hardly take one step after the other. Eventually I learned that when I shifted my focus to my shoulders, and controlled that my shoulders did not swing with each step, my legs could just keep walking without any difficulty. (This would be good training for actors or anyone who performs in front of an audience.) Later I was self-conscious about my shoulders being balanced, my posture and about my underarm perspiration. These kind of self-conscious thoughts are natural enough for adolescents, although they can become compulsive and irritating, but they are a form of natural meditation. When adults notice this in children, especially in shy children, they should not use language that diminishes this kind of reflective thinking because this is a natural beginning of meditation, which as Buddhist adults, we have to learn to do all over. Children should be told that their self-conscious, introspective thoughts are natural, that this kind of self-training is part of growing up and leads to appropriate action when gently guided.

Reading for the Day:

"Learning to appreciate the clarity of the mind is a gradual process, just like developing an awareness of emptiness. First you get the main point, slowly grow more familiar with it, and then just continue training in recognition. Some texts actually compare this slow course of recognition to an old cow peeing—an old cow doesn't pee in one quick burst, but in a slow, steady stream. It may not start out as much and it doesn't end quickly, either. In fact, the cow may walk several yards while in the process, continuing to graze. But when it's over—what a relief!" (Mingyur, pg. 99)

"Zen in Action: Exercise—Do Nothing. Find a situation that is troubling you and that you have been trying to work out. Think about it and Do Nothing. Think about it again, and Do Nothing again. Stop all unnecessary activity, thoughts, and machinations. Take a walk at the beach (or anywhere that is relaxing to you), enjoy the moment—then think about the situation. Still Do Nothing at all. Keep walking, keep enjoying."

"When this situation actually appears in your life, continue to Do Nothing. After about a week of this, notice the changes that have taken place without your interfering at all." (Shoshanna, pg. 53)

"Often the word kama [kharma] is used not only in reference to an intentional action, but also mistakenly to indicate the result thereof. This kind of confusion is common even among the educated . . . Kamma means an action, never its result. The Pali words for the result are phala, vipaka, or kammavipaka. It is important to be aware of this distinction to avoid misunderstandings about kama." (Plamintr, 2007, pg. 110)

"Once we have understood this clearly [about the conditioner—the breath] and are convinced by our experience of this process with each in-breath and out-breath, then we have realized success in our practice of step three." (Buddhadasa, 1988, pg. 47)

Protecting:

A pot of tea is to be shared, with small cups for each Practitioner and teacher, Oolong or Jasmine to help with retention of the dharma.

"This is what I heard," review by both practitioners and teacher.

Additional Teachings:

Proverb: Good manners sometimes means simply putting up with other people's bad manners. (wellpage.com)

The fruits of meditation can seem glorious and fulfilling, exciting and like an hallucination, like a drug trip. "The drug experience is forced, phony experience, but because we don't know the real, the phony seems to be right . . . [or somehow efficacious.] If you compare your life with an ordinary man who has never taken anything like LSD, marijuana, then you feel very high . . . If you are really interested in meditation, then drugs are dangerous . . . drugs are dangerous for the religious people because something delicate arises out of meditation. It is very delicate and it comes out of much effort. Just a small quantity of a drug and it is destroyed and you will have to start again from abc." (by Osho, quoted in Forman, 1987, pp. 71-72) (Formerly Bhagwan Shree Rasnish)

"It should not be thought that the eight categories or divisions of the Path should be followed and practiced one after the other in the numerical order as given in the usual list above. But they are to be developed more or less simultaneously, as far as possible according to the capacity of each individual. They are all linked together and each helps the cultivation of the others." Of course we can't initially incorporate everything at once, so taking them in order, one at a time is appropriate.

"These eight factors aim at promoting and perfecting the three essentials of Buddhist training and discipline: namely: a) Ethical Conduct (Sila) [Right Speech, Action and Livelihood,] b) Mental Discipline (Samadhi) [Right Effort, Mindfulness (or Attentiveness) and Concentration,] and c) Wisdom (Panna) [Right View (Understanding) and Thought (Intention).] . . . The Buddha gave his teaching 'for the good of the many, for the happiness of the many, out of compassion for the world'."

In summary: "Right Action aims at promoting moral, honorable and peaceful conduct. It admonishes us that we should abstain from destroying life, from stealing, from dishonest dealings, from illegitimate sexual intercourse, and that we should also help others to lead a peaceful and honorable life in the right way."(Walpola, pp. 46-47)

Sharing Merit:

Rejoicing In Others' Merit (Saying Sadhu)

Buddhist Sutra

Lesson Title: **The Eight-fold Path—Right Action**

Lesson Number: **Nine**

Key Vocabulary: Hanh, nying-jay, Jainism, clarity, believer, discipline, seven-points, objectification, Nagarjuna, diligence, Vairochana, celibacy, Taoism, Ontology, action potential, neurotransmitter, dopamine, epinephrine, synapses, serotonin, pliability, neurons, sankhara, dhyana (jhana)

Assignment: Practice meditating on each of the seven points of sitting as often as possible, and try to recognize and identifying "clarity."

The first point is to create a stable basis—crossing your legs . . . the goal is to create a physical foundation that is simultaneously comfortable and stable.

The second point—rest your hands in your lap just below your navel, with the back of one hand resting in the palm of the other. It doesn't matter which hand is placed on top of the other, and you can switch their positions at any time during your practice . . . or palm down over your knees."

The third point—allow a bit of a space between your upper arms and your torso; find a balance between your shoulders so that one is not dipping below the other.

The fourth point—is to keep your spine as straight as possible 'like an arrow.'

The fifth point—let the weight of your head rest evenly on your neck, let your chin tilt just slightly more toward your throat than it ordinarily does . . ."

The sixth point concerns the mouth—rest naturally so that your teeth and lips are very slightly parted [take a few breaths orally to test this] to allow the tongue to rest naturally.

The seventh point—the eyes. Keeping the eyes closed is okay, but it is easier to become attached to an artificial sense of tranquility, so it's better to keep your eyes open to stay alert, clear, and mindful.

Define each of the Key Vocabulary in your own words.

Give your own explanation of the meaning of 'right action' in Buddhism.

How does clarity become important in meditation?

Visualize how "group breath" conditions, nourishes and supports "the body."

How does discipline play a role in your spiritual practice?
Identify a situation in your life and practice "doing nothing."

How does our existence relate to our instinct to search for meaning in our lives?

In what ways do we school our instincts and perfect our actions (karma)?

What are the implications of accepting the fact (ontology) of our existence?

Material for next lesson: Epistemology, Tea Service

Buddhist Sutra

Lesson Title: The Eight-fold Path—Right Livelihood

Lesson Number: Ten

Rationale:

If our profession is a service, even those on assembly lines serve, it will be rewarded, and if we use our talents to capacity with hard work, we may be exceedingly well compensated. We can use that reward to satisfy our feelings of compassion. "The circumstances of our lives can help us water the seeds of patience, generosity, compassion, and love. The people around us can help us [as we can help them] water these seeds, and so can the practice of mindfulness." (Hanh, pg. 203) What about mentoring?

Discussion of Prior Lesson:

Getting clear on a subject usually means to gain understanding. Getting 'clear' is a technical term used in Scientology to identify the mental state when "engrams," mental blocks, are removed from the sub-conscious mind that inhibit desired or appropriate action, and personal achievement. But for Buddhists clarity has a more prosaic meaning: "When there is mere un-distraction, clarity of mind is generated." (Brown, pg. 297) How does this differ from "***epiphany***?" Or the proverbial light going off in our mind?

"Discipline is another word that we prefer not to use any more, but it is impossible to move forward in yoga [or in any spiritual practice] without it. It takes discipline to turn up week after week [day after day,] discipline to find the time to practice or meditate at home, discipline to follow spiritual teachings in a consumer society that considers them old-fashioned and irrelevant. Without discipline, most people give up on themselves, and live to regret it." (Forstater, pg. 69) This Right Action is also a key to success in business or in pursuing higher education. Can we improve our work habits as part of Right Action?

Training Objective:

Talents and education should be used in service to ourselves and to others. Apply Buddhist moral codes while engaged in commerce and the labor market. How to "***direct***" attention during contemplation as a beginning stage of meditation. Calming the breath is step Four. Creative Thinking.

Materials Required: Epistemology, Tea Service

Motivational Statement:

"Because the roots of ignorance are so intimately entwined with the fabric of the psyche, the un-awakened mind is capable of deceiving itself with breathtaking ingenuity. The solution therefore requires more than simply being kind, loving, and mindful in the present moment. The practitioner must equip him—or herself with the expertise to use a range of tools to outwit, outlast, and eventually uproot the mind's unskillful tendencies [in order to make significant progress.] For example, the practice of (1) ***generosity (dana)*** erodes the heart's habitual tendencies towards craving and teaches valuable lessons about the motivations behind, and the results of, skillful action. The practice of (2) ***virtue (sila)*** guards one against straying wildly off-course and into harm's way. The (3) cultivation of ***goodwill (metta)*** helps to undermine anger's seductive grasp.

[Beyond that] the ten recollections offer ways to (4) alleviate doubt, (5) bear physical pain with composure, (6) maintain a healthy sense of self-respect, (7) overcome laziness and (8) complacency, and (9) restrain oneself from unbridled lust. And there are many (10) more skills to learn." (Bullitt, internet)

First Progressive:

"All the suffering of living beings is our own suffering. We have to see that we are they and they are us. When we see their suffering, *an arrow of compassion and love enters our hearts.* We can love them, embrace them, and find a way to help. Only then will we not be overwhelmed by despair at their situation. Or our own." (Hanh, pg. 271)

"Though we must remain calm and stable in bad times as well as good, when things are going well, human beings not infrequently tend to be complacent or proud. Buddhism teaches that there are many different kinds of pride: in family background, in health, in youth and power, in good reputation, in influence, in wealth, [in employment status,] in personal beauty, in knowledge, in strength, in technical or artistic skills, and so on. Pride in one's sense of compassion and in merciful works indicates immature faith and lack of understanding of the true nature of compassion. Although it is wrong to be proud of powers and abilities, it is still worse to be proud of powers and abilities that one does not even possess [bragging, false advertising] . . . Pride causes a person to lose modesty and the sense of sympathy with others. Buddhism has long recommended the life of poverty and suffering not for its own sake but to serve as a precaution against pride in happiness and good fortune, to stimulate a constant feeling of modesty and humility, [the customer is always right,] and *to awaken a feeling of compassion and protection for unfortunate people* through actual knowledge of what it means to be unfortunate . . . One must be trained in faith and in physical strength to remain stable no matter what conditions are encountered." (Mizuno, pp. 133-134)

Nothing is fated in our lives, we have the hope of upward economic mobility, the effects of actions or potential (i.e. the law of cause and effect) consequences from our own actions (other than illegal) are usually optional. We can improve our lives by having compassion. However, actions that we take that relate to others (i.e. The Law of Causality) create complications (compounded things) which may not be optional, and thus the lack of compassion may have serious consequences.

How do we achieve the changes in our character and personalities according to these lofty goals that are taught in Buddhism? "Meditation is useful even in matters not relating to religion or Dhamma . . . Dhamma is useful both at the superficial or worldly level and also at the spiritual level. For example, when there is good concentration in the mind, there will be enough of mindfulness to drive one towards a life of good hygiene [which most people take for granted,] sound physical health [a more subtle concern relating to the self-discipline of fitness and correct eating,] and proper spiritual well-being [seriously moving toward a less complicated life with fewer attachments.] Anapanasati meditation helps to make the mind function well. It enhances the tranquility of the mind, thus enabling it to think well, remember well and also perform other duties well. The mind is gentle and tranquil and is most suitable for carrying out its function. It is thus called '***Kammaniya***' meaning 'fit for work'. Hence the mind is fit enough to think, memorize, decide or whatever function it sets about to do." (Buddhadasa, 2003, pp. 28-29) Often it is the compassion of others that gets us into the position in life where meditation is possible. What does it mean to pay it forward?

Second Progressive:

"As for [The Buddha's] character apart from his philosophy, little can be said, for in our sources his character is his philosophy." (Carrithers, 1983, pg. 12)

"The fundamental principle at play in right livelihood is the classic Indian virtue of ahimsa: harmlessness. The serious Buddhist does not wish to compromise his integrity by becoming involved in any activity that is going to cause harm to other people, animals, or the environment, or even outer space . . . To be an effective Buddhist, one needs that space and calmness [that comes with honest productive business practices] that can only come from being on reasonably good terms with oneself and with the world at large." (Snelling, pg. 50)

The Theravada teachings show the interconnectedness of the Eight-fold Path. "Our life will be in the stream of wholesomeness when we live our lives by right occupation. Thus, our life will be outwardly pure or bodily pure which is called 'bodily good conduct' or 'moral conduct' or 'precepts' (Sila) that is to keep body and speech wholesome." (Wee, pg. 29)

"Everything you think, everything you say, and everything you do is reflected back to you as your own experience. If you cause someone pain, you experience pain ten times worse. If you promote others' happiness and well-being, you experience the same happiness ten times over. If your own mind is calm, then the people around you will experience a similar degree of calmness." (Mingyur, pg. 235)

"Buddha's actions after his enlightenment . . . were all intended to help people abandon the law of the world and come to understand ***the Law of the Universe*** . . . Some of Shakyamuni's sermons emphasize secular morality and everyday life . . . the Sutra of Good Fortune . . . teaches: [call it Buddhist morality, or comparable to the Beatitudes.]

"Not to associate with fools but to associate with wise men and to revere people who are worthy of reverence. This is the highest blessing."

"To live in a suitable place, to have accumulated merits and virtues in previous lives, and to have correct wishes. This is the highest blessing."

"To be learned and skillful, to be trained and to have studied much, and to speak words of good teachings. This is the highest blessing."

"To care for parents, to provide well for wife and children, and to have a way of making a living that is pure and correct. This is the highest blessing."

"To give alms, to perform correct actions, to care lovingly for and to protect relatives, and to do nothing that is blameworthy. This is the highest blessing."

"To take no pleasure in wickedness and to refrain from evil acts, to control one's own consumption of intoxicants, [no mention of abstinence] and to be selfless in all things. This is the highest blessing."

"To respect others, to be humble, to know what is sufficient, to be grateful for what others do, and from time to time to hear the Law taught. This is the highest blessing.

"To be forbearing, to speak gently, to meet with people of religion and occasionally to discuss the Law and teachings. This is the highest blessing."

"To make efforts, to be trained in the Buddha's way, to comprehend the Noble Truths, and to find enlightenment in nirvana. This is the highest blessing."

"To remain unshaken by contact with the things of the secular world, to be free of anxiety, to be undefiled, and to be tranquil. This is the highest blessing."

"Those who do these things are undefeated in all things, prosperous in all things, and theirs is the highest blessing."

"This series of definitions represents Buddhist morality [Theravada tradition] on the plane of everyday life. A person living according to these principles is not upset by contact with the law of the world . . . Buddhism does not advocate rejection of the world." (Mizuno, pp. 153-156) Discuss each of these. We have all inherited Earth.

Third Progressive:

The effect or potential (i.e. cause and effect) from action usually creates more optional choices, however there may be unavoidable and unintended consequences of karma. Actions that relate to others (Law of Causation) create complications "compounded things" which may not be optional (i.e. partnerships create duties.) "Right living is obtaining food, clothing, and housing by proper means. This entails being faithful in one's work and living seriously without resort to shady methods, like gambling, for a living. But it further includes an orderly way of life in which hours for sleep; kinds, quantities, and numbers of meals; hours for work, study, rest, exercise, and entertainment are all properly regulated to suit individual needs. A controlled life that keeps a person in good health and enables him to work more efficiently is highly important, no matter what the environment. It can help determine success or failure." (Mizuno, pg. 56) If we do what we are lead to do by our talents and native ingenuity, there are millions of choices, there will be surplus wealth and leisure to support a rewarding life (at least in most developed countries.)

"If you keep practicing Zen spiritedly and dauntlessly in the midst of the objects of the senses and mind, plunging your entire being into your study, completely losing yourself in concentration, not making the slightest error and summoning up your entire spirit . . . you will surely gain a great joy as if you had crushed an iron mountain to pieces . . . You will be like the lotus blooming in the midst of fire, which increases its beauty and fragrance when it encounters the flame. Why is this so? Fire is no other than the lotus; the lotus is no other than fire!" (de Bary, pp. 392-393) This may explain the symbolism on the heads of some Buddha icons, but obviously it is possible to enjoy a fruitful practice with somewhat less intensity.

Epistemology is the study of how we know, or more deeply can we know, i.e. can we know that god exists? How do we come to know facts and phenomena of nature? Ludwig Wittgenstein showed that knowing the context of a discussion, and the language game involved silenced the misgivings about what it is to know. Most often the questions themselves are what cause the fundamental misunderstanding, and when we ask: "What kind of answer do we want?" in many situations we can come to ***clarity.*** Buddhism takes the pragmatic perspective, and accepts the world as we see it, teaches us to eliminate attachments and silences the sixth sense to the status of observer of phenomena and our perceptions of objects of nature that enter through the "body-doors."

"It has been argued, for example, that anyone who says that we never know anything but only believe—or suppose it robs the concept of belief of an essential contrast with knowledge, without which it would be meaningless. This argument—the so-called argument from polar concepts—is invalid, because a philosopher can use the concept of belief as long as he has a concept of knowledge, as long as he knows what it would be like to know; he does not have to admit that anyone knows anything as a matter of fact." (Edwards, pg. 38, Vol. 3) This is perhaps an academic argument. We all have beliefs and we act on these, as with the development of our Hearts. The Lotus can become a symbol of our beautiful, inspired beliefs.

Meditation Practicum:

(Guided meditation.) Breathe in a relaxed way with eyes closed. "***Concentration (Samadhi)*** [also translated as absorption] means one-pointedness [single-minded] of mind, steadfast concentration for mental tranquility or insight."

"Meditation by mindfulness on breathing means mental task in realizing inhalation and exhalation at the tip of the nose and the upper lip only. This is ***Concentration Meditation*** which brings about equilibrium and concentration. This is the most important meditation exercise which is suitable for the temperament of people in general. Therefore, mindfulness on breathing is the most standard meditation practice for Concentration Meditation in Buddhism." (Wee, pg. 125)

"When we realize inhalation, we feel the air touching the upper part of the nose tip. We have to watch it so that we can know the touch of the air. [wrinkle the nose if needed to focus attention] When breathing in, the belly rises. This is a bodily feeling of inhalation. Realizing inhalation, [air coming in] we chant 'Bud' [silently.] Likewise, when breathing out, we feel the air touching the lower part of the nose tip and the upper lip. When breathing out, the belly falls. This is exhalation. Realizing exhalation, we chant 'Dho' [silently.]" Elsewhere it is taught that this is to be thought of as hosting the Buddha for the purpose of inspiration.

Follow this instruction repeatedly in a soft voice, until it becomes a unison; that will be a sign to stand. "Continue the meditation practice by standing until mind is concentrated and some fruition is produced eventually. The fruition is indicated by mental images appearing in the mind. Resume the practice till the utmost of suffering, we [then] change the posture." (Wee, pp. 128-129)

Practitioners may sit now. "The ordinary mind constructs images and ideas for the range of sensory stimulation, and these mental constructions become more and more elaborate, in the form of ideas, conceptualization, and conflictual emotional states. [Whereas this kind of creativity is useful in business, creative writing and most work environments, it is not helpful when one is trying to develop a formal meditation practice. What works for one, doesn't necessarily aid the other.] . . . These elaborations arise because the ordinary mind scatters in various ways with seemingly little order and control. This particular quality of the mind makes it extremely difficult to keep it focused upon protecting certain truth." As with waking from a dream, we remember the details for only a few minutes, and the insights gained during meditation must be protected from disappearing.

"At the very beginning of meditation, attempts to focus attention on the intended meditation object cannot easily be separated from the coarse content of the mind, mostly elaborate thinking. The beginner easily confuses attention with thinking . . . this is referred to as contemplation, not as formal meditation. Nevertheless the attempt to isolate the act of focusing attention from the background of elaborate thinking does produce a certain benefit with practice . . . the mind stays on its intended object, at least somewhat. From the perspective of the mind's events, thinking becomes less elaborate—that is, it becomes a bit calmer." During the day the mind will reflect back on these efforts and benefit from this moral self-leadership.

"Contemplation and meditation are learning processes, much like learning to drive a car . . . Once learned, driving becomes second nature . . . Learning to meditate is very similar, in that it requires four similar skills—***directing, intensifying, pliancy, and intelligence***. [The meditation practice up to this point has been intended as preparatory.] . . . The Santideva describes the task as learning to tie up the mind, like tying a rope around the neck of an elephant . . . Once bound to the intended mediation object, the mind must be directed repeatedly back to the object time and time again . . . With practice, smaller and smaller adjustments are necessary to make the mind stay there . . . Developing skill in directing the mind to stay is like learning to use the steering wheel of a car." (Brown, pp. 151-154) Contemplate your breath and identify and record an estimate of the number of times you are distracted during several five minute periods.

"Solving the problems we face in every day life often calls for 'creative thinking.' Those who believe in a higher intelligence can call forth the assistance of [their concept of] deity, but the process for an Atheist is about the same. The first step in solving any problem is to organize as much information that is available in your mind—or possibly in columns on paper. Discuss the situation with experts and then allow the problem to stir in your mind, 'unconscious' thinking. "When we consciously seek a new or unusual tentative conclusion we tend to stay in familiar channels. But when we permit the unconscious mind to roam the frame of reference, free from restraint by the conscious mind, [or prejudice] it is often able to break out of familiar channels and put information together into new combinations." (Moore, 1955) This process is called ***incubation***, and depending on the situation the answer could come in the middle of the night, waking us with the power of an alarm clock, or on the spur of the moment while in the shower, etc. Incubation is one way to use meditation for practical benefit as well as to reduce complications and suffering on the path to enlightenment. This is not a super-natural power, it is a commonplace phenomenon.

Step four of the Sixteen taught in the Theravada tradition is 'calming the body-conditioner.' This means that as we inhale and exhale we make the body-conditioner (breath) calmer and calmer . . . The flesh body will become very gentle, relaxed and tranquil . . . Then there will also arise a calming of the mind . . ." To summarize, here are 'skillful means' for calming the breath, tools we have already used.

1. following the breath;
2. guarding the breath at a certain point;
3. giving rise to an (object) image at that guarding point;
4. manipulating these images in such a way as to gain power over them [directing]; and
5. selecting one image and contemplating it in a more concentrated way until the breath becomes truly calm and peaceful. [This is the culmination of four steps and when these are used repeatedly in sequence our practice can result in the alleviation of stress from the workplace.]

"[. . . Choose] one image to be the specific object of samadhi (concentration, collectedness) until there is complete calmness . . . This citta, this sati, is not allowed to go anywhere; it must stay at the chosen point [along the path of the breath.] It guards the breath passing in and passing out; hence, the results are equivalent to "following," except that guarding is more subtle . . . Generally, we use the furthest point on the nose where the breath makes contact." (Buddhadasa, 1988, pp. 47-49) This guarding is taught as being initially less important than **chasing**; however, eventually being "one-pointed" is the goal of samadhi and facilitates the elimination of suffering as well as moral development.

Biographical Sketch:

"Two or three years after the enlightenment of Shakyamuni, Buddhism had developed considerably, especially in and around the city of Magadha. Soon it spread northward along the Ganges . . . Shakyamuni's half brother Nanda left his family to join the Order as did his own son Rahula. Later, one by one, other members of the five hundred families of the Shakya clan followed suit. Many outstanding young men from Magadha and its environs found the teachings of the Buddha attractive, believed them, and left home to join the Order without parental permission. This caused families to suffer so much that they raised a bitter cry . . . causing family lines of inheritance to be broken. At this point, Shakyamuni established the ruling that a person must have parental permission to join the Order . . . If everyone abandoned the secular life and became a monk, the productivity of society would cease, and daily economic life would become impossible . . . the clergy presumes the laity, and life for the clergy without the laity is inconceivable." (Mizuno, pp. 99-100) This experience can be interpreted as proof of the necessity and virtue of Right Livelihood and associated economic success.

"In the village of Patali . . . Shakyamuni taught a sermon on the misfortune of breaking moral rules and the merits of abiding by them . . . He explained that a person who does wrong by breaking the rules of moral conduct suffers five kinds of misfortunes: 1. through sloth, he loses much property; 2. his evil conduct gains him an evil reputation; 3. he lacks self-confidence and is embarrassed in any society, whether it be that of kings, Brahmans, lay believers, or samanas; 4. he ends his life in psychological anxiety and ignorance; and 5. after a fearful death, he is reborn into one of the four temporary evil states. [like limbo?] A person who does good and abides by moral precepts, on the other hand, enjoys fivefold merits: 1. through diligence he gains great wealth; 2. his good actions win him a good reputation; 3. he has self-confidence and is unembarrassed in any society; 4. he is free of psychological anxiety at death; and 5. after death, he is reborn into a blessed state . . . Shakyamuni's teaching method was to move gradually from the worldly and easy to the abstract and difficult." (Mizuno, pp. 76-77) Rewards of wealth and success in business (fivefold merits) do not necessarily create evil, but can be the effect (reward) of doing good, and in fact if these rewards are valued in Buddhism, then we should think of these as goals for hard, intelligent work.

Reading for the Day:

"The ordinary lotus, being an aquatic plant, withers when it is brought near to fire; is not fire then a dreadful enemy of the lotus? A lotus flower [bodhi, enlightenment] which blossoms in the midst of fire increases its beauty and glowing luster the more it faces the blazing flame. A man who practices Zen [in quietude], detesting the pleasures of the objects of the five senses, even if he may have mastered the discipline of emptying both atman and the substantiality of things, and even if he may claim to have the clearest vision of enlightenment, once he has left quietude and become involved in activity, will be like a clam or shrimp out of water, or like a monkey without trees. He will have no vitality at all, and, like the lotus in water that is faced with fire, will wither immediately." (de Bary, pp. 392-393)

Directing: "Each time the ordinary mind gets distracted from the intended meditation object, the Practitioner learns to direct it back until the mind stays on its object. With practice, smaller and smaller adjustments are necessary to make the mind stay there." (Brown, pg. 154) Of course we return to this `directing` repeatedly.

Protecting:

"This is what I heard." Review by both Practitioners and teacher.

Finding time to meditate for prolonged period can be difficult for most people. One quick and poignant activity is to engage in "*Prayer Meditation* . . . Kneel, with my body upright . . . and arms raised to the sky. I was to feel that I was receiving energy, being rained on, from above; and when I felt filled, I should slowly lower my arms and body to the ground and pour energy into the earth. When I felt emptied I was to raise my arms and start again. This was to be done seven times; otherwise one left the process incomplete." (Forman, 1987, pp. 49-50) This is a cleansing ritual—Tonglen meditation.

Additional Teaching:

"When the ordinary worldly man [and woman] hears that nothing is worth getting or being, [s/he] is not convinced, [s/he] doesn't believe it. But anyone who understands the real meaning of this statement becomes emboldened and cheered by it. His[/her] mind becomes master of [material] things [and achievements] and independent of them. [S/He] becomes capable of going after things sure in the knowledge that [s/he] *will not become enslaved by them*. His[/her] actions are not motivated by desire [craving, lust, ambition] and [s/he] is not so blind with passion that he comes to be a slave to things . . . because there is nothing that we can really get or be as we might wish.

All things are transient [impermanence] and unsatisfactory and never belong to us [soulless.] . . . we act in a way that does not accord with the true nature of things, simply because we become involved in them while ignorant of their true nature [and the complications of our lives multiply.] The result is bound to be all manner of suffering and trouble [if we are] motivated entirely by [our] desires. As a result, [s/he] is not master of himself and cannot be consistently good, honest, and fair. In every case of failure and ruin, the root cause is slavery to desire [outside of natural calamities such as earthquakes.]" (Buddhadasa, 2005, pp. 103-104) So the issue is not what we do, presumably it is a valuable service to someone, but why and how we go about doing it; and if we are right-minded, choosing a Right Livelihood, we can be "emboldened and cheered" by our success and not demoralized by momentary setbacks.

Corollary: When we begin a cycle of action or new adventure and understand that it is temporary, impermanent; and that it will be incomplete and unsatisfying; and that it has been caused by elements perhaps outside our control, then we can enter this action without the fear of creating conditioned origination (dependent arising) for ourselves, thus we will have avoided creating future suffering from the decision to engage in this action (karma).

Sharing Merit:

Rejoicing In Others' Merit (Saying Sadhu)

Buddhist Sutra

Lesson Title: **The Eight-fold Path—Right Livelihood**

Lesson Number: **Ten**

Key Vocabulary: directing, epiphany, despair, humility, samanas, Samadhi, fruition, wandering, Contemplation, conflictual emotional states, law of the world, Law of the Universe, Concentration Meditation, elaborated, kammaniya, epistemology, incubation

Assignment: How can you use your breath to improve concentration?

Practice "Prayer Meditation" just before going to sleep, and just after rising.

Identify your true motivation—your true intention in studying Buddhism.

Can you distinguish between "guarding" the breath and "following." Discuss.

Why should we employ our talents and education in service to ourselves, to "the market place" and to others?

How can we recognize the different levels of the mind? or is thinking our only mental activity?

What should we do differently to take the next step toward enlightenment?

What changes do we need to make in our lives in order to more strictly apply Buddhist moral codes in commerce and the labor market?

Define each of the Key Vocabulary in your own words.

Does the fact of so many monks and "non-productive" intellectuals determine or influence the development of the Asian economies?

"Realizing inhalation, [air coming in] we chant 'Bud.' Likewise, when breathing out, we feel the air touching the lower part of the nose tip and the upper lip. When breathing out, the belly falls. This is exhalation. Realizing exhalation, we chant 'Dho'."

Record an estimate of the number of times you are distracted and needed to direct your attention back to your breath during several five minute periods.

Materials Required: Utopianism, (reversing painting), tea service

Buddhist Sutra

Lesson Title: **The Eight-fold Path—Right Effort**

Lesson Number: **Eleven**

Rationale:

With my first exposure to Buddhist teachings, I thought there was considerable overlapping in explanations of the requirements to fulfill the stages of the Eight-fold Path; but as much as these are connected, there are important differences which are only understood by a close examination (the right effort) of each stage individually.

Discussion of Prior Lesson:

"Sampajanna, means clear comprehension, consciousness, awareness [clarity]. In sitting meditation, clear consciousness manifests in mind due to realization of the feeling of the mind and matter appearing at the body-door [nose in the case of breathing]. We must be able to note the feelings rising from the sense objects of the mind and matter in time when it appears at the body-door. This is to note the current sense-objects. Doing so, we comprehend clearly what we are doing." (Wee, pp. 184-185) Just watch and notice these feelings to begin with, later we will do more.

"If we create a mental image (nimitta) at the guarding point, the breath will be further refined and calmer . . . You can close your eyes and 'see' it, you can open your eyes and still 'see' it. The image is like an hallucination the mind creates by itself to calm the breath . . . indeed all the faculties, must be refined in order for a mental image to arise [corollary: if you have a strong image you are already well refined!] The breath must become finer and calmer until the image is created." (Buddhadasa, 1988, pg. 50)

Training Objective:

Begin to eat small portions at the supper meal, and gradually in a week, eat only before noon, and sparingly. The essence of Buddhism is to change the way we live by changing the way we think. The concept of "do over." Understand how to control "intensity"—the level of effort in meditation and in your life—using imaging.

Materials Required: Utopianism, reversing painting, tea service

Motivational Statement:

"The Tibetan Buddhist term for mind is sem, a word that may be translated into English as 'that which knows.' This simple term can help us to understand the Buddhist view of the mind as less of a specific object than of a capacity to recognize and reflect on our experiences . . . the mind itself isn't something that can be seen, touched, or even defined by words. Just as the physical organ of the eye is not sight, and the physical organ of the ear is not hearing, the brain is not the mind." (Mingyur, pp. 41-42) Our physical limitations notwithstanding, with study of the Buddhist teachings and practice we can expand the mind without drugs.

"Zen practice [and Buddhism in general] approaches the deluded mind and the problems, struggles, and relationships we are faced with day by day . . . Rather than seeking to diagnose illness, prescribing medication to numb the pain, correcting deficiencies, or seeing ourselves as weak or sinning, Zen takes another tack. It points to our fundamental strength and beauty—our 'Buddha Nature'—and spends time strengthening that. As we do this, depression, conflict, and other disturbances fall away by themselves." (Shoshanna, pg. 3) As we meditate on compassion with clarity, we expand positive effort and the awareness of our essential buddha-nature.

First Progressive:

"I always believe that we human beings are all essentially the same—mentally, emotionally and physically . . . There are no miracles. I am very skeptical of such things . . . The fundamental thing is that *everyone wants a happy, successful life*. This is not only our goal but our legitimate right as well. The question then arises, how do we achieve this happy life? When material and spiritual development are combined, however, we can achieve our goal of a happy life. Therefore, while focusing on material development, it is essential that we pay attention to inner values as well." (Dalai Lama, pg. 30) This is to be the character of our Right Effort.

An attitude of *compassion and awareness can pervade our entire waking* life through different levels of informal meditation. "First, when you integrate practice [the breadth of our Effort] into your daily life, you avoid the trap of being calm and peaceful during formal meditation and then turning around and being tense and angry at the office [or with your family at home.] Second, and perhaps more important, practicing informally in daily life gradually eradicates the all-too-common misconception that you have to be someplace absolutely quiet in order to meditate." (Mingyur, pg. 202) This informal effort (integrated practice) enhances the integrity of our personality and permits our sense of compassion to expand as well.

How do we achieve the balance of the "middle way?" "The Buddha taught that the greatest act of all is the act of giving . . . to evolve spiritually . . . *True generosity* does not involve mindlessly handing over everything to anyone who asks. For example, the parent who gives his spoiled child every toy the child wants may be showing more laziness than generosity . . . The spouse who tolerates or even enables a partner's addiction in the name of love may be more codependent than generous, thus doing harm while trying to be helpful. The worker who allows an exploitative corporation to take advantage of his or her willingness to work overtime for free [or of customers] or without appropriate benefits is exhibiting more fear than generosity. One must find what Buddha often called the Middle Way, one of balance and appropriateness . . . combine compassion with wisdom in everything we do . . ." (Surya Das, pg. 27) Never give when under any coercion or emotional "blackmail."

Second Progressive:

So what should we be doing? "Next are inwardly wholesome deeds which are inside our minds. How shall we perform to be considered wholesome according to the Noble Path? The answer is that we can follow the Noble Eight-fold Path: Right Effort . . . means effort [also diligence] to perform bodily and mentally wholesome deeds. Precepts can control [guide] bodily wholesome actions. Regarding the mentally wholesome actions, we need to have four efforts as follows: 1. to avoid unwholesome states [i.e. drunkenness]; 2. to overcome unwholesome states [i.e. avoid laziness]; 3. to develop wholesome states [i.e. showing respect or reverence]; 4. to maintain or augment arisen good [i.e. being grateful and having compassion.] . . . Keeping our mind in the stream of wholesomeness can be practiced by observing each of these four efforts . . . We, therefore, have to understand the meaning of all of them so that we can follow them in a correct way."

"The important purpose of the Noble Path is to eliminate suffering. To be able to eradicate suffering according to Buddhism, we have to practice [and exercise] mind to develop concentration and insight so as to be able to reduce and eradicate cravings and desires in our mind . . . It is because all suffering we encounter comes from all defilements [we experience.] We have to lead our lives by following the Noble Path; we will then be able to eliminate suffering. Thus, when we understand efforts and use them as a guideline to control our physical and mental actions, we have to be careful of our mind [and thoughts] and always keep it in the stream of wholesomeness. The most important effort that brings utmost mental wholesomeness is the effort to develop wholesome states. It is the effort to cultivate wholesomeness in inborn trait [overcoming instincts and develop a beautiful character.]" (Wee, pp. 29-32) Our meditation practice will succeed in direct proportion to the "wholesomeness" of our deeds.

Compare the following with the above: "Right effort is described as of four kinds: 1. Striving to prevent evil from arising. 2. Striving to abandon evil that has arisen. 3. Striving to produce good. 4. Striving to increase good that has been produced. These actions toward evil and good pertain to more than considerations of morality. Evil is anything that runs counter to the ideal, and good is anything that agrees with ideal politics, economics, and health on either the individual or the society-wide basis . . . This aspect of the Eightfold Noble Path can be called courage, since courage is essential to spiritual development." (Mizuno, pg. 56) This author is writing from the Japanese tradition but is saying the same thing as the Theravada teacher. It often requires courage to persevere and take the Right Effort day after day.

"Just as a respectful attitude potentiates spiritual development, certain other attitudes or behaviors can interfere with this development . . . the six defilements: 1. pride, that is, looking without really listening, or listening disrespectfully; 2. lack of faith; 3. lack of effort toward the truth; 4. distraction toward external things, so as not to mirror the teaching in thought; 5. shutting down the mind, that is, falling asleep; and 6. fatigue, that is, listening with a wandering mind and failing to intellectually understand the meaning of the teachings. Such defilements must be abandoned, and the [Practitioner] must 'listen without *defilements* day and night.' Otherwise . . . 'you will cast aside the teachings.' The **effort** it takes to abandon the six defilements is the first significant step toward virtuous action. The greater the effort, the more one has given up, the greater the virtuous effect that ripens over time." (Brown, pg. 56) If we can overcome these defilements, and reach "accommodation" there is a good likelihood we will have the strength to improve the purity of our lives, begin to eliminate suffering, and thus also make merit. Our true intentions are demonstrated by what we actually do. Beginning with these six is just a start on the 108 defilements described later.

Perhaps compassion is the first step in our progress, just as Realization is the last step in our development of purification. "All the Brothers [and sisters] in this Great Assembly, and you too,

Ananda, should reverse your outward perception of hearing and listening inwardly for the perfectly unified and intrinsic sound of your own *Mind-Essence*, for as soon as you have attained perfect accommodation, [with compassion] you will have attained to Supreme Enlightenment. The Surangama Sutra" (Goddard, pg. 260) In this way we combine the aesthetic "listening inwardly" with ethical practice. What can this essence of mind be? Is the essence of our mind this kind of skillful spiritual development?

Third Progressive:

"Even though Buddhism extols gentleness and patience in practice . . . some energy has to be put out too. This brings us to the sixth item on the Eight-fold Path: right effort. Again, the word 'right' is important here, indicating the energy too should be strictly regulated." (Snelling, pg. 50) "Proper effort is not the effort to make something particular happen. It is the effort to be aware and awake in each moment, the effort to overcome laziness and defilement, the effort to make each activity of our day meditation." (Kornfield, pg. 51) Just as with meditation—if our efforts to improve our lives fall short for a time, we refocus and start with a new enhanced effort. This is a rational approach to living—this is called "do-over." When we fail or digress we often get to repeat our effort and do it a second time better.

There is a special effort required, most skillful effort is directed inward, a kind of introspection. "The ability to experience and understand truth depends a great deal upon the quality of the unfolding mental continuum. In the protecting exercise, the practitioner discerns some similarity between the truth represented by the teachings and the qualities of his or her own mental continuum. [This is done also after insight meditation.] Typically the practitioner's first attempts to protect only serve as a reminder of how far the emerging activity of the mental continuum has gone astray from any approximation of realized truth." (Brown, pg. 151) Two people who read the same book or set of instructions (or study *Buddhist Sutras: Lesson Book*) will often come away with different information, each seeing what they wanted to see or what they needed. The next time they may find other information they missed the first time. So it goes.

Many times through history leaders have sprung up to gather around them devotees who wish to live an ideal life, sharing work, food, minimal housing and the trials and rewards of life, i.e. Israeli Kibbutz system. To what extent is this striving for the ideal (or utopia) a motivation for the development of the Sangha 2500 years ago and for the monasteries of Buddhism today (as well as cloisters in other religions?) But Buddhism is primarily a self-directed, self-motivated discipline and teaching; those involved with the Theravada tradition number in excess of 70 million. Those who would claim association with Mahayana are as many or more than that, but only a few people can claim enlightenment.

"The good qualities that emerge and mature from [following] these practices not only smooth the way for the journey to Nibbana; over time they have the effect of transforming the practitioner into a more generous, loving, compassionate, peaceful, and clear-headed member of society. The individual's sincere pursuit of Awakening is thus a priceless and timely gift to a world in desperate need of help." (Bullitt, internet.) This pursuit is also a rational choice, especially for those who were not born into this religious tradition.

"Those of us who have some intelligence should be capable of investigating and examining things [concepts, objects and the complications of our lives] and coming to know their true nature. Each thing we come across we must study, in order to understand clearly its true nature. And we must understand the nature and the source of the suffering which it produces, and which sets us alight and scorches us. To establish mindfulness, to watch and wait, to examine in the manner described the suffering that comes to none—this is the very best way to penetrate to Buddha-Dhamma. It is infinitely better than learning it from the Tipitaka." (Buddhadasa, 2005, pg. 37) Experiential learning of Dhamma through practice involves using the non-rational aspect of our natures. This is a generalized guide for the Rightness of our Effort

Meditation Practicum:

"Mantra meditation is a very powerful technique that not only cultivates clear awareness, but also, through the potency of syllables that have been recited by enlightened masters for thousands of years, clears away layers of mental obscuration and increases our capacity to benefit ourselves and others. This connection may be hard to accept at first; it seems too much like magic. It might be easier to think of mantric syllables as sound waves that perpetuate through space for thousands, perhaps millions, of years." What good comes to the wolf when it howls? It is participating in a sense of community. Likewise in the Sangha as we join in a mantra chant, or other respectful meritorious rituals, then we are communicating both to ourselves and to our community about the benefits of spiritual practice.

"In Mantra meditation, the focus of your attention is on the mental recitation of a certain set of syllables that appear [from empirical and historical experience] to have a direct effect on calming and clearing the mind . . . OM AH Hung. OM represents the lucid, distinctive, perceptual aspect of experience; AH represents the empty, or inherently open, aspect [to purify our guarding point;] while Hung represents the union of distinctive appearance and the inherently empty nature [impermanence] of the appearance. You can start by reciting the mantra aloud, and then gradually slip into a more internal form of mental recitation. Continue reciting the mantra for about three minutes, and then just let your mind rest, alternating between recitation and resting for as long as you can. Whether you feel the effects immediately or not, you've set something in motion. That 'something' is the freedom of your mind." (Mingyur, pp. 156-157) Chant together for three cycles, to enhance receptivity to being interconnected.

Intensifying: "The degree to which the mind learns to stay on the intended meditation object is a function of another skill, intensifying. Just as . . . driving requires skillful use of the accelerator . . . progress in developing the skill of staying depends on similar skills of intensifying and easing up . . . the degree of energy needed to direct the mind at any given moment. Imagine being told to look at a particular painting . . . Then imagine being told to look at the painting much more carefully. What does the mind do at that point? Since the mind is already directed . . . the act of directing the mind does not explain what else occurs. But something else does occur. The mind supplies more energy to the act of looking . . . the mind stays more closely on the intended object as a result of the additional energy supplied . . . supplying too much intensity results in agitation of both body and mind, as a result of which the mind doesn't stay on anything. [Show a symbolic painting or reversing image.] At that point easing up on the energy increases the clarity of the meditation object, from the event-perspective . . . The skilled meditator knows when to intensify and when to ease up depending on the quality of the meditation at the time."

"There are two signs of progress. From the mind-perspective, the mind is said to stay longer and more completely on the intended meditation object. From the event-perspective, the mental continuum's coarse content [i.e. habit of superficial looking] comes forth with greater clarity. Visual objects are brighter, eventually becoming luminous. Bodily sensations are felt more vividly. Staying and clarity are independent but complementary signs of meditation progress viewed from two perspectives." (Brown, pp. 154-155) At some point, we may begin to recognize the subtle benefits of mantra meditation, for example, and feel the changes that are occurring in the moment.

In the previous chapter we learned: "From the perspective of the mind that observes, the ordinary mind fails to stay on its intended object of focus for anything but very brief moments. [Continue breathing and chanting in silence.] Even when it stays on the intended object, the mind typically only partially stays on it, in that attention is divided between the intended object and the background noise of ordinary mental activity . . . [Now the intended object is simply the passage of breath.] From the perspective of the unfolding events within the mental continuum, the very structure of the ordinary mind is disorganized. A mind that gets distracted from its intended object of awareness and gets lost in the construction of more and more mental content is said to become ***elaborated***. Continuous elaboration is called '***wandering***' from one thing to another, with the mind attaching itself to one sensory object or thought after another."

Return to the fourth step of the sixteen stage meditation practice of Theravada. (pg. 102) Continue the process of guarding using the five skillful techniques. Once we have done the preliminary three steps in meditation and we have created an image to guard, possibly at the tip of the nose ". . . change the image or alternate between images according to our requirements. We can change from one image to another . . . manipulate them, to play with them . . . As we do this we are developing our ability to master [intensify] the mind in increasingly subtle and powerful ways . . . Because we can now control the mind more than before, the citta automatically grows more subtle and refined by itself. The citta becomes more and more calm until eventually we are able to calm the mind completely . . . The fourth technique is controlling the mental images as we wish . . . We observe the calming process while practicing this step . . . Choose an image that is most fitting and proper, and then contemplate it with full attention in order to develop a complete measure of samadhi. We should choose an image that is soothing, relaxing, and easy to focus on. The image should not stir up thoughts and emotions or contain any special significance or meaning. A mere white point or dot will suffice . . . The citta gathers together on this single spot. Concentrating everything on this one point is the fifth of our skillful means . . . In Pali this state is called ekaggata, which means 'to have a single peak, focus, or apex.' Everything gathers [intensifies] at this single focus . . ." (Buddhadasa, 1988, pp. 50-55)

Biographical Sketch:

"When I first began meditating, I was horrified to find myself experiencing more thoughts, feelings, and sensations than I had before I began practicing. It seemed that my mind was becoming more agitated rather than more peaceful. 'Don't worry,' my teachers told me. 'Your mind isn't getting worse. Actually, what's happening is that you're simply becoming more aware of activity that has been going on all the time without your noticing it . . .' They taught me a short prayer known as the Dorje Chang Tungma . . .

> The Body of meditation, it's said, is non-distraction.
> Whatever thoughts are perceived by the mind are nothing in themselves.
> Help this meditator who rests naturally in the essence
> Of whatever thoughts arise, to rest in [the natural mind.]"
> (Mingyur, pg. 212)

An example of right effort of a more fundamental kind comes from this important Buddhist teaching. "After a stay in Vesali, Shakyamuni and Ananda went northward . . . at the Ananda shrine, Shakyamuni preached on the topic of the Four Great References. According to this sermon, the members of the Order are instructed to be critical of all reported teachings; to examine them diligently; to compare them with the scriptures and the genuine teachings; and, on the basis of such comparison, to decide whether they are true [external verification is a form of protecting.] Four kinds of reports to be subjected to such inquiry are cited: 1. words reported as having been heard directly from Shakyamuni himself, 2. words reported as having been heard from a group of elders, 3. words reported as having been heard from several elders, 4. and, words reported as having been heard from a single elder. Monks [nor Practitioners] must not accept blindly what has been said but must examine it on the basis outlined above [based on their own frame of reference.]" (Mizuno, pg. 183) This is a key element in Rational Buddhism.

An independence of mind and thought was encouraged by the Buddha. "By directing his spiritualized offering within, therefore, the silent sage was sacrificing to the internal and external devas, who were in fact one and the same . . . The new spirituality had grown organically and logically from the old . . . The new hero of the Age was not a heroic warrior, proudly vaunting his martial prowess, but a monk dedicated to ahimsa, who was determined to discover the absolute by becoming aware of the core of his being. The renouncers were seeking 'yathabuhuta', or 'enlightenment' that was also an 'awakening' to their authentic selves." (Armstrong, pg. 124) This independent attitude is still an example for our spiritual development today.

Reading for the Day:

"The heavy emphasis on theoretical philosophy in Buddhism—heavier than in many other religions—may result from the general Indian devotion to philosophical investigation. This and the Indian tendency to explain philosophy in terms of religious practice influenced Buddhism considerably. Shakyamuni himself was especially interested in philosophical issues and would employ nothing in his teachings that was not theoretically convincing." (Mizuno, pg.159)

The Buddhist is taught to challenge not only philosophy but also the way they ***think about thinking***. ". . . The practitioner takes the mind's real nature as the object of continuous and uninterrupted mindfulness in such a way that no artificial activity whatsoever is necessary to set up or sustain mindfulness of the mind's real nature. Since the mind's real nature is awareness-itself, this kind of mindfulness essentially implies uninterrupted awareness of awareness-itself, free of any artificial activity that might otherwise obscure such awareness. Thus, mahamudra meditation [Tibetan] is sometimes called non-meditation yoga to distinguish between ordinary meditation, which presumes some artificial [or other natural] activity and a conventional object of concentration, and extraordinary meditation, which goes beyond all artificial activity and takes awareness-itself as both the vantage point and the object. These non-meditation instructions only make sense, however, to a practitioner who has directly realized the simultaneous mind through either pointing out by the teacher or conventional meditation practices." (Brown, pg. 15) This is definitely meta-cognition, a special effort to think about the way we think.

Protecting:

"This is what I heard," review by both practitioners and teacher. Reflect on the effort you have made relating to meditation up to this point.

Proverb: Job security is being worth more than you're getting paid. (wellpage.com)

Prayer of Thanks: "Most excellent, Lord, are the words of thy mouth, most excellent!
It is just as if a man were to set up what was thrown down,
Or to reveal that which was hidden away,
Or were to point out the right road to him who has gone astray,

Or were to bring a lamp into the darkness so that those who have eyes can see:
—just even so, Lord, has the truth been made known to us by the Blessed One.
And we betake ourselves, Lord, to the Blessed One, to the Truth,
And to the Brotherhood, as our refuge.
May the Blessed One accept us as disciples, as true believers, from this day forth,
As long as life shall last." Tevigga Sutta (Goddard, pg. 72)

Another vocalization is the ancient Buddhist phrases:
"Buddham sharanam gachchhami . . .
Sangham sharanam gachchhamii . . .
Dhammam sharanam gachchhami . . ." (Forman, 1987, pg 288)

Additional Teachings:

If (as scientific studies have now shown) anxieties are absorbed from one's associates, may not persistence be assimilated as well? Robert Ingersoll once remarked that had he been God, he would have made health contagious instead of disease; to which an Indian contemporary responded: 'When shall we come to recognize that health is as contagious as disease, virtue as contagious as vice, cheerfulness as contagious as moroseness?' One of the three things for which we should give thanks every day, according to the Buddha, is the company of the holy. Just as bees cannot make honey unless together, human beings cannot make progress on the Way unless they are supported by a field of confidence and concern that Truth-winners generate." (Smith & Novak, 2003, pg. 40)

In summary: "Right Effort is the energetic will (1) to prevent evil and unwholesome states of mind from arising, and (2) to get rid of such evil and unwholesome states that have already arisen within a man[woman], and also (3) to produce, to cause to arise, good and wholesome states of mind not yet arisen [making merit,] and (4) to develop and bring to perfection the good and wholesome states of mind already present in a man[woman.]" (Walpole, pg. 48) This is how we utilize the Law of Cause and Effect to our advantage by making and sharing merit.

How much effort do we need to make, deliberately, (karma) to become more compassionate and caring? "Inner generosity also means cultivating non-attachment, acceptance, and contentment, so that we are more open to whatever the needs of others might be. Meditation and conscientious self-inquiry can greatly help us in this effort. Critics of meditation often say, 'Isn't meditation selfish" [if reclusive?] Doesn't it mean cutting yourself off from the rest of the world? Isn't it unproductive?' Nothing could be further from the truth. By meditating, we're learning to disengage ourselves from habitual clinging and disperse the defilements and obscurations that hinder our capacity to serve others, such as illusory feelings of scarcity and fears of deprivation. We gradually learn to be more conscious and make better choices. We develop simplicity instead of complexity, open-mindedness instead of narrow-mindedness [equanimity,] flexibility rather than rigidity. We free ourselves to be more available to others and to give more generously of ourselves . . . Finally, there is generosity as it relates to our secret or innermost spiritual level of being, the incandescent immensity of innate Bodhicitta, which Buddhists call our 'suchness,' our Buddha nature." (Surya das, pg. 32)

Sharing Merit:

Rejoicing In Others' Merit (Saying Sadhu)

Buddhist Sutra

Lesson Title: The Eight-fold Path—Right Effort

Lesson Number: Eleven

Key Vocabulary: Mantra, meta-cognition, utopia, Dorje Chang Tungma, sem, matter, optical illusions, pride, intention. intensity, nimitta, mind-essence, chant, defilements, skillful, ekaggata

Assignment:
Practice "Mantra meditation, the focus of your attention is on the mental recitation of a set of syllables that appear to have a direct effect on calming and clearing the mind . . . OM AH Hung." Do this at least five times for five to 10 minutes each time.

Return to the fourth step of the Sixteen stage meditation of Theravada Anapanasati. Continue the process of guarding using the five skillful techniques. Manipulate the image, or create new images. Feel the calming affect on your breath and body. Choose the one image that is most fitting and proper, and then contemplate it with full attention in order to develop a complete measure of samadhi.

Define each of the Key Vocabulary in your own words.

"Please take a pen and a sheet of paper. Go to the foot of a tree or to your favorite place, and make a list of all the things that can make you happy right now: the clouds in the sky, the flowers in the garden, the children playing . . ." (Hanh, pg. 189)

Give an example from the history you have studied of a utopian society or commune.

Have you ever (or wished to) made this kind of specialized effort?

Begin to eat only a small portion at the supper meal, and gradually in a week, eat only before noon and sparingly. (Continue to take vitamin supplements, prescription medicines if any, and drink plenty of fluids.)

The essence of Buddhism: can you change your life by changing the way you think?

Repeat this prayer prior to your practice sessions. (Dorje Chang Tungma)

> The Body of meditation, it's said, is non-distraction.
> Whatever thoughts are perceived by the mind are nothing in themselves.
> Help this meditator who rests naturally in the essence
> Of whatever thoughts arise, to rest in the mind as it naturally is."

Identify decisions or efforts you have made that you would like to *do over.*

Materials Required: Phenomenology, drinking water, candle, tea

Buddhist Sutra

Lesson Title: **The Eight-fold Path—Right Mindfulness**

Lesson Number: **Twelve**

Rationale:

"The practice of mindfulness leads to concentration and insight. Insight is the fruit of the practice, which can help us to forgive, to love. In a period of fifteen minutes, or half an hour, the practice of mindfulness, concentration, and insight can liberate you from your anger and turn you into a loving person. That is the strength of the dharma, the miracle of the dharma." (Hanh, pg. 255) Mindfulness is also translated as "*attentiveness,*" awareness, carefulness or being in the moment, but can also be thought of as right motivation which brings a slightly different twist to the subject, as we will see.

Discussion of Prior Lesson:

The freedom achieved during and after Mantra Meditation may feel strange or unpleasant. "That's because we're used to our chains. They might chafe, they might make us bleed, but at least they're familiar." (Mingyur, pg. 157) Our repeated efforts can become a rut!

"Compare your lists of things that can make you happy . . . the fact that you have met the practice of mindfulness, your beloved ones sitting in the next room, your two eyes in good condition . . . The list is endless. You have enough already to be happy now. You have enough to no longer be agitated by fear or anger." (Hanh, pg. 189)

"When the mind is one-pointed, there are no other feelings, thoughts, or objects of the mind . . . You should practice [the four initial steps] until these steps require no effort and you have become well-versed in these activities." (Buddhadasa, 1988, pp. 54-56)

Training Objective:

The importance of a gradual approach to developing concentration and insight meditation. Know the difference between the two. Understand walking meditation, using mindfulness of the body. How to utilize "pliancy." The second tetrad . . . Piti.

Materials Required: Phenomenology, drinking water, candle, tea

Motivational Statement:

"As long as you maintain *awareness* or mindfulness, [attentiveness, carefulness,] no matter what happens when you practice, your practice is meditation. If you watch your thoughts, that is meditation. If you can't watch your thoughts, that is meditation, too . . . If you remember that awareness of whatever occurs is meditation, then meditation becomes much easier than you may think." (Mingyur, pg. 166)

"Mindfulness means to be present, to be aware of what is going on. This energy is very crucial for the practice. The energy of mindfulness is like a big brother or big sister, holding a young one in her arms, taking good care of the suffering child, which is our anger, despair, or jealousy." (Hanh, pg. 67) Thus we connect to a source of strength that is likely greater than our own courage and self-discipline.

First Progressive:

We must "... keep in mind always the basic Buddhist tenets that all things are impermanent, that nothing has an ego, and that nirvana is quiescence. This in turn makes it habitual to remain undisturbed and calm in all considerations and actions . . . Everything apart from these firm, reliable truths—is inconstant and untrustworthy. Distrust, doubt, emotional problems, and discord arise even between man and wife or parent and child . . . People who understand the truth about the nature of all things, neither think nor act in this egoistic way, since they see everything from a high, all-encompassing standpoint enabling them to fuse their own interest with those of everyone else. In a society composed of such people there would be no fighting, no discord, no distrust, and no suspicion because everyone would know *the joy of union with his fellow human beings.*" (Mizuno, pg.133) This is at least part of what it means to make merit, to feel it, to live in merit, a sense of the numinous, then pass it on—to do the right things for the right reasons.

If we think with compassion for others every day: "Where our attention is, our life is—our energy . . . As sitting continues, we see—dreams, memories, fears, fantasies, commands—for what they are. Our choices, actions, and responses then become appropriate to the present situation, to what is actually happening now."

"All of this happens simply by our paying attention to our breath, [attention] to this very moment . . . *As we practice, our priorities shift [strangers become people.]* That which we thought was inconsequential, such as the next breath, becomes precious. That which we thought was so urgently needed, such as the next boyfriend or new car, becomes less pressing. We can do without more and more [which means we can share more and more]. We are not using others, ourselves, or the goods the world provides to 'make' our lives right. As we sit, we see how our lives are already right. And we say thank you." (Shoshanna, pg. 22)

Mindfulness training is often the first exposure people have to Buddhism. While it is essential and interrelated to nearly all other teachings, it remains one part of a hundred aspects of Buddhist teachings. Consider the Ten Perfections:

"One: May I perfect the sublime virtue of **generosity**, which liberates and releases craving, grasping, and attachment, and brings joyous contentment.

Two: May I develop and accomplish the pure virtue of ethical self-discipline, which dries up the boiling river of greed, hatred, and delusion . . .

Three: May I perfect the noble virtue of patience, which can face naked reality, forgive, accept adversity, and turn it into an ally.

Four: May I perfect the noble virtue of enthusiastic effort and fearless perseverance, which selflessly strives for the ultimate benefit of all.

Five: May I perfect the subtle virtue of concentration and alert **mindfulness,** which clarifies the heart and mind, body, and soul, and allows awareness and discernment to dawn within.

Six: May I perfect the profound virtue of transcendental knowledge-wisdom, which knows how things actually are, as well as how they arise and appear, interrelate, and function.

Seven: May I perfect the multifaceted virtue of skillful means and resourcefulness, which makes all things possible and swiftly accomplishes all that is wanted and needed.

Eight: May I perfect the virtue of unshakeable resolve, determination, and inspired aspiration, which has vast vision and universal scope.

Nine: May I perfect the wondrous virtue of spiritual empowerment and positive influence, which accomplishes unselfish service and love in action far beyond the limits of mortal beings.

Ten: May I realize the supreme virtue of primordial awareness, which intuitively recognizes the innate purity and perfection of all that is." (Surya Das, chapters) There are plenty of motivational statements here that join together with mindfulness.

Second Progressive:

"The more people develop mindfulness and wisdom towards the Teachings [and] make more progress for themselves, the more they create confidence in Buddhism. [When] people know how to think and examine carefully with their mindfulness and wisdom . . . [and] realize the facts of life and compounded things according to the Teachings, [they] will be able to attain knowledge and understand the truth that the Lord Buddha taught. The essential objective of the Buddhist Teachings is that people are able to develop mindfulness and wisdom so as to completely *eradicate defilements*, mental intoxication from mind and inborn traits." (Wee, pg. 4) This developing purity is beyond reasoning and conscious rationality. This is where the limitations and our use of language begins to fail, and we need to rely on ". . . profound virtue of transcendental knowledge-wisdom."

"One of the signs of ripening is the urge to meditate more . . . develop the spontaneous moments of meditative calmness now occurring into a solid foundation for formal meditation practice . . . [so far the] practices are designed to lay a solid foundation for formal meditation practice . . . [but] "Do not run full tilt at *tranquility and special insight*. First, cultivate a fertile ground for positive qualities within yourself'." (Brown, pg. 131) The virtue of good behavior is that it leads to a synergism of growth along the path to emancipation and enlightenment, thus we gain the capacity to make giant steps by taking small steps (as with walking meditation.)

This is also a way of showing self respect. Another lesson in Buddhist etiquette is the matter of not wearing shoes, and "Usually we never pay attention to our feet . . . our feet are among the most sensitive parts of our bodies . . . they are able to absorb wisdom and information we could not receive any other way . . . When we enter a zendo [a temple or wat, and our homes] the first thing we do is take off our shoes and place them neatly in a rack by the door . . . we do not want to trek dust and dirt . . . our feet are precious. We honor and respect our feet, and walk on them carefully. We do not discard what they have to teach. Zen practice is just like this. Nothing discarded, everything used in the way it was intended. We walk slowly, eyes on the floor, concentrating on each step, feeling the floor under our feet as we approach our seat." (Shoshanna, pg. 18)

This *carefulness* (as opposed to carelessness) comes from developing a breadth of mindfulness that involves (samma sati) greater than the mere attentiveness one might exercise during a class lecture. "In fact, numerous discourses mention 'wrong' mindfulness, which suggests that certain forms of sati can be quite different . . . sati requires the support of being diligent and ***clearly knowing.*** It is a combination of mental qualities [e.g. Right Effort and Right View] supported by a state of mind free from desires and discontent, and directed towards the body, feelings, the mind and dhammas, which becomes the path factor of right mindfulness." (Analayo, pg. 52)

"Your practice can begin with the simple aspiration to do better, to approach all of your activities with a greater sense of mindfulness, and *to open your heart more deeply toward others.* ***Motivation*** is the single most important factor in determining whether your experience is conditioned by suffering or by peace. Mindfulness and compassion actually develop at the same pace. The more mindful you become, the easier you'll find it to be compassionate. And the more you open your heart to others, the more mindful you become in all your activities." (Mingyur, pg. 249)

Right mindfulness involves right memory. "This has the double meaning of retaining in recall things one has experienced and of evoking and *remanifesting* these things. Commentaries on the sutras set forth four insights on which right memory works: the body, the emotions, the mind, and the world—that is, the entire physical and mental environment. In the Buddhist sense, right memory means constantly bearing in mind the four insights: 1. that the world is transient, 2. that the body is impure, 3. that perception leads to suffering, and 4. that the mind is impermanent. In secular terms, right memory means being always careful, clearheaded, and attentive. Slight lack of attention is frequently the cause of serious accidents or fires. Though ***carelessness*** in itself is a small, scarcely criminal matter, since it often leads to such things as airplane crashes, collisions of trains or ships, and serious fires; results in tremendous financial loss; and causes death and injury, it can [at these times] be considered many times more grave than murder or robbery." (Mizuno, pg. 57) This carefulness becomes a serious moral imperative especially for Zen Buddhists.

Third Progressive:

"Right Mindfulness (Samasati), means mindfulness on the Four Foundations of Mindfulness [also the same for Satipatthana and Anapanasati] which are *body, feelings, mind and mind-objects*. According to Buddhism, in reality, life has derangement [misconception]: 1. To regard what is impermanent as permanent; 2. To regard what is suffering as happy; 3. To regard non-self as self; 4. To regard what is not fine as fine . . . Minds of people in general has derangement relating to the reality of life, body and compounded things . . . Therefore, observing Mindfulness . . . will enable us to be aware of reality of our life that it is suffering. [If] we are not able to realize that life is suffering [it is] because we lack mindfulness and consciousness on our life in reality." (Wee, pp. 32-33)

Phenomenology is a broad philosophical curriculum that involves understanding how the mind perceives objects: ". . . the descriptive science of observable phenomena . . ." It was Hegel who ". . . traced the development of Spirit (or Mind) through various stages, in which it apprehends itself as phenomenon, to the point of full development, where it is aware of itself as it is in itself—as noumenon [a reflective object.] Phenomenology is the science in which we come to know mind as it is in itself through the study of the ways in which it appears to us [by self examination.]" (Edwards, pp. 135-136, Vol. 6) This category of philosophy also concerns itself with the study of more abstract mental concepts, such as revelation, intuition and the possibility of knowing religious truth. A great deal of Buddhist teachings have to do with phenomenology in the broadest sense of the study, and the concept of "mindfulness" is the central concept that connects the Eastern and Western schools of thought. The teaching of "making merit" is connected here, in the sense that this is a way of describing the special (numinous) significance we associate with our actions or worship activities.

"The old texts advise 'taking your life as the path' . . . Simply walking down the street can be a great opportunity to develop mindfulness . . . The opportunity here is to decide consciously to bring your attention to your surroundings. Look at the buildings, at other people on the sidewalk, at the traffic in the streets, at the trees that may be planted along your route . . . When you pay attention to what you see . . . Your mind becomes less agitated, and you begin to develop a sense of calmness . . . You can also bring your attention to the physical sensation of walking, to the feeling of your legs moving, your feet touching the ground, the rhythm of your breathing or your heartbeat . . . When you bring conscious awareness to your activity, distractions and anxieties will gradually fade and your mind will become more peaceful and relaxed . . . You can even meditate while sleeping or dreaming. As you fall asleep, you can either rest your mind in objectless meditation or gently rest your attention on the feeling of sleepiness. Alternatively, you can create an opportunity to turn your dreams into meditation experiences by reciting silently to yourself several times as you fall asleep, I will recognize my dreams, I will recognize my dreams . . ." (Mingyur, pp. 203-204) The attention we give to a dream is pure and continuous, often for extended periods. When these are written and recorded, they can be re-manifested for conscious inspection and analysis. Dreams are often given special significance like omens or prophecies, or for most of us these are simply the subject of curiosity.

However, "Meditation is not something to be toyed with lightly. It involves opening up the psyche and operating with it at depth. Problems, more or less difficult to handle, may arise. Therefore, to begin with at least, it should always be approached in conducive circumstances and with the guidance of an experienced and qualified teacher. The ***right motivation*** must also be present. It is a misapplication of meditation to use it to obtain personal benefits like 'mind power' or 'peak experiences'." (Snelling, pg. 51)

Meditation Practicum:

Pliancy: "Learning to meditate requires four similar skills—***directing, intensifying, pliancy, and intelligence*** . . . The third skill of a driver is the ability to adjust the gear ratio [shifting gears] . . . Meditation entails bodily and mental pliancy . . . A rudimentary type of mental pliancy is the ability to stay on the intended meditation object despite marked shifts in mental content or state of consciousness. Geshe Gedun Lodro defines pliancy as a 'mental factor that removes . . . bad mental states [i.e. moods] . . . and takes to mind a true object . . . joyfully and the mind is light [during each sitting.'] A 'bad mental state' is defined as a condition in which the mind . . . 'cannot bear . . . being aimed at its object of observation.' Another type of mental pliancy is the ability to generalize the gains of meditation to different meditation objects. A more advanced type of mental pliancy is skill in shifting perspective . . . between mind-perspective and the event-perspective."

"Still another type of *pliancy* is the ability to stay on the intended meditation object throughout shifts in levels of the mind. According to Buddhist psychology, there are three levels to the mind. 1. The coarse level pertains to ordinary content in the stream of consciousness, for example, thoughts, percepts, bodily sensations, and emotions. 2. On the subtle level there is no content. The skilled meditator learns to hold awareness on the mind's moment-by-moment fleeting movements prior to these movements being constructed into coarse content. 3. At the very subtle level of mind the skilled meditator learns to hold awareness on karmic propensities [i.e. inclinations, motivating factors] prior to their manifestation in the time-space matrix of the ordinary mental continuum [thinking before we act.]"

"Mastery of the concentration stages of meditation opens up the subtle level of the mind. Mastery of the special-insight stages opens up the very subtle or extraordinary level of the mind. *Advanced pliancy* entails shifting through these levels of mind with considerable skill, much like shifting gears in a car." (Brown, pp. 155-156) Shifting gears and steering become automatic mental activities once we know how to drive a car.

Walking Meditation: "After a period of sitting, of gathering our energy and concentration, we get up and resume activity. Rather than plunging into this [walking] mindlessly, we take the focus and awareness that has developed during the sitting and put it into what we do next . . . We walk slowly, one foot behind the other, hands clasped under our breastbone [or right over left across our navel,] back straight, eyes down, paying attention to the bottom of our feet and to our breathing. We pay attention to each step as we take it. That's all. We are not walking to get somewhere, but to be exactly where we are. Each step is precious and unique. As we walk it becomes clear that, 'This particular step will not come again.' [recognizing impermanence]" (Shoshanna, pp. 23-24) This can be an alternate to sitting and standing with a group, or practiced during individual meditation.

"Mindfulness on the mind and matter is mainly exercised at the body-door [for example the feet during walking meditation] where a distinct feeling of cold, heat, softness or solidness appears. The mind has to . . . [distinguish between different sense objects and instantly realize the kind of thought involved.] Do not let it be conditioned by the other sense-objects and wander anywhere outside the body at all. When the mind wanders, bring it back to note the physical body immediately." (Wee, pp. 178-179) Keep the mind focused (one-pointed) on the body and identify the Four Foundations of Mindfulness, namely body, feelings, mind and mind-objects. Do not focus on the external objects that create the sensory perception, but notice the activity of these four foundations only.

"The first two steps of this tetrad take piti (contentment) and sukha (joy) as the subjects of our detailed examination and study [about emotions "vedana-nupassana."] . . . Once the body-conditioner, the breath, is calmed, feelings of piti and sukha appear . . . proportionate to the extent of that calming . . . (contentment) arises from our successfully inducing samadhi in the previous steps [of meditation.] . . . Piti is not peaceful . . . There is a kind of excitement or disturbance in piti; only when it becomes sukha is it tranquil. Step one of the second tetrad, 'experiencing piti' consists of contemplating piti every time we breathe-in and breathe-out . . . Find out what this feeling is like. Fully experience it [don't expect it to be the same each time.] . . . This is the essence of the practice of step five . . . This work is fun to do; it is a most enjoyable lesson . . . If piti interferes, the contemplation of sukha is ruined and real tranquility will not arise . . . We should not let any other feelings interfere . . . We should feel saturated with happiness, certainly a wonderful way to meet with success in the practice of step six." (Buddhadasa, 1988. pp. 57-61) When do we feel this kind of happiness otherwise? As we follow the breath from end to end, slow/deep breaths, short breaths, we prepare our consciousness to experience jhana/absorption, which is best achieved in the lotus/sitting position. We can use any posture to practice step five, but walking is useful because it is also active.

Biographical Sketch:

The legends about Buddha must be considered mostly unreliable, especially those that invoke mystical powers and supernatural beings. These allegories and myths usually have important lessons and they may contain seeds of truth that we can sprout in the gardens of our own lives. Many of the sermons and sutras are not his but the work of teachers in later times, so what are we to make of these teachings? If there is considerable doubt as to the exact nature of his original message, how do we regard this religion? It asserts itself as the path to enlightenment, which means it presumes to lead us to our own, *impermanent* truth. "By the fifth century, these eastern peoples had realized that their improved trade and agriculture brought them far more wealth and status than the Vedic rites. (pg. 236) All beings shared the same nature, therefore, and must be treated with the same courtesy and respect that we would wish to receive ourselves." This gave rise to the chant "Neti . . . neti" (not this . . . not this) which is "Mu" in Japanese. (Armstrong, pg. 241)

During the course of my life and recent study of Buddhism, I have come to some similar, or at least parallel conclusions: When we understand that life is about finding meaning without doctrine and revelation, and we accept the art and wisdom of the Eight-fold Path without the threat of punishment, without even the warning of continuous lives of suffering, then we have arrived. When we find our own reasons to follow a path of "righteousness," and agree to teach that to other people, we no longer need to depend on Buddha, Christ, Mohammed, Lao-tzu, Confucius, Socrates, Aristotle, Zoroaster, Meher Baba . . . We will have arrived when we understand that dependence is a manifestation of emptiness.

"Most of what the Buddha taught was delivered spontaneously according to the needs of the people who happened to be around him at any given moment. The ability to respond spontaneously in precisely the right way is one of the marks of an enlightened master—which works quite nicely as long as the enlightened master happens to be alive." (Mingyur, pg. 135) For the rest of us, we are on our own in a life of continuing study and practice with the aid (and guidance—not commandment) of Buddhist oral traditions and subsequent (Tipitaka) writings.

Reading for the Day:

"Sati means mindfulness. The importance of the Dhamma practice is that we can train mind to attain perfect and efficient mindfulness to know the truth of the body: it is impermanent, suffering and subject to decay at last." (Wee, pg. 184) Thus we maintain purposeful motivation.

"According to the Abhidharma [Buddhist psychological] literature, the practitioner learns to observe the mind not as a continual flux but as discrete moments of awareness or mind-moments . . . To be distracted is to allow another mind-moment to draw awareness away from what is intended and toward something else . . . mindfulness as 'continuous imagining—that is, a certain style of holding' . . . Practicing mindfulness entails applying pure awareness to an immediate sense object [phenomenon] without getting lost in thinking about the object, and then holding that awareness moment by moment without distraction . . . The object of mindfulness is referred to as the support of mindfulness . . . [As for Wee above] there are four types of supports: 1. the body, 2. feeling tone, 3. state of consciousness, 4. and contents of consciousness. [body, feelings, mind and mind-objects] The latter type includes the virtuous and non-virtuous mental factors, perceptions, thoughts, and emotions. Each of these four is a distinct class of internal events within the mental continuum. Each can serve as a vehicle for mindfulness. Practicing mindfulness of the body [as with walking meditation] is considered to be easier than the others, so it is often practiced first in the series. To fully master mindfulness, all four types are recommended [and we will deal with feelings, mind and mind-objects each subsequently.]" (Brown, pg. 140) Different authors refer to the sixteen steps in different ways.

What is mindfulness? "Looking within is essential for an understanding of Dhamma or Buddhism. Failure to look at things in the right way can be a barrier to understanding, as when two people disagree because one of them has failed to look at a question in a certain important way and so is not in a position to understand the point that another person is making. Disagreement is usually caused by two parties looking at the matter in question in two different ways." (Buddhadasa, 1999, pg. 59) Thus being attached to your own outcome or beliefs, can create this impasse. Liberation is about using each defilement, hindrance, fetter or emotional problem, etc. as an internal object and overcoming or diffusing each.

Protecting:

"This is what I heard," review by both practitioners and teacher.

Additional Teachings:

"The Lord Buddha rebuked Ananda sharply and said:—Surely that is nonsense, to assert that your being is your mind."

"Ananda stood up with hands pressed together and said with astonishment:—Why, my Lord, if my being is not my mind, what else can be my mind?"

"The Lord Buddha replied:—The notion that your being is your mind, is simply one of the false conceptions that arises from reflecting about the relations of yourself and outside objects, and which obscures your true and essential Mind. It is because, since from beginning-less time down to the present life, you have been constantly misunderstanding your true and essential Mind. It is like treating a petty thief as your own son. By so doing you have lost consciousness of your original and permanent Mind and because of it have been forced to undergo the suffering of successive death and rebirths." The Surangama Sutra (Goddard, pp. 124-125)

". . . The modern tendency to believe that spiritual truths can be understood by those who have not been spiritually trained [is likely mistaken.] All intending students of Buddhism would do well to remember, however, that the heart of the Dharma, the spiritual essence which underlies and interpenetrates all doctrinal formulations, metaphysical disciplines and aesthetic expressions, will be revealed, not in proportion to the bulk of our scholastic equipment, but only to the extent to which we have cultivated Right Motive [mindfulness.]" (Sangharakshita, 1957, pg. 39)

In summary: Mindfulness "... is our connection with the infinitely abundant truth and inexhaustible source, the Dharma or universal law. When we realize its limitless possibilities, we know how little we need from the outside world or anyone in it and feel content, supported, fulfilled. With this delightful knowledge, we give freely of ourselves at all times, without preconceptions or specific goals in mind. When we surrender to what is and learn to let go and let be, we exist as agents of pure generosity, like a clear channel for the flow of cosmic energy of enlightenment." (Surya das, pg. 32) This is a synergism that connects us to life and to all aspects of Dharma.

Sharing Merit:

Rejoicing In Others' Merit (Saying Sadhu)

Buddhist Sutra

Lesson Title: **The Eight-fold Path—Right Mindfulness**

Lesson Number: **Twelve**

Key Vocabulary: remanifesting, sati, mindfulness, insight meditation, carelessness, phenomenology, awareness, samasati, tranquility, time-space matrix of the ordinary mental continuum, bad mental state, piti, sukha, pliancy, karmic propensities, motivation, clearly knowing.

Assignment:
Practice meditation "Mindfulness on the mind and matter is mainly exercised at the body-door . . ." as the beginning to insight meditation. After performing the first four steps, practice—"Step one of the second tetrad, 'experiencing piti' consists of contemplating piti every time we breathe in and breath out . . .

Find out what this feeling is like.

Fully experience it Is it heavy? Is it light? How coarse is it? How subtle? This is called "knowing its flavor." (Buddhadasa, 1988, pg. 59)

Use the same meditation and do walking meditation for at least ten minutes, five times.

Define each of the Key Vocabulary in your own words.

Describe the importance of a gradual approach to developing concentration and insight meditation. What is the difference between the two?
What difference did you experience with walking meditation, using mindfulness of the body (feet), compared to sitting?

Can you exercise pliancy while walking?

What part of our mental continuum is dreaming? Before you go to sleep repeat “I will recognize my dreams . . .” and write about one in the morning.

Look at a stone and describe the infinite “life cycle” of that stone as a way of describing a spiritual dimension.

In secular terms, right memory means being always careful, clearheaded, and attentive. When is this especially important?

Materials Required: Language games, (Buddhist sash-white), tea service

Buddhist Sutra

Lesson Title: **The Eight-fold Path—Right Concentration (meditation)**

Lesson Number: **Thirteen**

Rationale:

"Every time you feel lost, alienated, or cut off from life, or from the world, every time you feel despair, anger, or instability, practice going home. Mindful breathing is the vehicle that you use to go back to your true home." (Hanh, pg. 99) Concentration is only slightly distinct from insight or "vipassana" meditation, as two poles of a continuum with distinct goals and perhaps different mental activities. Whenever you feel a sense of boredom, a lack of stimulation or interest in your surroundings i.e. a dharma talk, then you can touch the beauty of Concentration.

Discussion of Prior Lesson:

"Meditation is the specialized activity that helps us to fully realize the Buddha's teachings, to make them an integral part of our being rather than just a new set of ideas to be entertained theoretically in the mind. It weans us away from our usual habit patterns, particularly our involvement with our thoughts and their emotional sub-themes. At the same time it sharpens and intensifies our powers of direct perception: it gives us eyes to see into the true nature of things. The field of research is ourselves, and for this reason the laser of attention is turned and focused inwards." (Snelling, pg. 51)

"We *study and train* as we experience piti in the mind." (Buddhadasa, 1988. pg. 59) Then we proceed to sukha. Each practitioner may share a dream story.

Training Objective:

Understand how *intelligence* supervises meditation coordinating directing, intensity and pliancy. Review the reflective mind. What it means to be a "Stream Enterer." Examine the "questions," and identify the special language. Step six, sukha.

Materials Required: Language games, Buddhist sash-white, tea service

Motivational Statement:

Having been asked to preach and make distinctions between people: Buddha replied: Stop, stop, no need to speak! / My Law is wonderful and difficult to ponder.

Those who are overbearingly arrogant
When they hear it, will never show reverent belief.

This stands as a warning to us all, especially those who think they have learned a great deal about Buddhism. Furthermore, there is the story of a young girl who came to the Sangha to astound the group with her level of understanding and achievement. Prior to that, it was held that women could not obtain Buddhahood. ". . . But all such assertions are here in the Lotus Sutra unequivocally thrust aside . . . she reaches the highest goal in the space of a moment. Once again the Lotus Sutra reveals that its revolutionary doctrines operate in a realm transcending all petty distinctions of sex or species, instant or eon . . . These joyous revelations concerning the universal accessibility of Buddhahood . . . from this we see that in the Lotus Sutra the Buddha, who had earlier been viewed as a historical personality, is now conceived as a being who transcends all boundaries of time and space, an ever-abiding principle of truth and compassion that exists everywhere and within all beings." (Snelling, pg. xviii-xix) A "principle of truth" however is not a god, but it is an ideal to be respected.

"The objective of [Rational] Buddhism is to enable teachable persons to be devoid of suffering or to attain the Teachings (for general people) or 'to attain enlightenment' (as for the Buddha)." (Wee, pg. 111)

First Progressive:

"If you touch suffering deeply in yourself and in the other person, understanding will arise. When understanding arises, *love and acceptance will also arise*, and this will bring the suffering to an end." (Hanh, pg. 283) This works both ways as we increase generosity and compassion in our lives, suffering declines and understanding expands.

"On the inner level, we experience our thoughts and feelings about our outer acts of generosity. These internal attitudes should harmonize with the acts involved. Otherwise, we are not engaged wholeheartedly in royal giving. [. . . giving the best of what we have, graciously and unstintingly, without reservations, hesitation, or regret.] The most important thing to clarify in our mind is the intention behind our act of generosity. Why are we taking this action? Is it a means of impressing the other person, bolstering our influence over him/her, or enhancing our own self-esteem? If so, we are still attached to and reinforcing our egocentric self rather than giving of self, and so we are not yet being really and truly unconditionally generous . . . These thoughts and attitudes can affect the shape and influence of our lives just as powerfully as the thoughts and states of consciousness we put into overt action. Examine our negative, unhelpful attitudes about ourselves, our lives, and the world in which we live, can we take the same proactive approach, turning wounds into wisdom and recognizing difficulties and hardships as one of the greatest precipitants to genuine growth and transformation?" (Surya Das, pp. 28-29) We can be aided by planning our giving annually as a rational plan, and thus removing impulse or spontaneous pressures.

"Wisdom and compassion are aspects of the same non-dual realization. Therefore the experience of certainty about the mind's real nature necessarily leads to compassionate desire that others find this same truth ' . . . pray that the highest realization will be known among all sentient beings, namely the virtue [of compassion] and the bliss [of awakened wisdom] coming from the virtue practice. Protecting, sets the groundwork for the devotional prayer's perfect purification. Then, as it is said, you will greatly increase the roots of virtue, which is no small accomplishment (Tashi Namgyel) . . . The 'lofty ideal' is to desire *to realize truth for the sake of all others*." (Brown, pg. 149)

Second Progressive:

"The essence of Buddhism is mind development by Concentration Meditation and Insight Meditation. Therefore, there must be techniques in studying and [the development of] understanding meticulously how to practice to develop mind . . . Of all wholesome deeds in Buddhism, the most advantageous one is mind development . . . we are to acquire religious knowledge especially the one about mind . . . We should know [what practice] means [and that it will lead to] fruits [and] the right result." (Wee, pg. 19) How many "essences" can there be in Buddhism or in any one teaching? Is this just a figure of speech that is used like an exclamation point to emphasize a single point? Or is it the first step of developing a theory of meaning, a move in a special *language game*?

Perhaps the most important obstacle to ethical development are the five "hindrances." "The following five factors are regarded as major obstructions to the development of concentration and so to penetration of ultimate truth: 1. Sensual desire; 2. Ill will; 3. Sloth and torpor: 4. Restlessness and worry; 5. Doubt.—The study of the dharma, its practice, cultivation of the company of the wise and profitable discussion all tend to diminish these **hindrances**, which will gradually fade out as progress is made. Also, specific antidotes may be applied. For instance, to counteract sensual desire one may meditate upon the repulsive aspects of the body; and to counteract ill will, one may consciously direct good will towards an enemy or other particular object of aversion. Cutting down on food intake and taking outdoor exercise may help to diminish sloth and torpor."

"Restlessness and worry are said to arise from an uneasy conscience and may be counteracted by repentance [***cleansing***] of past wrong deeds and a resolve not to repeat them. Moreover, as any Catholic priest or psychoanalyst would no doubt readily confirm, confession can be very helpful in easing the pangs of conscience . . . The confused form of doubt displays itself in a general inability to decide on any course of action and see it through. This hindrance may be resolved by the increasing clarity that comes from the study and practice of the dharma, and from discussions with spiritual friends. Buddhism places very strong emphasis on the importance of spiritual friends and the general company one keeps." (Snelling, pp. 65-66)

"We have to practice mind [development through meditation] to be so mindful and conscious that we can get rid of suffering by continuing exercising the Noble Eight-fold Path [by developing] Concentration. We have to know and understand more Dhamma to be fundamental in practicing mind by Concentration Meditation and Insight Meditation which are the most important issues in Buddhism. To practice to eradicate suffering, we require perseverance in performing mental wholesomeness; that is to meditate to cultivate wholesomeness [buddhahood] in inborn trait that is in mind [instincts and the mental continuum.]" (Wee, pg. 33) We may each have different ideas of what "wholesomeness" implies, but we can begin by following our best conscience.

Third Progressive:

"According to Buddhism, the person who can attain the first stage of holiness of the Teachings is called a Stream-Enterer (Sotapanna). That person can become a stream-enterer when he has faith in Buddhism, his mind has entered into the stream of the Teachings, can give up the first 3 fetters namely: 1. false view of individuality [i.e. Yoga;] to regard one's body as oneself. 2. Doubt: doubt in the Buddhist Teachings [at least the Rational side] 3. Adherence to mere rules and rituals [i.e. strict vegetarianism.]" (Wee, pg. 111)

Full awareness—*intelligence*: "The fourth skill required of the driving student is to keep watch that the other three skills are being performed well. Likewise, the skillful meditation use full awareness to watch the meditation and insure that its best qualities are brought out for the duration of the session. A common beginner's mistake is to meditate for an entire session without ever reflecting on the quality of the meditation. Such beginners develop subtle and not so subtle bad habits of meditation, the accumulation of which will arrest progress at some point. A wise practitioner uses full awareness to assess the quality of the meditation." (Brown, pg. 156) Is it possible to waste time and effort, probably not, but some sittings are necessarily better than others.

"It is understood that Concentration Meditation is aimed to make [the] mind calm. In practicing, we need *Bhavana* to make mind calm more easily. ***Bhavana means mental growth, mental cultivation, mental development, mental training to cultivate concentration such as by praying.*** Bhavana enables mind to be stronger. Continuous Bhavana will produce good result. It is mentioned in the Three Baskets that 'it is named Bhavana because it means regular practice'." (Wee, pg. 44) Much of Western religious training dealing with reverence and prayer renders us prepared for concentration. "Right meditation leads to spiritual unification, mental tranquility, and the attainment of the state in which thought and concepts [theorizing] no longer exist." (Mizuno, pg. 57) We can simply be at peace.

Throughout the day we can evaluate our mental status as a simple kind of meditation. "Mind (citta)—is **heart**, thing that perceives something, thinks and feels. It is a state of consciousness. It is the natural state that is aware of sense-objects or always perceives sense-objects. Mind can be named 'perceiver' only . . . In respect of practice to develop mind, there are three kinds of mind we should notice to know and understand. They are ***1) calm mind, 2) pure mind and 3) enlightened mind.*** Noticing [the status of our] mind will enable us to understand how to practice [to develop further the] mind, [we can see] how much we make progress in practicing [developing] it, whether we make any progress." (Wee, pg. 78) At this point the Practitioner should be able to achieve a calm mind, or know how to go there at any time, even during stressful periods. Each Practitioner should have a good idea what it takes to have a pure mind, and developing that will be the next task, applying the lessons we have learned. The Stream Enterer will begin to get a glimpse of what it means to obtain enlightenment as well.

A great deal of effort associated with *Buddhist Sutras* involves learning the specialized vocabulary of Buddhism. The meaning of the myths and allegories comes to light more easily when one is well versed in the specialized language that is used in the teachings, and not used in the same way in ordinary communications. This is known in philosophy (Wittgenstein) as a "language game," or it can be thought of as a jargon, and when one is using a specialized idiom with first time listeners, it is not unreasonable to expect difficulty communicating ideas. Thus it may be difficult for beginners in Rational Buddhism to understand the point of the teachings until they are well versed, even well read in many texts, and understand the specialized meaning of otherwise rather mundane words. This is only a brief discussion, and there is more to the discussion of language games, a more detailed discussion would show how switching word usages inadvertently, gives rise to the many philosophical problems (see Schopenhauer's category errors) that have preoccupied humanity for thousands of years. Often when we examine nagging philosophical problems and questions, and then identify the special language game from which they arise, the answers become less problematic. Two helpful questions are: "When would that statement be true, meaningful (or useful)?" and "What kind of answer do you want?"

Meditation Practicum:

A review of the mindfulness of breathing: "As its name implies, the mindfulness of breathing (*anapaNA'sati in Pali*) uses the breath as an object of concentration, and the practice takes one through four stages that require progressively greater attention. By focusing on the breath one becomes aware of the mind's tendency to jump from one thing to another. The simple discipline of concentration brings one back to the present moment and all the richness of experience it contains. It is a way to develop mindfulness, the faculty of alert and sensitive awareness. And it is an excellent method for cultivating the states of intense meditation absorption known as dhyana (jhana) that form the basis for seeing things as they really are. The mindfulness of breathing is an effective antidote to restlessness and anxiety and a good way to relax: concentration on the breath has a tonic effect on one's entire physical and mental state." (Vishvapani, pg. 48) We see at every step the integration between concentration and more active mindfulness.

The following can be used as a guided meditation. Concentration can be divided ". . . into nine substages called the *nine stages of the mind staying*. Concentration practice entails placing and holding the mind on the intended meditation object for longer and longer periods without distraction, learning to make the mind 'stay' continuously and completely on the intended object . . . [is a developmental process, like learning a skill.] The nine stages are likened to a winding road . . . There are five bends in the road and six straight roads between each bend. The five bends symbolize difficult transition points, each of which requires application of a special method. The six straight roads symbolize the six powers of concentrative stability along the way . . ." (Brown)

"Simply sit up straight, breathe normally, and allow yourself to become aware of your breath coming in and going out. As you relax into simply being aware of your inhalation and exhalation, you'll probably start to notice hundreds of thoughts passing through your mind. Some of them are easy to let go of, while others may lead you down a long avenue of related thoughts. When you find yourself chasing after a thought, simply bring yourself back to focusing on your breath. Do this for about a minute." (Mingyur)

1. "The first straight road, known as the road of hearing, (directing the mind) the meditator uses the teacher's instructions to repeatedly place the mind on the intended object. [guided meditation] The first skills to develop are the skill in recognizing distraction and the skill of recovery from distraction.
2. The second straight road is called the road of reflection because the meditator thinks about and has applied the teacher's instructions in such a way as to try to reflect—continuously directing the mind . . . The skills arising out of this stage are

the achievement of some continuity of staying and a marked reduction in mental elaboration.

3. The third and fourth of the nine stages—resetting and setting closely—correspond to the third straight road, known as the road of mindfulness, because now [already] the meditator rarely completely loses track of the intended object . . . Recovery of focus occurs shortly after becoming distracted . . . with greater continuity . . . The main problem at this stage is the problem of patchy or partial-staying . . .
4. Staying closely: the meditator has developed very powerful mindfulness, so staying is relatively continuous and complete . . . The main problems at this stage are coarse flightiness and dullness and their derivatives, sleepiness and heaviness . . . ***Dullness*** actually seems to increase at this stage because concentration is much more inward than outward.
5. The fifth and sixth . . . disciplining and calming—correspond to the road of intelligence [having the bigger picture] . . . ***Intensifying*** is vitally important because it effects the shift from the road of hearing to the road of reflecting, from the road of reflecting to the road of mindfulness, and from the road of mindfulness to the road of intelligence . . . the meditator rarely loses track of the intended object. Along this road concentration is pleasurable and uplifting, and at times intensely blissful . . . The practitioner must stay very alert and keep the mind bright and sharp . . .
6. Calming—subtle dullness has disappeared, but subtle flightiness remains a problem, in part because the ordinary mind remains habitually attached to sensory experiences, in part because the meditative mind has become attached to the uplifting sense of the road of intelligence . . .
7. The seventh and eighth of the nine stages correspond to the fifth straight road, the road of perseverance. Along this road the meditator has sustainable energy to continue meditation for long periods without distraction or fatigue . . . thoroughly calming, still distracted by dullness and flightiness, but they pose no risk . . . still needs to apply considerable effort to get the mind to stay continuously and completely . . . until it becomes automatic . . .

8. ***One-pointedness***: effort is only needed to set up the meditation session, but it becomes automatic after that . . . easing up on the effort will not cause distraction from the intended object." This is an identification of the role of Concentration.
9. ***"Equanimity*** or balance, corresponds to the sixth road, the road of mastery. At this final stage staying is complete and continuous and events arise with intense clarity. The signs of genuine mastery include continuous meditative stabilization during both waking and sleep; being done-with coarse-level appearances and negative emotional states during meditation; the sense of having acquired a new body upon waking from meditation; the occurrence of pure, illusion like appearances and meditative visions." (Brown, pp. 277-280) These latter "visions" might be considered the fruits or pleasant or desirable goals of practice for the Stream Enterer, but these are just delusions, or dreams, constructs of the Sixth Sense.

Again: ". . . the how of Buddhist practice—lies in learning to simply rest in a bare awareness of thoughts, feelings, and perceptions as they occur. In the Buddhist tradition, this gentle awareness is known as mindfulness, which, in turn, is simply resting in the mind's natural clarity . . . Simply looking at what was going on in my mind actually changed what was going on there." (Mingyur)

"You may also find yourself getting caught up in a particular train of thought and follow it while ignoring everything else. Then suddenly you remember that the point of the exercise is simply to watch your thoughts. Instead of punishing or condemning yourself, just go back to focusing on your breath . . . Experience follows ***intention.*** Wherever we are, whatever we do, all we need to do is recognize our thoughts, feelings, and perceptions as something natural. Neither rejecting nor accepting, we simply acknowledge the experience and let it pass. If we keep this up, we'll eventually find ourselves becoming able to manage situations we once found painful, scary, or sad. We'll discover a sense of confidence that isn't rooted in arrogance or pride. We'll realize that we're always sheltered, always safe, and always home." (Mingyur, pp. 43-45)

The indication that concentration meditation is beginning to be successful is to notice as follows: "After setting up the seed [or another object for meditation] the practitioner allows various perceptual attributes to 'emanate from and be absorbed back into it.' What emanates from the seed may vary in size, shape, intensity of light, color, fragrance, and so forth, but at any given moment of its emanation the seed has a particular set of perceptual attributes. These attributes quickly disappear and other attributes appear [yet the mind stays on the seed and does not wander elsewhere.] The seed does not change its pure nature, even though various attributes arise and pass away moment by moment. When concentration is strong, the mind is fixed without distraction on the presence of the seed in such a way as to recognize its various ever-changing attributes, unobstructedly . . . Since the ordinary mental continuum has already become rearranged through concentration training, various perceptual attributes emanate from the seed moment by moment in a more or less orderly fashion." (Brown, pp. 208-209)

In the last lesson, we studied and observed ". . . the power piti has over the mind . . . Finally, we realize that piti stimulates the mind in a coarse way; it lacks a refined and subtle effect like sukha . . . In the second step of this second tetrad—or **step six overall—'experiencing sukha,'** we contemplate sukha (happiness, joy) with every inhalation and exhalation. We focus on sukha as arising out of piti. [We ask the same questions about sukha.] . . . sukha does not stimulate or excite; it calms down and soothes. Here we contemplate sukha as the agent that makes the citta tranquil . . . Usually piti obscures sukha, but when piti fades away, sukha remains. The coarse feeling gives way to calm. Taste the tranquil flavor of sukha with every inhalation and exhalation." (Buddhadasa, 1988, pp. 59-60) Sukha is often associated with calm concentration, relaxing even sublime, with no intended effort or anticipated result; the calm of reverence, respect and restraint.

Biographical Sketch:

"Meditation may have had a very humble origin. In a land as hot as India, sitting in the shade of a tree is an excellent way to cool off. While relaxing in this way, some people no doubt gradually came to reflect on the world and human life and reached a state in which contact and fusion between the human mind and divinities were thought possible. Upanishadic philosophy taught a dichotomy between the material and the spiritual. According to this teaching, Yoga is a good method for freeing the spirit from the bonds of material things and from the flesh. By the time of Shakyamuni, meditation had already been studied and explained in detail. In Magadha lived two recluse religious ascetics who had left their homes to practice disciplines . . . Having reached the extremely high state of meditative concentration in which nothing existed for him [emptiness], he had many disciples to whom he taught that the attaining of such a state was the ideal. Entering the trance state of no-thinking—such a concentration is difficult for ordinary human beings. Among Alara-Kalama's hundreds of disciples, no one else had succeeded in it. Of course, the ability to do so depends on the level of the individual's training. But it also depends on the innate characteristics of the person: some people find it much easier than others. A meditative person from birth, Shakyamuni developed the habit of entering such states early in youth." (Mizuno, pp. 22-23) Many years later Buddha repudiated this yoga system.

Although it might be more accurate to make the claim that the Buddha perfected this Yoga meditation. "The Lord Buddha then warned Subhuti, saying:—Subhuti, do not think that the Tathagata ever considers within his own mind: I ought to enunciate a system of teaching for the elucidation of the Dharma. You should never cherish such an unworthy thought. And why? Because if any disciple should harbor such a thought, he would not only be misunderstanding the teaching of the Tathagata but he would be slandering him as well. Moreover, what has just been referred to as '*a system of teaching*' has no meaning, as Truth can not be cut up into pieces and arranged into a system. The words can only be used as a figure of speech." The Diamond Sutra (Goddard, pg. 104) What implication does this have for the existence of the many different Buddhist sects that espouse systems of teaching? Or do they? Practice is very individualized!

Consider: "If you . . . sit in a Buddhist shrine room while a lecture or a chanting practice is taking place, you'll undoubtedly see the monks restlessly scratching themselves, shifting on their cushions, or coughing. But, chances are, if they've taken their training seriously enough, they're shifting [etc.] mindfully—bringing their attention to the sensation of the itch, the sensation of scratching it, and the relief [from suffering] they feel when they're done scratching." (Mingyur, pg. 211) Practice is individualized.

Reading for the Day:

"If you can breathe in and out and [lie] in the spirit of 'I have arrived, I am *home*, in the here, in the now,' then you will notice that you are becoming more solid and more free immediately. You have established yourself in the present moment, at your true address. Nothing can push you to run anymore, or make you so afraid. You are free from worrying about the past. You are not stuck, thinking about what has not happened yet and what you cannot control. You are free from guilt concerning the past, and you are free from your worries about the future." (Hanh, pg. 199)

"In concentration meditation: From the perspective of the mind, the mind 'stays' on its intended object without distraction. [This is the culmination of step four of sixteen.] From the perspective of observable events, the events in the unfolding mental continuum become 'calm.' Shinay means 'calming/ staying'—from both perspectives... 'a technique for setting the mind, without fluctuation, on a single object of observation.' The purpose of concentration meditation is to bring the mind under control and make it serviceable. 'Serviceability means that you can direct your mind as you wish [pliancy] toward a virtuous object of meditation' [with the desired intensity.]" (Brown, pg. 152)

In Satipatthana: "The only way that leads to the 1. attainment of purity, [dwelling in contemplation of the body, full of energy, clearly conscious, attentive, after subduing worldly greed and grief] to the 2. overcoming of sorrow and lamentation [with awareness of in- and out-breathing,] to the 3. end of pain and grief [whilst setting the mind free with clear conscious, attentive] to the entering upon the 4. right path [contemplating impermanence, the fading away of passion, extinction of attachment,] and the realization of Nibbana, is [following] these *four fundamentals of attentiveness*." (Goddard, pp. 52-53) These are the first four chapters in my book *Bodhicitta: Higher Truth.*

Protecting:

Now after having studied and become familiar with the Four Noble Truths, and having applied each stage of the Eight-fold Path to your lives, write down what these are and a brief description; preferably in the order they were presented. Those who succeed will be identified as Stream Enterers, so you will feel and know what it means to connect to Buddhism in this meaningful way. (This will be a repeated activity for those who do not successfully accomplish the assessment.) When a student has succeeded, they will receive a white sash to wear as a learning aid (not an ordination) and acknowledgment of their humility and intimate connection to Buddhism. (In giving this title, the intention is both to say and feel what it means to connect to Buddhism in this meaningful way.)

"And by thus considering, three fetters vanish, namely: Self-illusion, Skepticism and Attachment to Rule and Ritual. But those disciples, in whom these three fetters have vanished, they have all entered the Stream (sotapanna), have forever escaped the states of woe, and are assured of final enlightenment.

> More than any earthly power,
> More than all the joys of heaven,
> More than rule o'er all the world,
> Is the Entrance to the Stream.
> And verily those, who are filled with unshaken faith towards me, all those have entered the stream." (Goddard, pg. 37)

"This is what I heard," review by both Stream Enterers and teacher.

Additional Teaching:

"Right mindfulness and right concentration are developed in tandem through satipatthana ("frames of reference" or "foundations of mindfulness"), a systematic approach to meditation practice that embraces a wide range of skills and techniques. Of these practices, mindfulness of the body (especially mindfulness of breathing) is particularly effective at bringing into balance the twin qualities of tranquility (samatha) and insight (vipassana), or clear-seeing. Through persistent practice, the meditator becomes more adept at bringing the combined powers of samatha-vipassana to bear in an exploration of the fundamental nature of mind and body. As the meditator masters the ability to frame his immediate experience in terms of ***anicca (inconstancy), dukkha, and anatta (not-self),*** even the subtlest manifestations of these three characteristics of experience are brought into exquisitely sharp focus. At the same time, the root cause of dukkha—craving—is relentlessly exposed to the light of awareness. [*The opposite of this is charity and compassion.*] Eventually craving is left with no place to hide, the entire karmic process that fabricates dukkha unravels, the Eight-fold Path reaches its noble climax, and the meditator gains, at long last, his/her first unmistakable glimpse of the Unconditioned—Nibbana." (Bullitt, internet) This is an exciting map for rational progress.

In summary: "Our secret level of being is the inherent domain of complete non-attachment, where we live with wide-open mind, heart, and hands. The more we cultivate generosity in our outer and inner lives, as clumsy as our efforts may sometimes be, the more we resonate with the secret and subtle level of our being, releasing its amazing, inexhaustible energy into our lives and into the world. When we realize the truth of the Buddhist adage that deep spiritual contentment [through concentration] is the ultimate form of wealth, we liberate ourselves to practice generosity to its fullest extent. We re-enter the marketplace with bliss-bestowing hands and a large bag of gifts on our backs, ready to dispense them." (Surya das, pg. 32) Generosity is the essential outside link between our internal talent and with the rewards of concentration.

Sharing Merit:

Rejoicing In Others' Merit (Saying Sadhu)

Buddhist Sutra

Lesson Title: **The Eight-fold Path—Right Concentration (meditation)**

Lesson Number: **Thirteen**

Key Vocabulary: anapanasati, dhyana (jhana), Bhavana, Stream Enterer, equanimity, dullness, heaviness, cleansing, purification, anicca, annatta, language game, home, fetters, vipassana, inborn trait, intensifying, calming, one pointedness, sotapana

Assignment:
Taste the tranquil flavor of sukha with every inhalation and exhalation. Ask the same questions as for piti to determine the flavor of sukha.

What road are you on?

Use a "seed" in object meditation: ". . . allow various perceptual attributes to 'emanate from and be absorbed back into it.'

Imagine the occurrence of pure, illusion like appearances and meditative visions. How will you recognize these events in meditation?

Define each of the Key Vocabulary in your own words.

How does our *intelligence* supervise meditation coordinating directing, intensity and pliancy?

What does it mean to you to be recognized as a "Stream Enterer?

Recall the four supports of mindfulness? And describe your experience with these.

Examine a question, and identify an example of the special language game of Buddhism.

Meditate again on compassion and reflect on the changes in your intentions.

What implication does it have to consider a system of teaching a "figure of speech?"

What implication does this have for the existence of the many different Buddhist sects, that espouse systems of teaching?

Materials Required: Candles for Ceremony, incense and an icon of Buddha

Buddhist Sutra

Lesson Title: **Kinds of People**

Lesson Number: **Fourteen**

Rationale:

"Buddhism places very strong emphasis on the importance of spiritual friends and the general company one keeps." (Snelling, pg. 66) What kinds of people are attracted to Buddhism in a serious way? The correct answer is probably all kinds, yet there must already be a certain amount of integrity and brilliance of character to bring someone from a Judeo/Christian background into a completely different perspective of religion and life, however, some people begin when they bottom out, completely exhausted with the routines or complications of their lives. Which kind are you?

Discussion of Prior Lesson:

We should not let any other feelings [vedana] interfere . . . We should feel saturated with happiness, certainly a wonderful way to meet with success in the practice of step six. "The key—the how of Buddhist practice—lies in learning to simply rest in a bare awareness of thoughts, feelings, and perceptions [concentration] as they occur." (Mingyur, pp. 43) Intelligent un-control of meditation: let it flow naturally.

A Stream Enterer knows: "Compassion is a beautiful flower born of understanding. When you get angry with someone, practice breathing in and out mindfully. Look deeply into the situation to see the true nature of your own and the other person's suffering, and you will be liberated." (Hanh, pg. 153)

Training Objective:

Taking Ownership. What are the attributes of a "Stream Enterer?" The importance of repetition. How to be a freethinker. Understanding images during meditation. Encouragement. Introduction to rapture. Vedana as mind conditioner.

Materials Required: Candles for Ceremony, incense and an icon of Buddha

Motivational Statement:

"The Buddha recognized that no two people are exactly alike, that everyone is born with a unique combination of abilities, qualities, and temperaments. It is a measure of his great insight and compassion that he was able to develop an enormous variety of methods through which all sorts of people might arrive at a direct experience of their true nature and become completely free from suffering." (Mingyur, pg. 137) How well do you know your own path and progress?

"When the practitioner [Stream Enterer] holds certainty in both meditation and daily activity, the protecting practice is said to be 'well-rounded' . . . While the preliminary practices prepare the mind for the realization of certainty, true realization comes only after rigorous meditation. The advanced preliminaries properly prepare the mind for formal meditation practice. Contrary to popular opinion, meditation is the outcome, or fruit, not the beginning of spiritual practice . . . The profound changes in lifestyle and view of the mind that constitute the preliminary practices help to generate meditation, and open the way to the essential meditations that follow." (Brown, pp. 148-150) This "formal practice" is what we are preparing for.

"If we were to make a list of people we don't like . . . we would find a lot about those aspects of ourselves that we can't face." (Pema Chodron, Start Where You Are, Mingyur, pg. 173) Are these people responsible for our suffering?

First Progressive:

"This is the practice. When you become mindful, understanding, and loving, you suffer much less, you begin to feel happy, and the *people around you begin to profit from your being there*." (Hanh, pg. 279) "You can start by *thinking kind thoughts* about everyone you have contact with every day. If you have mindfulness, you can do this every waking minute with everyone you deal with. Whenever you see someone, consider that, like yourself, that person wants happiness and wants to avoid suffering. We are all the same [in that respect.] We all feel that way . . . When you recognize that common ground, *you see how closely we are all connected*." (Gunaratana, pg. 42)

Light the incense [three] near the icon of Buddha now to remind us of the beauty and pleasant, all-pervading nature of dharma. Recall the three virtues of Buddha (pg. 85). ". . . Within the Order worldly considerations of position, class, and occupation were of no significance. *All members were the same*, according to the basic Buddhist tenet that all human personalities must be recognized on an equal footing. In Buddhism, it is not a person's birth, lineage, or occupation that determines his value, but his spiritual attitudes and his actions." (Mizuno, pg. 98)

Light a candle near the Buddha icon now to remind us to also be the spark of compassion, to develop a pure mind, and to originate loving kindness wherever we go. "The essential feature of Bodhicitta is genuine, heart-quivering compassion toward all. It's based on empathy and a deeply felt sense that we're each interconnected with everyone else in the universe, and that no one person can be free from suffering until everyone is. Feeling and expressing this compassion means going beyond ordinary benevolence toward those who are close to us, share our beliefs, elicit our sympathy, or attract our interest. Instead, a Bodhisattva cultivates loving kindness toward all beings, all the time, including enemies, and patient gentleness toward all things, even unpleasant and unwanted ones." (Surya Das, pg. 16)

"You [may] need to find reasons to develop loving-friendliness toward those you have problems with. A few traditional analogies describing five different types of people may help guide you here. The first type of person is someone whose deeds are rotten. He does bad things and has a very base manner. He does not know how to behave. He is not polite. His manners are rough. He does not show respect to anybody . . . Venerable Sariputta compared such a person to a dirty rag . . ." That person can be put to some use after you listen to his story of neglect and self-absorption. "All kinds of things you do not know about may be contributing to his rough behavior. These are his history . . . it is best to forgive him for all his misdeeds. Practice metta toward him."

"You may discover a second kind of person with bad words whose deeds are good. This is someone who has no polite words in his/her vocabulary, only foul language, yet he or she nonetheless does something good for you or for the world . . . This person is compared to a pond covered with algae. When you want to dive into it or get water out of it, you have to remove the moss by hand . . . You watch and you find out that her/his heart opens to compassion and loving friendship from time to time. She/he develops a pure heart from time to time. That is a good reason for you to develop loving-friendliness toward this second person." Eventually they may begin to speak and act like those around them.

"A third person may have both bad words and bad deeds, yet a flickering impulse toward kindness within. This person is like a puddle on the road . . . You are desperately thirsty and tired . . . You find a little water in a cow's footprint . . . If you try to take that water by hand, you make it muddy. So, you kneel down and slowly bring your mouth close to that bit of water. Then sip it without disturbing the mud . . . In this way we can see at least the potential, from time to time, for even such a person bad in word and deed to, in certain circumstances, open his/her heart to noble things, friendly things, and [yes] compassionate things. You should practice loving-friendliness toward such a person, in spite of all his weaknesses." There is a breath of life in that person that may save another.

"You meet a fourth person. This person's words are bad, his/her behavior is bad, and his/her heart does not open at all for anything noble. This person is like a patient, a sick man, walking on a road where there is no hospital . . . This person is afflicted and suffering from a severe sickness . . . You think, 'How can I help this suffering being? What can I do for him? He needs water, medicine, and clothes . . . Let me help him get rid of his hatred."

"A fifth person's thoughts are sweet and wonderful. His/her words are beautiful and friendly. His deeds are friendly, beautiful, and pure. Everything is ideal. It is, of course, very easy for us to cultivate loving-friendliness toward that person. Even so, doing this mindfully can be of great value." (Gunaratana, pp. 44-46) But where is the challenge, where is the merit? When we cultivate loving-friendliness with each of these five people, there is also merit in our own consistency.

Second Progressive:

"A person with the **Eye of the Law** sees life and the world in the Buddhist way and can never again fall into superstitions or false beliefs or be tempted by other religions or philosophies. [Stream Enterer] has reached the state that is called non-retrogression [no back sliding.] Those who have reached this state are certain to attain the highest level of enlightenment." (Mizuno, pg. 41) They are in a position to share their confidence with others.

There are times, especially in our personal relationships ". . . when the act of observation of an event [or a dialogue] can influence the outcome of an event . . . [this] can seem like too much responsibility. It's much easier to assume the role of the victim and assign the responsibility or blame for our experience to some person or power outside oneself. If we're to take the discoveries of modern science seriously, however, we have to assume responsibility for our moment-by moment experience [thus taking ownership.]"

"While doing so may open up possibilities we might never before have imagined, it's still hard to give up the familiar habit of being a victim . . . if we began to accept responsibility for our experience, our lives would become a kind of playground, offering innumerable possibilities for learning and invention. Our sense of personal limitation and vulnerability would gradually be replaced by a sense of openness and possibility. We would see those around us in an entirely new light—not as threats to our personal security or happiness, but as people simply ignorant of the infinite possibilities of their own nature. Because our own nature is unconstrained by arbitrary distinctions of being 'this way' or 'that way,' or having only certain capabilities and lacking others, then we would be able to meet the demands of any situation in which we might find ourselves." (Mingyur, pp. 90-91) The only limitation is our innate ability and talent which we can improve upon.

We all have enough talent to behave well, so "Buddhist ethics are not codified into a rigid moral code; nor are they about making judgments and arousing sin and guilt, though every willed action produces consequences... Buddhists try to be aware of any particular failing to live up to an ethical principle and resolve to do better next time. [Developing a pure mind from day to day, each day better as a "rebirth".] They also note in such cases that they have still a long way to go towards finally overcoming their faults, which breeds a healthy humility. There have always been in every religion those self-righteous people who refuse to recognize their own faults but instead nurse delusions of moral superiority. We all fall into these traps at times. Christianity has its 'whited sepulchers' who praise the Lord that they are not sinful like other men; Buddhism has its 'whited stupas' too. Clearly honesty and keen mindfulness of one's actions are of the essence as a foil to these snares." (Snelling, pp. 47-48) When we are concerned about others and offer encouragement, we share our attributes humbly.

"Live your daily life in a way that you never lose yourself." (Hanh, pg. 183) What kind of person are you?

Third Progressive:

Buddha taught about different kinds of people with respect to their spiritual qualities. "... Whoever has mindfulness and wisdom to know and understand the Buddhist Teachings will have good confidence in Buddhism and will understand the profound Teachings of the Lord Buddha . . . 'mindfulness and wisdom' of human [nature] beings is another important factor. The Lord Buddha compared the mindfulness and wisdom of human beings to four groups of lotus flowers . . . 1. The Genius like a 'mature lotus flower:' it is the lotus flower above water level. When the sun shines on it today, it opens today. 2. The Intellectual like a 'less mature lotus flower:' it is the lotus flower at water level. When the sun shines on it today, it will open tomorrow. 3. The Trainable like a 'pre-mature lotus flower:' it is the lotus flower under water level. It will come up and open the day after tomorrow. 4. The Idiot like a 'newly born/unhealthy lotus flower:' this kind of lotus flower hardly has a chance to grow up. It rather becomes food for turtles and fish."

"Therefore, people who will have confidence in Buddhism and understand the Buddhist Teachings must rely on their 'mindfulness and wisdom' to study and peruse the Teachings . . . [they] will try to find out reasons [explanations for their lives] in studying and understanding the Teachings in Buddhism in order to attain right thoughts about life/compounded things . . . then have more and more prosperity in Buddhism." (Wee, pp. 3-4) This promise should encourage us to study.

Buddhahood is available for every kind of person. "These joyous revelations concerning the universal accessibility of buddhahood . . . constitute the second important message of the work [the first being, that practically everyone can attain buddhahood eventually.]" (Watson, pp. xviii-xix) One popular symbol for Buddha's teachings is the Rolling of the Wheel of the Law. "The Buddha guides and saves mankind by rolling the Wheel of the Law. All of the sermons of Shakyamuni are referred to as Rolling the Wheel of the Law." (Mizuno, pg. 33) Thus our lives turn over again and again each time on new ground. This is a symbol that is found frequently in artwork that adorns temples.

"In Zen we do the same things a hundred times and more. Learn to love repetition. A raindrop that falls on a piece of rock may have to fall a thousand times before the rock becomes a little softer and can absorb the rain . . . We sit down, day after day, in the same way and we stop moving, chasing, fixing, thinking. We no longer run away from our pain or act it out. Instead, we allow ourselves to be with whatever is going on without judgments. Then, whatever has arisen passes, and we have to be with something else. Then that passes and something else appears."

"As we do this, we're actually pulling the plug on our suffering, taking our attention back from the outside world, and returning it to ourselves. Zen is the practice of returning you to yourself." (Shoshanna, pp. 21-22) When we offer encouragement to others in the Sangha we are true to ourselves too. "To share the Dharma does not necessarily mean to preach to people. Preaching can easily get out of control and turn into shoving dogma down people's throats, mixed in with all kinds of dualistic illusions, impure motivations, and unconscious drives and desires. Tradition tells us that there are four ways a Bodhisattva-like teacher helps convey Dharma wisdom to others so that they can mature and develop spiritually. The first 1) is through the generous sharing of ourselves, in order to establish a trusting relationship with others and be both attractive and accessible. The second 2) is through interesting and meaningful discussions with others regarding what is of true benefit to them, as opposed to self-serving chatter, idle gossip, or the dissemination of distorted and hurtful views. The third 3) is through encouraging others to implement and internalize what they have learned and understood. The fourth 4) is through walking the talk, practicing what we would otherwise preach and, in the process serving as an example, a beneficent role model." (Surya Das, pg. 26)

Obtaining the designation of Stream Enterer while following these lessons is not an official Buddhist ordination, but is intended to be a personal acknowledgment of commitment, confidence and recognition of having obtained the basic understanding of the fundamental truths of Buddhism. It would be nice for anyone to attend a wat or temple and seek official ordination from an historical tradition. "Traditionally this sense of community was manifested in the religious orders [of Buddhism], consisting of those who had left their homes to follow the way of the Buddha. Many resided in monasteries, and may fairly be called 'monks.' They underwent an ordination ceremony and undertook to observe disciplinary precepts in a manner somewhat similar to the vows of holy orders in the West. There were, in addition, lay communities or societies whose character and activities varied with time and place. To call the former group 'priests,' however, would be misleading. The Buddha had set aside the traditional sacrifices of Brahmanism and there is no remnant of the sacerdotal tradition in Buddhism, unless it be through a process of *syncretism* by which this traditional function is reabsorbed even though nonessential . . . *Buddhist ritual focuses upon the attainment of a state of mind*; the Christian liturgy is a people's expression of praise and thanksgiving to their Creator and Redeemer." (de Bary, pp. xx-xxi) It is perhaps difficult on the surface to see the difference between the work of Western priests and the monks in Thailand where I have visited my family frequently. The difference if any, is about the same difference between various sects of Christianity where lay members are also members of the priesthood. All this comparison is so much hair splitting and not very useful. What do **you** feel when you kneel in private to repeat the Three Refuges?

"This first enlightenment experience, known as stream-entry (sotapatti) [for those who have chosen to accept Dharma,] is the first of four progressive stages of Awakening, each of which entails the irreversible shedding or weakening of several fetters (samyojana), the manifestations of ignorance that bind a person to the cycle of birth [daily or weekly] and death. Stream-entry marks an unprecedented and radical turning point [this is the preeminence of the Heart] both in the practitioner's current life and in the entirety of his or her long journey in samsara. For it is at this point that any lingering doubts about the truth of the Buddha's teachings disappear; it is at this point that any belief in the purifying efficacy [i.e. emptiness] of rites and rituals evaporates; and it is at this point that *the long-cherished notion of an abiding personal 'self' falls away*. The stream-enterer is said to be assured of no more than seven future rebirths (all of them favorable) before eventually attaining full Awakening." (Bullitt, internet) Later we well examine this 'traditional teaching' relating to rebirth, but for now, we're getting closer to our goal.

Meditation Practicum:

"An ancient Zen story tells that centuries ago, a physician, faced daily with death and suffering, sought out the guidance of a famous Zen Master who was living quietly in an inaccessible mountain hut. The physician climbed the mountain . . . found him raking leaves at the side of his tiny house. The teacher did not look up when the student arrived, but kept raking slowly. "I have come to understand the essence of Zen,' the physician proclaimed."

The Zen master looked up for a moment. 'Go home and be kind to your patients,' the Master replied. 'That is Zen.' (Ancient Zen story) (Shoshanna, pg. 9)

"After spending several days sitting beside someone during a silent meditation retreat, you know all there is to know about that person, and feel as close to him or her as to yourself, even though the two of you haven't spoken. It is easy to realize that our words, actions, and false mannerisms, rather than bringing us closer to one another, can serve as walls to keep others away. At this time you begin to know what it means to 'go home and be kind to your patient,' [to yourself as you follow the 'cure' of meditation practice] and to actualize the command—to love your neighbor as yourself [yourself first.]"

> "All beings are flowers
> Blooming
> In a blooming universe. Soen Nakagawa Roshi."
> (Shoshanna, pg. 16)

Remember the symbol or image of a lotus flower as an object, considering the symbolism taught here, it shows that this is an important object to visualize.

"There is a sign indicating whether we develop concentration, to which level our concentration progresses and whether we are developing Jhana. That sign is mental image (Nimitta) which is mental reflex or boundary marker . . . Thus, if we study and understand mental images, we will be able to know by ourselves whether we succeed in training mind to be concentrated, to which level we are making progress. Nimitta is a sign, an omen, a mental image reflecting mind state while practicing Concentration Meditation and Insight Meditation, for example, seeing a light or a candle light."

"Different mental images appear depending on how much the mind (citta) is concentrated, to which level concentration is developed. Appearance of mental images depends on the practice method. For example, in Concentration Meditation, concentration is induced by gazing at any of ten objects; [progressively through the fifth jhana] the mental images appearing thereafter are different from the ones by mindfulness on breathing [-object meditation incorporating using the breath.] When we practice, we have to [recognize the qualities and] realize how [we got] the mental image appearing during such a practice. This will enable us to understand and know to what level our Concentration Meditation and Insight Meditation progress and whether our practice is correct . . . We should know and remember [protect] by ourselves the characteristics of [whichever] mental image appears in each meditation practice." It is less important to share, understand and analyze immediately—than to simply keep track of them and experience them.

"Hereinafter is an explanation about mental images during mindfulness on breathing which is a type of Concentration Meditation: 1. During momentary concentration; no mental image appears at this stage. We only realize inhalation and exhalation. Sometimes we can do [this], sometimes we cannot. Mind is concentrated only momentarily. 2. During proximate concentration; many mental images appear at this stage:

a. we feel as if we saw a light. Sometimes it seems that there was a candle light near us. Sometime we feel as though a light was flashing on our face. If you experience these mental images, be aware [you will know] that your mind develops proximate concentration.
b. While our eyes are open as usual, we see as if a cigarette smoke billowed for a while [a haziness.]
c. While sitting, eyes closed, doing meditation, we see a skeleton moving back and forth for a while and disappear. If we feel [joy] like to see it, we will not see it again.
d. We see divine images inside while sitting, eyes closed, doing meditation. We see image of the past events.
e. During proximate concentration, we experience a mental image called rapture (five levels of jhana) about Dhamma. Rapture about Dhamma occurs before mind becomes so established that Jhana is developed. Rapture [like love] is a feeling of natural phenomenon . . . Jhana means a state of serene contemplation attained from meditation." (Wee, pp.

38-40) The images and stages of rapture are developed in subsequent lessons.

"When piti [fifth step] conditions a thought, that thought is coarse [raw satisfactions and pleasures] . . . when a thought arises through sukha [sixth step], that thought is calm and tranquil. Thus we realize the way that Vedana condition thoughts—'conditioning [preparing] the mind.' [Compare to sankhara, conditioning of the body with the breath. It is important] to have an 'understanding of the citta-sankhara sufficiently' . . . It is an art, a spiritual art of controlling piti and sukha so that they benefit our lives. This is the secret that we ought to know concerning piti and sukha."

"We have discovered that piti is a foe of vipassana, whereas sukha, happiness-joy, is a friend, a supporter. Vipassana means 'seeing clearly"—having direct insight into the truth of aniccam (impermanence), dukkham (unsatisfactoriness), and anatta (not-self). We must acquire the ability to regulate piti and sukha. We contemplate this fact [with calm emotions] in the mind every time we breathe in and breathe out. This is the practice of step seven." (Buddhadasa, 1988, pp. 61-64)

To accomplish this kind of tranquil meditation it may be necessary to over-exert first to then quieten the mind. Dynamic Meditation, to physically dramatize thoughts, is taught by the Osho community—

Step One: Deep fast chaotic breathing for up to ten minutes;
Step two: Playfully act out all your madness or anger;
Step Three: Jump straight up and down for five minutes or so, and shout 'Hoo!'
Step Four: Stop, freeze exactly as you are in an extended vertical position;
Step Five: Celebrate and rejoice through dance. (Active Meditation)

Insight meditation was introduced during the lesson on mindfulness (Lesson Twelve). "Insight [Vipassana] means the development of wisdom to realize the impermanence, suffering and non-selfness of the Compounded Things (Sangkhara) and the true state of compounded things by knowing that compounded things are under the law of the Common Characteristics namely [the above] . . ." (Wee, pg. 153) This 'insight' means literally looking inside oneself, rather than the interpretation of being inspired or coming to an understanding (through contemplation), although this happens as well.

Biographical Sketch:

"If the Buddha himself was impressive and inspirational to a wide spectrum of people, it is clear that the bhikkshus of his sangha were so too. On one occasion King Prasenaji of Kosala contrasted them with other monks and Brahmans, who appeared to be 'lean, wretched, unsightly, jaundiced' and so forth. The Buddhists, on the other hand, were 'smiling and cheerful, sincerely joyful, plainly delighting, their faculties fresh, unexcited, unruffled . . . dwelling with minds like the wild deer." (Snelling, pg. 26) Those who have achieved the level of confidence as well as wisdom, are identified as "Stream Enterers" and must now apply these virtues in their lives. Stream Enterers will be acknowledged in this same way by their peers and family members.

What comes to us from the tradition is a highly innovative and unique teaching both for India and for the entire world; even unique today. ". . . In the Buddhist and Jain texts which reveal the Buddha's immediate environment a multitude of contending voices speak, as though in a tumultuous market-place of philosophical opinions and ascetic practices. There were indeed public debating halls where ascetics of all stamps gathered to dispute. The public lecture or sermon, directed to disciples but also to potential supporters, was a common institution . . . Buddha was later to inveigh against those who were 'clever, subtle, experienced in controversy, hairsplitters who writhe like worms in argument' . . . There were different schools of skeptics, philosophers doubtful of the possibility of effective knowledge in this or that matter, and their existence was perhaps the surest sign of the heat and sophistication of the intellectual climate." (Carrithers, 1983, pp. 25-26) This would argue against the claim that Buddhism could not have been original and is just warmed over and reformed Brahmanism.

"Consequently, 'confidence' is a very important fundamental doctrine. (see Lesson Two) If we want to categorize people according to their confidence in Buddhism, we can do as follows: 1. People with confidence or people with right view (understanding): i.e. those who believe in Buddhist Teachings. 2. People without confidence or people with wrong view (misunderstandings): i.e. those who do not believe in the Buddhist Teachings . . . For example they do not believe in the existence [or consequences] of vice, virtue, merit and demerit . . . The best way to create confidence in Buddhism is to practice for mind development to create religious mindfulness and wisdom . . . according to three Wisdoms: 1. Wisdom resulting from listening/ studying . . . 2. Wisdom resulting from reflection (protecting) . . . 3. Wisdom resulting from mental development . . . from practicing the Teachings—using the Four Foundations of Mindfulness." (Wee, pp. 8-9)

From the Tibetan tradition: "Thrangu Rinpoche explains: 'The development of loving kindness for all sentient beings is necessary because we all have one thing in common, the wish to experience peace and happiness and not experience pain and suffering . . . Therefore, we have to include every single being in our development of Bodhicitta . . .' Shantideva, the Peace Master of ancient India, says that all the suffering in the world comes from one culprit, self-clinging and egotistical attachment, and that all the happiness in the world derives from thinking unselfishly of the well-being of others. Helpfulness is the prime product of Bodhicitta, the awakened heart-mind." (Surya Das, pg. 16)

Reading for the Day:

"The first important means is to practice [by] ourselves [develop the ability] to reflect *intentionally* [in the right direction] about our life. We need reasoned ***attention*** to enlighten the mind to cultivate primary wisdom which is called Right Understanding (Samaditthi). [This is going full circle back to the first step of the Eight-fold Path.] Firstly, with Right [view] Understanding, we have to think analytically and understand suffering according to the Four Noble Truths. Succeeding in doing so, the mind will become somewhat enlightened. It is the mind [of] ignorance which is a fetter making the mind blind and misled to lead a life of suffering. [Understanding] is the first means to make the mind enlightened to cultivate mindfulness and wisdom fruitfully in Buddhism." (Wee, pg. 85)

Practice can be simple or esoteric. "The chant 'Om' was not merely a transcendent reality external to the priest who intoned it. It was also one with the human body, with the atman, with breath, speech, ear, eye, and mind . . . A person who chanted this immortal and fearless sound while contemplating these bandhus would himself become immortal and free from fear." (Armstrong, pg. 126)

Protecting:

"This is what I heard," review by both Stream Enterers and teacher.

Additional Teachings:

"Of all these various aspects, [Buddhism as Truth, Religion, Psychology, Philosophy, Culture, as the Art of Living] the one a real Buddhist ought to take most interest in is Buddhism as Religion. We ought to look on Buddhism as a direct practical method for gaining knowledge of the true nature of things, knowledge which makes it possible to give up every form of grasping and clinging, of stupidity and infatuation, and become completely independent of things. To do this is to penetrate to the essence of Buddhism. Buddhism considered in this aspect is far more useful than Buddhism considered as mere morality, or as truth which is simply profound knowledge and not really practical; and more useful than Buddhism considered as philosophy, as something to be enjoyed as an object of speculation and argument, but of no value in the giving up of the mental defilements; and certainly more useful than Buddhism considered simply as culture, as attractive behaviour, noteworthy from the sociological viewpoint." (Buddhadasa, 2005, pg. 22)

According to the teachings of Bhagwan Shree Rajneesh, renamed before his death as Osho: "In the West you try to force the problem, you reduce it to the cause. In the East we try to put consciousness back to its source, and we don't touch the problem at all. You try to force the problem away, and we try to bring consciousness home. We don't touch the problem, but rather remove ourselves from it."

"Focusing the mind on thoughts gives them energy; witnessing was simply stepping back and observing the mind with its perpetual penchant for problem creating. 'When a guest is uninvited, unwelcome, and the host does not bother about him, doesn't even say hello, how long will the guest go on knocking at the door? One day he simply goes. Each thought, each problem, is a guest. Don't do anything with them, but remain a host—unconcerned, indifferent and centered'." 'Hammer on the rock' (Forman, pg. 89)

In summary: Most religions try to improve the way people live their lives according to their own principles. "Above all, any discussion of moral and ethical values today must include tending not only to lapses in our own personal virtue but also to social, political, and economic evils on a global level, such as racism, sexism, chauvinism, imperialism, poverty, crime, injustice, genocide, health care inequalities, and environmental degradation. We do this by striving ceaselessly to manifest the power of ethical and moral goodness in everything we think, say, and do [or we don't.] There is a Tibetan saying, 'The upright, like a precious jewel, never change at all.' In a world of constant change, I find this statement quite comforting . . . The Sanskrit word sila means 'that which cools or calms.' In this context, cooling or calming refers to taming the virulent, seething passions that can easily overwhelm us, sometimes damaging ourselves as well as others. Specifically, the practice of ethics serves as an antidote to our tendencies to be careless, meretricious, irresponsible, cruel, false, exploitative, and unfair. Moral living exemplifies compassion in action." (Surya, das, pg. 56) Thus the moral suasion of Buddhism as a religion may be the most important part of the Dharma.

Sharing Merit:

Rejoicing In Others' Merit (Saying Sadhu)

Buddhist Sutra

Lesson Title: **Kinds of People**

Lesson Number: **Fourteen**

Key Vocabulary: Nimitta, proximate concentration, samaditthi, Eye of the Law, Vipassana Bhavana, Rolling the Wheel of the Law, jhana, figure of speech, Osho, tranquility, Vedana—emotions (the second group of 4 foundations), attention

Assignment: Remember the images you encounter as you meditate using the Buddha icon as an object. (Compare this to the result of Lesson Two.) Practice the art, a spiritual art of controlling piti and sukha so that they benefit our lives by learning tranquility—We contemplate this art in the mind every time we breathe in and breathe out.

Use Dynamic Meditation to help train your mind to control piti and emphasize sukha.

Are these results different than when you use only your breath as an object of meditation?

Define each of the Key Vocabulary in your own words.

Can other people cause your suffering? ". . . make a list of people we don't like . . . [or just their most obnoxious characteristics, do we]

find a lot about those aspects of ourselves that we can't face." Pema Chodron, Start Where You Are. (Mingyur, pg. 173)

What does it mean to "Take Ownership?"

How well do you know your own path and progress?

What are the attributes of a "Stream Enterer?"

We are using the Four Supports of mindfulness as a sequence of objects for meditation as we learn the sixteen steps of Anapanasati Bhavana meditation step by step.

The object of mindfulness is referred to as the support of mindfulness . . .

1. the body,
2. feeling tone,
3. state of consciousness,
4. and contents of consciousness. [body, feelings, mind and mind-objects]

The latter type includes the virtuous and non-virtuous mental factors, perceptions, thoughts, and emotions.

What does it mean to have a religious nature? If you believe on a spiritual level, how is that different than believing on an intellectual level?

Materials Required: Hinduism, tea service

Buddhist Sutra

Lesson Title: **Pre-existing Causes of Suffering**

Lesson Number: **Fifteen**

Rationale:

This is a review of the causes of suffering, the second of the Four Noble Truths. How much of whom we are is associated with our inheritance from parents or—the nurturing from them, from our siblings and from other influential mentors during our childhood? (i.e. our conditioned mind.) Knowing the causes of our past suffering is important, but preventing further causative factors (defilements) is for Buddhism just as—or even more—important. "Not really knowing 'what is what' or the true nature of things, we act [karma is action] inappropriately in every way. Our actions are appropriate all too rarely. They are usually 'appropriate' only in terms of the values of people subject to craving, who would say that if one gets what one wants, the action must have been justified. But spiritually speaking, that action is unjustifiable." (Buddhadasa, 2005, pg. 31) When ambitions are shared they are easy to justify.

Discussion of Prior Lesson:

Doubts are often identified as a hindrance (see Lesson Thirteen) to progression toward enlightenment. "The confused form of doubt (rather than healthy skepticism) displays itself in a general inability to decide on any course of action and see it through. Instead there is uncertainty, vacillation [lack of confidence], mixed motivation, [objecting to the religious nature of Buddhism] and muddled thinking. Specifically there may be lack of certainty about the Buddha's teaching, its practice and related matters [i.e. perhaps the role of karma in your life?] This hindrance may be resolved by the increasing clarity that comes from the study and practice of the dharma, and from discussions with spiritual friends . . ." (Snelling, pg. 66)

Training Objective:

What do we carry with us from our predecessors (or from our own past lives?) Review contemporary moral behavior. Buddhism is a collection of many, some strange, teachings. Does the idea of rebirth (in the past or reincarnation in the future) affect your practice? How to analyze Piti into assada and adinava.

Materials Required: Hinduism, tea service

Motivational Statement:

The deepest mystery of all is understanding what our life force is—and how (if at all) is it connected to nature and Universe around us? "The thing that [scientists] know least about is this great mystery that is right here with each one of us all the time . . . Thus in a very real sense they fail to see what's right under their noses . . . Buddhism, however, is centrally concerned with this mystery and how to unravel it . . . It is necessary to see through the great delusion of 'I,' of the so-called person [as well as the Yoga 'Self']. Then it's a matter of finding out what is really there . . . the mystery at the heart of all things, and confront what the Christians call God, the Muslims Allah, the Hindus Brahman . . ." (Snelling, pg. 7) For many Buddhists there are images which identify a god or higher power, i.e. Amida Buddha. Does it matter?

"The Lord Buddha replied:—Ananda! The true Essence of the wonderful enlightening Mind is self-intuiting, perfectly accommodating, and pure. In its nature it has no such defilements as conceptions of deaths and rebirths, contaminations and taints, neither has it any such attribute [as a need for a belief in a god] as emptiness. All these are arbitrary conceptions that have arisen from prior false conceptions. But the original immaculate intuitive and enlightening Essence becomes defiled by the accumulating of these false conceptions and because of them manifests all the phenomena of the world . . . So those who are ignorant of the real cause build up in their mind an imaginary cause. Even the nature of space which we think of as empty is an imaginary conception. So it is with every cause, condition and nature, it is always a mental illusion cherished by sentient beings." The Surangama Sutra (Goddard, pp. 221-222)

"However, through the fading away of delusion, through the arising of wisdom, through the extinction of craving, no future rebirth takes place again." Majjhima-Nikaya (Goddard, pg. 41)

First Progressive:

When considering the life force, "Buddhists, however, hesitate to put a name to it [a god] or say anything at all about it. It is, they maintain, something that cannot be grasped by the intellect or described in words. It can only be seen directly; but that seeing brings about something truly miraculous: a total transformation, [an individual matter] no less. The veils of delusion fall away and at last the world is perceived as it really is. At the same time *a deep compassion also crystallizes:* a pure, selfless kindliness and caring born of an understanding of the unity of all beings." (Snelling pg. 7)

"Because his mind is always calm, *it is easy for the person with the heart of benevolence to enter the concentration* state of meditation. This same calm protects him from perplexity, suffering, and mental confusion when death is near and enables him to die with the peacefulness of falling asleep. The heart of benevolence can be a way of attaining enlightenment and of escaping from the cycle of transmigrations of birth and death. But even if this does not happen, the person with the heart of benevolence is certain to be born in a happy state of the *Brahma* heaven." (Mizuno, pg. 65) How does one reconcile these promises of an improved afterlife, with the teaching of no reincarnation? Is part of Enlightenment when you no longer need this kind of myth to guide the decisions of your life, and you are benevolent and of high moral character notwithstanding?

"Once we can regulate the feelings, we will be able to keep our life on the correct path. When we are foolish about the vedana, [emotions] we become slaves to materialism. This happens when we indulge in material pleasures, that is, the flavors of feelings. All the crises in this world have their origin in people not understanding the vedana, giving in to the vedana, being enamored with the vedana. The feelings entice us to act in ways that lead to *disagreements, quarrels, conflicts, [the opposite of compassion]* and eventually, war . . . because people act unwisely through the deceptions of vedana." (Buddhadasa, 1988, pp. 67-68)

It takes time to change the raw instinct of humanity into a refined and compassionate Heart. "Zen practice is authoritarian and anti-authoritarian at the same time. It is anti-authoritarian in the sense that Zen students are taught how to totally reclaim their lives and their minds. They become able to take back all the scattered power and energy they have given to the thousands of 'authorities' they have found or projected in the outside world [i.e. diety?] After years of practice, a Zen student is finally able to walk on this earth with his own two feet, to live the life given to him. He is able to laugh when he laughs, cry when he cries. He is wholehearted and without deception." (Shoshanna, pg. 10) This *personal power creates leadership ability in the Stream Enterer that can possibly be used to help solve a few of the problems facing the world.* It is the improvement of this simple daily life which was and is the concern of Buddhist teachings.

Second Progressive:

Moral codes change over the years and the context of a society and its developed culture determine what is acceptable behavior, just as courts change their judgment about pornography and obscenity. ". . . Even the highest teachings seem invariably to undergo a fall [i.e.

Vedic traditions] when they are packaged for popular consumption by a professional priestly class. Thus it was with the Upanishads. The formless Brahman became formalized and eventually came to wear an anthropomorphic face, that of the great god Brahma. And the equally elusive *Atman* that once great sages had hesitated to mention save in negative terms, that too congealed into a permanent personal entity or immortal soul, the jivatman. It was part of the Buddha's project to point out these debasements of the once noble teachings of the Upanishads, which in their original and highest forms were quite consistent with his own teachings." (Snelling, pp. 14-15)

Thus Buddhism has been adapted to different circumstances, and this explains the numerous and different interpretations of Buddhist doctrine that presently exist around the world. The uniting concept is the Four Noble Truths ". . . Buddhism teaches the everyday common-sense law that a good cause produces a good effect, a bad cause a bad effect; and both kinds of causes, suitable rewards and retributions. Even small acts of good and small acts of evil unrelated to other acts of good and evil do not disappear without a trace. Instead, each is stored up to form the intellect, personality [complexes,] customary behavior, and physical makeup of the individual committing them. They become part of the personality, which they daily alter in the direction of good or bad. Acts of good and evil are intimately related to the individual's happiness and fate. All human beings must understand that everything in this world is related according to the inflexible law of cause and effect . . . It is the basis on which Buddhism teaches the impossibility of true happiness for an individual without development in the direction of happiness for all the other people in that individual's environment." (Mizuno, pp. 95-96)

Just so you know, at this point in our study and practice ". . . full Awakening is still a long way off. As the practitioner presses on with renewed diligence, he or she passes through two more significant landmarks: once-returning (sakadagati), which is accompanied by the weakening of the fetters of sensual desire and ill-will, and non-returning (agati), in which these two fetters are uprooted altogether. [We call this stage Samadhi, absorption] The final stage of Awakening—arahatta—occurs when even the most refined and subtle levels of craving and conceit are irrevocably extinguished. At this point the practitioner—now an *arahant,* or "worthy one"—arrives at the end-point of the Buddha's teaching. With ignorance, suffering, stress, and rebirth having all come to their end, the arahant at last can . . ." (Bullitt, internet) live a life of service and contentment.

Third Progressive:

"In essence, then, Buddhism is quite simple. But simple things are often hard to fully realize, so people need all kinds of aids and supports. A vast superstructure has therefore grown up around the basic heart-core of the Buddha's teaching: mountains of philosophical speculation, a voluminous literature, monastic codes and ethical systems, histories, cosmologies, different types of ritual and meditation practice, institutions, and hierarchies. All or any of this may be helpful in enabling the sincere [Stream Enterer] to zero in upon the central issue—who or what is here, now—and to keep doing so until that great mystery has been completely realized. But it can also become a massive hindrance, entangling the all-too-errant mind in a thick undergrowth of secondary accretions [vestments, ordinations, penances] . . . books just contain more potential clutter for the attics of the mind . . . When we are fully aware and awake to [the great mystery], then we confront the very heart of the matter." (Snelling, pp. 7-8)

"Closely linked to the notion of karma is that of rebirth. This should not be confused with reincarnation, which is the view that there is a soul or subtle essence imprinted with an enduring personal stamp that transmigrates or commutes from body to body down through the eons. Buddhism of course rejects that view. What it does admit, however, is causal connection between one life and another. Thus the karmic accumulations, good and bad, of a particular life (itself the culmination of an endless series of causally-connected past lives) will condition a new birth. [Can this be distinguished from physiological/biological inheritance or instincts?] Sequences of such interconnected lives form a continuum. Nothing is handed on, however but the conditioning: the influences, the karmic charge."

Is this the potential and pre-disposition for certain actions. (Can we be pre-disposed to breaking the law and becoming a felon?)

"To clarify this notion various standard illustrations have been developed. There is the example of the flame that is passed from one candle to others. It is not exactly the same flame that carries on down the line, but it is not a different one either. Another is the cannoning of billiard balls . . . It is a single movement, [a force describable by physics] passed on through a sequence of temporary vehicles." (Snelling, pp. 59-60) This sounds almost like materialistic atheism, and many Buddhists are comfortable with that, however, many believers in Southern Asia and elsewhere accept oral teachings on faith that are more closely related to reincarnation as a reality.

"Buddhism, it should be noted, took over from earlier Indian thought the belief in karma . . . According to the Indian view, living beings pass through an endless cycle of death and rebirth . . . only by striving to do good in one's present existence can one hope to escape even greater suffering in a future life." The story of DNA and RNA are considered in Lesson Eighteen.

"Buddhism vehemently denied that there is any individual soul or personal identity that passes over from one existence to the next—to suppose there is, is simply to open the way for further craving—[though many superstitions about rebirth abound especially in the Mahayana tradition] this meant that one did not necessarily have to struggle for release from suffering within a single lifetime, but could work at the goal of salvation step by step, performing good moral and devotional acts that would insure one rebirth in more favorable circumstances in the future, and in this way gradually raising one's level of spiritual attainment." (Watson, pg. xi) If you believe in reincarnation for yourself, how does this coincide with the teaching of enlightenment—reaching nirvana when you have arrived at that point in your karmic development—when you will say as did Buddha that there is no rebirth for your present mind or body, just emptiness?

"The Rig Veda is a collection of one thousand and twenty-eight poetic hymns . . . [considered] 'the earliest document of the human mind, [for Hinduism] representing, according to most scholars, the religion of an unsophisticated age, the creation of inspired poets and seers. Many of the hymns, it is said, are simple and naïve, in praise of nature gods and goddesses; some deal with formal ritual; and others, especially the last book . . . present the results of conscious reflections on the origin of the world and of the Supreme Being . . . They embody penetrating intuitions. But no system of philosophy is presented at this stage, for mythology and poetry precede philosophy and science . . . At the center of religious life during the Vedic Age lay the ritual of sacrifice . . . completely controlled by the hereditary Brahmin priesthood . . . [they] jealously guarded the secrets of its rituals . . . At the social center of the new culture . . . there developed a caste system, [a closed hereditary designation] which divided the population up into various hierarchical groups . . . If a person lived dharmically, then, in his next incarnation, he might receive the reward of birth into a higher caste [traces of these social divides can still be found in India]." (Snelling, pp. 12-13) It is interesting to identify the roots of Buddhism, and see where Buddha's teachings diverge diametrically.

"It should be noted that modern Hindus do not regard the Buddha as an outsider to their tradition. In fact he is considered by them to be a manifestation of the great god Vishnu, one of the Hindu trinity, who descends into the world in various forms at particularly difficult times to help set things right. The Hindu system certainly derived much from Buddha's teaching, and indeed Buddhism, during the more than fifteen hundred years during which it was a significant part of the Indian spiritual scene, also derived much from Hinduism. Buddhist Tantra, for instance, has a great deal in common with the Shiva-Shakti tradition of Hindu [and Yoga] Tantra." (Snelling, pg. 29)

Meditation Practicum:

"The Buddha found what he was looking for by means of vipashyana [insight meditation] . . . a meditation session [requires] a workable degree of mental calm and concentration in preparation for vipashyana . . . the mind is opened and awareness is directed to all that enters its sphere. Often at first a great deal of hitherto submerged psychological material arises into consciousness. This is a very positive process; the darkness is becoming conscious. Old fears and phobias, traumas and repressions can now be hospitably entertained in full awareness. The meditator is neutral towards them, neither rejecting nor repressing—nor, on the other hand, identifying and hence becoming carried away by them. If merely treated to 'bare attention,' they will pass away. This is a very real and effective form of psychotherapy." It is possible and desirable to protect these results at the end of the meditation session.

The various authors quoted here seem to agree about the importance of the following: "Later, as the mind quietens down, attention may be directed in a more systematic way. Traditionally there are said to be four foundations of mindfulness: 1. Bodily activity, 2. Feelings, 3. States of mind, 4. Mental contents. [Each of which are rationalized in these Lessons in four parts (4x4=16).] Whatever enters the field of attention is observed and analyzed. Invariably it will be found to be subject to three conditions or marks: 1. Dukkha—unsatisfactoriness [suffering], 2. Anicca—impermanence, 3. Anatta (Anatman)—not self . . . '*Anatta*' is perhaps the most profound discovery that can be made in meditation: that, **search as hard as we will, we can never point to anything in ourselves that we can definitely say is the self.** Neither the body, nor the thoughts, nor the feelings can be self, for they are dukkha and anicca, unsatisfactory and impermanent. All this we can observe, while the observer, the one who knows, remains ever elusive, standing outside the field of sense perception, outside the world . . . in the end he always eludes us—always remains a great mystery. This is Anatta (anatman)." (Snelling, pp. 52-53) The very thought of there being no soul or human spirit may be a significant cause of suffering for many Western people who have been acculturated by Christianity, although they gloss over this fact. Most westerners are taught from childhood to believe in a soul, and most people agree this belief gives them comfort—thus they avoid acknowledging this as a potential source of suffering.

"Though pure, formless contemplation would seem in itself to be simple, it is not easy. Therefore . . . many types of meditation practice have been developed that use forms to a greater or lesser extent. There are, for instance, meditations involving emotional arousals and imaginative visualizations. One may perhaps try to feel *maitri, loving—kindness*, for oneself and for the whole world. Or one may picture a beautiful person and then, as an antidote to lust, visualize their body full of obnoxious secretions and by-products, as undergoing the process of aging, death, and decay. One may contemplate the qualities of the Buddha [as in Lesson Fourteen,] or the Four Noble Truths, or other doctrinal formulations. When in due course we examine Tantra, we will see how elaborate deities and mandalas are created in detail by internal visualization and then dissolved away again into nothingness. A full survey would be very extensive . . . At times it has all conspired to obscure the formless [abstract] **heart** towards which, in theory at least, it's all meant to point . . ." (Snelling, pp. 54-55) For many, "anatta" may be the most difficult aspect of Buddhism if it conflicts with other religious beliefs. (Discuss by all.) We develop the Heart as an important allegory.

Another very useful posture for meditation is: "Lying meditation: lie supine [on either side] with eyes closed, stretch both legs, do not lie prone, lie in a comfortable posture, do not lie stiffly, lay the head on a pillow with both hands on the chest, one on top of the other, do not move, do not turn the body to change the posture, continue the first posture till the extremity [discomfort is too intense then move to] sitting meditation."

"We can lie in whatever position we feel convenient but the significant point is that we lie with eyes closed and mindfully note inhalation and exhalation at the tip of the nose only . . . At the same time, we chant 'Bud' when feeling inbreathing air touching the upper part of the nose tip and 'Dho' when feeling out-breathing air touching the lower part of the nostril and the upper lip . . . keep chanting . . . The reason why we chant at the same time as we realize the breathing is that chanting empowers concentration to be able to fight with the power of defilements. We will not be easily enamored and fall into the unwholesome power of defilements when the mind is touched by external emotions." It is beneficial to understand the "why" of chanting. Perhaps our Hearts are changed in subtle ways, such as being more receptive.

"To change the posture can be done like when practicing by other postures . . . till the utmost of suffering . . . Understand well why we have to change the posture . . . due to utter suffering [analogous to our suffering in life.]" (Wee, pp. 151-152)

"If we do not practice till the highest limit of suffering, we will not understand how suffering is since we do not feel the suffering that occurs. This is the reason why we have to practice till the utmost of suffering. [This practice is not universally accepted.] Another reason is that to practice dogged perseverance till the utmost of suffering is one way to burn down defilements [this is a Theravada equivalent of a mandala offering.] . . . We have to practice till the utmost of suffering of that posture—we do as the Lord Buddha stated: 'you all; come to be Bhikkhu. The Dhamma is well expounded. Lead a sublime life to perform righteousness till the utmost of suffering by the right way'." (Wee, pg. 89) Not all sects of Buddhism subscribe to this severe ascetic interpretation, and most eschew physical suffering during meditation as a distraction. However, this Theravada tradition offers an explanation of the "why" some tolerable suffering is useful, especially to learn how Piti can change. Why is suffering useful, when the objective is to eliminate and promote the "cessation of suffering?"

When we work on 'calming the mind-conditioner' during our breathing ". . . We make the citta-sankhara, the Vedana (feelings), calm and peaceful . . . either by samadhi—a higher level of concentration; or by the wisdom—panna [insight]—method. We aim at the one pinnacled mind that has sati or Nibbana as its object. Panna realizes the true nature (characteristics, qualities, conditions) of all things to understand how piti arises and what will cause it to cease." This is step eight.

"Another wisdom method is to contemplate [insight] the *assada and adinava* of piti. Asada is an element's attractive quality, its charm that deliciously tempts the heart. [In this case we are getting directly to the emotions that relate to craving, greed, envy, ambition and desires.] Piti has an enchanting flavor [as we have already noticed.] Adinava is an element's unhealthy consequences [think of the 108 defilements.] The adinava of piti is the fact that it excites and disturbs, that it drives away tranquility and is the foe of vipassana. Once we realize this, piti dissolves [like turning on a light to expose and foil a thief.] This is how to drive off piti with the panna technique . . . At this point, the mind is able to regulate the feelings. It has developed the kind of mastery and self-control where the feelings no longer have the power to drag us this way or that." (Buddhadasa, 1988, pp. 65-67) Putting together the desires with the consequences can prevent further suffering, and can we burn off past suffering by seeing it, exposing its roots?

Biographical Sketch:

There are many schools of thought, so to speak, that come under the umbrella of Buddhism. I prefer to think of this as a problem of success, rather than a problem of failure. Consider that the Druid and early Native American teachings which were more or less contemporary with the development of Buddhism, by contrast, haven't been so influential or well preserved. Hinduism is possibly more fragmented than Buddhism. "Counter-movements have also sprung up periodically that have sought to sweep all the accumulated accretions and superstructures aside and go back to the basic essentials of pure formless contemplation with a minimum of superfluous trappings. In Tibet (and in medieval India too) there was Mahamudra and Dzogchen, and in China Ch'an, which became known as Zen when it was propagated in Japan. Meditators also occasionally encounter rddhis (Pali, iddhis). These are paranormal powers, like clairvoyance and telepathy, the ability to multiply one's body or transform one's shape, to levitate or walk on water, to recall former lives and such . . . magic . . . generally speaking [it is] thought to be in bad taste to boast of occult powers or to show them off, particularly for worldly gain . . . The special danger they present [aside from the aspect of fraud and self-delusion] is that common to all forms of power: they are open to misuse, may inflate the ego, and may also sidetrack the meditator and cause him/her to forget his main concern: nirvana." (Snelling, pg. 55)

"The Buddha was born in the ancient village of Lumbini—Sanskrit for the lovely—in the Southwestern part of the Terai region of Nepal at the foothills of the Churia mountain range . . . At the time of Buddha's birth, there was a grove of sala trees there. The site of the birthplace remained unknown until 1886, when a German archeologist, Alois Fuhrer, discovered the Asoka pillar located there."

"In Buddhist tradition the Buddha was born at Lumbini 563 BC [elsewhere 623 BC-543BC . . .] When he was born an immeasurable light appeared throughout the world. His body and that of his mother were washed with two streams of water, one cold and the other hot, falling from the sky. (The hot water symbolized the harshness of asceticism, the cold water the coolness of Enlightenment) . . . The future Buddha, once born, looked in all four directions. (The *scanning of the four quadrants*, according to the commentator, meant unobstructed knowledge.) He saw no one who was his equal. He then took seven steps and stopped. (The seven steps symbolized he would acquire the seven Enlightenment factors.) He spoke the following words with a bull-like voice: 'I will be the chief one, the supreme one, the eldest one in the world. This cycle of birth will be my last. There will not be another existence for me'. (Even the 'bull-like' speech is significant as setting in motion the irreversible Dhamma wheel. The statement that there would not be another existence signified the 'lion's roar' of the coming Nibbana of the arahant.) The future Buddha was born with the thirty-two Brahmanical distinctive marks of a great man, for instance, a bright, golden complexion, and blue eyes." (Inthisan, pp. 20-21) These myths sound like stories for children, but more than anything indicate the cultural tendency in India to exaggerate details in favor of important personages. These myths are mere curiosities along side Buddhism, not an essential element of the dharma.

"As an archeological site Lumbini is significant today for the Asoka pillar; the sacred pool of Pokarani; the temple of May Devi, built, in turn, over one of Great King Asoka's four stupas; the stone presumably placed by Asoka to mark the exact spot where the Buddha was born; the manyu stupas; the monasteries; and the bas-relief of May Devi giving birth." (Ithisan, pg. 23) Giving this location, or other historical places, a special accord is at times a way of "holding-on" when Buddhist Practitioners might think twice about finding ways of "letting-go." Or is this just a matter of perspective?

Some scholars teach that Buddha was a reformer rather than an innovator in ethical and philosophical terms. "The . . . improbability of a great Teacher breaking away completely from the highest and deepest thought of his nation and his age, is very great. The great Teacher is always a reformer as well as an innovator; and to reform is to go back to an ideal which had been forgotten, or otherwise obscured. The chances are, then, that Buddha, who was unquestionably one of the greatest of all moral teachers, went back from what was corrupt and degenerate in the thought and the consequent practice of his age to what was pure and spiritual." http://www.sacred-texts.com/bud/cob/cob07.htm

Reading for the Day:

In the mahamudra view: ". . . awakened wisdom which manifests in the three buddha bodies (the truth body, enjoyment body, and emanation body), is the mind's natural condition. However, our karmically created mistaken conceptions and negative emotions defile the mind's inherent purity and obscure us from our Buddha-nature. Enlightenment is in fact already inherent in our experience, if we can only recognize it. Concentration and special insight meditation lay the foundation for recognizing this awakened wisdom. The teachings of Buddha-nature were characteristic of the Yogacara school in India [with its roots in Hinduism] . . ." (Brown, pg. 7)

"The [Stream Enterer] now wishes to 'seek only what is rare' [as with the wish granting-gem] and wants only that which will bring enlightenment, the Dharma teachings. Furthermore . . . we yearn more and more for direct experience of the truth, so much so that all else loses importance . . . we are not satisfied with ordinary un-virtuous mental states and behaviors." (Brown, pg. 61) However, "Only when [we] realize that the final aim of the teaching is to eradicate all suffering will desire grow into a deep longing [quite different than one with attachment, i.e. lust;] [when we] reflect upon the teachings 'as if hearing words that could cure a disease.' The more the benefits of spiritual practice are realized, the less likely the resistance to the process . . . These reflections must be purified. Purified reflections are those that are capable of grasping preciousness." (Brown, pg. 55)

Protecting:

"This is what I heard," review by both Stream Enterers and teacher.

Additional Teaching:

"Ananda! When you come to know where illusion has its rise, then you will clearly understand these universally false causes and conditions . . . And furthermore, if ignorant people had only true nature from which to make deductions, what would they have to talk about, anyway? Therefore I show you this interpretation in order to have you see clearly that at the base of the five-sense ingredients [aggregates] there are always false conceptions."

"Ananda! Regarding your body . . . You ought to know that your present body is your first manifestation in substance of your false conceptions that have been accumulated in your [DNA] karma. It may be called the first false conception of '*firmness*'."

"Again, in likeness to the trembling that comes to the feet when one stands on a lofty place [fear of heights,] so in the presence of causes and conditions that can influence your body, there is corresponding reaction in the body . . . a pleasant one . . . when propitious and to your advantage, and an unpleasant one that rises when the causes and conditions are disadvantageous or painful. This may be called the second false conception of '*discrimination*' or 'knowledge'."

"By means of conceptions [theorizing] your physical body is always in bondage to the thinking mind, and this is because there is an affinity between the discriminating mind and the body . . . For instance: when you are awakening, it simply means that you have begun to think again; when you are sleeping you dream according to some unconscious mental strain or passion that is agitating your mind. This may be called the third false conception of '*accommodation*' or 'response' or 'activity'."

"As the process of changes in everything is forever going on, there are secret and unconscious displacements throwing things out of balance [aging] . . . all these changing causes and conditions and reactions are but the shadows of the activities of your own mind and your own mind is but a shadow of Essential Mind as defiled by the mind's activities. This may be called the fourth false conception of '*secrecy*' and 'silence'."

"Then by your practice of Dhyana there comes into your mind an enlightening essential point of tranquility and stability, and you take that point of tranquility as a permanently abiding place . . . But is that true? . . . It is in likeness to the current of a deep river which, as you glance at it, seems to be quiet and motionless but in fact is steadily and relentlessly moving onward . . . This dependence upon a partial state of tranquility as being the perfect attainment is the fifth refined and concentrated thought of 'topsy-turviness' of mind. The Surangama Sutra—Sixth Chapter." (Goddard, pp. 222-224)

Suffering begins in our lives when we have cravings and fail to follow virtuous ethical practices. "As Patrul Rinpoche says in *Heart Advice on the Two Ethic*s (spiritual ethics and worldly ethics) . . . 'If you desire to enjoy happiness in this life and the next, don't keep talking about others' qualities, but watch yourself and examine your own path. This is the entire means of achieving both a spiritual and worldly accomplishments.' As the Buddha himself said: 'Seeing myself in others and others in myself, Whom would I harm, whom could I exploit?' The moral self-discipline of sila [that which cools or calms] involves training through familiarization and repetition, which is what we Buddhists call practice. If a bear can learn to ride a bicycle, as I have seen at a circus, just imagine what a human being can accomplish! All the various kinds of vows and precepts in Buddhism are training guides or spiritual exercises to be used in taming and refining our own rough, intransigent tendencies toward greed, anger, meanness, cruelty, and jealousy. They are not whips or scourges to be applied to others, but like mirrors to better see and know ourselves . . . The virtuous man or woman is the very heart of every society. This is universal law—truth itself. Character is at the root of action." (Surya das, pg. 57)

Sharing Merit:

Rejoicing In Others' Merit (Saying Sadhu)

Buddhist Sutra

Lesson Title: **Pre-existing Causes of Suffering**

Lesson Number: **Fifteen**

Key Vocabulary: maitri, Anatman, mandalas, iddhis, stupa, Lumbini, four quadrants, Tantra, Anicca, afterlife, Brahma, condition a new birth, assada, adinava, vedic traditions, firmness, discrimination, accommodation, sila

Define each of the Key Vocabulary in your own words.

Assignment: "The mind is opened and awareness is directed to all that enters its sphere." What does this mean?
Feelings must be understood, by unmasking the piti and 'burning off' emotional baggage.

Practice lying meditation, and note your impressions using your breath as an object.
Practice and understand the two aspects of Piti—assada tempting pleasures and momentary thrills. Adivana—the unhealthy consequences i.e. losing at gambling.

What do we carry with us from our ancestors (or our own past lives?)

How many of our emotions are related to our body chemistry? and how can we utilize this fact to our advantage?

What are peculiar requirements of contemporary moral behavior in Western society?

Recall the way to create confidence in Buddhism by developing the three wisdoms:

1. Wisdom resulting from listening/ studying . . .
2. Wisdom resulting from reflection (protecting) . . .
3. Wisdom resulting from mental development . . . from practicing the Teachings

How has each of these been a factor in your practice.

Buddhism is a collection of many, some strange, teachings. Does the idea of rebirth (even reincarnation) affect our practice?

Why do we chant at the same time as we realize the breathing? ("Bud"—in; "Dho"—out)

What is your notion of happiness?

Describe (don't interpret) and record the images (if any) you see during meditation.

Materials Required: Spontaneity, A piece of art paper to draw on. Tea service

Buddhist Sutra

Lesson Title: **Alleviation of Suffering**

Lesson Number: **Sixteen**

Rationale:

This is a review in more depth about the third of the Four Noble Truths. "How to cease suffering is very essential in Buddhism because cessation of suffering is the utmost goal in Buddhism . . . In order to cease suffering, we have to know the means to do so. Training our mind to be concentrated, well established to develop wisdom is the direct means to extinction of all defilements, but it takes time." (Wee, pg. 69)

It is important to review and expand on the material covered in Lesson Five.

Discussion of Prior Lesson:

Chanting empowers concentration to fight with the corrosive power of defilements. "Please remember that your notions of happiness may be very dangerous. The Buddha said happiness can only be possible in the here and now. So go back and examine deeply your notions and ideas of happiness. You may recognize that the conditions of happiness that are already there in your life are enough. Then happiness can be instantly yours." (Hanh, pg. 205)

"It is clearly important that we take advantage of this ability to control the feelings for the rest of our lives. This tetrad [5-8] has been included in the practice of anapanasati because of the great power and importance of the Vedana." (Buddhadasa, 1988, pg. 68) We at least know how to develop the mind's ability to be independent of feeling and to have control over the Vedana. "Once we fully know the various mental states and conditions, both positive and negative, then we can put the citta into any state that is appropriate or desirable." (ibid. pg. 74)

Training Objective:

Emotional blackmail, and the straw-man arguments. Hindrances—that come ironically from success, as suffering comes ironically from joy. The role of religion. The status of the Mind in step nine. Role of craving and defilements.

Materials Required: Spontaneity, A piece of art paper to draw on. Tea service

Motivational Statement:

"The facts of our lives, when we are able to know them, will free us from the torment we are in. When we can bear reality thoroughly, suffering is over . . . Suffering is what we add to pain." (Shoshanna, pg. 13)

"Psychologically speaking, when an individual is living under the pressure to constantly achieve, a subtle message is communicated—that he or she is not good enough, not loveable just as they are. Love and value must be earned. Of course this is never experienced as love or true nourishment. No matter how much praise or love such an individual seems to receive, deep down they feel that it is only their achievements that are being cared for, not them." Each day is a new day to love the humanity in each other.

"As we practice [Buddhism] we grow to realize that **we are sufficient as we are,** more than sufficient, whole and complete . . . As we return to the moment . . . we are returning to the essence of life itself. Daily life itself is complete. It deserves full attention." (Shoshanna, pp. 39-40) Understanding this is a way of acknowledging the buddhahood inside each of us.

"People in general lack reflection and do not exercise their mindfulness and wisdom to be aware of the truths as they are. They, thus, do not believe in nor understand what the Buddha discovered and taught. To understand well about suffering, we need to ponder over the truth of [our] lives whether it is as the Buddha taught: life is all suffering." (Wee, pg. 63) And work to change this circumstance. To what extent is this simply a gross oversimplification?

First Progressive:

We focus on suffering only to the extent that we aim at a target, we must know the problem in order to solve it and we learn early on that all our friends and family members suffer from similar suffering from similar causes. "All of our lives are suffering. It is true like the Teachings of the Lord Buddha . . . All lives on the earth are overborne by suffering in the aspect of impermanence (uncertainty, constant flux), suffering (difficulty, physical and mental discomfort, unsatisfactory) and state of non-self [everything we are has a cause.] These are called the ***Three Characteristics***. They are common characteristics of all lives." (Wee, pg. 64) *When we develop compassion to help others and relieve their suffering*, (if only by sharing merit) *we are indeed relieving our own suffering.*

"As the Awakened One, Buddha exemplified to millions of his followers a living Truth, a dynamic wisdom, and an *active compassion*. It was these qualities which inspired hope and courage in believers who were asked to face the stark reality of man's finitude and his inevitable involvement in suffering. Without the *powerful affirmation* of his own example, nothing but despair could follow from the pessimistic premises concerning existence which Buddhism takes as its starting point." (de Bary, xvii) To what extent is the premise that we are all suffering—therefore we need to be Buddhists—a *straw-man argument*. Are there other valid formulas or religious systems that are effective at relieving suffering? Is there more to life than suffering? Of course there is, but even the joy we feel from moment to moment is impermanent, and for people unwilling to change and adapt to new circumstances, even this joy has its antithesis in suffering. Is this a form of *emotional blackmail*? To make us think we are suffering so a priesthood can grow and live off our donations, keep control and gain power over our emotional as well as social lives? Compare the history of Buddhism with the many Christian faiths where a clergy dominate the membership. Buddhism is not, and never was a cult that supports a single well-rewarded charismatic leader, because it is an individual journey, and there is nothing for a hierarchy to gain whether we believe, practice or not.

"Compassion is reciprocal. As you develop your own mental and emotional stability and extend that stability through a compassionate understanding of others and dealing with them in a kind, empathetic way, your own intentions or aspirations will be fulfilled more quickly and easily. Why? Because *if you treat others compassionately*—with the understanding that they have the same desire for happiness and the same desire to avoid unhappiness that you do—then the people around you feel a sense of attraction, a sense of wanting to help you as much as you help them. They listen more closely to you, and develop a sense of trust and respect. People who might once have been adversaries begin to treat you with more respect and consideration, facilitating your own progress in completing difficult tasks. Conflicts resolve themselves more easily, and you'll find yourself advancing more quickly in your career, beginning new relationships without the usual heartaches, and even starting a family or improving your existing family relationships more easily—all because you've charged your batteries through shinay meditation and extended that charge through developing a kinder, more understanding, and more empathetic relationship with others. In a sense, compassion practice demonstrates the truth of interdependence in action [and the law of cause and effect.] The more openhearted you become toward others, the more openhearted they become toward you." (Mingyur, pg. 229) When do we start this process? Make a vow and start today.

Proverb: "Kindness is like snow, it beautifies anything it covers." (Wellpage)

Second Progressive:

Is acting out a way to alleviate suffering? As a teacher I have on numerous occasions observed students with emotional problems act out, be defiant and fail to thrive both emotionally and intellectually, this inadvertently signals the problems from which they suffer. Harsh punishment and scolding is not the answer for the well trained teacher or parent, there are always other, better choices. Certainly corporal punishment has gone by the way because of ethical "enlightenment," as we have learned numerous ways to control our classrooms with positive motivation, alternative consequences and appropriate interventions. This same technology—finding alternative choices—works in the workplace to make our human environments more effective. Identifying and implementing better choices can be the saving grace for our most intimate relationships as well.

Where do these choices come from? Buddhism gives us a menu of sorts. "Another point concerning concentration we should know and understand is hindrances (*Nivarana*) which are obstacles preventing us from attaining virtue. We do not succeed in training mind to be concentrated because hindrances—as various mind states—obstruct mind. We have to fight to defeat unwholesome mind states, we will then be able to practice mind to be one-pointed. There are six hindrances:

1. Sensual desire; pleasure and satisfaction in sensuality:
2. Ill will; hatred, malevolence, aversion:
3. Sloth and torpor; stolidity and drowsiness:
4. Distraction and remorse; restlessness of mind and anxiety:
5. Doubt, uncertainty:
6. Ignorance; lack of knowledge, delusion." (Wee, pg. 37) (Also pg. 263) If these issues are strong, of course we don't meditate.

"How do you 'kill' a hindrance? You 'watch it to death.' You bathe it regularly in the fiery light of awareness and it melts away. You often don't notice hindrances dying. While you are doing the awareness process there is a sense of, 'It's still there. It's still there. When will it ever go away?' But one day you say, 'You know, I haven't seen such-and-such around lately. I wonder why? By George, it's gone at least!' We often see it when it is present and see it when it is gone, but fail to notice that 'going away' stage in which it is becoming weaker and less frequent." Overcoming a mental phase is like gaining maturity.

"The hindrances are eliminated in three stages: Stage one—is observing moral and ethical principles and restraining the senses. During this stage, gross expression of these tendencies is prevented from arising and the senses become relatively calm. This is the stage in which you employ mindful reflection by consciously thinking about the deep nature of what is meeting your senses.

"Stage two—is attaining jhana, during which the five hindrances are in abeyance. At this stage, conscious thought about the nature of your perceptions does not take place. Your senses are turned inward and recognition of the fundamental nature of your perceptions is wordless and automatic."

"Stage three—is final and complete. It is the attainment of full enlightenment. In this stage, all underlying tendencies are uprooted from the mind." (Gunaratana, pp. 79-80)

As a contrast to these "don'ts" consider the **Six Perfections: 1. giving [which is the basis for compassion], 2. ethical behavior, 3. patience, 4. diligence, 5. contemplation and 6. special insight.** These comprise the standard training of a bodhisattva, as found in numerous sources . . ." (Brown, pg. 484) From this raw information we add experience and construct wisdom.

Take a piece of art paper and draw a situation that is joyful and rewarding.

"What we must do is practice looking at the subjective side, the mind. We have to look at the doer [karmic side, action, to make positive changes in our lives] more than the recipient . . . So it is essential that we practice looking at the side [of the mind] which puts us in the advantageous position [rather than being a victim or fatalist,] the side which has the upper hand—the subjective side." (Buddhadasa, 1999, pg. 65) We can expect to receive inspiration, and solutions to our problems during or shortly after meditation.

Third Progressive:

What is suffering all about? "In ordinary conditions, human beings turn to religion when they suffer from illness, poverty, unhappy love affairs, domestic problems, [death of a loved one] or trouble at work. When they are [apparently] free of dissatisfactions and [overt] suffering and in good mental and physical condition, they do not seek help from religion . . . Even those with reason to worry cover up by means of such things as sports, amusements, drink, or [sexual relations]. Indeed, much of the dissatisfaction and suffering of the world is solved [at least temporarily] and eliminated by nonreligious means . . . Furthermore, social advances and the institutions of social-security systems have reduced general poverty by raising the ordinary standard of living and making daily life more comfortable . . . Just as in the past, [people] continue to suffer and die from sicknesses that are either difficult or impossible to cure . . . How can such anxiety be relieved?" (Mizuno, pg. 94) In an important way, all religions intend to relieve suffering and enhance our emotional satisfaction; does it always work? What is the role of the Sangha for the elimination of suffering in Buddhism.

How can our emotions be beneficial rather than obstacles? As we move past the study of emotions (vedana) to the phases of the mind, what are the most important considerations? "This expansion of our emotions [i.e. happiness, jhana] is a religious feeling, which does not need a belief in God to be expressed. Although yoga has traditionally been theistic, it comes from a Hindu tradition that does not discriminate between believers and atheists. Since yoga pre-dates Hinduism, it is not tied to any one religion, so is applicable to any religious faith, or none at all. [Buddhism accepts many of its disciplines.] A belief in God is not necessary for the practice of yoga [nor for Buddhism] but . . . one of the results of yoga is a profound feeling that I can only call religious. Yoga induces in me (and others) a feeling of sacred, by giving us the experience of a unity, an oneness, with everything else. Since this feeling of oneness is difficult to achieve, [perhaps even more difficult to lose,] those who manage to find it hold yoga in the highest esteem." (Forstater, pg. 37) Two goals of yoga are to reduce the causes and impact of suffering. In this respect yoga and Buddhism have in common these important goals.

Our emotions influence the way we perceive realities as well as react, thus these determine our ability to perceive reality objectively. "Looking within, examining all things within ourselves—is essential for an understanding of Dhamma or Buddhism. Failure to look at things in the right way can be a barrier to understanding, as when two people disagree because one of them has failed to look at a question in a certain important way and so neither is in a position to understand the point that another person is making. Disagreement is usually caused by two parties looking at the matter in question in two different ways." (Buddhadasa, 1999, pg. 59) This is like missing the train at the station.

Meditation Practicum:

We have six senses with which to "view" the world. "The technical name for using the sense of sight [associated with right view] as a means for resting the mind is 'form meditation.' But don't let the name scare you. Form meditation is actually very simple. In fact, we practice it unconsciously every day whenever we stare at a computer screen or watch a traffic light. When we lift this unconscious process to the level of active awareness, deliberately resting our attention upon a specific object, the mind becomes very peaceful, very open, and very relaxed . . . [recall from Lesson Two, meditation using the Buddha icon.] It's possible to focus on mental forms—objects recalled simply in your imagination [or memory.]" This is engaging our sixth sense.

"Whatever object you choose, you'll probably notice that it has two characteristics: shape and color . . . The idea is simply to rest your attention on either its color or its shape, engaging the mental faculty only to the point of barely recognizing the object. Nothing more than that. The moment you bring attention to the object, you are aware . . . Keep your focus loose, with just enough attention to hold the bare awareness of the object you're looking at. Don't try to make anything happen or try to force your mind to relax. Simply think, Okay, whatever happens, happens. This is meditation. This is what

I'm doing. It doesn't have to be anything more than that . . . And when you recognize that your mind has drifted away from the object of focus, just bring your attention back to the object." (Mingyur, pp. 149-150)

"Mental images resulting from mindfulness on breathing are most important because mindfulness on breathing is the fundamental meditation exercise in Buddhism and it suits everybody's character. If we exercise meditation by insight development, we will experience mental images also but they are called 'imperfections of insight' which are defilements of insight or immature insight that makes us misunderstand that we are enlightened. This prevents practitioners from making progress in insight knowledge. There are ten imperfections of insight namely: 1. illumination, *luminous aura* 2. knowledge *(trance)* 3. rapture (*unprecedented joy*) 4. tranquility (*calmness*) 5. bliss (*pleasure*) 6. conviction, *assurance, resolution* 7. exertion, *well-exerted energy* 8. established mindfulness 9. equanimity 10. delight . . . This prevents practitioners from resuming the practice because they would think that they achieve the final goal of the practice . . . Do not pay too much attention to them, just realize how they are and resume the practice. If we do not know about this, they will be hindrances, mislead us and make us misunderstand." (Wee, pp. 43-44) Thus the very success and beauty we perceive during meditation can be a hindrance if we cease the practice prematurely.

Follow this Guided meditation: "The great Zen Buddhist Thich Nhat Hanh [Vietnamese] says . . . keep a half-smile on your face. Breathe slowly and deeply, following each breath, becoming one with each breath. Then let go of everything. Imagine yourself as a pebble that has been thrown into a river. The pebble sinks through the water effortlessly; detached from everything, it falls by the shortest distance possible, finally sinking to the bottom, the point of perfect rest. You are like a pebble that has let itself fall into the river, letting go of everything. At the center of your being is your breath. You don't need to know the length of time it takes to reach the point of complete rest on the bed of fine sand beneath the water. But when you feel yourself resting like a pebble that has settled [weightlessly] on the riverbed, that is the point when you begin to find your own rest, your own peace. In that peace you are no longer pushed or pulled by anything." (Forstater, pg. 83)

"Our study of the third tetrad of anapanasati is concerned with the citta, the mind-heart, and is known as cittanupassana (contemplation of citta) . . . Many different states of mind have arisen since the beginning of the practice. We must observe the state of the mind at each step. What arises in the citta? What is the condition of the mind now? What are the mind's characteristics at this moment?" We observe the mind and its phases in the very moment of its existence. (This is step nine.)

Raga—"There are many different characteristics of the mind to contemplate . . . whether the mind has *lust (raga*) or is free of lust—sexual, or of money, jewelry, gold, food, housing, and possessions is also called raga . . . lust for love [from others . . .] If there is lust, then thoroughly contemplate its presence to distinguish what kind of lust it is . . . If there is no lust, then contemplate its absence. Breathe in and breathe out while experiencing the actual state of mind in this moment."

Dosa—"The next characteristic of mind to contemplate is *dosa (anger, hatred, aversion)* . . . Any dislike in the mind is dosa; it can even arise from within, without any external object [self-loathing or lack of self-esteem . . .] When the mind is oppressed, irritated, offended, or resentful, it is called dosa. If the citta is free of anger and hatred, then know that state. This is the second characteristic to observe."

Moha—"The third characteristic to observe is *moha (delusion and confusion).* Moha is feeling infatuated with something because of not knowing that object as it really is [as with a new acquaintance.] Doubt, hope, delusion, expectation—we cannot avoid dwelling on it. When one kind of thought or another ferments in the mind, it is called moha . . . If citta is empty of delusion, then contemplate its absence. Always contemplate this state of mind while breathing in and breathing out."

A feeling of wanting, grasping is a sense of raga. Dosa does not like, does not want, it is negative, pushing away. Moha is ignorant, it does not know what is wrong and right, good and evil, running in circles.

"Next, we need to know whether the mind is distracted or undistracted . . . We contemplate the mind's character while breathing in and breathing out. We practice in order to know all types of citta . . . Is the mind sharper than usual, more satisfying than usual, higher than usual? If so, contemplate it. If not, it is a common state of mind. Contemplate this pair [superior or common citta] while breathing in and breathing out."

"Another pair of states to consider is whether or not this mind is supreme and unsurpassed . . . where there is nothing better?" Or are there finer things yet to come? Have we achieved final satisfaction that of an arahant? "If there is this highest mind, contemplate it clearly in order to understand it. Breathe in and breathe out with this kind of awareness." That superior mind exists in each of us, but possibly we have not come to accept it or utilize it consistently.

"The next pair is whether or not the mind is concentrated. Is it or is it not in samadhi? . . . Know whether the mind is concentrated or not while breathing in and breathing out." Compare this to watching "attention span" in active children. Some can only manage to focus for a minute, while a few can be absorbed in a project for hours.

"The last pair [of phases] is to see if the mind has been liberated, if it is empty of attachment, not grasping or clinging to anything, or if it is not yet liberated and still clinging to something. Does the mind have attachment or not? . . . Right now, is there anything arresting the mind or is it free? Whatever the case, know it clearly. Breathe in and out with this awareness, Make it as distinct as possible . . . By practicing like this, we learn to know ourselves and the kinds of thoughts that are typical for us . . . Our primary aim, however, is to know our mind as completely as possible." (Buddahadasa, 1988, pp.70-74) Is it useful to think of these as phases?

Biographical Sketch:

"The Mahayana movement appears to have begun in India around the first or second century BC. In part it was probably a reaction against the great emphasis upon monastic life that marked earlier Buddhism and against the arid psychological and metaphysical speculations that characterize much of early Buddhist philosophy. It aimed to open up the religious life to a wider proportion of the population, to accord a more important role to lay believers, to give more appealing expression to the teachings and make them more readily accessible." (Watson, pg. xii)

"The Madhyamaka School: This was founded by Nagarjuna (c. 150 A.D.) a south Indian philosopher of genius whose birth was, according to some, predicted by the Buddha himself and who is also reputed to have received instruction from the nagas (serpent kings) in their place beneath the sea. His major work is the 'Verses on the Middle Way'." (also Garfield)

"In the great tradition set by the Buddha, Nagarjuna devised new ways for driving us into the arms of the inconceivable. Rather than propounding a philosophy as such, he advocated a method, the technical term for which is dialectic, which if rigorously applied would reveal the inherent absurdity of all propositions. In this way the practitioner would ideally be liberated from all views. 'The right teaching is the Middle Path devoid of name and character where no speech or thought can reach. It transcends all points of dispute . . .' Dependent origination is also important in Nagarjuna's philosophy, and he connects it with shunyata. To see that nothing exists 'from its own side,' but always in dependence, that nothing is absolute but that all is relative: this is to see emptiness." Compare to the concept of absolute truth.

"Nagarjuna's philosophy has often been compared to the modern linguistic philosophy of Ludwig Wittgenstein. At the end of this great work, the Tractatus Logico-Philosophicus, Wittgenstein argues that his philosophical arguments [of his earliest period] are self-annihilating. [Later, W. just thought his early philosophizing was simply mistaken and he showed a better way by teaching about meaning and language games.] . . . Nagarjuna is similarly trying in his dialectical way to lead us beyond words and concepts to a new level of consciousness." (Snelling, pp. 89-90) Suggesting there is an ". . . inherent absurdity of all propositions" is perhaps a little cynical, and a rather unfortunate over-generalization. It suggests that perhaps one needs to find some new friends, rather than any particular fact about our ordinary use of language.

"It has to be borne in mind that in general a word can have several different meanings according to the context. [Based on its use.] Two principal cases can be recognized: 1) language referring to physical things, which is spoken by the average person [often referred to as 'ordinary language'] and 2) language referring to mental things, psychological language, Dharma language, which is spoken by people who know Dharma (higher Truth, buddha's teaching.).'birth' refers to the arising of the idea 'I am . . . In everyday language 'path' refers to a physical road; in Dharma language it refers to . . . the Noble Eightfold Path . . . Anyone who fails to grasp this point will never succeed in understanding anything of the Buddha's teaching." (Buddhadasa, 2005, pp. 201-203)

Reading for the Day:

"For the sake of putting in order one's own mental continuum it is necessary to listen. If you desire to know how to eradicate [mental] defilements, which are like the evil deeds of a criminal, then when you have looked into the mirror, you'll know how. When you listen to the Dharma, the arising conditions of your own undefined practice will appear to you in the mirror of the Dharma. At that moment, you will generate a longing in your mind. This is known as your own mental continuum [a Stream Enterer] going according to the Dharma. Hereafter, because you are now capable [both] of removing faults and bringing about the benefit, you must follow the teachings." (Kunga Tendzin, pg. 45 as quoted by Brown, pg. 54)

"We know well how to do bodily wholesome deeds [no killing, no stealing, no sexual misconduct.] The next step is to do mental wholesome deeds which are the ultimate wholesomeness in Buddhism [giving praise and sharing, forgiveness and taking right for righteousness.] The purpose of Buddhist Teachings is to train mind to be free from all defilements. In order to do internal wholesome deeds, we need to have knowledge on religious essence which provides right practices through body and mind. If we do not have such knowledge, we will tend to practice wrongly [too] easily. In this regard, studying the Buddhist Teachings to train mind is very important . . . [using] Concentration Meditation and Insight Meditation. Therefore, we have to study the Teachings that will be fundamental for the practice." (Wee, pp. 24-25) Step by step we are learning how to and the importance of becoming free from all defilements.

Protecting:

"This is what I heard," review by both Stream Enterers and teacher.

Now at the end of the lesson, turn the page of your drawing, look through to the light at what you have drawn, see and draw the inverse showing impermanence and/or suffering from the same situation. "When, by following the Buddhist method, we come to know things aright, to see clearly that they are all impermanent, unsatisfactory and not selves, that there is really nothing about things that might make it worth attaching ourselves to them, then there will immediately come about a slipping free from the controlling power of those things." (Buddhadasa, 2005, pg. 29)

Additional Teaching:

"Why is there no obtaining of Nirvana? Because Nirvana is the realm of no 'thingness.' If the ego-soul of personality was an enduring entity it could not obtain Nirvana. It is only because personality is made up of elements that pass away, that personality may attain Nirvana. So long as man is seeking highest perfect Wisdom, he is still abiding in the realm of consciousness. If he is to realize Nirvana, he must pass beyond consciousness. In highest samadhi having transcended consciousness, he has passed beyond discrimination and knowledge, beyond the reach of change or fear; he is already enjoying Nirvana. The perfect understanding of this and the patient acceptance of it is the highest perfect Wisdom that is Prajna-paramita. All the Buddhas of the past, present and future having attained highest samadhi, awake to find themselves realizing Prajna-paramita. Maha-Prajna-Paramita-Hridaya." (Goddard, pg. 86)

In chapter 17 we return to discussing the importance of faith as in chapter 2. "Almost all religions are built on faith—rather 'blind' faith it would seem. But in Buddhism emphasis is laid on 'seeing', knowing, understanding, and not on faith, or belief. In Buddhist texts there is a word saddha which is usually translated as 'faith' or 'belief'. But saddha is not 'faith' as such, but rather 'confidence' born out of conviction. In popular Buddhism and also in ordinary usage in the texts the word saddha, it must be admitted, has an element of 'faith' in the sense that it signifies devotion to the Buddha, the Dhamma (Teaching) and the Sangha (The Order)." (Walpola, pg. 8) In order to remove suffering we need to have this kind of confidence based on practical success.

Sharing Merit:

Rejoicing In Others' Merit (Saying Sadhu)

Buddhist Sutra

Lesson Title: Alleviation of Suffering

Lesson Number: Sixteen

Key Vocabulary: internal wholesome deeds, straw-man argument, emotional blackmail, nagas, dialectic, spontaneity, reflection, dosa, raga, moha, nivarana, cittanupassana, pranja-paramita, saddha, phases

Assignment: Every time you begin practice, start with long breaths . . . each session is new . . . then short breaths etc . . . each step depends on the previous one until you arrive at step nine: introspection, examine mind—experience mind and what it is like in this moment.

Imagine yourself as a pebble thrown into a river; identify the teaching of un-attachment.

Imagine yourself as a pebble that has been thrown into a pool and watch the splash and the resulting ripples and identify the Law of Cause and Effect.

Define each of the Key Vocabulary in your own words.

Ask yourself what it is you truly want, that you think temporary acquisitions fulfill?

Give an example of Emotional blackmail.
Give an example of the straw-man counter arguments.

Describe how hindrances that come ironically from success, can delay enlightenment.

Proverb: "Failure is the opportunity to begin again more intelligently." (wellpage) Discuss in the context of alleviating suffering.

Give an example of how suffering comes ironically from joy.

What is the role of the Sangha for the elimination of suffering in Buddhism.

Six Perfections:

1. giving [which is the basis for compassion],
2. ethical behavior,
3. patience,
4. diligence,
5. contemplation and
6. special insight.

How does each of these relate to your practice?

In an important way, all religions intend to relieve suffering and enhance our emotional satisfaction; does it always work?

Materials Required: tea ceremony, photo of a lotus flower

Buddhist Sutra

Lesson Title: **Choosing a Meditation Practice**

Lesson Number: **Seventeen**

Rationale:

Buddhism offers a 'vehicle' for following the path to enlightenment for every taste and predisposition. A few of the prominent choices are discussed here with the idea of pointing out what a rich and diverse culture Buddhism has become. In this lesson we seek to prepare the path for great faith to manifest. Does Buddhism try to homogenize us?

Discussion of Prior Lesson:

It is inappropriate to get caught in a mental state of self-pity about the suffering with which you have been involved. The reason for that is because there is a way out, not usually leaving the situation, but looking inside it, as we do with insight meditation, and utilize the Four Foundations or supports of Mindfulness. "The Third Noble Truth points out that deliverance, freedom from suffering, Nirvana, consists in the complete extinguishing of desire. People don't realize at all that Nirvana is something that may be attained at any time or place, that it can be arrived at just as soon as desire has been completely extinguished. So, not knowing the facts of life, people are not interested in extinguishing desire. They are not interested in Nirvana because they don't know what it is." (Buddhadasa, 2005, pg. 30)

Is there an afterlife for Buddhism if "rebirth" refers to the repeated arising of the idea "I am" instead of reincarnation?

Training Objective:

Understand "feeling tone." The path to enlightenment is slow and pleasurable as one sheds suffering one feather at a time. What, if anything, can Tantra offer? The five aggregates. Step Ten of meditation. 10 Fetters. The lotus symbol.

Materials Required: tea ceremony, photo of a lotus flower

Motivational Statement:

"The seventh and eighth items on the Eight-fold Path, right mindfulness and right concentration, bring us fully into the sphere of meditation. Meditation is the specialized activity that helps us to fully realize the Buddha's teachings, to make them an integral part of our being rather than just a new set of ideas to be entertained theoretically in the mind. It weans us away from our usual habit patterns, particularly our involvement with our thoughts and their emotional sub-themes. At the same time it sharpens and intensifies our powers of direct perception: it gives us eyes to see into the true nature of things. The field of research is ourselves, and for this reason the laser of attention is turned and focused inwards." (Snelling, pg. 51)

This explanation should be obvious by now, and further "Zen practice is not exotic and difficult, but an amazingly simple and powerful way to enhance one's everyday life. Whatever presents itself to us is not rejected, but becomes our practice. We do not judge or condemn anything, just seek to understand the essential nature of experience itself." (Shoshanna, pg. 3) How much of our experience or desires are based on super-natural events or wishes, i.e. praying to reduce the suffering in the world—what connects our prayer with the possibilities for so many millions of lives? How is that different than just accepting the world as it presents itself to us?

By now we may agree that, as taught in Lesson Two, "Faith is the prerequisite. Small faith takes an object, such as a god or Buddha. *Great faith does not need an object.* It is a quality of mind [feeling tone] that does not need to evaluate the immediate perceptual experience nor anticipate what will happen next. Concentration training requires great faith. The [Stream Enterer] does not allow thoughts to elaborate regarding the supporting object of meditation, but simply attends to it. The preliminary prayer lays the foundation for this type of faith." (Brown, pg. 191)

First Progressive:

"The natural transition from guru yoga to the *advanced preliminaries*, is an outgrowth of a number of signs—fleeting moments of special insight, *spontaneous virtuous acts toward others*, and refreshing moments of inner stillness. Such signs inevitably appear for the serious [Stream Enterers], and are said to be the 'guarantee of the *preliminaries*'." (Brown, pg. 132) Thus the way we measure the success of our practice is how well we serve the needs of other people and loved ones in our lives.

"Tibetan Buddhist teachings say that ideally a donor is endowed with the seven jewel-like Bodhisattva qualities: *Faith, integrity, nonattachment, learning, discrimination, modesty, and conscience.* This endowment helps make possible a prototypical Bodhisattva's pure power of selfless generosity . . . free from condescension and pride. In addition, it does away with any chance of humiliating the recipient, feeling regret about the gift, or being personally attached to what the recipient does with it. Practically speaking, however, most of us need to give what we can, as we can, and not wait until we have all these perfectly pure and exalted qualities." (Surya Das, pg. 25)

Thus as we progress in Buddhism "The most important benefit, however is the acquisition of a solid foundation of virtuous propensities within [Stream Enterers'] mental continuum. Over time the practitioner will become a spreader of virtuous action in the form of a greater *tendency to do good deeds* and to emulate the bodhisattva ideal. As the power of the virtuous states increases, the practitioner more spontaneously and naturally acts like a bodhisattva." (Brown, pg. 119) Each of us acts differently progressing at our own pace, based on the diverse circumstances we confront.

Buddhism ranges from the ideal of the bodhisattva to such teachings as: "In . . . *Tantra [Yoga]* . . . adult, thinking men and women work together *for each other's benefit*. Sex, making love, and mutual orgasms are some of the most beautiful and pleasurable things two people can do together. Whatever creator God you believe in, it must surely blaspheme Her/Him/It to deny the gifts you are given." (Frost and Frost, pg. xxii) How does this improve our moral conduct? Or improve our knowledge and wisdom? Is this use of sexual stimulation disingenuous on the part of those who choose it? This is a unique form of compassion, giving your very privacy to help someone else achieve nirvana. It's doubtful if that is what Buddha had in mind when he encouraged sharing your talents, alms giving or compassion, however.

Second Progressive:

The more work we do to prepare our minds, the more we improve our ethical conduct, the closer we get to enlightenment. "A process is initiated that slowly builds [making merit] a positive karmic force and eventually ripens into perfection." (Brown, pg. 115) The more effort we sustain, the more our minds diverge from the routine life from which we are departing.

Just studying and meditating is not enough, we have to make changes in our lives of course. "Removing weeds and rocks doesn't guarantee that a seed will grow into a tree. It is far more important to supply the right positive conditions for the seed's development, such as water, sunlight, and nutrition. Likewise, eradication of obstacles to spiritual development does not automatically lead to progress . . . Genuine progress is a function of active cultivation of positive mental factors . . . In the earlier Theravada Buddhist tradition these factors are known as the factors of enlightenment. In the later Mahayana tradition such potentiating factors are found in the sutra tradition of the six perfections and in the Tantric mandala offering . . . the Mahamudra refers to these positive changes in the mental continuum as 'building a suitable vessel'." (Brown, pg. 113) When we grow as a tree, we grow in our own unique way.

The practice of yoga is popular especially in the West. "The popular image of a yoga is of someone, usually a young and svelte woman, holding a graceful asana [physical] position and looking positively beatific . . . This concern for a specific body look has led many [people] into yoga, where they hope that diligent practice will trim and tone their body to the required shape. I don't have to point out how far removed a body-based yoga practice like this is from the spiritual ideal proposed by Patanjali, and this is surely *a case of missing the goal by concentrating on the technique.* The ultimate goal is freedom but who is less free than a person trapped by the dictates of a fashion designer." (Forstater, pg. 72) But even if people are working on the surface of improving their lives, perhaps that is something distinctive happening for the better.

In Lesson Five we saw: "The Fetters (samyojana): This teaching enumerates the ten factors that bind individuals to samsaric existence: 1. Belief in personality [egocentric;] 2. Skepticism [unwillingness to believe;] 3. Attachment to[other] rules and rituals [self-righteousness;] 4. Sensuous craving [as co-opted in Tantra;] 5. Ill will [bias;] 6. Craving for material existence; 7. Craving for non-material existence; 8. Conceit; 9. Restlessness; 10. Ignorance . . . Rules and rituals certainly have their uses, and they are considerable, but essentially they are means for furthering spiritual development. They can, however, become ends in themselves [the opposite of compassion.] . . . In such cases, a particularly strong form of attachment has probably been forged, one that is not easily recognized as detrimental because its object is ostensibly so worthy. Fear, ignorance, and a simultaneous grasping for security are more or less certain to be present too . . . The person of the way travels light and lets no opportunity to further lighten his luggage slip by." (Snelling, pp. 66-67) Each of these "Fetters" can be dealt with in the sixteen step meditation practice as we use our breath to essentially burn off bad habits and eliminate cravings. Each of these can be subjected to "turn arounds" with the opposite trait being given a priority for our lives. Just as in ancient times: "The ego . . . was ephemeral, because it was subject to time—not our real self . . . in an intense act of cognition, we would achieve moksha (liberation)." (Armstrong, pg. 193) A step toward enlightenment.

Third Progressive:

What is the most skillful way to practice meditation? "His Holiness the Dalai Lama gives this advice to those wishing to be initiated into a Tantric path: . . . take refuge in the Three Jewels **from the round orb of your heart** [have faith], then take a vow of individual emancipation [free of family ties, and follow a rigorous moral discipline,] and after that generate the aspirational and practical minds of enlightenment [adept at concentration and insight meditations.] Then, when you arrive at the point where it is suitable to hear Tantra, you should receive teachings on Ashvaghosha's 'Twenty Stanzas on the Bodhisattva Vow' and 'Fifty Stanzas on the Guru.' Then you may receive initiation." (Snelling, pg. 100) This is a rather long term preparation, by which time the practitioner will likely find more skillful ways to learn.

What suffering does Tantra Yoga generate? If any? "Ananda delivered to Channa a sermon that, long ago, Shakyamuni had delivered for another . . . This sermon explained how one must observe the causes of suffering and their extinction so as to avoid falling into the mistaken belief that the causes are an actual reality [or necessary events that cannot be prevented] and that their elimination is nihility. According to the sermon, this is *the way to understand the nonexistence of a permanent self* and the error of becoming attached to conditioned phenomena [including sexual pleasures and the bliss, etc. of meditation. From this] Channa clearly perceived the meaning of the five aggregates that constitute the individual and of the impermanence of the self . . ." (Mizuno, pg. 119) Another possible synonym for "conditioned phenomena" is complications. What are the complications that keep you from progressing in your Buddhist training?

How skillful is this? "Through Tantra we gain complete control of our own emotions, and those around us learn similar control. Some of the strongest human emotions are those raised by sexual differences. Once we learn to control them, the lesser emotions—such as anger and pain—are more easily controlled as well. Students work through disciplined control toward Nirvana." (Frost and Frost, pg. xvi) What kind of complications would be created by developing a practice based on sexual stimulation and toying with human emotions?

"The five aggregates . . . means attachment to 1. form (physical things) 2. perception (operation of the perception of pleasure and pain) 3. mental conceptions and ideas (the operation of conceptions and symbols) 4. volition (the operation of various mental processes including that of wishing or craving) and 5. consciousness (the operation of conscious judgment and of awareness itself.) Since *clinging* to them binds the sentient being to the world [seeking pleasure and material satisfaction in the mundane parade of life.]" (Mizuno, pg. 48) The five aggregates is how the raw human as a sentient being is defined in Buddhism. How can we help but be attached to our existence as a human? How can we overcome our crude natures if we indulge and enable these? By anticipating changes, and recognizing these are the same for everyone, and not being self-indulgent or overly proud, thus developing our Hearts.

"When a person lacks steadiness and is unable to control his mind, his senses are like wild horses. But the mind, like horses, can be trained . . . The purpose of yoga, as defined in the Yoga Sutras [compiled by *Pantanjali*,] the most ancient (fourth- to third-century BCE) text of yoga philosophy, is to stop the wandering and craving mind and return it to a serene and calm state . . . [they] explain how the mind works, and how to train it. Paradoxically, the power of the mind is unleashed not by allowing it to be increasingly active, but by encouraging it to become centered and stilled . . . 'Yoga means to control and still the swirling currents of thoughts in the mind. If you can control the thoughts that arise, and still them completely, you are able to observe the world clearly and directly without the distortions of the ego. The ability to discipline the chattering mind is what takes us to the state of yoga [union.] . . . This control is not repressive and strict, but represents a more balanced and harmonious approach to life, one that can restore in us a sense of joy." (Forstater, pg. 24) This is a more skillful aspect of yoga and can be useful, yet it stops short of giving us a stepwise process for accomplishing its stated objectives.

In Nagarjuna's Examination of the Four Noble Truths, he succinctly explains the message of Buddha's lesson about the abstract nature of suffering:

> "If suffering had an essence,
> Its cessation would not exist.
> So if an essence is posited,
> One denies cessation." (Garfield, Nagarjuna, pg. 70)

Neither the causes nor the suffering are actual reality, like the concept of a tree. They are more like a kiss, when not being given it does not exist, it is nothing, yet when given its impact may last forever. The suffering from grief can last for a very long time, whereas the cause, i.e. death of a loved one, may or may not happen in our own lifetime. Grief can have a substantial impact on our lives, even in anticipation, yet it need not exist at all. If one accepts the meaning of life and death in Buddhism, there is no persistent grief, it contains emptiness not essence.

Meditation Practicum:

The lotus is a popular adornment for Buddhist shrines, and has been given many different symbolic meanings. "Meditating on the Lotus: The Lotus is the Eastern symbol of duality and transcendence. The thrusting spike develops into the beautiful opening flower with its central thrusting stamen. The symbolic lingam and yoni [male and female genitalia] that the lotus represents produce great beauty. Each petal is part of your spiritual understanding, yet the stem anchors it to the earth. In this mode the lotus represents the growth of understanding from humble soil and water. If made fertile with muck, the muck makes the growth of the lotus more healthy and vigorous, ascending from its filthy beginnings to achieve beauty." (Frost and Frost, pg. 69) This, from Tantric Yoga, may be as close to those teachings as one might care to go. The seven point sitting position used in meditation is often called the lotus position.

Renderings of Buddha are often 'androgynous' that is combining both genders, with the idea that both male and female are naturally contained in each human being on a continuum from aggressive to passive (or receptive); therefore there is no need to unite externally with the opposite gender to gain unity of spirit.

Again, Buddhist practice is an important source of ethical-behavioral guidance that works on the individual level to change the way people and societies function. These same fundamental teachings have been influential for centuries according to another ancient manifesto developed in Japan: ". . . By these teachings the dust and stains of the world are cleansed away, revealing the splendor and solemnity of the world of the Mandalas. As the performer of the Mantra meditates on the syllables Ma and Ta, the buddha's nature shines forth and dispels the darkness of ignorance. In the lasting light of sun and moon appear the Bodhisattvas of Wisdom, while the Five Buddhas reign supreme, each making his characteristic sign of the hand [mudra.] The universe is filled with the radiance of the Four Mandala Circles representing the Buddha-world." (de Bary, pg. 307) Try using these sounds and images in your meditation practice.

Once this series of lessons is completed, ". . . the time that one gives to meditation must depend upon the individual although less than 15-20 minutes is of little benefit unless the mind is very well concentrated. Also, it is a good discipline to resolve to practice every day and at the same time (in so far as outside circumstances like work allow). One should not—practice on some days but not on others. This shows a wavering mind and cannot accomplish much. And when one has determined to meditate every day, one should also resolve to practice for the same length of time each day, not one day twenty and next only five minutes. If one's practice is not regular then this shows weakness of the mind and such a mind is good at suggesting 'Today it is too hot,' 'Today I am too tired . . .' and a thousand and one other excuses. The best time for formal meditation is early morning when everything is quiet and while the mind and body are rested. If one meditates only once a day then this is the best time to do it. Some people like to meditate twice and do some practice also in the evening. However personal experience will soon make it clear that while hunger is not conducive to meditation, neither is a full stomach. Tiredness may also be a limiting factor in the evening." (Khantipalo)

Consider an alternative—meditating all day long throughout the day—making every activity a meditation. This is not disabling and may even reduce cognitive dissonance, and thus this is enabling and empowering as if constantly being plugged into a superior source of energy. This meditation would not be deep nor distracting to the requirements of employment or housework, etc. But it can be used to focus on one specific goal for the day, perhaps; use your thriving imagination. What does it mean when we feel boredom during meditation, or we become annoyed at "insomnia" at night? I now regard this as the first step to successful, peaceful meditation. Children report being "bored" at school when they are not experiencing the same kind of interesting stimulation during a lecture or lesson as they might get from watching an exciting movie or TV, etc. This means their minds have become calm at least for a few minutes, and this is the kind of slowing down of the mental activity we should look forward to during meditation.

Be aware and keep track of the results of meditation, particularly if there are images or "signs." "There is a sign indicating whether we develop concentration, to which level our concentration progresses and whether we are developing Jhana. That sign is mental image (Nimitta) which is mental reflex or boundary marker." (Wee, pg. 38) The specifics of Jhana are discussed later, along with these signs. Another more mundane sign ". . . of progress is that the practitioner becomes *more devoted* to practice and more detached from the world. Yet another sign is that the practitioner begins to develop a new perspective on everyday suffering: ' . . . imagine all pleasant experiences to be the guru's blessing. Meditate that all painful experience are the guru's compassion. It is essential that you make use of such experiences to enhance your devotion and reverence and do not look elsewhere [entertainments] for a remedy [for suffering].' Furthermore, the practitioner may get spontaneous 'glimpses of realization' or 'moments of calmness' during meditation . . . 'The one who meditates without view [comprehension of emptiness] is like a blind man wandering the plains'." (Brown, pp. 130-131) Remember we are in the middle of a progression of learning, and it is important to have patience and expect that when all sixteen steps are mastered and repeated, these hints will have more meaning.

"During concentration training the act of internally representing the object properly is more important than the specific object used . . . 'supporting representation' . . . A support is anything that the mind can use to learn how to make a representation during concentration training. The practitioner begins training with substantial supports [i.e. the icon of Buddha, forms—meditation described in chapter 16,] but must also learn to use insubstantial supports in order to complete the meditations with support. Insubstantials, are objects generated solely by the imagination without a corresponding external stimulus [i.e. by the sixth sense.]" (Brown, pg. 185) Most of the work in meditation practice is with internal objects rather than with external aids even though we have done some of this kind of work for orientation. "The usual objects . . . start with the body points . . . [steps one through four.] Then fervently pray to the lama. This is considered the way to begin, namely with a respectful meditation to your understanding lama [or Amida]. 'Absolute truth occurs of itself through the very devotion that must be understood.' Therefore the only entrance [to concentration] is through devotion." (Brown, pg. 188) Think of this devotion as the 'feeling tone' or receptivity to obtaining mindfulness, and use this feeling to strengthen your resolve to "chase" your breath during the fundamentals of vipassana meditation!

"Nagarjuna taught that the way of Salvation by one's own efforts is like a toilsome journey by land, that the Way of Faith in the Merits of Another [by contrast] is as an easy voyage in a fair ship over smooth waters, that if a man puts his trust in the Fundamental Vow of Amida, he will enter at once, by buddha's power, into the class of those destined to be born in the Pure Land. Only let him ever call upon the Name of the Tathagata, and gratefully commemorate the great all-embracing Vow." (de Bary, pg. 337) There is no easy path to enlightenment, and making Buddhism into a religious practice, similar to a Christian religion with saints and god, is not skillful either. But the faith that you can "commemorate" to aid in obtaining this goal, is necessary.

Yoga meditation has similarities physically to Buddhism. "In the early days of yoga, the asanas [physical positions] were less important for physical exercise and were intended for purposes of meditation. The classic asana for meditation is the Lotus position, with legs crossed, one foot placed on top of the opposite thigh, the hands placed on the knees facing upwards, and the thumb and first finger touching. In this position the body becomes so comfortably seated and firmly locked on the floor that it allows the mind and emotions to quieten, and pranayama [breath control] exercises and then meditation can be performed . . . 'The wise person holds his body straight, with head, neck and chest in line, withdraws his mind and senses towards the heart, and on the raft of the spirit crosses safely through dangerous waters'." (Forstater, pg. 45) But *Buddhist Sutras* offers a more detailed meditation regimen than the physicality of yoga.

"Step two of this [third] tetrad [step ten] is delighting the mind [from Dharma] . . . to make the mind joyful, delighted, and content. It is important to be able to control the mind so that it feels satisfied and glad while breathing in and out . . . We do not have to endure a sorrowful mind because we can control it . . . [not that satisfaction] rooted in materialism and sensuality . . . We require the delight that comes from knowing and using Dhamma . . . Thus, there are two kinds of joyfulness: defiled joyfulness [temporary, piti, excited,] and joyfulness free of defilement (kilesa)." This higher joyfulness may be what is meant by "devotion" and corresponds to sukha.

"Joyfulness comes from the feeling of being successful, [from the feeling of being loved or appreciated,] of having correctly and successfully completed an activity. An easy way to delight the mind is to return to practicing steps one, two, and three again. Go back to the beginning and practice each step successfully. Then there will be contentment and joyfulness with each completed step. This kind of gladness is associated with Dhamma." We should be able by now to feel delight from being relieved of a good deal of suffering, by achieving success in our meditation practice, or at least seeing the light at the end of the tunnel. ". . . We are the most fortunate of human beings, one who has found Dhamma and is able to eliminate dukkha." (Buddhadasa, 1988, pp. 74-76) This is like the seventh inning stretch in a baseball game, a prelude to some very rigorous work in the subsequent steps. Later we will learn why this

Anapanasati meditation scheme is important in terms of learning about impermanence in a quasi-esoteric way.

Biographical Sketch:

"Sona, the rich man's son . . . became a disciple . . . he now underwent disciplines more rigorous than those of any of the other members of the Order . . . his tender feet were wounded by the rough ground till the places where he trod were bathed in blood . . . Going directly to the house where Sona was, the World-honored One sat in the seat provided for him. Sona bowed before him and sat at his side . . . Shakyamuni then asked Sona if he had played the lute when he lived at home. Sona said he had played it, and Shakyamuni asked, 'If the strings are stretched too taut, will the lute produce a pleasing sound?' "No."

"If the strings of the lute are too slack, will the instrument produce a pleasing sound?"—"No."

"But if the strings are neither too taut nor too slack, but just right, the lute will produce a pleasant sound?"—"Yes, it will."

"Well, Sona, in Buddhist discipline, if one is too eager, the mind will be shallow and unsettled. If one is too lax, the mind will become lazy. The proper way is to be neither too eager nor too lax but to make spiritual efforts and progress at a suitable pace." (Mizuno, pp. 116-117) This is the principle involved in the sixteen steps enunciated by the Theravada teacher Buddhadasa as quoted.

Just as the historical record of the origins of Buddhism are sketchy at best, "The usual kind of explanation is given for the origin of Tantra: that it was originally taught by the Buddha himself, but, because of its highly specialized nature, not for general application. Hence it is sometimes labeled 'Esoteric Buddhism.' . . . Tantric scriptures are a kind of late-arriving fourth addition to the original three pitaka of Vinaya, sutra, and Abhidharma . . . Tantra is primarily concerned with the attainment of buddhahood . . . What is original and distinctive is what it has to offer in terms of methods. Tantra is in fact about transforming the gross body, speech, and mind into those of a buddha by means of special practices, some of which involve working consciously with extremely subtle processes beyond the range of normal awareness [super natural]. This must be done within the context of a special relationship with a guru. If the ideal of the Hinayana is the arhat and that of the Mahayana the bodhisattva, the spiritual hero of Tantra is the siddha or adept." How and why does one *attain* buddhahood if this feature is innate?

"There are varieties of Hindu Tantra . . . which center on the great god Shiva—'Great Ascetic'—Shiva is the prototype of the dedicated yogi . . . but Shiva also has an antithetical erotic aspect and iconographically he is often depicted as coupling with his consort or Shakti. [This sexual union symbolizes the process whereby the passive male aspect of ultimate reality is brought into manifestation by the powerfully creative female aspect.] Sexual symbolism [and erotic ceremonies] plays a conspicuous part in Tantra . . . it is the self-division [dialectic] of the primal unity into a bipolar dualism and the subsequent dynamic interaction of the two poles that generates the creation of the ten thousand things; and of course that very process of creation can itself be reversed and a conscious return to unity achieved." (Snelling, pp. 93-94)

"Tantra practice is divided into six levels: Outer Tantra; 1. Action, 2. Performance, and 3. Yoga tantras: Inner Tantra (highest); 4. Maha Yoga, 5. Anu Yoga, and 6. Ati Yoga . . . These different categories exist because of the differing spiritual abilities of human beings. [There are less formal approaches to Tantra where teachings and practices proceed in a more intuitive way.] Highest Yoga Tantra is the apogee of the Buddhist path; but it is not for everyone. Each person must therefore find which level is appropriate to them. It may indeed be that they are suited to no Tantric path at all, in which case they would be advised to practice a sutra path [Mahayana and Hinayana]." (Snelling, pg. 98) The claim that "tantra is the apogee of the Buddhist path" must certainly be examined critically.

There are much more subtle ways to develop spiritually. "Zen's influence was no where more marked than in the evolution of the Japanese tea ceremony. The cult of tea was not exclusively affiliated with Zen Buddhism; the tea ceremony came to be considered an effective means of training young women in the concept of ri, 'ritual' . . . The tea cult also had its commercial aspects from the outset. Zen priests not only introduced the new beverage to Japan but also the pottery in which it was served . . . 'the cup that cheers but does not inebriate'." (de Bary, pg. 395)

The value of the ethical training that is a priority in the practice of Buddhism, has been recognized for a very long time. Since the introduction of Buddhism via China to Japan, the dharma has had a huge influence on Japanese culture and even politics as early as the fifth century AD. The Constitution of Prince Shotoku is a combination of "Confucian ethical and political philosophy. Buddhism . . . offered a personal discipline leading to emancipation from the world, it had never provided the basis of a political and social order . . . At the same time, however, Shotoku insisted that Buddhism was . . . relevant to the problem . . . He exhorts his people: 'Sincerely reverence the Three Treasures. They are the final refuge of the four generated beings and the supreme object of faith in all countries. Few men are utterly bad. They may be taught to follow [Buddhism]; but if they do not betake themselves to the Three Treasures, wherewith shall their crookedness be made straight'?" (de Bary, pg. 260) So, as early as the fifth century, political leaders recognized that Buddhism was a moral force to help people.

"In Japan . . . following World War II . . . the people came to feel that they must always act independently on the basis of their own interpretations of given situations . . . consequently, unconditional belief in the efficacy of chanting formulas and engaging in Zen meditation is not as widespread as it once was. People today hesitate to chant the old formulas or meditate in the Zen fashion without understanding what relations these acts have to human life in general . . . Nonetheless, the sound theoretical basis of Buddhism can inspire belief in these acts even today when few people approve of trusting without questioning." (Mizuno, pg. 160) Buddhist practice has evolved in different ways in different social environments. Zen has been popular in the USA, but many people move from it to other less restrictive practices; using Zen as an apprenticeship of sorts.

Reading for the Day:

"According to the Yoga Sutras, the Spirit does nothing, it is just a silent observer that sees everything that takes place. It is light, a light that shines through the mind, body and beyond. This light is the true Self that we seek, but, paradoxically, there is no need to see it, because the sages say it is always there, waiting silently. We only need to discover it, and to uncover it, so that its light can radiate with no obstructions." (Forstater, pg. 55) Does this Spirit or "true Self" exist for Buddhists?

"Buddhist Doctrine (kyogi): We are all children of the Buddha and come into this world endowed with the Buddha-Mind (busshin). However, failing to realize this, we live selfish, willful lives, causing ourselves much suffering. If we make repentance to the Buddha [return to humility] and take refuge in him, our spirits will come to rest, our lives will experience harmony and light, and we will rejoice in being of service to society. We will also experience the deep faith . . . to stand up under any hardship. To discover happiness and a life worth living is the teaching of the Soto Zen School." (Kokusai)

Protecting:

"This is what I heard," review by both Stream Enterers and teacher.

Additional Teachings:

"The Lord Buddha replied: Subhuti, any good pious disciple who undertakes the practice of concentrating his mind in an effort to realize Anuttara-samyak-sambodhi, should cherish only one thought, namely, when I attain this highest perfect Wisdom, *I will deliver all sentient beings into the eternal peace of Nirvana* . . . if [you have] any such arbitrary conceptions as one's own self, other selves, living beings, or a universal self, [you] could not be called Bodhisattva . . . It means that what I [Buddha] attained is not something limited and arbitrary that can be called, 'Anuttara-samyak-sambodhi,' but is Buddhahood whose essence is identical with the essence of all things and is what it is—universal, inconceivable, inscrutable." The Diamond Sutra (Goddard, pp. 97-98)

Even when we have achieved the realization of the above we can feel some satisfaction and feel successful. "Obtaining what is good, achieving the good life, being a good human being, discovering enough Dhamma to ensure that we will not suffer—this kind of reflection is a simple way for the citta to experience joy." (Buddhadasa, 1988, pg. 76) This is consolation for the inevitability of impermanence, un-desirableness of things, and anatta or not having an eternal soul. ". . . The characteristic functions of sati and concentration (Samadhi) are quite distinct. While concentration corresponds to an enhancement of the selective function of the mind, by way of *restricting the breadth* of attention, sati on its own represents an enhancement of the recollective function, by way of *expanding the breadth* of attention. These two modes of mental functioning correspond to two different cortical control mechanisms in the brain." (Analayo, pg. 63)

As a preview: soon to come will be a serious focus on the most intense aspect of Buddhist meditation, jhana. "This scheme is that of the four Absorptions (jhana), a graduated series of increasingly deep meditative states. In the first Absorption the meditator becomes oblivious to everything around him, though still capable of both casual and concerted thought, and his attention dwells unbrokenly on the object of meditation. In this state he enjoys both bodily comfort and the more refined mental pleasure attendant on such relaxed concentration . . . In the second and third Absorptions the meditator gradually leaves off thinking entirely, becoming more and more absorbed in the object of meditation alone, and with this increased concentration and simplification he also transcends his feelings of comfort and intellectual pleasure . . . And finally, in the fourth Absorption, the meditator is aware only of the object, and of an abiding sense of firm *equanimity*, beyond feelings of pain or pleasure. Indeed from this point of view he might be said to have increasingly become the object of meditation . . . [this jhana is] representing specific useful skills in the manipulation of one's own experience." (Carrithers, 1983, pp. 32-33)

Sharing Merit:

Rejoicing In Others' Merit (Saying Sadhu)

Buddhist Sutra

Lesson Title: **Choosing a Meditation Practice**

Lesson Number: **Seventeen**

Key Vocabulary: samyojana, Amida, volition, Tantra Yoga, Great Faith, advanced preliminaries, supernatural, Pantanjali, androgynous, bliss, Esoteric Buddhism, kilesa, equanimity, positive mental factors

Define each of the Key Vocabulary in your own words.

Assignment: Meditate on the form and growth of the lotus bud and its blooming as an "insubstantial supporting representation." This is a symbol of impermanence.

After following the first nine steps arrive at step ten: To allow the mind to rest in joy, delighted and content, supported by Dharma. (Images of Buddha are often smiling.)

Look at a photo of a lotus flower as you meditate and feel any difference; understand the uniqueness of each.

Use the mantra "Ma and Ta" and sense the effect on feeling tone, if any.

Choose a partner and sit in front of each other, and feel the attraction, repulsion or simply identify the effect of their presence. This is as close to Tantra as we need to get.

The path to enlightenment may be slow and pleasurable—as one sheds suffering one feather at a time. Do you agree?

Write a short devotional poem or prayer that you can repeat using the name "Amida" (optional) as the redeeming force for all ages. Prepare the path for great faith to manifest.

Memorize the Five Aggregates:

1. form (physical things)
2. perception (operation of the perception of pleasure and pain)
3. mental conceptions and ideas (symbols, i.e. Jung's archetypes?)
4. volition (the operation of mental process including creativity, karma as will) and
5. consciousness (the operation of conscious judgment and of consciousness itself as the sixth sense.)

Look back at your notes for Lesson Two, how has your faith changed? What are the complications that keep you from progressing in your Buddhist training?

Materials Required: tea ceremony, reaching ceremony, DNA and RNA

Buddhist Sutra

Lesson Title: **Techniques of how to study.**

Lesson Number: **Eighteen**

Rationale:

Intellectual development of understanding—and knowledge of Buddhism is accomplished by studying and reading original sutras, authoritative commentaries and texts. This is an important component of developing faith and making progress on the path toward enlightenment, but there are techniques that can be employed to make this effort more effective. When study is mixed with at least an equal amount of practice, it is likely to be more rewarding and successful.

Proverb: The gift of happiness belongs to those who unwrap it. (wellpage)

Discussion of Prior Lesson:

"Staying—calm practice, is the foundation of all subsequent spiritual development... The Stream Enterer who attains one-pointed concentration masters staying-calm practice." (Brown, pg. 181)

Sharing of haiku poetry or prayer.

"When we are certain that we can extinguish dukkha, or when we have gained the best that humans can possibly achieve, then it is normal for us to be joyful and content. We study the Dhamma to understand what will eradicate suffering, to realize our maximum human potential. Then we are content. We are able to delight and gladden the citta using this skillful technique." (Buddhadasa, 1988, pg. 76)

Training Objective:

Review Mindfulness and "state of consciousness." More about the meaning of refuge. Having Integrity, Acknowledging Samadhi, realizing Interdependence. About karma. Step Eleven, and kammaniyo—ready to work.

Materials Required: tea ceremony, reaching ceremony, DNA and RNA

Motivational Statement:

In Buddhism the teachings are at once a vehicle and a vessel. The value of a vehicle lies in its function of transporting man to his destination, such as an automobile. If it does not function, it is no longer a vehicle. The teaching (and the developing moral way of living) must be practiced if it is going to be of value in transporting us from the life of anxiety to a life of serenity. Each of us has his own vessel of Buddhism, and we fill it with our understanding of the teachings and by protecting our insights from meditation as we expand our frame of reference.

When the teaching is not practiced, it is like carrying around a vehicle on our backs without ever putting it into use. Your vessel remains empty. It is meaningless to discuss faith, enlightenment, and other goals if we do not commit ourselves to integrating the spiritual practice with the teaching in our homes and communities. "The journey of a thousand miles begins with a single step." And with each step thereafter we fill our Buddhist vessel.

"Successful spiritual development entails finding a balance between intellectual understanding of each stage of meditation and actual meditative experience. Placing too much emphasis on either alone significantly decreases the likelihood of genuine progress." (Brown, pg. 3) Is it difficult to proceed one step at a time? or would it be better to do all sixteen steps of Anapanasati at once?

First Progressive:

One problem we face with Buddhism is actually applying the Buddhist teachings to our lives. This involves the topic of *refuge*; in the early stages of the Buddhist path students may trivialize and just skip past the significance of *refuge*. When *refuge* becomes trivial and meaningless, we're missing and depriving ourselves of the benefit of the very foundation of all the Buddhist practice. We are social beings after all, and having the benefit of peers and cohorts to help us along the way is a skillful choice.

Taking *refuge* is not about repeating a formula and cutting a little piece of hair as some traditions do and maybe getting a Buddhist name, it's a whole basic change of attitude toward life. It involves changing the way we study because all of our intellectual effort becomes a spiritual practice that we can share—as much as meditation is. We open ourselves to *helping others* and to being vulnerable to risk, asking for help in the Sangha. And we develop and exercise faith—interest and admiration for the teachings.

Refuge is a state of mind (state of consciousness) with which we actively point our lives toward a safe direction [with humility,] which is the direction of working on ourselves—trying to develop ourselves to make our samsara a little bit better, to actively reduce suffering. *Refuge* is an invitation to a state of consciousness that gives us comfort as well. When we accept refuge our goals become attaining liberation (liberation from what?) and reaching enlightenment so we'll *be able to help others as fully as is possible*. Then we are focused on sharing refuge as well. This is not accepting or belonging to a cult, nor is it a personality cult for the psychic benefit of some teacher. But rather, taking refuge to the Three Gems entails a change in our state of consciousness, our receptivity, a whole new orientation that we put into our lives. This consciousness becomes stable in us, as with awareness, it influences all the sensory perceptions we interpret. It especially influences the way we relate to other people, peers, family and those less fortunate than ourselves. We come to know what we're doing with our lives because we are living in the big picture. We determine where our lives are going, rather than having this determined for us. We have a firm idea of the purpose for our lives as we grow, change and become a different person.

"Someone whose primary vehicle on the path is faith [those with a less intellectual orientation,] this faith is his[/her] vehicle for the attainment of enlightenment. He[/she] follows a devotional path based on deep faith in the Triple Gem taking refuge. If he has strong faith in the Triple Gem, he can attain the stream-entry path without attaining any of the mundane jhanas." (Gunaratana, pg. 192) You win with compassion what you might otherwise try to make up for by spending more time reading or discussing with friends.

Second Progressive:

When we have an idea of where we're going in life—what we're supposed to be doing—all the teachings we encounter become real, and our acceptance is based on this foundation. This changes the way we study. Specifically, we're looking at the teachings of the Buddha and the example of the Buddha to fill in the gaps of our own effort and give us that safe and positive direction. As our frame of reference grows, our direct dependence on Buddha lessens, until we reach enlightenment and we become one with the energy of Buddha, as with a dancing partner once we practice and learn the steps.

The important point about refuge, is the attitude we develop toward our study and practice of the teachings based on having this *safe direction of refuge in our lives.* [This intellectual refuge is especially important to Rational Buddhists looking for direction for their lives, and for people who tend to rely less on mysticism or mythical teachings.] What it means is; we look at all the teachings as being relevant to either lessen or eliminate suffering and as relevant to improve our capacity to help others. We take the teachings very seriously and we have confidence that the Buddha taught them, or a later disciple taught them, solely for the purpose of helping us to eliminate suffering and to create in us a person better able to help others. That's the whole purpose of any Buddhist teaching. With this refuge we learn—what's in this teaching that helps us accomplish these aims. (Berzin)

"The *pandit* stereotype is the scholar who devotes considerable energy to understanding the philosophy associated with a particular form of spiritual practice but who never practices. The term *kusali* is derived from the name of the grass commonly used to make meditation cushions. The *kusali* stereotype is the fervent meditator who clocks long hours on the cushion trying to deepen meditation experience. The kusali rarely reflects on the quality of the meditation experience, rarely shares the experience with other meditators, and rarely reads the authoritative literature on meditation or compares his/her experiences against classical descriptions. Without any perspective and without systematic reflection, the kusali risks developing subtle and not so subtle bad habits that eventually arrest his/her progress." (Brown, pp. 3-4)

Central to Buddhism is the elimination of defilements. "To gain experience with ethical training is to become familiar with the mind-which-lets-go. There is more to learn about increasing virtue through restraint, namely [learning restraint] is enhanced through mindfulness and intelligence. It is . . . necessary to let go of all immoral and evil behaviors and to carefully protect [the gains derived from] the ethical training . . . behavioral restraint [emphasized by] ethical training is enhanced both by the act of sensory restraint [prior restraint] and by mental training in mindfulness . . . Behavioral restraint is intended to simplify life. On the external level . . . it reduces engagement in exactly those situations that might otherwise increase afflictive emotions or attachment and aversion . . . The complementary practice is sensory restraint . . . observing moment-by-moment perceptual events with the attitude of the mind-that-lets-go, until the mind is less inclined to grasp any given attribute of perception over another . . . thus protecting the mind from being afflicted by attachments or aversion." (Brown, pp. 134-135) This process is one of developing integrity of the personality such that our ethical training "rules" and guides our entire lives and prevents us from falling back into old destructive habits.

Striking the right balance in our lives is what amounts to living life as an art form as discussed elsewhere. This takes on a moral dimension when we apply these considerations to every aspect of our lives, i.e. "increasing virtue through restraint."

Third Progressive:

"Teaching (and learning) are said to be the real 'miracles' of Buddhism." (Inthisan, pg.15) "If Buddhism is considered as a place of refuge for all teachable persons to come to take refuge in order to assuage suffering and create mental happiness for themselves according to their strength of mindfulness and wisdom at their disposition, it will not be incorrect really . . . The people who obtain benefits from Buddhism are those who understand the essence [have faith] in Buddhism and really *apply to their practice* [to work conscientiously] for their own benefits and happiness . . . [others] follow what is not substantial and they will not fully obtain benefits from Buddhism. It is not the right purpose of Buddhism." (Wee, pg. 54)

Pause for a moment and consider this perspective: Science during the time of Buddha was non-existent. There were no textbooks nor written commentaries on Buddhist teachings to study. He observed, no doubt, that there were hereditary tendencies passed from parents to offspring in every species, and this was evidence to support the generally accepted belief that humans, as well as other animals, had previous lives. The Effects, or similarities that were readily observed had to have a Cause. How else would the thinkers of ancient times explain how they acquired instincts, talents and traits that were so similar to their parents? Of course now, but only in the second half of the 20th century, we know that our biological heredity is a primary factor in determining who we are. New species have evolved and stabilized, and all these organisms use DNA to encode genetic information that they pass on to their offspring. They all use RNA molecules as messengers to transfer the information from DNA to cellular factories called *ribosomes,* which then build proteins, which in turn drive our metabolisms and form the structures of our cells. This indicates, further, that every species seems descended from a common ancestor whose attributes define what scientists mean when they say "life as we know it." RNA is an unusual molecule that can both store genetic information and act like an enzyme, cutting apart other molecules or putting them together. (Borrowed shamelessly from Discover Magazine) Mutations in either the RNA or DNA definitely occur, albeit at an un-predictable rate, and give rise to improvements, deterioration and distinctions within species (by selection pressure,) to new species and to mutations in human organisms.

So believing in transmigration, a mental continuum, and "karma" 2,500 years ago was a no-brainer, as they say, no other competing theory existed to explain how human beings followed in their parents' footsteps so predictably. Add to that the conjuring of the mystic which often seemed to work, the ability of the human body to cure itself from diseases and injuries, and the difference in the use of language between initiates and common usages, and you have a viable explanation for the theory of karma and some of the misunderstandings and historical misuses that have surrounded this term. Do we still need this explanation today? It is a leap of faith (and a misuse of terminology) to believe that some aspect of our minds preexisted in some form that created karmic influences to which we are now unavoidably subject. (Recall the discussion of the use of the word "births," and karma means action or deed.)

As suggested, understanding these "karmic influences" is what we do when we engage in Teleology—trying to figure out why? Can Buddhism thrive without this particular artifact of ancient religious superstition? We need to refine our understanding of karma based on modern scientific discoveries, Buddha anticipates and advises this when he said that we must test information that we receive, from whatever source. We have to update our understandings in light of new scientific discoveries, with more to come! Is the religion of Buddhism diminished if we consider "karma at birth" the biological inheritance from DNA and RNA? Certainly the Law of Cause and Effect applies here, i.e. inheritance of congenital diseases. Although we have come to accept that each child is innocent and "all [people] are created equal," at least as respecting political rights. It was a huge innovation for Buddha to accept that all people are created equal as to religious and social rights as well. This went against the hereditary caste system of India which can still be found today only slightly changed from 2,500 years ago.

Certainly the Law of Cause and Effect applies in our temporal lives if we follow a path of greed, craving etc., and allow "defilements" to fester and engulf our lives in destructive ways. We create complications, compounded events, conditioning factors, and circumstances with each wrong minded decision. Similarly, when we are diligent, conserve our resources, work hard, and make merit in many different ways, we create a better life for ourselves and our families (i.e. saving for retirement.) Even according to the virtues described by Buddha, in spite of his otherwise ascetic appetites, he valued these material accomplishments as appropriate rewards for righteousness. Now we learn all about this from books.

Are these questions so important as to detract us from the main emphasis of Buddhism? Is practicing meditation to develop our minds to prevent suffering that is clearly central to everyone's life in so many ways, a good idea nonetheless? Apologizing for these anachronisms in Buddhism is not as difficult to rationalize as the mental gymnastics, and purported miracles in order to accept the internally contradictory teachings of The Bible for example. Let the show go on, after this brief detour into a scientific cul-de-sac.

What is important is to understand the basic interdependence of Mankind with nature, between man/woman with woman/man, and with ourselves and the world. "Interdependence is fundamental principle in both Buddhism and ecology. The core belief is that all things are connected in some unfathomable but tangible way [i.e. we share DNA.] Ultimately, all things are dependent on one another. We are all enmeshed in Ingra's Net. 'We understand that our future depends on global well-being. Having this viewpoint reduces narrow-mindedness. With a narrow mind, [we are] more likely to develop attachment, hatred. I think this is the best thing about the theory of interdependence—it is an explanation of the law of nature. It affects profoundly, for example, the environment.' (Dalai Lama)" (Chan, pg. 118)

Meditation Practicum:

Previous religious experience and training gives one insight into what it is like to work on spiritual growth (mental isometrics), however misguided that religious faith might have been. Another exercise for the mind is the common meditation technique of counting breaths from one to ten (often one to seven is used.) ". . . after ten, start again at one, following your natural breath. Don't interfere with that. Don't make it anything special . . . The important thing is to sit regularly, for as long as you can." (Shoshanna, pp. 19-20) If you feel you are having too much trouble being distracted, use this technique.

"Commentaries on the sutras explain four stages of meditation, all leading to high states of spiritual unification [integrity] impossible for ordinary people in everyday life [without this kind of effort.] Meditation was widely practiced in India before the time of Buddhism. Shakyamuni himself mastered it while in his father's home and during his period of spiritual discipline, and Buddhism can be said to have made use of four stages of meditation [the four supports of mindfulness we are studying as the outline of the sixteen steps] that had already been taught in India."

"Aside from the specialized concentration involved in these four stages of meditation [or possibly the four levels of rapture discussed in detail beginning in Lesson Twenty-two,] spiritual unification is very important in daily affairs like thinking, reading, [we become more effective] writing, and making talks before audiences. Without it, one is unable to adopt a cool, calm attitude; and objective thought and speedy, appropriate action [removing cognitive dissonance] are impossible. Correct meditation is necessary to the acquisition of correct wisdom and to putting that wisdom to effective use. As I have already mentioned, right meditation leads to the paramount stages of right wisdom and *right liberation*." (Mizuno, pp. 57-58) We study our lives and predispositions in meditation.

As review: "Whatever serves as the object of mindfulness is referred to as the supports of mindfulness . . . 1. the body, 2. feeling tone, 3. state of consciousness, and 4. contents of consciousness." (Brown, pg. 140) The four supports of meditation.

As to *liberation* (chapter 19), Nagarjuna taught an important linkage:

"Without a foundation in the conventional truth [having a decent education relating to scientific and social information,] the significance of the ultimate cannot be taught. Without understanding the significance of the ultimate, *Liberation* is not achieved." (Nagarjuna, pg. 68) We cannot protect and gain new knowledge when we cannot compare this to other teachings because we are ignorant. We need [or we need a teacher with] a broader frame of reference.

"The expectations you bring to meditation practice [possibly based on lack of sufficient knowledge] are often the greatest obstacles you will encounter. The important point is to allow yourself simply to be aware of whatever is going on in your mind as it is. Another possibility is that experiences come and go too quickly for you to recognize them. It's as though each thought, feeling, or sensation is a drop of water that falls into a large pool and is immediately absorbed. That's actually a very good experience. It's a kind of objectless meditation, the best form of calm-abiding practice. [shinay] So if you can't catch every 'drop,' don't blame yourself—congratulate yourself, because you've spontaneously entered a state of meditation that most people find hard to reach. After a little bit of practice, you'll find that the rush of thoughts, emotions, and so on begins to slow, and it becomes possible to distinguish your experiences more clearly." (Mingyur, pg. 214) In this way you prepare for Samadhi.

"Step eleven is to concentrate the mind (smadaham cittam). This step is not difficult because we have been practicing with concentration from the beginning, especially in step four (calming the body-conditioner) [Lesson Nine] and step eight (calming the mind-conditioner) [Lesson Sixteen.] If we could do it before, then we can do it now. So we concentrate the mind in samadhi and immediately drive away any unwanted feelings."

"Most people misunderstand, thinking that if the mind is in samadhi, we must sit absolutely still—stiff and unable to move. Or they think that in samadhi we should experience no sensations whatsoever. This is wrong understanding. To sit still and stiff like a log is only a training exercise in higher levels of samadhi . . . Here in ***step eleven***, concentrating the mind means to train the mind so that it has good qualities and is ready for work. It is prepared to perform its duties as needed. [Such as being absorbed in reading a book.] We should not misunderstand and think that when the mind is in samadhi, we must be rigid like a rock or a log . . . If the mind has correct samadhi, we will observe in the mind three distinct qualities. 1) The quality of mind that is firm, steady, undistracted, and focused on a single object is called *samahito* (stability, collectedness). 2) That mind is clear and pure, not disturbed by anything, un-obscured by defilement, parisuddho (purity). And 3) A citta is fit and supremely prepared to perform the duties of the mind, kammaniyo (activeness, readiness)." (Buddhadasa, 1988, pp. 76-77) Recall the training and discussion of "clarity, calming, intensifying, and pliancy." When we think of citta as "Heart" that instruction takes on a deeper, more poignant and useful meaning, as with the development of an instructive and practical allegory. Return often in meditation to "chasing" the breath as taught in steps 1-3. (Stability, purity, and prepared.)

Biographical Sketch:

"Dogen (1200-1253) the seminal master of the Japanese Soto Zen School . . . earnestly enjoined his own followers to forsake the pursuit of fame and fortune, and, remaining ever keenly aware of death and the general unpredictability of things, [he had lost his parents at an early age, and] to wholeheartedly apply themselves to the practice of sitting Zen. He was less averse to scriptural study than his Rinzai counterparts . . . [he wrote] To study the way is to study the self. To study the self is to forget the self [at least in the Heart.] To forget the self is to be enlightened by all things. To be enlightened by all things is to remove the barriers between one's self and others." (Snelling, pg. 159) in the Heart.

Near the time of his death, Buddha ". . . was overtaken by 'violent and deadly pains,' but he suppressed these symptoms because it was not fitting that he should die without having taken proper leave of the Sangha. Recovering temporarily, he spoke to Ananda, stressing that it was not his intention that the community should become dependent upon him personally. Each bhikshu should try to be as self-reliant as possible and when in need of guidance should turn to the dharma. He, the Buddha, had in fact taught them everything that they needed to know; ***there were no secret or esoteric dimensions . . .*"** (Snelling, pg. 32)

"After the Buddha's death the teachings continued to be passed down orally within the monastic community, in keeping with an Indian oral tradition that long predated the Buddha. By <u>250 BCE</u> the Sangha had systematically arranged and compiled [more than 200 years later] these teachings into three divisions: the <u>Vinaya Pitaka</u> (the "basket of discipline"—the texts concerning the rules and customs of the Sangha), the <u>Sutta Pitaka</u> (the "basket of discourses"—the sermons and utterances by the Buddha and his close disciples), and the <u>Abhidhamma Pitaka</u> (the "basket of special/higher doctrine"—a detailed psycho-philosophical analysis of the Dhamma). Together these three are known as the Tipitaka, the "three baskets." In the <u>third century BCE</u> Sri Lankan monks began compiling a series of exhaustive commentaries to the Tipitaka; these were subsequently collated and translated into Pali beginning in the <u>fifth century CE</u>. The Tipitaka plus the <u>post-canonical texts</u> (<u>commentaries</u>, <u>chronicles</u>, etc.) together constitute the complete body of classical Theravada literature."

"Pali was originally a spoken language with no alphabet of its own. It wasn't until about <u>100 BCE</u> that the Tipitaka was first fixed in writing, by Sri Lankan scribe-monks, who wrote the Pali phonetically in a form of early Brahmin script. Since then the Tipitaka has been transliterated into many different scripts (Devanagari, Thai, Burmese, Roman, Cyrillic, to name a few)."

"No one can prove that the Tipitaka contains any of the words actually uttered by the historical Buddha. Practicing Buddhists have never found this problematic. Unlike the scriptures of many of the world's great religions, the Tipitaka is not regarded as gospel, as an unassailable statement of divine truth, revealed by a prophet, to be accepted purely on faith. Instead, its teachings are meant to be *assessed firsthand, to be put into practice* in one's life so that one can find out for oneself if they do, in fact, yield the promised results. It is the truth towards which the words in the Tipitaka point that ultimately matters, not the words themselves. [Of course words and intentions do matter, and any vagueness or ambiguity has to be looked at carefully.] Although scholars will continue to debate the authorship of passages from the Tipitaka for years to come (and thus miss the point of these teachings entirely), the Tipitaka will quietly continue to serve—as it has for centuries—as an indispensable guide for millions of followers in their quest for Awakening." (Bullitt, internet) When we understand what there is about Buddhism that is essential and unique, many of the details and the intellectual debates become moot. We need to spend at least as much time in practice as we spend reading or studying.

Reading for the Day:

Saicho, a leader of the Tendai Buddhist movement in early Japan, stated: "A devout believer in Buddha's Law who is also a wise man is truly obliged to point out to his students any false doctrines, even though they are principles of his own sect . . . If . . . he finds a correct doctrine, even though it is a principle of another sect he should adopt and transmit it. This is the duty of a wise person. If a man maintains his partisan spirit even when his teachings are false; conceals his own errors and seeks to expose those of other people; persists in his own false views and destroys the right views of others—what could be more stupid than that: From this time forward, monks in charge of instruction in the Law must desist from such practices." (de Bary, pp. 281-282)

"The subject of meditation is like the kick-board. It is used until the skill is built and then abandoned . . . After a period of effort comes a noticeable strengthening of concentration. The mental attributes that will eventually mature into jhana—things like one-pointedness and bliss—become quite noticeable. This is your first major attainment. It is a state on the brink of genuine jhana. It is called 'access' concentration because it is the doorway to the real thing . . . Your attention touches the breath repeatedly, strikes at it, flicks away and then begins to dwell upon it. You may feel lightness or floating. In the mind's eye you may see shimmering forms or flickers of light. These are not visual phenomena in the eyes. These phenomena are totally in the mind . . . [Sometimes called delusions.] This is the realm of visions. If a deity or an entity is ever going to speak to you, this is where it will happen. Your normal thought patterns are being disrupted and deep imagery can come forth. Your visions may be beautiful or terrifying or just strange kaleidoscopic sequences without meaning. Whatever they are, you just let them be there and bring the mind back to the breath. They are nothing special, just more discursive thought in disguise." (Gunaratana, pp. 115-116)

Protecting:

(Guided Meditation)

Stream Enterers take a good look all-around, sit in the seven point Lotus position with closed eyes. Sense the presence of each other, circle the Sangha with your sixth sense and visualize each other, stretch out the right arm with the hand held palm-open, straight, feel the presence of each other with your fingers, reach for this refuge, reach for the understanding of dharma, examine the Amida Buddha influence in the air, feel the touch of refuge and support, acknowledge the change in your state of consciousness since you began to follow *Buddhist Sutras*, reach for enlightenment, as your arm tires you recognize the parallel to the suffering in your life, if you need to drop your arm that is okay, you choose to cease the suffering, and raise it again and reach for nirvana, for the comfort of knowing that you can live well and safe without the threat or incentive of any future life, then reflect on all that for a moment.

"This is what I heard," review by both Stream Enterer and teacher.

Proverb: Kindness is a language the deaf can hear and the blind can see. (Gene Bedley)

Additional Teaching:

"Ananda replied:—My Lord! At the time I experienced the sensation of being pleased, it was both through my eyes and my mind. When my eyes saw my Lord's excellences, my mind immediately experienced a feeling of being pleased. It was then that I made up my mind to become thy disciple so that I might be delivered from the cycle of deaths and rebirths."

"The Lord said:—From what you have just said, Ananda, your feeling of being pleased originated in your eyes and mind. But if you do not know where lies the perception of sight and where the activities of the mind originate, you will never be able to subjugate your worldly attachments and contaminations [sense your own Heart and witness its growth in your being.]. It is like a king whose city was pestered by robbers and who tried to put an end to the thieving but was unsuccessful because he could not locate the secret hiding place of the robbers. So it is in the lives of human beings who are always being troubled by worldly attachments and contaminations [defilements,] causing their perception of sight to become inverted and unreliable and seducing their thoughts and causing them to wander about ignorantly and uncontrolled. Ananda, Let me ask you? Referring to your eyes and mind, do you know their secret hiding place? The Surangama Sutra." (Goddard, pg. 113) Is this a description of solipsism?

Sharing Merit:

Rejoicing In Others' Merit (Saying Sadhu)

Buddhist Sutra

Lesson Title: **Techniques of how to study.**

Lesson Number: **Eighteen**

Key Vocabulary: pandit, kusali, Integrity, serenity, refuge, reflections, liberation, isometrics, essence, samahito, parisuddho, kammaniyo, solipsism, vessel, vehicle

Assignment: Reflect, using insight meditation, on your own "state of consciousness."

Do this by reviewing the three qualities of concentration. These three qualities (of step eleven) can be present while walking, standing, sitting, or lying down.

What does it mean to have Integrity? Stability, purity and prepared?

What is spirituality in your life?

How does integrity apply to the way you approach your intellectual study?

Behavioral and sensory restraint follow mental (thinking) restraint. Do you agree? And discuss each.

If one of our goals becomes attaining liberation (liberation from what?)

Use the counting to ten technique at least once for five or more minutes. (Counting to 7 may also be used.)

Recall and acknowledge Samadhi, the state of absorption; are you there? and what difference will it mean when you get there?

Is Zen related to the concept of Tao? (Think of ‘emptiness’ as a synonym.)

Repeat the reaching ceremony several times in your own practice.

Define each of the Key Vocabulary in your own words.

Write a paragraph on taking refuge in the Three Jewels.

Proverb: No person is so poor that they cannot give a compliment. (wellpage.com)

Describe the last time you did this?

Materials Required: tea ceremony, solipsism, two hand mirrors

Buddhist Sutra

Lesson Title: **Buddhism vs. Yoga**

Lesson Number: **Nineteen**

Rationale:

Yoga (the Sanskrit word Yuj, for union) was widely practiced and taught before, during the period of Buddha's life and subsequently. He would have learned it as a youth and he immersed himself in yoga as an extreme ascetic before his enlightenment. He respected the teachings as one respects an elaborate entry way or a decorative door, but in his teaching (Dharma) pointed-out the limitations of yoga as well. Yet Yoga persists and in the West is often confused with Buddhism.

Discussion of Prior Lesson:

Koan: "8. The question of ignorance . . . A monk asked Hsuan-sha, 'I am a newcomer in the monastery; please tell me how to go on with my study'."

"Do you hear the murmuring stream?' 'Yes, master'."

"If so, here is the entrance." (Suzuki, pg. 253) *How is this an example of refuge?* (1. Having the humility to ask for advice, 2. accepting help, and 3. sharing the song of the murmuring stream that all can hear.)

If the three qualities of concentration (1. Firmness (stability), 2. purity, 3. Readiness (activeness, prepared) are present while walking, standing, sitting, or lying down, that is called "divine standing, etc . . . If there are any problems in life that we cannot answer, then concentrate the mind and the answers will automatically come . . . We can observe that these three qualities are interdependent; they are interconnected in a single unity. There cannot be purity of mind without stability of mind. If there is no purity, there is also no stability. And there must be stability and purity for there to be activeness. The three work together as the three factors of the concentrated mind." (Buddhadasa, 1999, pp. 77-78)

Training Objective:

Identify Contents of Consciousness. Similarities and differences between Yoga and Buddhism. Which semantic maps to memorize. Step twelve—liberating the mind.

Materials Required: tea ceremony, solipsism, two hand mirrors

Motivational Statement:

The essence of Yoga is communion with the Universal Spirit and often practiced as ecstatic meditation. "It is unlikely that an ant would ever ask the four fundamental questions of Tantra Yoga: Who am I? Where have I come from? Where am I going? Why am I here? These questions go to the heart of what it means to be human . . . [and what it means to be an ant even though there is some doubt about the content of their consciousness.] This research becomes a search for spiritual knowledge [for yogi] . . . it is an inner quest, one that we pursue naturally . . . We are in danger of losing contact with our souls, [has the ant lost its soul?] and without that link we can't seem to find the purpose and meaning of existence."

"Can we find a way to get it back? Can we discover in ourselves a rich and vibrant soul, a creative spirit that initiates and receives love, comfort and joy out of our ordinary mundane existence? Can we in fact transform our seemingly mundane lives into a form of the sacred?" (Forstater, pp. 21-22) Elsewhere in Yoga teachings as in Buddhism, we are given assurance that we are perfect and whole at birth, how did we come to almost lose this sacred essence? Is it harder to lose it—consider losing guilt, the very concept testifies to the existence of conscience—than to get it back? What would it take to lose one's soul? A Faustian question. Is this empty rhetoric as The Buddha suggested?

"The basic tenet of the Buddhist position is this: there is no need to be concerned with solving questions about the existence or nonexistence of things unrelated to faith or religious practices [such as the a-four-mentioned questions.] Instead, we must concentrate only on the world of phenomena—the world in which we live and suffer, the world where we seek liberation from suffering. Since this world of phenomena and of birth, destruction, and change is related to faith and religious practices, we must observe and deal with it correctly [in the present moment.]" (Mizuno, pg. 29)

First Progressive:

"What is the home of a wave? The home of the wave is all the other waves, and the home of the wave is water. If the wave is capable of touching himself and the other waves very deeply, he will realize that he is made of water. Being aware that he is water, he *transcends all discrimination*, sorrows, and fears." (Hahn, pg. 233)

"Buddhism was the first of the Indian religions to take deliberate steps for the sake of *teaching and converting the ordinary masses* . . . while still meditating under the bo tree, Shakyamuni came to the decision that he must impart his unprecedented doctrine to all people [as one with all the other waves] in order to transform human society into a realm of peace and happiness . . . He wanted to share it and to rejoice together with everyone, and this desire remained with him throughout his more than forty years of enthusiastic missionary activity." (Mizuno, pp. 104-105) Caste-less society was compassionate revolutionary.

Having *compassion for humanity* is made easier when we acknowledge our inseparable connection to the ". . . Universal Soul

[that] is the real self of each one of us." To suggest that we are all part of this total, is to say nothing particular about each of us. Even if we were to accept Brahma as an overarching, infinite deity ". . . each man/[woman] in turn must take his life into his own hands and work out his destiny for himself." (Sacred-texts, internet) And there are other more esoteric benefits of having and showing compassion in a general sense.

"Metta meditation has the potential to carry you into jhana. The pure feeling of metta as an experience can be used to carry you across the barrier into the wordless. It is very close to the feelings that predominate in the first jhana and it can be used as a tool to reach them . . . 'May I be well, happy and peaceful. May no harm come to me. May I always meet with spiritual success. May I also have patience, courage, understanding, and determination to meet and overcome inevitable difficulties, problems, and failures in life. May I always rise above them with morality, integrity, forgiveness, compassion, mindfulness and wisdom . . . May my parents be well . . . etc. May my teachers be well . . . etc. May my relatives be well . . . etc. May my friends be well . . . etc. May all people to whom I am indifferent be well . . . etc. May all unfriendly persons be well . . . etc. May all living beings be well . . . etc.'." (Gunaratana, pp. 51-52)

Second Progressive:

The Yoga teachings about rebirth and the inner soul are reasonably specific: "The Self is not male or female, but it takes the form of a body with desires, attachments and delusions. The Self is born again and again [indestructible therefore permanent] in new bodies to work out the karma of past lives. The quality of the soul determines whether its future body will be earthly or airy, heavy or light. Its thoughts and actions can lead it to freedom or lead it to bondage, life after life. Love the Lord and become free. He is an incorporeal Spirit but can be seen by a heart that is pure [like having a babysitter for eternity.] He is God, the God of love, and when a person knows Him he leaves behind his past life bodies and becomes immortal." Shvetashvatara Upanishad (Forstater, pg. 210) If "the Self is not male or female," how can this business about using sex to join the yin and yang in Tantra Yoga be useful?

The teaching of the need for moral behavior is similar for Yoga as for Buddhists, but for Buddhists the concept of immortality is quite different (i.e. impermanence—nothing is immortal). Many Buddhists would agree that a yogi is bound to future existences of suffering, as they believe are most Buddhists, but that begs the four questions as originally stated. Furthermore, the belief in an "immortal" anything is heedless of the goal of obtaining enlightenment and nirvana in this lifetime—thus ending this "cycle." Surely to see God with one's heart is meant in a figurative sense, but is loving the Lord the equivalent of knowing Him? (or is that figurative also?) This is very different language usage than is found in Buddhism generally. How does this belief affect our moral conduct.

"The Buddha was evidently willing to accept many paths to release, [from attachments] even ones very near those of his yogic teachers; but the final goal still had to be achieved by a quite different step, a change in quality of thought and feeling, not in quantity of meditative effort." (Carrithers, 1983, pg. 37)

"Self-inflicted pain, it was believed, brings an immediate experience of the accumulated negative karmic retribution from the past, and thereby accelerates its eradication. The Buddha disagreed with such mechanistic theories of karma. In fact, any attempt to work through the retribution of the entire sum of one's past unwholesome deeds is bound to fail, because the series of past lives of any individual is without a discernible beginning . . ." These kind of superstitions are anachronistic in today's more scientific world. "What awakening requires is the eradication of ignorance through the development of wisdom." (Analayo, pg. 168-169)

Third Progressive:

"Originally developed in India nearly 6,000 years ago as a method of integrating the entire person and of freeing the spirit, yoga is sometimes seen today as another form of aerobics, a stress reducer or a means to a flatter tummy. It's true that yoga makes our bodies stronger, more agile and flexible, and our minds more relaxed, but the ultimate aim of yoga practice is to go beyond these limited results and to unite all aspects of the person: mind, body, heart and spirit. It is in this sense that it can be called a spiritual practice." (Forstater, pg. 15) How did these "aspects of the person" become separated, disunited or even hidden from each other? Is this a straw-man argument? Or just a popular misconception on a rather large scale (or cynicism) defect of our modern, materialistic society? Is this representative of yoga teachings. These excerpts were intended to be representative of what the author wrote and quoted fairly; there is no deliberate intention to distort the message of Yoga.

In his early teaching to the five ascetics, his former yogi companions, Shakyamuni said: "O brothers, there are two extremes that must be avoided. One of them is living a life of passion. This is by no means holy [referring to hedonism of any sort.] It does nothing for the sake of achieving the ideal of enlightenment. The other extreme to be avoided is devotion to ascetic practices that punish the body [this is a likely reference to his former—and to yoga—practices of the time.] This is nothing but empty suffering and does nothing for the sake of attaining the ideal of enlightenment. I have departed from these two extremes and, by having the Eye of the Law opened, have discovered the Middle Path leading to nirvana and liberation. Putting this into practice, I attained the highest enlightenment . . . [then] Shakyamuni taught them the doctrine of non-self according to which the five aggregates . . . are transient and soulless . . . this is a major Buddhist tenet . . . [in contrast to yoga.]" (Mizuno, pp. 32-34) For review I have over-layered the five aggregates with the Four Foundations of Insight Meditation.

"1. form (physical things i.e. the *body doors and brain*)
2. perception (operation of the perception of pleasure and pain i.e. the nexus of the body doors and *feeling tone*)
3. mental conceptions and ideas (the operation of conceptions and symbols, i.e. *states of consciousness*) (mind)
4. Volition (the operation of various mental processes including that of mind in action—karma—will) and
5. consciousness (the operation of conscious judgment and of consciousness itself i.e. intelligence and *content of consciousness.*)" (Mizuno, pg. 48)

Another version of the aggregates has "properties and capacities" as 1. matter, 2. sensation, 3. perception, 4. intellect, and 5. dispositions. (Nagarjuna, pg. 142) These are two of those "semantic maps" or taxonomies that ought to be committed to the "content of consciousness,"—to be accessible memory—since these are such fundamental explanations of the nature of the impermanent mind and the Buddhist "non-self." How many Buddhist taxonomies can one conceivably memorize? Which are the most important? Compared to the apparent vagueness of Yoga teachings, Buddhism is a bit compulsively organized.

For Buddhists "Contents of consciousness . . . includes the virtuous and non-virtuous mental factors, perceptions, thoughts and emotions . . . Regardless of the type of support used to train mindfulness [i.e. chasing and/or guarding the breath,] the primary goal is to develop continuous awareness without discontinuities or lapses in awareness. From the perspective of mind, the goal is uninterrupted mindfulness of everything as it occurs in the unfolding mental continuum. This is . . . protecting the mental continuum." (Brown, pp. 140-141) ". . . Continuous awareness . . . uninterrupted mindfulness . . ." Is probably the most popular retreat course offered by Buddhist monasteries and training centers. The best method involves walking meditation with the focus on slow stepping. Yoga retreats tend to focus on body exercises, exaggerated breathing and ecstatic experiences based on trance like activity, all unused by Buddhism in my experience.

Meditation Practicum:

"Your mind can behave as a good friend, but also as your enemy. The uncontrolled mind acts as your enemy." In Buddhism this is the same as the monkey mind, the elephant or the wild horse, all useful analogies.

In Yoga "As you gain control of your mind with the help of your *higher Self*, you are a friend of your *higher Self*, and your mind and ego become your friends. When your mind is disciplined and your soul is at peace, so you are in peace and remain unaffected by heat or cold, pleasure or pain, praise or blame . . . *There is no need to believe in yoga philosophy to get real benefit from yoga practice* . . . As the Amritabindu Upanishad states: 'The mind can be both pure and impure. Driven by the senses it becomes impure, but with the senses under control the mind can become pure. It is the mind that frees us or enslaves us. When we are driven by the senses we become bound; if we seek freedom we must master our senses. When the mind is detached from the senses we reach the height of awareness. Mastery of the mind leads to wisdom'." (Forstater, pp. 28-30) If the mind is out of control, what good does it do to master our senses? Is this another solipsism? Is being "detached" the same as mindfulness? an often used concept in both Yoga and Buddhism. The very first lessons in *Buddhist Sutras* were about having faith to make the practice of meditation both purposeful and effective to create the "mind that frees us." We have learned that doubt and ignorance are hindrances, even in Rational Buddhism.

There are similarities and differences in perspective and vocabulary between yoga teachings and Buddhist dharma. Praying to Amida Buddha, for example, can be compared to calling on a higher power, or chanting OM, but that is not the higher Self, except in a way of suggesting that we each contain buddhahood as an innate capacity. The Yoga *higher Self* is likely at the endlessness of the double mirror images. What is the difference between the 'higher Self and God; between *Self and soul*; between *soul and spirit*; between *mind and spirit*; and between *Self and ego* for Yoga? Possibly an organized explanation exists elsewhere? Buddha came to know that looking for his higher Self in yoga, the "self-existing self" was an empty, pointless search. Looking for the lost Self for yoga is like looking at the image of an image, ever smaller in two mirrors, to find the last one. Take the mirrors and experiment first with one, then with two.

The only sense in Buddhism that "drives us" is the sixth sense with memories and the content of consciousness as its playground. The sixth sense interprets input from the body-doors, recalls memories, has more or less awareness; leads us into day dreams, elaborations, distractions and can naturally filter or embellish creative impulses as easily as sensory input. The Samahito doesn't master, shut down or "control" the five senses, we seek to master this non-dual (it's not separate, it is part of our whole) sixth sense through concentration and insight meditation, at the same time we influence our mental continuum. Wisdom comes from practice (in the broadest sense) combined with instruction from mentors, with a healthy dose of intellectual study of dharma, (possibly even esoteric intervention) and letting free the trained mind to offer insight—rather than the mind being mastered in a strict sense. But possibly this is just a different language game?

"Through vipashyana [insight] meditation, the mind arrives at the understanding that 'everything that arises passes away and is not self,' which is what buddhas know. But this, as we have already indicated, is not merely a negative insight: the discovery of a pure nothingness. Nor is it the uncovering of a mysterious 'something' [the Yoga Self.] It is nirvana—ineffable, infinitely subtle, fleetingly glimpsed at first but returned to again and again until it is fully established as the fulcrum of one's being and lived out in action. 'Real' meditation is direct, formless contemplation of this reality." (Snelling, pg. 54)

For Yoga: "All is OM. Om is Spirit. Everything is OM. OM is the beginning of the ancient chants. The priests start with OM, the teachers start with OM. The student murmuring OM seeks the Spirit and finds it in the end." If you think this terminology is a little confusing, just wait.

"The Word. Let us meditate on OM, the beginning of prayer. The essence of all beings is the earth; the essence of the earth is water; the essence of water is plants; the essence of plants, the human; the essence of the human, speech; and the essence of speech is OM." We can come back to this in a moment.

"OM represents the highest Spirit, so it is the essence of essences, [the set of all sets] that which we humans take as being holy. At the heart of prayer, like a couple coming together to fulfill each other's desire, speech and breath come together as the imperishable OM . . . [How does this work for celibates?] When we chant OM, we honour the sounds of the word which is the key to knowledge and the higher Spirit, which we call Brahman . . . when we chant OM with knowledge, inner awareness and faith, we grow in power." Chandogya Upanishad (Forstater, pp. 177-178) The emptiness (or impossibility) of the set of all sets is that it cannot, paradoxically contain itself, thus the incompleteness theorem by Gödel.

Coming back to "The word . . ." If you look closely you will notice that the description of the essences of OM makes more sense when it is read backwards: OM is the essence of speech (i.e. a phoneme,) speech is the essence of the human (i.e. communicator,) the human is the essence of plants (i.e. the highest organism,) plants are the essence of water (i.e. life sustainer,) water is the essence of earth (i.e. compare to other planets) and earth is the essence of being—alive (i.e. tectonic plates.)—"To dust we shall return." Curious that reading it backwards makes more sense. Which is the solipsism?

The use of the sound OM is a verbal painting of the infinite with a broad brush, if a name refers to all, non-differentiated, it is just another word, albeit a special word, for infinity or Universe. OM seems to more closely represent a concept of replicated fullness, the opposite of non-differentiated emptiness, the recognition of which for Buddhism is the last step to nirvana. Yoga has given a numinous meaning to this mantra, a meaning greater than the sum of its many essences and conceivable explanations, and it carries special significance for the Yoga initiate, but not for those outside with simple intellectual curiosity. This seems to be an expression of a *tautology,* and as such this description is—logically speaking—trivial, but more likely it could simply be at best a poetic expression, at worst, nonsense.

The highly organized and sensible nature of Buddhism gives many monks a well deserved sense of confidence. In the Tibetan practice of Buddhism, the lama in mahamudra is renowned: "To intensify the internal dissonance in his listeners, Tashi Namgyel then systematically refutes all other spiritual practice. He tells them that whatever practices they may be engaged in are faulty because they are based upon ignorance instead of on certain truth. Such accusations are designed to instill doubt in the listener. When someone experiences a healthy doubt about his or her life condition, he or she is likely to become more receptive to genuinely hearing the advice of a holy being: 'If you do not know the way the enlightened mind stays, then you will not attain the fruit of liberation, even if you were to know one hundred thousand other practitioners' practices. But if you understand this, [and the relationship to the content of consciousness] you will become [the Buddha] Dorje Sempa." (Brown, pp. 42-43)

"Step twelve . . . is liberating the mind (vimocayam-cittam). Liberating the mind means not letting the mind become attached to anything. We make the mind let go of anything it is grasping . . . Liberating the mind from all attachments has two aspects: the mind can let go of all these things, or we can take these things away from the mind. The results are the same. Then we observe if there is anything to which the citta continues to cling. If so, we try to release those things from the mind . . . Scrutinize the dangerous and painful consequences that all attachment (when we cling to something as 'I' or 'mine') inevitably brings. Then examine and realize the benefits and advantages of non-attachment. What kind of happiness is present [with non-attachment?] . . . Examine both sides of the coin . . . Observe this every time you breathe in and out." (Buddhadasa) Liberating the mind is the brightest form of mind development, the epitome of mental cleansing. This conditions the Content of Consciousness and mental continuum.

"The objects of attachment are numerous . . . and there are four types, or modes of attachment . . . These four main categories of attachment include all the things that we grasp [crave or obsess about:]

1) material objects valued by sensuality (kama), such as possessions, necessities, gems, jewelry, gold, and money; or in other words, the things we see, hear, smell, taste, feel, and think about . . . These are objects of attachment to sexuality [thus we objectify someone when we are merely sexually attracted to them.] The other three categories are *immaterial* objects of attachment . . .
2) our correct opinions, beliefs, views, and theories. These are the things [or ideas] that we cannot understand, that we cannot possibly know, but because of avijja (ignorance) we accept and are attached to them. We have many such incorrect opinions and views . . . (i.e. fear of charnel—funeral grounds)
3) The third category includes the traditional activities and practices that we follow. All of them, both the religious

and the secular, are superstitious. There are many of these customs with which we identify. (i.e. making offerings to 'hungry ghosts')

4) all the things that we are attached to as 'I' or 'mine' (i.e. stylish clothing). Observe them and see the pain and suffering of clinging to them. See the value of not clinging to them. Continually examine every kind of attachment with every inhalation and exhalation. In this way they are released in an automatic letting go. Release the objects of attachment. Let go, let go . . .

The mind must also let go of the things that are disturbing the citta right at this moment, such as the *nivarana (hindrances).* These are moods that arise in the mind out of habit and tendencies of thought. The five nivarana are 1) feelings of sensuality, 2) aversion, 3) depression and drowsiness, 4) agitation and distraction, 5) and doubt and uncertainty . . . Furthermore, the *kilesa (defilements)*—the emotions of *lobha (greed), dosa (anger), and moha (delusion)*—must go. Any feelings of liking and disliking, any moods of satisfaction and dissatisfaction, and attachments to dualistic things must be removed. Eventually, we will realize that no problems remain that will put the citta into dukkha . . . When the mind is empty of attachment, it experiences no dukkha because there is no foundation for dukkha." (Buddhadasa, 1988, pp. 79-82) This activity of liberation is a huge task and must be repeated over and over for every defilement.

Biographical Sketch:

"Patanjali's yoga philosophy differs from that of the Advaita Vedantists [and from Yogachara] not only in yoga's idea of the isolation of the Self. To Patanjali the Self and the world are both real and have a real existence, whereas for the Vedantists the world is unreal, being a manifestation of *maya, or illusion.*" (Forstater, pg. 47) Yoga is like a mixed fruit tree created from many graftings on the same tree. We find different fruits depending on what we are looking for.

"Patanjali's Yoga Sutras are a kind of self-help manual to help us dissolve our ignorance, gain true wisdom and find joy in living. The Sutras explain the theory behind the method of all types of yoga, which Patanjali describes as an ashtanga system. Ashtanga means eight-limbed, and each limb constitutes one part of the practice, although all the parts must be practiced simultaneously for it to be really yoga . . . Yoga is not a theoretical system but a practical one, in which the practice must lead to an end result: a new way of looking at the world . . ."

"(Ethical and spiritual practices) 1. Yama (self-restraint) 2. Niyama (personal observances);

(Physical Practices) 3. Asana (physical training) 4. Pranayama (breath control);

(Meditation Practices) 5. Pratyahara (withdrawing the senses) 6. Dharana (Concentration) 7. Dhayana (meditation) 8. Samadhi (absorption)." (Forstater, pp, 58-71) (Compare to The Eight-fold Path.) This multiple limb symbolism is a frequent feature of Indian and yoga iconography. Rational Buddhists can certainly embrace the goal of changing an individual's perspective on the world, and benefit from the practices and discipline taught by Yoga.

But Buddha's perspective on the world, once he experienced enlightenment, sounds quite different; the Buddha said: ". . . The other extreme to be avoided is devotion to ascetic practices that punish the body. This is nothing but empty suffering and does nothing for the sake of attaining the ideal of enlightenment." (Mizuno, pg. 32) The Chinese icon that portrays Buddha as happy (and corpulent) is possibly intended to draw a contrast to the asceticism of yoga.

"So, when we talk about the Buddha, we're talking about a man who understood that life doesn't always afford the opportunity or leisure to practice formally. (Most of us have to plow the fields and plant the rice.) One of his greatest gifts to humanity was the lesson that it's possible to meditate anytime, anywhere. In fact, bringing meditation into your daily life is one of the main objectives of Buddhist practice. Any daily activity can be used as an opportunity for meditation. You can watch your thoughts as you go through your day, rest your attention momentarily on experiences like taste, smell, form, or sound, or simply rest for a few seconds on the marvelous experience of simply being aware of the experiences going on in your mind." (Mingyur, pg. 201) Buddhism and Yoga practice merge in this area of teaching.

Reading for the Day:

"Yoga means to still the swirling currents of thoughts in the mind. If you can control the thoughts that arise, and still them completely, you are able to observe the world clearly and directly without the distortions of the ego. The ability to discipline the chattering mind is what takes us to the state of yoga [union.]"

"When the turbulence stops and the lake of the mind becomes clear and still, our true essence, our Self or Spirit, is reflected. Then the Self can abide in its own true nature. This is the goal, this is what we want to attain." This was possibly the source of Buddha's frustration with yoga.

"When we fail to still our minds we mistakenly identify our Self with the activities of the mind, and become lost in our thoughts. We lose the true sense of who we are because we have lost sight of our true essence, our real inner Self." (Forstater, pg. 82) It might be clear from this comparison, to the extent that it is a fair (albeit brief) presentation of Yoga, why so many people rely on Yoga for physical training and eschew the religious and esoteric teachings.

Protecting:

"This is what I heard," review by both Stream Enterer and teacher.

Additional Teaching:

"As you continue to breathe [first long breaths then shorter breaths,] take note of the beginning, middle, and end of each inhalation, followed by a brief pause. Then note the beginning, middle, and end of each exhalation. This will assure that your mindfulness is strong as you approach jhana. If you do not pay careful, mindful attention, you will not be able to discern these separate stages in each breath.

Each of these stages should be noticed as the place where you feel the touch of the breath. For that reason, it's very important to really find the place where the breath touches before jhana develops, and pay total mindful attention to that particular spot. By paying total attention, you also can notice the intrinsic nature of any phenomena as they arise." This is consistent with the teachings of Suan Mokkh Mindfulness Retreat.

"As your breath becomes subtler and subtler, the details begin to be noticeable. Finally they disappear altogether, and the mind naturally stays only at the place where you noticed the touch of the breath. At that point, you begin to experience inhaling and exhaling as one single sensation." (Your emotions begin to subside.)

"Each time the mind wanders away from the breathing, you bring it back and keep it at the touch-point. Repeat that process, as often as necessary, until the mind stays easily with the breath, as it flows in and out, passing the place where you established your attention. Then you will be able to see every tiny part of the breath . . . And as the breath changes, so does the feeling. You perceive the changing breath and the changing feeling. The thought, 'This is the breath—this feeling, this perception,' is called volitional formation. You intentionally (or 'volitionally') change and condition the activity of the mind, and pay attention to the breath and its sensations. Your awareness or consciousness also changes as your breath, feeling, perception, and thought change. You realize that any state of consciousness also changes, whether it arises dependent upon sight, sound smell, taste, touch or thought . . . When all the hindrances have subsided, joy arises. [You condition the content of consciousness. This is the perfection of your karma—this is a positive action.] Develop that joy further and let go of your restlessness. Let the joy spread all through your mind and body. This is a right thought, too." (Gunaratana, pp. 116-118) This is the perfection of your Karma.

Sharing Merit:

Rejoicing In Others' Merit (Saying Sadhu)

Buddhist Sutra

Lesson Title: **Buddhism vs. Yoga**

Lesson Number: **Nineteen**

Key Vocabulary: tautology, numinous, solipsism, cynicism, ego, higher Self, soul, Self, Yoga's God—Lord, ecstatic meditation, Yama, Niyama, Brahman, taxonomies, simultaneous mind, kama, dosa, moha, nivarana, kilesa, conditioning, metta

Assignment: What is meant by Contents of Consciousness, as it concerns insight meditation? Meditate on compassion at least once.

Practice applying step twelve to your mind. Identify attachments and by breathing in and out, eliminate their impact on your life. This is a self-cleansing.

Write down a list of objects, ideas, beliefs, superstitions, angers, delusions, obsessions, and run these through the mill of Liberation.

Try the OM mantra during meditation as an imagined sound in the sixth sense, as well as verbally as an object of speech and hearing for meditation. (Review Lesson Eight)

Evaluate the effect of OM in terms of the Four Foundations of Insight Meditation.

Identify several important similarities and differences between Yoga and Buddhism—from your own experience / if any.

Which semantic maps should you memorize?

Define each of the Key Vocabulary in your own words.

How is the concept of interdependence important?

Review for Lesson Twenty: The six defilements from Lesson Eleven:

1. pride, that is, looking without really listening, or listening disrespectfully;
2. lack of faith;
3. lack of effort toward the truth;
4. distraction toward external things, so as not to mirror the teaching in thought;
5. shutting down the mind, that is, falling asleep; and
6. fatigue, that is, listening with a wandering mind and failing to intellectually understand the meaning of the teachings.

Materials Required: Michelangelo Print. Music or soundtrack for meditation. Cottonwood (or bodhi) tree leaves. Photo of bodhi tree.

Buddhist Sutra

Lesson Title: **Aesthetics and Happiness**

Lesson Number: **Twenty**

Rationale:

The relationship between ethical conduct and *aesthetics* is an important philosophical consideration. The moral codes of Buddhism are general guides, but for the most part outside the monastery, Buddhists are left to their own devices on how to interpret the guidelines established by the Five Precepts, the Eight-fold Path and other teachings. This is where the study of human virtue enters an arena competing against practical considerations, and the moral discussion takes on an urgent and pragmatic tone.

Discussion of Prior Lesson:

Living ethically is in a very serious way connected to creating fine art, it is the art of living well. "This is a similar process to Michelangelo's fanciful theory of sculpting. We usually think that a sculptor carves away at a rough block of marble to make it resemble a shape that he holds in his imagination. But Michelangelo half-jokingly said that the shape was already in the marble, waiting to be let out. His job was just to carve away the excess and let the marble reveal the shape . . . liberating it. This is also the way of yoga, a means of liberating our Self [our identity and our ethical lives.] It is a negative process leading to a positive result, a way of making progress by going into reverse." (Forstater, pg. 36)

"Whenever the mind sees something clinging to it, it releases that object [by focusing on it and applying liberating breathing.] These are the four steps [of meditation] that deal with the mind: 1) experiencing the different states of mind, 2) gladdening the mind, 3) concentrating the mind, and 4) liberating the mind. Through them we successfully complete our study (9-12) of the mind." (Buddhadasa, 1988, pg. 82)

Proverb: Poise is the ability to raise your eyebrows instead of your voice. (wellpage.com)

Training Objective:

Discuss the art of living. The instinct to live is more than merely survival. Take charge of your life to be the best person you know how to be. No more excuses! This is another passageway to enlightenment. Eliminate angry venting by talking about it.

Materials Required: Michelangelo Print. Music or soundtrack for meditation. Cottonwood tree leaves. Photo of bodhi tree.

Motivational Statement:

"Having mastered the ordinary and extraordinary practices and built the mental continuum as a suitable vessel for spiritual realization, the [Stream Enterer] is now in a position to deepen his or her spiritual knowledge. The developing knowledge goes beyond mere intellectual understanding, and ripens first into direct experience and eventually into understanding." (Brown, pg. 120)

"Much of the Lotus Sutra is taken up with injunctions to the believer to 'accept and uphold, read, recite, copy and teach' it to others, and with descriptions of the bountiful merits to be gained by such action, as well as warnings . . . In the view of religion there are other approaches to truth than merely through words and intellectual discourse. The sutra therefore exhorts the individual to approach the wisdom of the Buddhas through the avenue of faith and religious practice. (Watson, pg. xxi)

> "If one upholds the Lotus Sutra
> His body will be very pure,
> Like pure lapis lazuli—
> Living beings will all delight to see it.
> And it will be like a pure bright mirror
> In which forms and shapes are all reflected.
> (Watson, pg. 262)

First Progressive:

". . . The profound influence which the Lotus Sutra has exerted upon the cultural and religious life of the countries of eastern Asia is due as much to its function as a guide to devotional practice as to the actual ideas that it expounds. It calls upon us to act out the sutra [teachings] with our bodies and minds [*developing compassion for all members of society* along the way] rather than merely reading it, and in that way to enter into its meaning . . ."

Why are the outer rituals and traditional patterns of the culture of Buddhism important? Mnemonic devices? Reminders of our own humility in the face of an infinite Universe? "In addition, one is encouraged to make offerings to the buddhas and bodhisattvas, to the stupas or memorial towers, and to the monastic Order. Flowers, incense, music, and chants of praise *are the customary offerings cited in the sutra*, along with food, clothing, bedding, and other daily necessities in the case of members of the Order. Gold, silver, gems and other valuables are also listed among the offerings . . . but it is the spirit in which the offering is made rather than the article itself that is important . . . The animal sacrifices so central to the Vedic religion were rejected by Buddhism as abhorrent [far ahead of his time]." (Watson, pp. xxi-xxii) Much of the Lotus Sutra is exaggerated poetry, although it is written also in prose and the message is repeated in verse. It follows the mystic tradition of the Hindu practice, and largely departs from Buddha's otherwise pragmatic, more logical approach. As a hugely influential cultural relic, now 2500 years after Buddha, it is equivalent to the Iliad and *La Divina Comedia* for its cultural influence. It can still give comfort even to those who are not in the sway of its mystic voice.

To summarize about compassion: "The next important hindrance and allurement is the tendency of all sentient beings of all the six realms of existence to gratify their pride of egoism [through achievements and progress]. To gain this *one is prone to be unkind, to be unjust and cruel,* to other sentient beings . . . right control of mind will enable them to keep the Precept of kindness to all animate life. The reason for practicing dhyana and seeking to attain Samadhi is to escape from the suffering of life, but in seeking to escape from suffering ourselves, why should we inflict it upon others? Unless you can so control your minds that even the thought of brutal unkindness and killing is abhorrent . . . No matter how keen you may be mentally, no matter how much you may be able to practice dhyana, no matter to how high a degree of Samadhi you may attain, unless you have wholly annihilated all tendency to unkindness toward others, you will ultimately fall into the realms of existence where the evil ghosts dwell." (Goddard, pg. 264) This is right here on Earth, if you are caught in continuous "births" of ego and "I-ness," suffering and the complications in your life increase rather than disappear.

Second Progressive:

"Not only in Buddhism, but in all human affairs, there is a great difference between performing an act as a result of orders from somewhere else and performing even that same act on one's own initiative . . . Kant said that the highest ethical morality is free obedience to dictates of conscience . . . [doing one's duty, even if carried out unwillingly.] . . . If the 'Instruction of the Seven Buddhas' [the core of Buddhist ethical practice] is interpreted not as a commandment but as a statement, then Buddhist ethical morality is seen to be one of joy and courage . . . The founder of the Soto Zen sect, Dogen (1200-1253), said that the power of religious training is manifest in a process whereby the person wishes to do no evil, does no evil, and finally becomes incapable of evil . . . one must purify one's own mind." (Mizumo, pp. 161-162)

To make others happy is thought to be a practice taught by Buddha. Yet in an important way, it is an empty hope, because each of us as adults is responsible for our own happiness. This is a simple truth, but how can we rationalize the two different concepts? In part the answer lies with the very discussion of happiness, and understanding that there are two very different kinds of happiness. The happiness on the surface that one obtains when socializing with friends, reading a good book, playing video games, listening to music, making love, participating in a sport, etc. is temporary, often fraught with grasping or leads to or results from addictive behaviors. There is a deeper happiness that results from successfully living with the Triple Gems, engaging with Dharma, progressing with meditation, participating in a Sangha, recognizing ones own buddhahood; these can bring a deep abiding happiness. When we empathize with another's plight, it means to place ourselves in the position of another and give service with joy and gratitude, unselfishly. When we share Rational Buddhism with others we empower them without enabling and improve their capacity to be happy. This is the most fitting solution along with practicing the *Four Immeasurable Attitudes: friendliness, compassion, joy and equanimity.*

1. *Friendliness* is the constant endeavor to share [deep] happiness;
2. *Compassion* is the source of empathy and leads to a concerted effort to alleviate discomfort and suffering in those we know, or meet deliberately or by chance;
3. *Joy* is an aesthetic agreement that derives when people share intimate and spiritual aspects of their lives;
   and
4. *Equanimity* is the result of wisdom (from insight) which helps us follow the moral principles taught by Buddha evenhandedly, fairly and consistently.

The illusion of trying to deliberately make someone happy, is to treat an adult like a child, or if not patronizing, at least sympathetic in the wrong sort of way. Listening, being emotionally available and sharing insights are usually enough to practice, with a healthy dose of humor thrown in naturally.

Not trying to deliberately interfere with others, is a step removed from the impossible task of trying to make someone else happy, but often there is a better, intermediate solution. Once one develops their own character through meditation, they will also develop a keen insight into the character of others they meet. It is an uncanny sensitivity that develops, and it requires a certain self-restraint to avoid taking over another person's life. When we share the clear understanding of life from the Buddhist perspective, we can comfortably promise that suffering and sadness can be overcome, and we simply point the way toward a long lasting, deep happiness. Being happy oneself is a moral choice. There is simply no need for a Samahito to wallow in sadness or depression. The most important practice is to be mindful and take to heart the Eight-fold Path, the steps of meditation leading to Liberation, and the other ethical teachings (including the six defilements from Lesson Eleven.)

Third Progressive:

"The ability to recognize the feelings and sensations of others is a property specific to mammals which are endowed with the limbic region of the brain. There's no doubt that this capacity can sometimes seem more problematic than it's worth. Wouldn't it be nice to just respond to every situation in simple, black-and-white terms of kill or be killed, eat or bet eaten? But what an incredible loss this simple approach to existence would be! The limbic region of our brains affords us the capacity to feel love, and the awareness of being loved. It allows us to experience friendship and to form the basic structures of society that provide us with a greater measure of safety and survival, which helps ensure that our children and grandchildren will thrive and grow. The limbic system provides us with the capacity to create and appreciate the subtle emotions evoked by art, poetry, and music. Certainly these capacities are complex and cumbersome; but ask yourself the next time you see an ant or cockroach scuttling across the floor if you would rather live your life in terms of the simple dimensions of fear or flight, or with the more complex and subtle emotions of love, friendship, desire, and appreciation of beauty [the aesthetic side of life.]" (Mingyur, pg. 226)

The Lotus Sutra is full of these positive emotional expressions as well as pragmatic instructions. ". . . It is not so much an integral work as a collection of religious texts, and anthology of sermons, stories and devotional manuals, some speaking with particular force to persons of one type or in one set of circumstances, some to another . . . This is no doubt one reason why it has had such broad and lasting appeal over the ages and has permeated so deeply into the cultures that have been exposed to it." (Watson, pg. xxii) Like most poetry, it is to be appreciated for the mood it creates, the poetic devices (i.e. exaggeration) it employs, and for the musical quality that can enhance the aesthetic appreciation, rather than a literal interpretation.

One cannot say that the Lotus Sutra sees life as it truly is, but as a fairytale life. "Shakyamuni explained that philosophies considering the world and the self to be eternal entities, philosophies considering the world and the self perishable and reducible to nothing, philosophies that are an eclectic blend of these two approaches, and skeptical philosophies rejecting both are all mistaken ways of thinking arising from attachment to *transient entities* [family and friends or other complications?] He then explained the Law of Causation and the need to abandon attachments to such entities and to see the world and human life as they truly are." (Mizumo, pg. 88) What are these problematic transient entities?

"The Victorious Conqueror has said that whatever is deceptive is false. *Compounded phenomena* are all deceptive. Therefore they are all false. Compounded phenomena—that is, all phenomena constituted of parts or brought into being dependent upon causes—[further] . . . Emptiness is the lack of essence and that emptiness itself is wholly negative in character." (Nagarjuna, pg. 207) The fly in the ointment of this theorizing and generalization is identified by asking the question—When would this statement actually mean anything? Or possibly: Can you give an example that would make what you just said understandable? It is very tedious to try understanding what phenomena apply here and which do not.

(Are these the ordinary complications that compound in ones life?) How do we find answers to these questions?

When we read theories that are too broad and too generalized for their own good, and pretend to tell absolute truths that apply in all situations, this should sound a bell of warning. What are we talking about here? It was Ludwig Wittgenstein who demonstrated that whether an object, such as a chair, is a simple object or a compound object (made of legs, a back, a bottom, etc.) is decided by the context of the discussion, what language game is engaged, what is at stake. "Of course, what confuses us is the uniform appearance of words when we hear them spoken or meet them in script and print. For their application is not presented to us so clearly. Especially not, when we are doing philosophy!" (Wittgenstein, pg. 6) One might clear up the matter by answering the question "What kind of answer do you want?" But until we can do this, the philosophical argument and theorizing are empty of merit. Wittgenstein's suggestion has a way of dismissing the questions and evaporates the theorizing (searching for the essence) that we also find prolific in Buddhist philosophical texts (consider the last two quotations.)

To explain in another way, one error behind the motivation to theorize is to identify the one thing that all the potential "compounded phenomena" have in common, for example. "I am saying that these phenomena have no one thing in common [no shared essence, nor a single essence] which makes us use the same word for all,—but that they are related to one another in many different ways. And it is because of this relationship, or these relationships, that we call them all ['transient entities,' for example.]" (Wittgenstein, pg. 32) This introduces Wittgenstein's famous "theory" of "family resemblance." Paradoxically enough, this helps point us to the emptiness that "essentially" underlies philosophizing and many generalized teachings. By knowing this are we a step closer to nirvana?

"The essence of Zen Buddhism [once again an essence] consists in acquiring a new viewpoint on life and things generally. By this I mean that if we want to get into the inmost life of Zen, we must forgo all our ordinary habits of thinking which control our everyday life, [that doesn't sound like very much fun,] we must try to see if there is any other way of doing things, or rather if our ordinary way is always sufficient to give us the ultimate satisfaction of our spiritual needs . . . Zen proposes to . . . [supply] a new point of view in which life assumes a fresher, deeper, and more satisfying aspect. This acquirement, however, is really and naturally the greatest mental cataclysm one can go through within life . . . This acquiring of a new point of view in our dealings with life and the world is popularly called by Japanese Zen students 'satori.' It is really another name for Enlightenment, which is the word used by the Buddha and his Indian followers ever since his realization under the Bodhi-tree by the River Nairanjana."

"Satori may be defined as *an intuitive looking into the nature of things* in contradistinction to the analytical or logical understanding of it. Practically, it means the unfolding of a new world hitherto unperceived in the confusion of a dualistically trained mind. Or we may say that with satori our entire surroundings are viewed from quite an unexpected angle of perception . . . the opening of satori, obtaining an eye to see into the spirit of the Buddhist teaching." (Suzuki, pp. 83-84) All the metaphors in Suzuki's writing confuse me, frankly. Can we likewise raise ourselves to view life and the dharma with an aesthetic mind rather than a mind that functions based on absolute truths or universal theories? This is not Suzuki's meaning, nor a paraphrase, it is an added explanation. Looking for the 'essence" of Zen, is probably his first mistake, giving up Buddha's pragmatic approach is another, and jumping to claim enlightenment on such a slim and precarious footing (my metaphor) is yet a third.

Meditation Practicum:

Call this the meditation on getting it done and reclaiming your personal power over your life; from a rather prosaic perspective: "What's lying around unattended to in your home or life? Pick it up right now and put it in its rightful place. [Make a list of all the incomplete projects that you need to finish, or wish to start when the time comes. The time has come.] Is it a piece of clothing [sort it and get rid of what no longer fits], paper, toothbrush [its time for a new one], person, relationship [call that former friend or neglected relative?] Is it an old dream that has been hanging there a long time? Just pick it up, wash or dust it off and put it where it belongs [or finish it to your own satisfaction.]" (Shoshanna, pg. 45) If all this takes a week of frantic doing to get caught up, it will be the best week of active meditation this year. Feel the power oozing back into your psyche as you progress, with awareness, through all these procrastinated tasks. Then congratulate yourself, you are ready for enlightenment!

"From the Zen point of view, anger is one of the three poisons, a great affliction. The rush [or psychic release or benefit] is counterfeit, [a myth] a substitute for real strength. [It's just a bad habit and destructive personality trait.] And the fragile self it is seen to protect, doesn't even really exist. It is a figment of our imagination. Others and ourselves can only be harmed [according to the law of cause and effect] by negative outbursts." This advice is not just a biased version of saying: "Asian mentality is a passive aggressive personality" stereotype we read about in tourist guide books, it is advocated by many counselors and psychologists in Western cultures as well.

"Anger is often justified by saying that some individuals are 'bad' and deserve the punishment inflicted upon them [by our ranting.] In fact, punishment is thought to straighten them up, give them due, or in some way or other teach the bad guys a lesson." Do people hear you better and respond more appropriately in the way you want them to when you yell at them? Does this acknowledge the sacred in them as well as in yourself?

"Zen rejects the hypothesis that individuals are either good or bad. Human life is fluid [and possibly `sacred`.] Zen points to the fact that one moment we can be saints, the next moment, devils. Good turns to bad and the other way around—our lives can be described as a process that contains all permutations. As we practice we learn not to hate hell, but to recognize it for what it is [right here surrounding us when our anger controls our personality] and recognize the danger and pain it contains." It's like dealing with toxic chemicals or radioactive material, and can harm and cause irreversible negative consequences.

"When anger and hate arise within us, when domination, cruelty, and ambition arise, we maintain balance and simply experience them for what they are. [Let them go their way like a wild, scared bear.] We do not repress and deny the energy, [or emotion knocking at our internal body door] but experience it fully [be aware of it, let it fizzle] and let it go. To stay steady and centered during the experience of anger, not to lash out, is a mark of the ripened person." (Shoshanna, pg. 98) When we can do this consistently, this is a sign that we are poised with class for enlightenment. This self-determination, this external change in our lives, is a stronger sign of progress toward realizing life as art, than any image we may have during meditation. If we need to create some ritual posture or *mudra* for our own use to help us develop this capacity; that is certainly a good idea.

Use some calming music or recreation when a long-term anger strikes that needs some serious ritual assistance. Listen to the sound of tropical birds, Native American drumming or Kenny G meditation music. Whatever it takes; take control of your own expression of anger, describe it, name it rather than act it out, (so there are no subsequent undesirable consequences that lead to an endless chain of suffering) as you would presume to take control of your own happiness.

Biographical Sketch:

Sanjaya was a skeptic who came to The Buddha "... to investigate whether Shakyamuni . . . was indeed an outstanding teacher . . . The uncle turned to Shakyamuni and said, 'I am a skeptic and cannot recognize any conclusive doctrine.'

"Shakyamuni replied, 'Do you, who say you cannot recognize any conclusive doctrine, recognize your own conclusive doctrine?' The uncle did not know what to say."

"At the rear of Mahabodhi Temple there is a *Bodhi tree* (as well as among the relics of Ayutia and Sukimvet), like the one under which The Buddha achieved Enlightenment. The bodhi (or called bo tree) is a variety of fig tree (bodhirukkha, Ficus *religiosa*) the Indian fig tree (peepul/pipal/peepal) . . . The shape of the *bodhi tree leaf* became a common motif in Buddhist (and even Hindu) architecture. For example, the main entrance to Ajanta includes the bodhi tree leaf pattern. Furthermore, such statues of the Buddha as the one in the Thai temple at Bodh Gaya feature the same leaf pattern: the crest of the leaf becomes the point of the Buddha's crown, and the two cut-away lower parts of the leaf relocated at either side, become the Buddha's ears." (Ithisan, pg. 37-8) At those temple sites where such trees exist there is a special ambiance that is hard even for a non-believer to dismiss. The leaf of the tree is, curiously, the shape of a "spade" (as cottonwood, aspen and others) in a common deck of cards, and is frequently used in artistic presentations, often as a symbol of enlightenment. During my experiences in Thailand each time, I visited bodhi trees and saw them stand unassuming, gnarled, complex, always unidentified, but with a simple grandeur. And even now I have a fondness for these trees (and a collection of leaves) after many years and enjoy having a picture of one around often.

Matsuo Basho (1644-1694) was not a Zen monk but a poet who consciously transformed the practice of poetry into an authentic religious way. By nature prone to wanderlust, he loved the life of the open road that led him to where he could commune with unspoiled nature. From these lonely wanderings came his poems. His preference was for the highly economical seventeen-syllable haiku form, which he took to unparalleled heights of poetic subtlety. Many of his finest haiku are thought to succinctly catch the elusive, often melancholy magic of the passing moment, and thereby express the true spirit of Zen." (Snelling, pg. 163) Most haiku poets in North America have become aware that 17 English syllables (5-7-5) convey a great deal more information than 17 Japanese syllables, and have come to write haiku in fewer syllables, most often in three segments that follow a short-long-short pattern without a rigid structure. This style is called by some "free-form" haiku. Simply writing short poems. Writing unstructured odes is a more popular Western approach; there being no right or wrong way to write a poem, only that one be engaged in this activity every day, at least mentally. I think of being a Buddhist as living in a poem.

Reading for the Day:

Part of Enlightenment may be simply knowing that rewards in an afterlife are fictional and furthermore not necessary to motivate compassion and sustain a virtuous life. Thus, nirvana is obtainable on Earth as the ultimate, continuous, self-directed aesthetic experience; the peace of mind resulting from self-consciousness that exists in the heart and mind of each buddha. This involves knowing with confidence a way of living, day after day, that is its own reward—and comes naturally to the aspiring Samahito. Can this Enlightenment be the result of progress in former lives?—who knows and does it matter?—but for sure in this life—as a result of cleansing, virtuous living, calm meditation, showing compassion and faith that this all makes life important and worth living and sharing.

> "The brilliance of his [her] wisdom/
> will be like the shining of the sun;
> Even in his dreams/
> he [she] will see only wonderful things."
> (Watson, pg. 210)

> I have no wings, yet
> I fly across the ocean
> An albatross, a gull.
> (IHJ, 18/5/09)
> Written in route to Thailand.

> My Pain talks to me
> About growing old, slowly
> But I ignore it.
> (IHJ, 18/5/09)

From the yoga perspective we learn the same thing—which now makes more sense when viewed from the perspective of Buddhism: "When the fluctuations of our minds subside, and the mind becomes clear and balanced like a jewel, the object of our concentration can then be reflected. We can concentrate on an object, such as a flame, or an organ of perception, like the eye, or an abstract idea, like the sense of ego. A state of fusion or identity between the Self and the object of concentration is known as Samadhi. The mind is completely absorbed and loses itself in the object or idea of meditation." (Forstater, pg. 288)

Visualize: "At dawn when we woke up [today], the joyous atmosphere of the nature in the morning enables us to be cheerful, so physically and mentally happy that we cannot describe. We did not see a busy crowd because we disassociate ourselves from them preserve our training mind at a calm place [possibly] along the fringe of woodland where light breeze blows regularly everyday . . . After we finish breakfast when we cannot stand hunger, we exercise meditation by walking to warm up the body to be awake to perceive sense-objects externally and internally efficiently. [By now] we understand well enough the method of the practice for mind development by Concentration Meditation and Insight Meditation. After the practice by walking, we practice by sitting. We alternate walking with sitting [or just standing] at our convenience till it is dark then rest." (Wee, pp. 114-115) This is the first day of our week of dedication to enlightenment.

Protecting:

We all have a need for, or at least we most often respond well to ritual and abstract ceremony. Like listening to our favorite song over and over, there is some psychic massage going on. There is no need to shy away from this, even for a Rational Buddhist. Uniquely in Buddhism, one is encouraged to be on the outside looking [mindfully] in on rituals, recognize both the aesthetic quality and the devotional experience, as opposed to avoiding them. Some esoteric power might just rub off, hold that possibility open by attending, or at the very least, a ritual service can be a time for meditation in an open mode of concentration, the ritual being the object. Most often Buddhist ceremonies are meant as mnemonic devices or teaching opportunities, more than superstitious practices, although there is a good deal of that, at least on the surface. Those who have a devotion to the ceremony and approach it with a feeling of the numinous, are no more welcome than the Rational Buddhist who can use this opportunity to look inside him/herself to see what is happening because of the ceremony. What happens to the practitioner is what is most important.

Repeat: "Now I accept this leaf—the same shape as the Bodhi tree leaf—as a symbol of my impermanence, and my accomplishment, having made ready for advancement to Samahito." It is up to you.

"This is what I heard," review by both Samahito and teacher.

Proverb: True wealth is what you are, not what you have. (wellpage.com)

Additional Teachings:

"When the mind is in samadhi, we can walk or stand or sit or lie down or work or taste the fruit of our labor or help others or help our-selves. The samadhi-citta can be used on any problem, in any situation. It can be used to solve all problems. Be interested in this word samahito—one who has samadhi and is able to perform every kind of duty."

"According to the discourses, what is a necessary condition for being able to gain stream-entry is a state of mind completely free from the five hindrances. Although a convenient way to remove the hindrances is the development of absorption, this is not the only way to do so . . . the hindrances can also be removed and the mind become concentrated even during walking meditation . . . another passage shows that the hindrances can be temporarily absent even outside the context of formal meditation, such as when one is listening to the Dhamma." (Analayo, pg. 80)

Sharing Merit:

Rejoicing In Others' Merit (Saying Sadhu)

Buddhist Sutra

Lesson Title: **Aesthetics and Happiness**

Lesson Number: **Twenty**

Key Vocabulary: satori, aesthetic, life as an art form, haiku form, identity, esoteric power, incompletes, personal power, compounded phenomena, equanimity, Bodhi tree

Assignment: Meditate during a calming sound experience of your choosing, possibly a rendition of tropical birds or the sounds of waves at the ocean. Be aware of the sounds, and let these prompt you into a shinay concentration. Alternate walking and standing with sitting. Use repeatedly, review and memorize the twelve steps you have learned. There are four more yet to come.

What beliefs do you maintain like Sanjaya the cynic, that are dogmatic, that do not allow for the hearing of contradictory views?

Discuss the art of living with another member of the sangha. Note your conclusions.

If the only thing you had to do to reach enlightenment and nirvana was to take charge of your life, deal with anger and sadness in the Buddhist way, to be the best person you know how to be; no more excuses! Is it worth it? Can you do it?

Define each of the Key Vocabulary in your own words.

Make a list of your incompletes, large and small, and possibly do some of the small ones first to give yourself the power to tackle the big ones.

Start this best week (finishing incompletes) in active meditation. This will give you the personal power to overcome suffering.

What are these problematic "transient entities" indicated by Buddha to Sanjaya? (Concepts, deities, humans?)

Develop a private mudra or ritual that you alone know, that can be a mnemonic device to recall your desired response to anger.

Can your Enlightenment be the result of progress in former lives?—who knows and does it matter?—but for sure in this life—as a result of cleansing, virtuous living, calm meditation and faith, this all makes life important and worth living and sharing. Discuss.

Materials Required: Tea ceremony. Begin tomorrow with a walking meditation. Beads for tying.

Buddhist Sutra

Lesson Title: **Nutrition—The Mind**

Lesson Number: **Twenty-one**

Rationale:

"The real Buddhism is not books, not manuals, not word for word repetition from the Tipitaka, nor is it rites and rituals . . . One ought not to rely on rites and rituals, nor anything else external, including spirits [special clothing] and celestial beings [or myths.] Rather one must be directly concerned with bodily action, speech and thought . . . to control and eliminate the defilements so that clear insight can arise. One will then be automatically capable of acting appropriately, and will be free from suffering from that moment right up to the end." (Buddhadasa, 2005, pp. 25-26)

By now each Samahito has hopefully adjusted to the austere practice typical of the Buddhist monastery and eats small portions and only prior to noon. There are exceptions for people of very low body fat who should perhaps eat more frequently, but for the rest of us, this will enhance meditation *as a fruit of our practice* by allowing the body to produce more of the natural "hallucinogens" or neurotransmitters than normally occur.

Discussion of Prior Lesson:

"The uncle [Sanjaya] did not know what to say [to Buddha]. If he recognized his own theory, he would be self-contradictory in that his own skepticism could not be applied to what he himself advocated. On the other hand, if he said that his own standpoint was dubious, he would no longer have any reason for maintaining it. As [contemporaneous] Greek philosophy also pointed out, this weakness is inherent in all skepticism, and Shakyamuni posed his question because he knew this." (Mizuno, pg. 88)

Training Objective:

How a vow can help you make progress? Know the five aggregates and the mind well. Know well the Four Foundations of Insight Meditation. Vegetarian diets—moderation. Step thirteen.

Materials Required: Tea ceremony. Begin the morning with a walking meditation for about two miles. Beads for tying.

Motivational Statement:

When (and if) we overeat, are we just feeding the monkey in our minds? Certainly the requirements of our bodies are fairly minimal depending on our work or level of activity. "We become sick because we act in sickening ways . . . What is it that is causing despair, anxiety, and constriction of [our] life? . . . As we practice Zen [or Rational Buddhism] a new part of ourselves emerges and grows strong [the best that we can be becomes all that we can be], bringing freedom from this inner tyrant. We call this new part our Buddha Nature . . . something that has been there [in us] all along, simply covered by the ignorance and restlessness . . . we simply reclaim that which we had always been [as a sign that we are ready to be called *Samadhi*.]

"In fact, our original mind is pure and beautiful. It is called '*splendid mind.*' It is a mind without defilements comprising greed, aversion and ignorance as well as sixteen impurities and five hindrances . . . Concentration will be able to overcome the [negative] power of the following five hindrances so that they cannot manifest themselves as unwholesomeness through body and speech: 1. sensual desire 2. ill will 3. sloth and torpor 4 distraction and remorse 5. doubt, uncertainty . . . one more to add to the above five is lack of knowledge . . . Major defilements that make mind impure are 1. greed, 2. aversion and 3. ignorance . . . there is another cause that can make mind impure and is important to our practice. That is diet or food that we eat as per our desire for deliciousness to pander to our wish for the sake of the body. If we eat without mindfulness, it is consuming [for the purpose of] feeding defilements . . . For this reason, we should pay attention to our daily diet so that it can become [one of our] habits for our practice for mind development." (Wee, pp. 81-82)

First Progressive:

Before Siddhartha (Shakyamuni) became enlightened as a buddha, he spent six years in extreme asceticism accompanied by five bhikkhus or companions (Kondanna, Vappa, Assaji, Mahanama, and Bhaddiya.) The tradition suggests that he became emaciated, and figurines showing him as skin and bones are often found among the Buddhist images and artworks. He eventually realized that there was nothing wrong with eating a reasonable amount of food. Throughout his 45 year period as a teacher *he was a mendicant and collected alms for his meals*, in addition to which he accepted the beneficence and attended banquets provided by wealthy donors and followers. Chinese traditions show the happy Buddha as a corpulent and even obese character who obviously enjoyed a good meal.

At some point soon it may be desirable to choose a Buddhist tradition and immerse oneself with a Sangha and respected teacher. "Since, ultimately, *wisdom and compassion are manifestations of the same non-dual condition of the fully realized mind*, guru yoga becomes a skillful means by which the seed of awakened wisdom is planted, which then complements the seed of compassion previously planted through the development of an enlightened attitude . . . [at some point] you must first receive the guru's blessing." (Brown, pg. 120) This kind of assessment and protection is an essential step for all sincere aspirants. In the meantime, one can donate money or otherwise choose to support a Sangha. Something to look forward to in the future.

> "If you wish to abide in the Buddha way
> And successfully gain the wisdom that comes of itself,
> You should be constantly diligent in offering alms
> To those who embrace the Lotus Sutra."
>
> (Watson, pg. 162)

"*When compassion begins* to awaken in your own heart, you're able to be more honest with yourself. If you make a mistake, you can acknowledge it and take steps to correct it. At the same time, you're less likely to look for flaws in other people. If people do something offensive, if they start screaming at you or treating you badly, you'll notice (probably with some surprise) that you don't react in the same way you once might have."(Mingyur, pg. 229) Smiling, laughing, apologizing and patience are true signs of compassion.

Second Progressive:

"In the armies of Mara (the traditional evil spirit) among the hazards and tribulations are listed: sensual pleasures, discontent, hunger and thirst, craving . . ." (Inthisan, pg. 33) So starvation and extreme asceticism sometimes associated with Yogis, is not a tradition among most Buddhist orders, nor is it expected or required of lay members.

There is a certain irony how some groups of people are preoccupied and suffer from starvation, and others with obesity that can become lethal (i.e. diabetes). Is being overweight a moral issue? Does it help to write a vow such as a New Year's resolution to lose weight? Perhaps, if we wish to lose weight we have to learn to gain our comfort from other than eating.

Sit well rooted
In the tree's shade daily
Birds—sing nirvana.
(IJ, 2007)

"When we start to understand that life is suffering, though we do not understand clearly, it does not matter. We can gradually practice. However, we need to have knowledge in practicing the teachings and let it lead our life always. This will enable us not to be imprudent in life and prone to errors. If we always are in the stream of wholesomeness, it is very beneficial for us . . . studying the Buddhist Teachings and using them as guide for the practice means that we lead our lives prudently every day, every minute and we may meet in the future with happiness resulting from wholesomeness we have been accumulating as per our mindfulness and wisdom." (Wee, pp. 26-27)

'Taking life not only includes the murder of human beings [taking away their breath] of course, but killing other living beings as well. This inevitably raises the question of whether meat-eating is permissible or not in Buddhism [as discussed in Lesson Nine, Right Action] . . . it was technically permissible for [the monks at the time of Buddha] to eat meat, but only if they knew that an animal, bird, or fish had not been killed specially to provide them with food. Many find this rather permissive attitude unsatisfactory . . ." (Snelling, pg. 48) Most Asians eat meat, perhaps more sparingly and with more respect than do Westerners?

Absolute insistence on vegetarian diets, including no eggs or milk, is a case of the rule becoming over-reaching and a hindrance to the development of enlightenment. Animals consume roughage, waste and seeds that humans cannot properly digest, and they have a short and limited life cycle (like most fish and birds). There is also the issue of the natural food chain to contemplate. However, in Buddha's day there were many unknown parasites and diseases which could be contracted from improperly feed animals, inadequate storage and unsanitary processing of meat, and even after cooking e-coli and salmonella etc., can contaminate meat. (Anyone who has walked through a street market almost anywhere in Asia, will surely tend toward vegetarianism.) The occurrence of these diseases (as with worms in pork which might be associated with the taboo against pork, and "kosher" for Semitic peoples) can easily explain the rise of superstitions against eating meat. When taken to the extreme, becoming a moral obligation, and creating a sense of self-righteousness, this becomes a hindrance to progress in spiritual development.

Third Progressive:

Our hunger and need for nutrition are what connects food to our minds. Again: "According to Buddhism, our body is five aggregates (Khandha) or it can be called Sankhara. Khandha is part of body and mind. Khandha is composed of: 1. corporeality (Rupa), 2. sensation (Vedana), 3. perception (Sanna), 4. mental formations (Sankhara), 5. consciousness (Vinnana)."

1) "Corporeality is the thing that can be perceived through [the five senses]. (matter, form) Another component of life is *Nama. Nama* comes along with Rupa. *Nama* is an invisible [sensation] thing. It can be perceived through mind only."
2) "Sensation is feeling: feeling of happiness, suffering or neutrality." These are composites, complex emotions even abstract conceptualizations felt at the intuitive level.
3) "Perception is idea, remembrance; idea of what that can be [and has been] perceived through 6 sense doors."
4) "Mental Formations are thought, volitional activities, essential condition [of] mind to be wholesome, unwholesome or neutral."
5) "Consciousness is awareness of senses perceived through the sixth sense-doors. They are eye consciousness, ear consciousness, nose consciousness, tongue consciousness, body consciousness and mind consciousness. This aggregate is Mind." (Wee) Proof of this is how we can remember smells and tastes, and make judgments about them, such as identifying the difference between bitter, salt and sweet and our similar preferences each time we experience them.

"Five aggregates in Buddhism means our life which consists of body (Rupa) and mind (Nama). Knowledge about body and mind is essential for Insight Meditation (Vipassana) because Vipassana is practice by mindfulness on Rupa and *Nama [remember this is about looking inside.*] Next is fundamental knowledge required for Insight Meditation, that is the Twelve Sense-Bases (Ayatana). Ayatana are sense-organs and sense-objects. For example, eye is a sense-organ and visible objects are sense-objects. The twelve Sense-bases are divided into two groups: Six internal sense-bases [same meaning as body-door] and six external sense-bases. Six internal sense-bases comprise eye, ear, nose, tongue, body and mind. Six external sense bases comprising visible objects, sound, smell, taste, tangible objects and mind objects [concepts] . . . Internal sense-doors are the channels for eye, ear, nose, tongue, body and mind . . . Tangible object is what is perceived through body such as cold, heat, softness, hardness, roughness, fineness. We can perceive sense-objects through sense-bases or sense-doors because Nama, which is mind, functions. We sense objects because we have mind inside the body. That is why mind is extremely important for all lives and for the meditation; both concentration and insight." (Wee)

"Citta is mind [elsewhere it also means Heart.] Its function is to perceive, think and reflect. It is mentality. It is [heart] formless. [unlike Nama—interpretations] It cannot be perceived through eye, ear, nose, tongue and body. It comes along with materiality (Rupa Dhamma). In Buddhism, mind is mentality. It is invisible. It is a nature which perceives sense-objects. It has four functions: 1. to be aware of, 2. to perceive, 3. to remember sense-objects and 4. to think about them."

"If we do not have mind in our body, it means that we pass away. What can indicate that we have mind as part of life is the feeling rising when we perceive touch from external sense-objects . . . the hard core of Buddhism is mind development. The Lord Buddha taught people to practice [exercise the] mind so that it can be perfectly pure and can develop wisdom to be able to attenuate, give up and eradicate completely all defilements in mind. That is why mind is essential for life and Buddhism." (Wee, pp. 46-50) That is what makes the practice of Rational Buddhism so useful, not only on a "spiritual" level, but on a pragmatic level. Using the allegorical concept of Heart (e.g. thinking, consciousness, compassion, conscience, memories) as part of the linguistic map of "citta" makes many of the teachings more poignant.

"We eat when we are really hungry [but only before noon]. Start the day by walking then sitting or standing (not lying) . . . We practice to make the body ready and healthy; that is efficient. We sit for the practice right immediately after we walk. This day we have to fight against uncomfortable feelings rising because we have never [lived on such little food.] . . . We have to defeat [cravings] which is destroyer caused by aggregates (Khandha-mara). It is an enemy of the practice. This destroyer is caused by the body . . . we may feel itchy on the body and the face as if a small chicken mite walked on us. Sometimes it makes us annoyed and uncomfortable. It troubles us and prevents us from easily practicing meditation." (Wee, pg. 115) Meditate for as long as possible in each position until the pain forces you to change to another position, and this way you can understand (internally, physically) a little bit more about suffering and cessation of suffering. Furthermore, the stress of suffering (and being hungry) helps the body produce excess neurotransmitters that can induce the emotional reactions associated with rapture and Jhana.

Meditation Practicum:

". . . The whole purpose of calmness meditation is to gain the ability to enter absorption as a stepping-stone for the development of insight, a sort of preliminary duty that either needs or does not need to be fulfilled. The discourses offer a different perspective. Here calm and insight are two complementary aspects of mental development. The question of practicing only insight meditation does not arise, since the important function of calmness meditation, as a practice in its own right, is never reduced to its auxiliary role in relation to insight meditation." (Analayo, pg. 89)

Review the discussions on the Four Foundations of Insight Meditation because this is the big picture.

"1. We must mindfully note the [stimulation] at the body-door . . . every moment to develop the mind to always focus on the sense-object of the mind and matter [first aggregate]."

"2. The supreme purpose of the Dhamma practice is to attain insight knowledge; that is ability to see suffering. Attaining insight into the truth of life, mind will find the way out of the body . . . separate from the body is called the Fourth Jhana (The Fourth Absorption)." But that is jumping ahead.

"3. Do not worry about ten imperfections happening. We just mindfully note the mind and matter [inside the body] as sense-objects."

"4. Do not cling to the mental images especially ten imperfections."

"5. In practicing the four Foundations of Mindfulness, the mind can be concentrated. We must know the feeling state of five raptures especially diffused rapture telling the feeling that the body is relieved, relaxed, bigger, and taller unusually. When passing the level of the diffused rapture state, the mind attains the Jhana state." (Wee, pp. 186-187) This Thai author is referring to Satipatthana rather than Anapanasati as a meditation scheme; this is discussed and explained in *Bodhicitta, Higher Truth.* We begin the preliminary explanation of jhana in the next lesson.

"In meditation practice, we have to eat only when we are so hungry that we suffer. [In this way we reinforce the lesson that life has been full of suffering.] Paying no more attention to food is thus correct according to the discipline of the practice to develop mind to be pure and free from internal defilements. Body belongs to defilements which create the body primarily and the body needs food to survive. Therefore, when we can cut off the concern for food consumption, it means that we can eradicate defilements indirectly." (Wee, pg. 82) When we eat a balanced, modest diet we have neutralized this craving; take it as a sign of approaching enlightenment.

"The contemporary mahamudra master Bokar Rinpoche makes a distinction between correct and incorrect staying-clam practice. He explains that the relative cessation of elaborated thought and emotion in-and-of-itself is incorrect in that it can easily lead to further obscurity. Yet the relative cessation of thought and emotion combined with clarity becomes the way of preventing obscurity. The respective terms *clarity, and awareness-itself* refer to the corresponding aspects of the mind's natural condition that manifest once purified of coarse-level perceptions, emotions, and thoughts, respectively. *Brightness* refers to a quality of mind that manifests once no longer obscured by elaborated thought . . . you 'generate the force of samadhi' . . ." (Brown, pg. 168) with respect to objects of perception, by improving clarity. When emotional objects are stabilized, this permits the development of bliss. When thoughts are purified "no longer obscured by elaborated thought" the awareness-itself and brightness are manifest. These details give useful hints to the Samahito, and this gives one confidence that their meditation practice can be advanced. Each step of the way, we must choose, "Yes, I want to take the next step."

Another perspective is: "Samadhi with deliberation is when we consciously identify the object of concentration by its name, shape and our knowledge of it. Samadhi without deliberation is a higher stage where we identify the object of our concentration with only our intuitive inner knowledge of the object. We are able to still our reactions to the object and focus on it as it truly is without any preconceived ideas." (Forstater, pp. 288-289) This clearly describes What we do, now we also know How to do it. We can examine any aspect of our lives, and work to eliminate each remaining source of suffering such as the 108 defilements.

Step thirteen: "The mind has [by now] a great deal of kammaniyo, readiness or activeness, from the practice of concentrating the mind . . . the mind is mudu (gentle and supple) . . . we return to the beginning step. First, we contemplate just the breath until we see that it is impermanent. We observe [following] that the breath changes and becomes long. Its long duration is impermanent, always changing, getting longer or shorter. Its shortness is impermanent as well . . . The breath's effect on the body is also impermanent." (Yet continuous and pervasive.) As you practice through the first twelve steps of Anapanasati Bhavana, notice that each step is impermanent. "Eventually, the feelings of piti and sukha arise. Watch them one by one. See impermanence in each . . . The calming of these feelings is impermanent as well . . . Next, we watch the citta itself; it, too, is impermanent. [etc.] . . . Even the liberating of the mind is only a temporary liberation here and thus is also impermanent." This explains why we must engage in meditation for the rest of our lives to maintain the gains we make and touch repeatedly the great joy we are beginning to realize.

"Now, observe that in the realization of impermanence there is the simultaneous realization of many other aspects. When *impermanence* is truly seen, it also has the characteristic of dukkham, namely, it is painful and *unbearable*. We can also find the characteristic of *not-self (anatta)* [external causes] in it. As these things are always changing, impermanent, unsatisfactory [the source of suffering,] and beyond our control, we realize anatta as well . . . We see they are void of self-hood, which is sunnata . . . Impermanence is just thus, just like that, thus-ness [a fact of all nature.] And so, tathata is seen as well."

"Please understand that the realizations of these truths are interrelated. From seeing impermanence, we see unsatisfactoriness . . . and see idappaccayata (conditionality, the law of cause and effect) as well. Each continues into the next . . . To see aniccam alone, in an incomplete way [it is not enough] that does not include dukkham and anatta, is neither profound nor sufficient to solve our problems. Thus, 'realizing aniccam' [impermanence] in this context must encompass a realization as deep as dukkham, anatta, sunnata, tathata, and idappaccayata . . . The short phrase aniccanupassana (contemplating impermanence) includes the realization of unsatisfactoriness, not-self, voidness, thusness, and conditionality as well."

"Now, observe—study closely until you see it—*that the realization of annicam dissolves upadana, dissolves attachment*. This is crucial. Realizing aniccanupassana dissolves attachment because we realize the pain and suffering of the attachment. Upadana dissolves until less and less remains. Such is the [end] result of realizing impermanence [and completing the idea.]" (Buddhadasa, 1988, pp. 83-88) No one said it would be easy, just understanding all the Pali words is an accomplishment.

Biographical Sketch:

Along with freedom, even mental freedom, comes responsibility. "The experience of this much freedom can have different consequences. [Becoming a Samahito] For some it becomes an addiction. Ordinary life seems meaningless and they spend their time chasing after enlightenment, or bliss. All they want is the freedom, oneness or peace. This is called *Zen sickness, or stinking of Zen.* It happens to those who are in early stages of practice. Just because one has an enlightenment experience does not mean that the person is far along . . . If anything, now he or she needs to practice more."

"Joshu, the great Zen Master, had his first great enlightenment at the age of sixty. He then stayed in the monastery and practiced until he was eighty, so his enlightenment could grow ripe. When he was eighty he left and established his own school and taught until he was one hundred and two, spreading his light far and wide."

"Another form of Zen sickness is a person believing, because of some enlightenment experience, that he is special, better than anyone else. He utters Zen phrases and looks at others with a strange glint in his eyes. This kind of sickness needs treatment immediately."

"A famous Zen teaching says, 'If you see the buddha, kill the buddha.' This has been widely misunderstood. It simply addresses this particular Zen sickness. It means, if you see someone acting like a great, enlightened being, pay no attention to him. Look within for the enlightened one. Do not venerate others and lose yourself." (Shoshanna, pp. 208-209) A good dose of humility is a healthy tonic.

Reading for the Day:

"One means to purify mind is to cut off the desire for food. As a result, when we eat food, it must not be for the desire. We eat only when we are hungry [to supply nutrition.] We must not eat a lot and we have to realize the taste of food. By doing so, we will obtain fruitful results easily from the practice for mind development. Especially in Concentration Meditation, we will be able to mentally see mental images clearly like we see clearly an object that fell to the bottom of a well but the water in the well is so clear and transparent because there is not much sediment or lichen."(Wee, pp. 82-83) Just like swimmers are warned not to swim for an hour after eating, meditators will notice over-fullness as a distraction.

"Such understanding [samadhi] prompts awareness of the need to strive for the perfecting of one's own personality and of all society. If society as a whole improves and develops, the happiness of the individual will be guaranteed. If society is happy, the individual and all of his fellows will be happy. This is the meaning of true happiness and of the realization of the ideal Buddhist realm. Buddhist training is for the sake of realizing such a realm." (Mizuno, pg. 96) But this idealism aside, samadhi is about developing the mind to achieve the goal of nirvana.

"Since all conceptions of phenomena are nothing but activities of the mind, so, speaking truly, the mind is not a fantastic thing but it becomes a fantastic thing. If you are not in bondage to these contaminations [attachments or arbitrary conceptions,] of your own mind, there will be neither arbitrary conceptions or fantastic things, or of things that are not fantastic." You will be able to perceive the world as it is.

"As there is no rising in your Essential Mind of such arbitrary conceptions as non-fantastic things, why should they be raised at all? This teaching is the wonderful 'Lotus Flower.' It is as gloriously enlightening as the diamond, as mysteriously potent as highest Samadhi. This is the incomparable Teaching! Anyone practicing it with sincerity and earnestness will out do the graduate disciples in a single moment, as suddenly as a rap on the door. Such a one will become Honored of all the Worlds! Indeed! This Teaching is the only path to Nirvana. The Surangama Sutra." (Goddard, pg. 216)

Protecting:

"Concentration (samadhi—absorption) is one-pointedness of mind, mental concentration practiced to make mind calm and develop insight. It can be stated that concentration is exercised to make the mind well established and calm without six hindrances." (Wee, pg. 92)

As a review: "The word samadhi is used in the Pali literature on meditation with varying degrees of specificity of meaning. In the narrowest sense, as defined by Buddhaghosa, it denotes the particular mental factor responsible for the concentrating of the mind, namely, one-pointedness. In a wider sense it can signify the states of unified consciousness that result from the strengthening of concentration, i.e., the meditative attainments of serenity and the stages leading up to them. And in a still wider sense the word samadhi can be applied to the method of practice used to produce and cultivate these refined states of concentration, here being equivalent to the development of serenity." (Access)

Each person wishing to be acknowledge as a Samahito will take 16 beads and tie a string or mala to use in their prayer/meditation practice.

Please repeat: "What kind of freedom is this, from which more is expected?"

"This is what I heard," review by both Samahito and teacher.

Additional Teachings:

"The next important hindrance and allurement is the tendency of all sentient beings of all the six realms of existence to gratify their pride of egoism. To gain this, one is prone to be unkind, to be unjust and cruel to other sentient beings . . . The reason for practicing dhyana and seeking to attain Samadhi is to escape from the suffering of life, but in seeking to escape from suffering ourselves, why should we inflict it upon others? . . . No matter how keen you may be mentally, no matter how much you may be able to practice dhyana, no matter to how high a degree of Samadhi you may attain, unless you have wholly annihilated all tendency to unkindness toward others, you will ultimately fall into the realms of existence where the evil ghosts dwell."

". . . But how can any faithful follower of the Lord Tathagata kill sentient life and eat the flesh?" The Surangama Sutra (Goddard, pg. 264) Are "lower" animals sentient beings? or was this an ancient lesson against cannibalism and human sacrifice that was practiced in the time of Buddha?

The role of meditation in the elimination of defilements is as follows. "You need to sit in the place where the whole world of your experience is coming up and passing away so rapidly that there is just nothing to hang on to. Nothing lasts long enough for you to mentally glue it together into 'something.' As soon as you turn your attention to any occurrence, it goes 'poof'! It vanishes as soon as pure awareness touches it. It all just comes up and goes away, leaving no trace. There is no time for such a trace to be left—as each thing comes up, it pushes the last thing out of the mind and there is no residue. You come out of this experience with no solid memory of anything that occurred. There is just the lingering impression of everything arising and passing away more rapidly than the mind can hold. This is termed 'seeing things as they really are.' You are not verbalizing or conceptualizing. You are just 'seeing.' This happens in the awareness of your deeply concentrated mind . . . When you see things this way, you lose interest in trying to hold on to things [at least in the sensitivity of your Heart.] You see that it is futile and harmful and cannot lead to any truth or happiness." (Gunaratana, pg. 87) Parts of the "world of your experience" are often contained in the mental distractions that buzz through your head, and as you recognize the suffering intrinsic in each one, one at a time, then you see it for what it is and some aspect of it can be neutralized and desensitized; poof!

Sharing Merit:

Rejoicing In Others' Merit (Saying Sadhu)

The 108 beads of a Buddhist necklace coincide to the 108 defilements as follows: (Virtue)

ostentatiousness	grudge	gambling	ingratitude
dipsomania	ambition	dominance	faithlessness
manipulation	stinginess	pessimism	hostility
Abuse	debasement	sexual lust	sarcasm
Humiliation	jealousy	gluttony	unruliness
Hurt	cruelty	unkindness	obstinacy
Envy	indifference	negativity	furtiveness
Sadism	enviousness	derision	falseness
high-handedness	know-it-all	rage	aggression
Rapacity	effrontery	disrespectfulness	hard-heartedness
Eagerness for power	lying	insidiousness	self-denial
inattentiveness	contempt	wrath	haughtiness
greed for money	seducement	vindictiveness	insatiability
voluptuousness	excessiveness	censoriousness	dissatisfaction
Egoism	ignorance	hatred	greed
Impudence	imposture	cursing	imperiousness
lecherousness	callousness	malignancy	torment
Intolerance	blasphemy	shamelessness	irresponsibility
Obsession	prejudice	arrogance	violent temper
Garrulity	dogmatism	presumption	intransigence
Oppression	prodigality	lack of comprehension	obstinacy
Pride	conceitedness	delusion	quarrelsomeness
self-hatred	violence	vanity	hypocrisy
stubbornness	baseness	pretence	mercilessness
Disrespect	ridicule	masochism	tyranny
capriciousness	deceit	anger	discord
Calculation	unyielding	desire for fame	deception

Buddhist Sutra

Lesson Title: **Nutrition—The Mind**

Lesson Number: **Twenty-one**

Key Vocabulary: nama, vow, splendid mind, torpor, sense-bases, Zen sickness, brightness, citta, addictions, dukkham, sunnata, tathata, annicam, idappaccayata, upadana, aniccanupassana, kammaniyo, mudu

Assignment: Meditate on the hunger we feel at the sixth sense-door (of our stomach), as insight meditation using it as an internal object inside the body.

Realize the impermanence in its extended form—aniccanupassana—and take a beginning step toward dissolving attachments.

How important is being a vegetarian to you?

View the food we do not eat at night (and the sensation of hunger in our stomach that seeing it engenders) use this external source as an object of concentration meditation.

After the Lesson, Samadhi will choose a partner, who should be a different person each day, to accompany silently during the day.

What does it mean to say: The instinct to live is more than merely survival?

Memorize and understand the five aggregates. Explain these.

Define each of the Key Vocabulary in your own words.

Prepare (or review) a vow to do those things in your life that are standing in your way to enlightenment.

Write a haiku on the significance of arriving to the level of Samadhi.

> There is one idea
> That dwells in my mind each day
> Happiness to all.

Tomorrow wake early and start your practice at dawn, before eating, then eat sparingly.

Review the attached list of 108 defilements. Identify those most urgently needing work in your own life and take one all the way through the thirteen steps.

Materials Required: Vows, bottle of electrolytes

Buddhist Sutra

Lesson Title: Rapture—Lesser Thrill

Lesson Number: Twenty-two

Rationale:

This is where the rewards of meditation begin. "I state that the middle path does not lean closest to [either of] the two sides, I know that. It is the path to develop mental eye, Jhana (absorption), it is for tranquility, utmost knowledge, enlightenment and Nibbana. Why did I state so? It is because the Noble Eight-fold Path [teaches us the way] . . ." (Wee, pg. 27)

"When we hold the hindrances in abeyance, we can attain jhana. Concentration then weakens our greed [hatred, and delusion,] and greed is the principal cause of our suffering." (Gunaratana, pg. 82)

Proverb: Blessed are they who can laugh at themselves, for they shall never cease to be amused. (wellpage.com)

Discussion of Prior Lesson:

A "Technique and tip for food consumption at each meal is 'stop completely worrying about food consumption at each meal. Eat each time only when feeling so hungry that suffering due to hunger arises. Eat to end suffering [as analogy for suffering we wish to end in our lives,] eat only enough, do not eat too much'." (Wee, pg. 90)

Each Samahito may read their vow or haiku.

"A complete realization of impermanence must include unsatisfactoriness, not-self, voidness, thusness, and the law of causality. When we see all of these, then we have seen impermanence completely and in the most profound way. This is how we fully realize the impermanence of the sankhara." (Buddhadasa, 1988, pg. 86) (see steps three and seven)

Training Objective:

Know the images and signals of first rapture. Experience suffering and cessation of suffering using hunger. Pliancy and full awareness—to reduce attachments. Step fourteen of Anapanasati Bhavana. Schopenhauer on emptiness.

Materials Required: Vows, bottle of electrolytes

Motivational Statement:

"Being able to realize the breathing, the mind becomes concentrated to the level of Proximate concentration . . . Minor Rapture (Khuddaka-piti): it is lesser thrill during which we experience goose pimples, tear drops . . . The First Jhana: mind has five sensations: thought, discursive thinking (the mental feeling of ordinary people), rapture [which can be faith or devotion,] happiness (due to solitude or quietude) and mental one-pointedness." (Wee, pp. 143-145) This level of relaxation and joy should be easily obtained.

"Respectful admiration, which is associated with 'faith like the ancients,' is the prerequisite to empowerment [constantly respect the lama.] The way to pray for empowerment is to 'pray over and over, uninterruptedly . . . Empowerment as a skillful means eclipses the entire set of previous skillful means, and the effects of each are now qualitatively stronger due to the practitioner's progress in building the vessel." (Brown, pg. 123) In this case, during extreme admiration, the Samahito is said to receive help from an esoteric force coming from the outside. This comes from the supreme confidence that one possesses, however, it is possible to a lesser extent to benefit from the charisma of the Sangha participants acting in unison to help each member who is prepared to receive assistance with their development.

First Progressive:

"There are those who are so discouraged that they no longer have the *courage to love*. They suffer a great deal just because they made an attempt to love and failed. The wounds within them are so deep that it makes them afraid to try again. We are aware of the presence of these people among us, all around us. We have to bring them the message that love is possible. Our world desperately needs love." (Hanh, pg. 237) This remembrance can certainly be a source of tears for many people. When we really develop compassion we forgive and forget the words from past slights and insults from years past, as well as from yesterday. Each day is a new day in love.

"Contentment and tranquility [on the other hand] are the Holy Grail of the spiritual path. We can achieve this state of calm and stillness when we manage to *let go of our limited selfish desires* and instead find a healthier relationship with the world . . ." (Forstater, pp. 68-69) Yet some of the social obligations and personal relationships (and complications) that hang onto us may still interfere with our complete "tranquility." One way to lessen the impact of these negative factors is to reduce are attachment toward them, and know that we can place them into a different category in our lives where we are not diminished by them.

Proverb: Worry [as well as remorse] is like a rocking chair; it will give you something to do, but it won't get you anywhere. (wellpage.com)

As we make this initial progress with compassion for ourselves, we begin an upward spiral, as it were. "The progression goes like this: you temporarily restrain the hindrances to attain jhana; then you use jhanic concentration to gain wisdom; with the combined power of your concentration and wisdom, you eradicate the fetters and begin to eliminate ignorance more easily from the roots; concentration weakens your greed, which is the cause of suffering; finally, wisdom and concentration weaken and destroy both the hindrances and the fetters altogether; when the hindrances and fetters are destroyed, destroying ignorance is easy." (Gunaratana, pg. 82) It is our compassion based on mindfulness, developed by following our breath, that prompts us into this "upward" spiral that leads to the perception of jhanas.

We must also keep our meditation into a global context. ". . . Remember that the universe is filled with an infinite number of beings, and to think, just as I want happiness, all beings want happiness. Just as I wish to avoid suffering, all beings wish to avoid suffering. I am just one person, while the number of other beings is infinite. The well-being of this infinite number is more important than that of one. And as you allow these thoughts to roll around in your mind, you'll actually begin to find yourself actively engaged in wishing for others' freedom from suffering." (Mingyur, pg. 187) This helps us feel our humility, but just as important is the realization that yes we are one of these many, and we do count, and we do matter, and yes we deserve to be free of suffering too, so we can grasp enlightenment and nirvana for ourselves unashamedly.

Second Progressive:

"An ethical sense is a biological feature of our species . . . His remarks resonate . . . with the essence of the Buddha's teachings: The more clearly we see things as they are, the more willing and able we become to open our hearts toward other beings. When we recognize that others experience pain and unhappiness because they don't recognize their real nature, we're spontaneously moved by a profound wish for them to experience the same sense of peace and clarity that we've begun to know." (Mingyur, pg. 106)

"We are not necessarily all ascetics [nor idealists,] but I do not know if there is not in every one of us an eternal longing for a world beyond this of empirical relativity, where the soul can quietly contemplate its own destiny." [A pure land, a perfect fantasy place.] We can do this here and now as Samadhi.

"When Basho was still studying Zen under his master Buccho, the latter one day paid him a visit and asked, 'How are you getting along these days?'

Basho: 'After a recent rain the moss has grown greener than ever.'
Buccho: 'What Buddhism is there prior to the greenness of moss?'
Basho: 'A frog jumps into the water, hear the sound!'

"This is said to be the beginning of a new epoch in the history of Haiku.

Explanation: "Basho, questioned by his master about the ultimate truth of things which existed even prior to this world of particulars, saw a frog leaping into an old pond, its sound making a break into the serenity of the whole situation. The source of life has been grasped, and the artist sitting here watches every mood of his mind as it comes in contact with a world of constant becoming, and the result is so many seventeen syllables bequeathed to us." (Suzuki, pg. 286) A marvelous virtue.

Proverb: True wealth is what you are, not what you have. (wellpage.com)

The price of admission to higher states of meditative peace (jhana) is exemplary ethical conduct. "The material jhanas are four states of experience that lie just beyond our ordinary cognitive, sensory world, but still have some relationship to it. Normal words can be used to describe some of the events and phenomena here, but we must remember that much is metaphorical. You 'see' certain aspects of your experience, but it is not visual perception. Some people can attain liberation [from attachments and craving] without the material jhanas through the path of insight meditation alone." (Gunaratana, pg. 104) It would perhaps be the case, although it is not certain, that explaining what jhana is or might be is easier for someone for whom the experience comes often or easy. But to the extent that such experiences are beyond words, the best we might expect is to be led to the door, read the sign: "Jhana, here, today." and then have the experiences for ourselves.

Third Progressive:

"Mastery of the concentration stages of meditation opens up the subtle level of the mind. Mastery of the special-insight states opens up the very subtle or extraordinary level of the mind. Advanced pliancy entails shifting through these levels of mind with considerable skill, much like shifting gears in a car. Overall, mental pliancy pertains to the developing skill of having the mind stay optimally on its intended object despite changes in mental content, state, or level of consciousness, or perspective of observation [The Four Foundations of Mindfulness,] just as adjusting the shift and clutch maintains an optimal level of a car's progress despite continuous changes in speed and road condition . . . Likewise, the skillful meditator uses full awareness to watch the meditation and insure that its best qualities are brought out for the duration of the session . . . A wise practitioner uses *full awareness* to assess the quality of the meditation." (Brown, pg. 156)

"As [we] enter the first jhana, something remarkable happens. There is a total break with normal thought and perception. Your mind suddenly sinks into the breath and dwells. The breath is still there, but it is no longer a 'thing,' just a subtle thought, much like a memory or an after-image. The world goes away. Physical pain goes away. [We] do not totally lose all sensation, but the physical senses are off in the background. Wandering conscious thought stops. What remains are subtle thoughts of good will toward all beings [as suggested above.]"

"Your mind is filled with rapture, bliss, and one-pointedness. 'Rapture' or 'joy' [piti] is like the leaping elation you feel when you finally get what you have been after. 'Bliss' or 'happiness' is like the rich, sustained satisfaction you feel when you have it. Joy may be physical, like hair rising all over your body. It may be momentary flashes or waves that shower you again and again. Happiness is more restrained, a gentle state of continuing ecstasy . . . Happiness is like relaxing in the shade of a tree . . ." (Gunaratana, pp. 104-105)

What are the adverse circumstances in our lives that can cause us to have the emotional reactions to produce goose bumps and tears? (List them.) As we meditate we can take ourselves there, relive these experiences, nullify the causes and extinguish the suffering? We know we have achieved this turn around, when we have the same physical reaction during meditation as we had during the event itself. The *tears* will be instead tears of joy, the goose bumps will be caused by the coolness (the touch of nirvana,) and sensations beginning at the back of the neck from the sheer sense of relief and *euphoria*. The feeling of infatuation and erotic touch can bring on goose bumps (so can a sneeze); we can laugh so hard that we cry.

As we develop our good Hearts, we are becoming awakened (steps in purification) and realizing our Buddha nature. ". . . Each of us instinctively seeks to live a life of higher principles, universal values, and cosmic radiance and, in so doing, to help create a loving family and a better world. I call this drive 'spiritual tropism': we grow up turning as naturally toward spiritual light as a flower turns toward the sun. Buddhists would say that this inclination is the spontaneous stirring of our inherent Buddha nature. In fact . . . it's only when we allow our Buddha nature to unfold [through awakening and practicing mindfulness] in its most natural way that we truly bloom and blossom into life." (Surya Das, pg. xix) This is also accomplished by study of Dharma, including reading commentaries and discussions based on Lessons such as this one.

Meditation Practicum:

Our meditation practice should be as often as possible and as long a time in each position in each session as possible to ". . . ensure that you succeed in overcoming the *destroyers* caused by aggregates [the raw uncultivated human nature.] The important point of this day is to try to stop thinking about meals. We have to notice our hunger. We have to wait till we suffer from hunger; we then eat [but only before noon, but drink liquids every hour.]" (Wee, pg. 116)

"When we concentrate reflectively on finer and more subtle objects . . . or the correct vision of reality, we understand that the object is limitless and as such [in our minds we] can trace it back to its very source. These kinds of samadhi [absorptions] are said to be accompanied by the small seeds of desire and attachment. The ultimate goal has not yet been reached. Even when we have acquired these states, we can still be seduced by our desires because the impressions of them remain latent in our consciousness. This is why we have to meditate with a pure mind." (Forstater) This is what we work for each time we cycle through the sixteen steps of `Anapanasati Bhavana. We have three more steps to learn.

We can begin to experience jhana as early as after following the breath extensively and after the perfection of step four of Anapanasati. "The first taste of jhana is usually just a flash, but then you learn to sustain it for longer and longer periods. Eventually you can experience it whenever you meditate. It lasts as long as you have decided that it should last. In the first jhana, 'joy' or 'rapture' predominates." (Gunaratana, pg. 105) "When we reach non-reflective samadhi the mind becomes clear and serene, and the clear light of our [virtue] shines out. This is absolute awareness, in which the mind is pervaded by true knowledge and understanding. We become [as profound as] our deepest knowledge, the wisdom of inner truth." (Forstater, pg. 289) This is the goal for both yoga and for Buddhist meditation through the fifth and sixth steps of Anapanasati.

The Dalai Lama said: "I use meditation technique called giving and taking, [it is about forgiveness—See Lesson Two, Tonglen.] . . . I make visualization: send my positive emotions like happiness, affection to others. Then another visualization. I visualize receiving their sufferings, their negative emotions. I do this every day. I pay special attention to the Chinese—especially those doing terrible things to the Tibetans. So, as I meditate, I breathe in all their *poisons—hatred, fear, cruelty*. Then I breathe out. And I let all the good things come out, things like compassion, forgiveness. I take inside my body all these bad things. Then *I replace poisons with fresh air*. Giving and taking. I take care not to blame—I don't blame the Chinese, and I don't blame myself. This meditation [is] very effective, *useful to reduce hatred, useful to cultivate forgiveness*." (Chan, pg. 74) It is interesting that once one knows the Theravada tradition in detail, it is possible to see common threads and techniques in other practices, including in the Tibetan practice.

But how do we get there? "Before the mind enters into Jhana state at the first Jhana, the mind has to experience mental phenomena in Pervading Rapture States every time of the practice. Pervading Rapture, therefore [the fifth rapture], is the indicator confirming that the mind is on the threshold of entering Jhana State. On the contrary, if the mind is concentrated but no mental images in pervading Rapture are experienced, it means that our concentration is not developed to Jhana state." (Wee, pp. 144-145) This is likely a reference to stages of concentration, samadhi.

"If you're distracted by strong emotions, you can try focusing, as was taught earlier, on the mind that experiences the emotion. Or you might try switching to tonglen practice, using whatever you're feeling—anger, sadness, jealousy, desire—as the basis for the practice. [If you get sleepy] There are a couple of ways to deal with this situation. One, which is simply a variation on being mindful of physical sensations, is to rest your attention on the sensation of dullness or sleepiness itself. In other words, use your dullness rather than being used by it. If you can't sit up, just lie down while keeping your spine as straight as possible." (Mingyur, pg. 211)

Proverb: Everyone has the key to happiness . . . you just have to choose the right lock. (wellpage.com)

Step fourteen: ". . . is contemplating fading away (viraganupassana) [similar to the dissolving of attachment.] Now we focus upon and study dissolving, or viraga. Vi, in this case, means 'not' or 'not having.' Raga is another name for attachment [also upadana.] Watching attachment dissolve is like watching the stains in a cloth slowly fade away, bleached out by sunlight, until the cloth is white . . . We know that attachment is lessening when we are even-minded toward sankhara, namely, toward all things to which we were once attached . . . Contemplate this with every inhalation and exhalation."

"There exist several obstacles to this further progress [through the four jhanas,] which usually arise in the course of Vipassana practice. While the mind is in a concentrated state, there are likely to arise various strange phenomena with which the meditator may become overawed, such as wonderful impressive auras seen in the mind's eye (the physical eyes being shut.) If these effects are purposely encouraged, they can become highly developed; and if the meditator jumps to the conclusion that 'this is the Fruit of Vipassana practice,' or congratulates himself saying: 'This is something supernatural; this will do me' and the like, the arising of these phenomena is liable to bar the way to the true Path and Fruit. Consequently, teachers consider it a side track, a blind alley." (Buddhadasa, 2005, pg. 118)

Biographical Sketch:

Arthur Schopenhauer (1788-1860) "... was a German philosopher of pessimism," whose writings were noted for their description of Buddhist and Indian teachings. (Read "will" as action or karma.) "Total release from the enslavement of the will, [something that society does to us] as compared with the identification of himself with others that is displayed in the conduct of the morally good man, in fact occurs only when a person finally ceases to feel any attachment to earthly things and when all desire to participate in the life of the world completely vanishes. Such an attitude of mind, which Schopenhauer attributed to ascetics and mystics of all times, becomes possible when a *man's will 'turns and denies itself,'* and when what in the eyes of ordinary men is the very essence and substance of reality appears to him as 'nothing' . . . This 'turning of the *will*' comes to him, as it were, 'from outside' and springs from an insight which wholly transcends the will and the world. [possibly from Amida Buddha?] Such mystical insight, moreover, is necessarily incommunicable and indescribable; all the knowledge, including that attainable by philosophy, here reaches its limit, and we are left with only 'myths and meaningless words' which express no positive content. 'The nature of things before or beyond the world, and consequently beyond the will,' Schopenhauer declared at the close of his main work, 'is open to no investigation.' The end of philosophy is silence." (Edwards, pg. 331 Vol. 7) This is not a message of desperation, but a message of hope for the enjoyment of the simple details of our lives, not "before or beyond the world," but in the world now, our momentary actions are important, the theories are not. This focus is part of what the Samahito does during meditation, even in Rational Buddhism as they approach an understanding of emptiness. When Schopenhauer is read with the understanding of "will" as "kharma" or action, it is easier to see the affinity of what he thought with Buddhism, and his theorizing and generalizations seem to have more usefulness.

Reading for the Day: from Lotus Sutra

"After I have entered extinction, there will be other disciples who will not hear this sutra and will not understand or be aware of the practices carried out by the bodhisattvas, but who, through the blessings they have been able to attain, will conceive an idea of extinction and enter into what they believe to be nirvana . . . For it is only through the Buddha vehicle that one can attain extinction . . . Monks, if a Thus Come One knows that the time has come to enter nirvana, and knows that the members of the assembly are pure and clean, firm in faith and understanding, thorough in their compression of the Law of emptiness and deeply entered into meditation practice, then he will call together the assembly of bodhisattvas and voice-hearers and will preach this sutra for them. In the world there are not two vehicles whereby one may attain extinction. There is only the one buddha vehicle for attaining extinction and one alone. Phantom City" (Watson, pg. 135)

Protecting:

"This is what I heard," review by both Samahito and teacher.

Proverb: You can't have rosy thoughts about the future when your mind is full of blues about the past. (wellpage.com)

Short poems: This is a special day if you make (or listen to) music!

Samahito names a flower
When our colorful clothing shines
as the gleam in our eyes.
(IJ 2007)

Additional Teachings:

"The issue at stake, simply stated, is whether the first absorption is a deep state of concentration, achieved only after a prolonged period of practice and seclusion, or a stage of relaxed happy reflection within easy reach of anyone and without much need for meditative proficiency."

"The later assumption stands in contradiction to the commentarial presentation . . . the Buddha himself encountered considerable difficulty when he attempted to attain the first absorption . . . one who has entered the first absorption is no longer able to speak. This would not apply if the first absorption were merely a state of calm mental reflection. Not only speech, but also hearing does not occur during the deeper stages of absorption; in fact, sound is a major obstacle to attaining the first absorption . . . it is an 'unworldly' experience; it constitutes another world in the psychological and the cosmological sense . . . a 'superbly extraordinary state'." (Analayo, pp. 77-79)

"Nagarjuna's astonishing inference was that since both samsara and nirvana are empty of own-being, they are in the last analysis one. In his own words, 'there is not the slightest difference between the two.' They are not two separate realities, but one vast field of empty arisings seen either through a veil of ignorance (and thus binding) or in the light of wisdom (and thus freeing) . . . Only the blinders of egoism hide this truth from us." (Smith & Novak, 2003, pg. 192)

"When you enter the first jhana you are still in touch with your physical senses. Your eyes are closed but you can still hear, smell, feel, and taste. This is one definite indication of the first jhana, as opposed to others. You don't fully lose thought either . . . They are one of the things that will pull you out of jhana . . . Mindfulness is present in your jhana. You are awake." Consider this reporting:

> "Quiet, secluded from sense pleasures, secluded from unwholesome states of mind,
> one enters and dwells in the first jhana,
> which is accompanied by applied thought and sustained thought,
> with rapture and happiness born of seclusion."

". . . [the joy you experience] is called 'non-sensual joy.' It does not gush into the mind suddenly. You have been experiencing pain arising from the hindrances for a long time. You have been working very hard to overcome those that have caused you pain. Now, every time you overcome one of them, you experience a great relief that that particular pain has subsided. It is this relief, this freedom from that particular hindrance, that brings you joy . . . It is gone. You rejoice."

"When you seek and know the impermanence, the change, the fading away, and the cessation of all these things [household pleasures: sounds, smells, tastes, touching and pleasurable mental images,] a different joy arises. You perceive the forms etc., as they actually are. You see with proper wisdom. You know they are all impermanent, suffering, and subject to change. You see that they are like this now and that they always were. Then a new joy arises. This called 'joy based on renunciation'."

"These five factors hold the first jhana together:

Vitakka—laying hold of a thought with applied attention. It is a directed thrust of the mind, a turning of attention toward a meditation subject, such as the right thoughts of renunciation, loving-friendliness, and compassion . . . Likened to the striking of a bell."

"Vicara—is the mind roaming about or moving back and forth over thoughts. It is a sustained dwelling upon the meditation subject. It is likened to the reverberation or resounding of the bell after it is struck."

"Piti—Sometimes translated as 'joy, rapture, enthusiasm, interest, or zest.' It is not a physical feeling. It can be described psychologically as 'joyful interest.' It is strongest in the second jhana."

"Sukha—Sometimes translated as 'happiness, pleasure, or bliss.' It may be either a physical or mental feeling. Sukha is an indispensable condition of attaining jhana. It is present in the first, second, and third jhanas and is strongest in the third."

"Ekagatta—One-pointedness; [as with step four of anapanasati] unification of mind. It implies serenity and tranquility as well as single-pointed concentration." (Gunaratana, pp. 121-125)

Sharing Merit:

Rejoicing In Others' Merit (Saying Sadhu)

Buddhist Sutra

Lesson Title: **Rapture—Lesser Thrill**

Lesson Number: **Twenty-two**

Key Vocabulary: extinction, tears, goose bumps, skillful means, euphoria, optimal, destroyers, poisons, Will, bodhisattvas, mystical, pliancy, full awareness, attachments, giving and taking—Tonglen, viraga, empowerment, awakened, renunciation

Assignment: After the Lesson, Samahito will choose a partner, who should be a different person each day, being together in silence, to accompany during the day, and safeguard each other.

Practice dissolving, or viraga, 'not having.' Watch attachment dissolve like watching the stains in a cloth slowly fade away. Have your partner read the fourteen steps slowly as you practice moving through these as with a guided meditation.

Our meditation practice should be as often as possible and for as long a time in each position in each session as possible. Caution: stop each practice before there is any muscle or tendon strain, this will not aid meditation. The important thing is that the body is stressed by pain (as well as hunger) to contribute to the production of natural chemicals that facilitate high levels of mental functioning. This will happen with repeated periods of stress rather than coming from self-inflicted injury.

Consult your notes and use meditation technique called giving and taking. Use this to overcome overeating and to eliminate the preoccupation with hunger.

Define each of the Key Vocabulary in your own words.

Relive difficult experiences, nullify the causes and extinguish the suffering [use Tonglen.] Note your reactions physically.

Tomorrow wake early and start your practice at dawn, before eating.

What are the adverse circumstances in our lives that can cause us to have the emotional reactions to produce goose bumps and tears?

Materials Required: electrolyte fluids, tea ceremony

Buddhist Sutra

Lesson Title: **Rapture—Momentary Joy**

Lesson Number: **Twenty-three**

Rationale:

Gradually our meditation deepens as we follow the guidelines of this very explicit sixteen step Theravada tradition / meditation technique.

"In the second jhana you drop even the subtle thought of the breath. The subtle thoughts of good will drop away. Your mind is not totally free of any verbal or conceptual thoughts, even that of the breath. All that remains is subtle reflection of thought and sensation that is more like a memory or an after-image. Joy predominates. There is happiness, mindfulness, and concentration." (Gunaratana, pg. 105) We don't control our meditation as we did with the in-out breathing, the breath is too subtle, now we just be.

Discussion of Prior Lesson:

The "mind has to experience mental phenomena in Pervading Rapture State every time of the practice" before we meditate to the level of jhana—our goal. (Wee)

"The result of this fading away of attachment is the even-minded stillness of non-attachment . . . as our erotic love for things to which we were once attached begins to fade. Anger toward past, or even present, objects of our displeasure dissolves away. We are no longer afraid of the things we once feared . . . hatred, envy, jealousy, worry, anxiety, longing after the past . . . each of these indicators lessens and shrinks until the mind is able to keep still and silent . . . not to grasp, cling, or regard anything as 'I' or 'mine.' Contemplate impermanence until the attachment dissolves, until we can remain still, silent, and even-minded [equanimity.]" (Buddhadasa, 1988, pg. 89)

Training Objective:

To understand our own Nature. To understand the epiphany of gaining knowledge. The beginnings of happiness—but don't stop here. Quenching, Step fifteen.

Materials Required: electrolyte fluids, tea ceremony

Motivational Statement:

"Momentary Rapture (Khanika-piti): it is instantaneous joy during which we experience penetrating feeling like *lightning*. . . The Second Jhana: mind has three sensations: rapture, happiness (delight) due to concentration and mental one-pointedness." (Wee, pp. 144-145)

"It is a rare and beautiful quality to feel truly happy when others are happy. When someone rejoices in our happiness, we are flooded with respect and gratitude for their appreciation. When we take delight in the happiness of another, when we genuinely rejoice at their prosperity, success, or good fortune rather than begrudging it in any way, we are abiding in *mudita, sympathetic joy* . . . The root of the Pali word mudita means 'to be pleased, to have a sense of gladness.' The Buddha called mudita 'the mind-deliverance of gladness,' because the force of happiness actually liberates us." (Salzberg, pg. 119)

Happiness is like a lunch pail full of appetizing and nutritious food that we can carry with us wherever we go during the day and it nourishes us.

First Progressive:

"When you are motivated by the desire to transcend suffering, to get out of a difficult situation, and to *help others to do the same*, you become a powerful source of energy that helps you to do what you want to do to transform yourself and to help other people." (Hanh, pg. 285) I'm reminded of the instructions of flight attendants when they give the safety briefing, that each person puts on their own oxygen mask first before attempting to help children or the person next to them.

". . . *Mudita is boundless.* As it develops in us, we are able to rejoice in the happiness and well-being of others, whether we like them or not. *It is through compassion that we begin to extend sympathetic joy beyond our prejudices.* Compassion reminds us that everyone suffers. Since that is true, do we really want some person whom we do not like to experience only more and more suffering? Should they have only pain in ever-increasing amounts until the day they die? What would such a wish mean in terms of what we value in our minds and hearts? Remembering the truth of the vast potential for suffering in this world, we can feel happy that someone, anyone, also experiences some happiness . . . Everyone's life is by nature continually vulnerable to pain. Remembering this is our gateway to mudita." (Salzberg, pp. 124-125)

". . . Spend a few moments generating bodhicitta, the desire to attain some degree of *realization for the benefit of others.* Don't worry about whether the desire is especially strong; the motivation alone is sufficient, and after working at it for a while, you'll probably begin to find that the desire has taken on a real significance, a deeply personal meaning." (Mingyur, pg. 198) Having an awakened Heart (in which we can loose the sense of "I" and "mine") and a gentle mind comes from this activity.

"The Dalai Lama personally taught me that the wish-fulfilling jewel that brings us all we need and seek is the unselfish heart and compassionate mind intent on benefiting others rather than preoccupied with ourselves. This is what Tibetan Buddhists call the indispensable or precious Bodhicitta, the highest intention, **the good heart**, our best self, our innermost, interconnected Buddha-being. It is the key element in the powerful magic of transformative spirituality: [Shantideva's *The way of the Bodhisattva,* is a manual on compassion and] describes it as the state of being 'mounted on the noble steed of awakened heart-mind, riding from joy to joy.' The dynamic way of the Bodhisattva swiftly delivers us to the pinnacle of reality, the goal of spiritual life. A Bodhisattva is what we need to be today." (Surya Das, pg. xv) In this stage of jhana we are living at least momentarily in our Hearts.

Second Progressive:

Putting it another way: "If you wish to seek the Buddha, you ought to see into your own Nature; for this Nature is the Buddha himself. If you have not seen into your own Nature, what is the use of thinking of the Buddha, reciting the Sutras, observing a fast, or keeping the precepts? By thinking of the Buddha, your cause (i.e. meritorious deed) may bear fruit; by reciting the Sutras your intelligence may grow brighter; by keeping the precepts you may be born in the heavens; by practicing charity you may be rewarded abundantly; but as to seeking the Buddha, you are far away from him. If your [identity] is not yet clearly comprehended, you ought to see a wise teacher and get a thorough understanding as to the root of birth-and-death. One who has not seen into one's own Nature is not to be called a wise teacher." (Suzuki, pg. 87)

"Judgment: It is all too easy to believe, or even insist, that other people should behave just as we want them to, that they should pursue lifestyles and sources of happiness in precisely the ways we deem appropriate. With this orientation, no wonder we find it difficult to be happy for the countless people we can never control . . . To be nonjudgmental means having flexibility of mind and the ability to let go of our attachment to what seems right to us [our mundane beliefs] . . ." (Salzberg, pp. 120-121)

Proverb: Carrying a grudge is like a run in a stocking . . . it can only get worse. (wellpage.com)

"Ignorance [one of the basic 'mental afflictions' or 'poisons'] is a fundamental inability to recognize the infinite potential, clarity, and power of our own minds . . . As we become accustomed to distinguishing between 'self' and 'other.' We lock ourselves into a dualistic mode of perception, drawing conceptual boundaries between our 'self' and the rest of the world 'out there' . . . We begin looking at other people, material objects, and so on as potential sources of happiness and unhappiness, and life becomes a struggle to get what we need in order to be happy before somebody else grabs it [the basic definition of economic scarcity.]"

"This struggle is known in Sanskrit as samsara, which literally means 'wheel' or 'circle.' . . . chasing after the same experiences again and again, each time expecting a different result . . . The opposite of samsara [suffering] is nirvana, a term that is almost as completely misunderstood as emptiness . . . [nirvana means] 'extinguishing' or 'blowing out' . . . A more precise interpretation of nirvana is the adoption of a broad perspective that admits all experiences, pleasurable or painful, as aspects of awareness. Naturally, most people would prefer to experience only the 'high notes' of happiness. But as a student of mine recently pointed out, eliminating the 'low notes' from a Beethoven symphony . . . would result in a pretty cheap and tinny experience . . . Samsara and nirvana are perhaps best understood as points of view. Samsara is a point of view based primarily on defining and identifying with experiences as wither painful or unpleasant. Nirvana is a fundamentally objective state of mind: an acceptance of experience without judgments, which opens us to the potential for seeing solutions that may not be directly connected to our survival as individuals, but rather to the survival of all sentient beings." (Mingyur, pp. 117-118) Understanding nirvana as a point of view should equip each Samahito with the confidence of achieving this state in only another week or more of lessons!?

Third Progressive:

From the Satipatthana meditation scheme we learn to look directly at awakening factors. ". . . And how does he . . . abide contemplating dhammas in terms of the seven awakening factors?" In order to enter the second jhana these seven factors must be well established in the Heart of the Samahito.

1. "Here, if the ***mindfulness*** awakening factor is present in him, he knows 'there is the mindfulness awakening factor in me' [if not] he knows how the unarisen mindfulness awakening factor can arise . . . and be perfected by development."
2. "If the ***investigation-of-dhammas*** awakening factor is present in him, he knows 'there is the investigation-of-dhammas awakening factor in me' [if not] he knows how the unarisen investigation-of-dhammas awakening factor can arise . . . and be perfected by development."
3. "If the ***energy*** *awakening factor* is present in him, he knows 'there is the energy awakening factor in me'; [if not] he knows how the unarisen energy awakening factor can arise . . . and be perfected by development."
4. "If the ***joy*** *awakening factor* is present in him, he knows 'there is the joy awakening factor in me' [if not] he knows how the unarisen joy awakening factor can arise . . . and be perfected by development."
5. "If the ***tranquility*** *awakening factor* is present in him, he knows 'there is the tranquility awakening factor in me' [if not] he knows how the unarisen tranquility awakening factor can arise . . . and be perfected by development"
6. "If the ***concentration*** *awakening factor* is present in him, he knows 'there is the concentration awakening factor in me' [if not] he knows how the unarisen concentration awakening factor can arise . . . and be perfected by development."
7. "If the ***equanimity*** *awakening factor* is present in him, he knows 'there is the equanimity awakening factor in me' [if not] he knows how the unarisen equanimity awakening factor can arise . . . and can be perfected by development." (Analayo, pp. 11-12) Meditate on each of these separately.

"Yet another kind of obstacle [to progress through meditation, paradoxically,] involves faith. **Faith** [as explained in Chapter Two] or confidence never felt before becomes firmly established, for example confidence in the Threefold Gem, Buddha, Dhamma, and Sangha, *or in theories the meditator thinks out for himself* [i.e. concepts.] There may even come about a most intense satisfaction in Dhamma. The ability to remain unmoved by anything becomes so strongly developed that it may even delude the meditator into believing he has already attained the Fruit of the Path and Nirvana itself. These things are a great difficulty for anyone encountering them for the first time. As you can see they constitute a barrier in the way of Vipassana. The meditator, however, is likely to regard them as highly desirable until such time as he develops the un-obscured knowledge that these things are in fact obstacles and succeeds in cutting out these finer defilements completely. This knowledge of what is the right path and what is not constitutes the third stage in Vipassana and the fifth Purification." (Buddhadasa, 2005, pg. 120) This is a call to return to humility and preserve the beginners attitude.

Knowing what to expect related to the second jhana is perhaps helpful. "The attainment of the second jhana does not take place by wishing or willing or striving. When the mind is ready to attain the second jhana, it automatically lets go of the first jhana. You don't even have to wish to go to the second jhana. When the mind is ready, it glides into the second jhana by itself. But only if you let it . . . The moment your thinking or subtle thoughts vanish from your mind, you are aware that you have entered the second jhana. But as soon [paradoxically] as the thought, 'This is the second jhana,' appears in your mind, you lose it. Try again and again until that thought does not appear. You can stay with the awareness of second jhanic experience without the concept 'this is the second jhana.' This is a very delicate balance. Only with full awareness can you maintain it." (Gunaratana, pg. 143)

This subtle balance is found throughout Universe. "The universe is [to be] looked upon as an enormous web woven of innumerable strands of thread . . . Disturbances in one area of the net galvanize a ripple effect that impacts, however subtly, on other parts. It is like the 'Butterfly Effect' . . . On a human level, my daughters will not sleep safely in their beds if kids in Kabul or Baghdad are not safe in theirs. For the Dalai Lama, the reality of life is an integrated whole: all things are interrelated, and nothing exists independently. There is a well-known Tibetan saying: all beings have at some time been our mothers, just as we have at some time been theirs. It encourages us to work hard at self-restraint and to cultivate consideration for the welfare of others. I grasped the idea intuitively, but I still find myself struggling for a deeper understanding."

"The Dalai Lama continued: 'In my own case, in Tibet, all this destruction, death, all happened. Painful experiences. But revenge... this creates more unhappiness. So, think wider perspective: revenge no good, so forgive. Forgiveness does not mean you just forget about the past. No, you remember the past. Should be aware that these past sufferings happened because of narrow-mindedness on both sides. So now, time passed. We feel more wise, more developed. I think that's the only way'." (Chan, pp. 108-109)

What are the adverse circumstances in our lives that can cause us to have the emotional reactions to "experience penetrating feeling like lightning?" As we meditate we can take ourselves there, relive these experiences, nullify the causes and extinguish the suffering? Review your journal and identify the learning gains and insights. We know we have achieved these turn-arounds when we have the same physical reaction during meditation as we had during the event itself. The "lightening" will be empathy for our own previous ignorance, and the impact of this sensation will give the sheer sense of relief and euphoria, and produce a lasting humility and objectivity.

How many times have changes in our lives affected us with drastic emotional consequences [like lightening?] "Contemplation of impermanence has to be comprehensive, for if any aspect of experience is still taken to be permanent, awakening will be impossible . . . This is the case to such an extent that a stream-enterer is incapable of believing any phenomenon to be permanent. Understanding of impermanence reaches perfection with the realization of full awakening. For Arhants, awareness of the impermanent nature of all sensory input is a natural feature of their experience." (Analayo, pp. 105-106)

If impermanence is a constant it can perhaps be best described as the personality of infinity. "Awareness of infinite space requires infinite awareness [or visualization.] The thought of infinite space drops away and what is left is infinite awareness without an object. You dwell in boundless consciousness, pure awareness of awareness." (Gunaratana, pg. 108) Conscious of consciousness. Thus, "The second jhana also has a deeper level of concentration. You do not have to watch out for hindrances. The first jhana is still close to the hindrances and to all material experiences. The second jhana is still close to vitakka and vicara, but remote from hindrances. 'With the subsiding of applied thought and sustained thought one enters and dwells in the second jhana, which has internal confidence and unification of mind, is without applied thought and sustained thought, and is filled with rapture and bliss born of concentration' . . . When thought drops away, you experience your entire body and mind filled with joy and happiness. This joy continuously replenishes itself with more and more joy." (Gunaratana, pg. 144)

Meditation Practicum:

The truth we gain as a Samahito, ". . . is totally different from the knowledge we gain from hearing a lecture, or reading scriptures or from reasoning. This is the higher knowledge that [cannot] be understood without the mind. Transcending the mind and revealing the knowledge of your inner essence [according to the Four Foundations of Mindfulness]—the ancient teaching of the yogis . . ." will secure your happiness and give confidence in your practice.

"The impressions made on the mind from this samadhi of absolute awareness remove all other past impressions, which disappear. We now understand our true nature and cannot return to an earlier state of ignorance." (Forstater, pg. 289) Even though this realization may happen as a flash of insight, it has happened and you gain from it.

"Wonderful experiences can occur when you rest your mind in meditation [in or out of jhana.] Sometimes it takes a while for these experiences to occur; sometimes they happen the very first time you sit down to practice. The most common of these experiences are bliss, clarity, and non-conceptuality."

"Bliss . . . is a feeling of undiluted happiness, comfort, and lightness in both the mind and the body. As this experience grows stronger, it seems as if everything you see is made of love. Even experiences of physical pain become very light and hardly noticeable at all."

"Clarity is a sense of being able to see into the nature of things as though all reality were a landscape lit up on a brilliantly sunny day without clouds. Everything appears distinct and everything makes sense. Even disturbing thoughts and emotions have their place in this brilliant landscape."

"Non-conceptuality is an experience of the total openness of your mind. Your awareness is direct and unclouded by conceptual distinctions such as 'I' or 'other,' subjects and objects, or any other form of limitation. It's an experience of pure consciousness as infinite as space without beginning, middle, or end. It's like becoming awake within a dream and recognizing that everything experienced in the dream isn't separate from the mind of the dreamer."

"Some people, furthermore, feel a sense of disorientation, as though their familiar world of thoughts, emotions, and sensations has tilted slightly—which may be pleasant or unpleasant . . . When distractions of this sort occur, just make them a part of your practice. Join your awareness to the distraction." (Mingyur, pp. 209-210)

". . . It's very important during each session to alternate between focusing on an object and simply resting your mind in objectless meditation. The point of working with supports for meditation is to develop a degree of mental stability that allows you to be aware of your own mind as it perceives things. Resting your mind between objectless meditation and object-based meditation gives you a chance to assimilate whatever you have experienced. By alternating . . . no matter what situation you find yourself in—whether you're dealing with your own thoughts and emotions or with a person or a situation that appears 'out there'—you'll gradually learn to recognize that whatever is going on is intimately connected with your own awareness." (Mingyur, pg. 195)

Step fifteen: ". . . *nirodhanupassana* is the study and contemplation of quenching of attachment. We observe the cessation of attachment, the nonexistence of attachment, while breathing in and breathing out . . . the quenching of greed, anger, and delusion; and the quenching of all experiences of dukkha . . . When we speak of quenching, remember that the ending of dukkha is what the practice of Dhamma is all about . . .

1) The first aspect is the ending of fearfulness, the horror of birth, aging, illness, and death . . . [these] will never again terrify our mind . . .
2) Next . . . the cessation of the various symptoms or condition of dukkha, such as sorrow, grief, lamentation, despair, sadness, pain, frustration and depression.
3) . . . our hopes and wants to attractive and unattractive things [is quenched.] Experiencing things we do not like is dukkha. Being separated from the things we like is dukkha. Not getting what we want is dukkha. These aspects of dukkha are quenched as well."

"4) Clinging to one of the five khandha (groups, aggregates, clusters), grasping the 'self' (body, feeling, perception, thought, and sense-consciousness) as 'I' or 'mine' is dukkha. [Eliminating the pride in who we are, for example.] These are the summation of all dukkha, the burdens of life. A full realization of this step must include all four aspects of dukkha's quenching . . . We should not underestimate this important realization." (Buddhadasa, 1988, pp. 89-90) Quenching is like drinking water beyond the point of thirst. Of course we can use the pronouns "I" and 'mine' in ordinary speech, but they will have no power over us. We are no longer thirsty for the feelings (or fetishes) associated with possessions.

"Another example [of an illusion of accomplishment during meditation] is the arising of feelings of joy and contentment which continually overflow the mind to such an extend that it becomes incapable of any further introspection, or jumps to the conclusion that 'this is Nirvana, right here and now,' so that . . . further progress is impossible. This is another obstruction to insight. Teachers say, furthermore, that even insight into the nature of body and mind may sometimes lead to self satisfaction and the delusion that the meditator has a remarkable degree of spiritual insight, so that he becomes over-confident. This too is an obstacle to progress in Vipassana." (Buddhadasa, 2005, pg. 118)

Biographical Sketch:

The following extract from *Jack and Lucky*, refers to the kind of meditation I did when as a child I was afraid of an uncontrollable vision—beginning around the age of eight—then as a teenager the ability to see and experience emptiness in this way became a desirable challenge and continued to occur with less frequency with each passing year until I was in my early twenties. "Jack woke slowly, letting his mind drift in and out of a blank, shapeless, vast Arctic expanse with no end. He could hear someone stirring outside the room, but had no inclination to get up. He had captured the vision of the 'far-away' and relished the tranquil moment between sleep and consciousness."

"When he could no longer maintain the trance, he searched his mind to recall where and who he was. He had been shuffled around so much and the circumstances were so unfamiliar that he had to concentrate to recall his recent steps. It was almost completely dark in the room as he lifted himself and stumbled toward the door. He opened it reluctantly wishing he could return to the vision of infinity." (Jacob, 1991) This autobiographical sketch describes a meditative experience that in the beginning was frightening and later developed into a sense challenge and calm rapture. I was unaware of what this experience was all about at the time. There is a lesson here; we need to identify the thinking and visualizing of young people, encourage them to recount their thoughts and meta-cognitions, and help them develop these into a useful spiritual practice. No one around during my youth was conversant with or aware of meditation or Buddhism, thus this experience just wore away and the productive value of it was minimized.

Lack of knowledge can hide our most formative experiences. "According to the Buddha's survey of wrong views in the Brahmajala Sutta, misinterpretations of reality can often be based on meditative experiences, not only on theoretical speculation. To prevent such misinterpretations, a firm acquaintance with the Dhamma is an important factor for proper progress along the meditative path. In one instance, the Buddha compared such sound knowledge of the Dhammna to the armoury of swords and spears used to defend a fortress. Clearly, for the Buddha the mere absence of concepts does not constitute the final goal of meditation practice. Concepts are not the problem, the problem is how concepts are used. An arahant still employs concepts, yet without being bound by them." (Analayo, pp. 113-114) Yet we can return to these accomplishments and rerun the tape, so to speak, even if we cannot necessarily be in that same state of rapture. The lessons for us may simply be lying there waiting for us to pick them up.

Reading for the Day: Lotus Sutra

"The skillful development of non-sensual joy and happiness was an outcome of the Buddha's first-hand realization, which had shown him the need to differentiate between wholesome and unwholesome types of pleasure. The satipatthana [and anapanasati] instructions for contemplating feelings reflect this wisdom by distinguishing between worldly and unworldly types of pleasant feelings." (Analayo, pp. 166-167)

"Medicine King, if someone should ask what living beings will be able to attain Buddhahood in a latter-day existence, then you should show him that all these people in a latter-day existence are certain to attain Buddhahood. Why? Because if good men and good women embrace, read, recite, expound and copy the Lotus Sutra, even one phrase of it, offer various kinds of alms to the sutra, flowers, incense, necklaces, powdered incense, paste incense, incense for burning, silken canopies, streamers and banners, clothing and music, and press their palms together in reverence, then these persons will be looked up to and honored by all the world. Alms will be offered to them such as would be offered to the Thus Come One. You should understand that these persons are great bodhisattvas who have succeeded in attaining anuttara-samyak-sambodhi. Pitying living beings, they have vowed to be born among them where they may broadly expound and make distinctions regarding the Lotus Sutra of the Wonderful Law. How much more so is this true, then, of those who can embrace the entire sutra and offer various types of alms to it!" The Teacher of the Law (Watson, pg. 161)

"You will recall that the first tetrad (steps one-four) concerned the breath and the body. The second tetrad dealt with those feelings that result from the calming of body-conditioners, the breathing. We studied the mind's feelings although not yet the mind (citta) itself.

We studied the mind-conditioner and learned about the conditioning of the citta. Then we learned to control the citta-sankhara, the mind-conditioners. The third tetrad we studied the citta and practiced various ways of controlling the mind. Now that this well-trained mind has been brought under control, in the fourth tetrad we use it to study Dhamma, the truth of nature . . . Once the mind is under our power and within our control, we put this mind to work [as Samahito.] Please observe how the four tetrads [the sixteen steps] are interconnected: first, the kaya-sankhara; second, the citta-sankhara; third the citta itself [samadhi;] and finally Dhamma, the facts (saccadhamma) of nature (Dhamma-jati)." (Buddhadasa, 1988, pg. 83)"

Proverb: Spreading happiness is like painting . . . you can't help but get a few drops on yourself. (wellpage.com)

Protecting:

"This is what I heard," review by both Samahito and teacher.

Additional Teachings:

In our meditation we should not expect to feel an ecstatic swoon or trance state. We should expect perhaps to replay emotions and physical reactions we have had associated with pleasant and dreadful experiences. This reliving is what helps us get rid of defilements and suffering. "Thus, we realize the voidness or nonexistence of attachment through the quenching, disappearing, and ending of attachment. We experience the absence of attachment in any of the aspects [or our lives] while we breathe in and breathe out. Or more simply, we drink, taste, and savor the flavor of Nibbana. Nirodha and Nibbana are synonyms; we can use them interchangeably. Thus, to contemplate the quenching of attachment is to contemplate Nibbana." (Buddhadasa, 1988, pg. 90)

What is Merit? "Merit can be classified into two categories as follows:

1. Merit in the distant past. This means the . . . accrued merits we had performed from our past lives, up to the time [which is the ancient metaphor to account for the similarities between family members due to DNA and RNA] we were born to bear the optimistic opportunities . . . [from the intelligence and talent we inherited.] As long as we are not careless and continue making merit [developing our talents and performing service,] we will rapidly meet success and progress in life. On the contrary, if we are heedless in doing good deeds, our life can be compared to a tree with the peaks of its branches broken that can no longer grow taller [until it mends itself.]" One possible way to think of "merit" is to think of it as "advantages".

2. "Merit in recent past. This refers to all of the good deeds or merits which have been done from the time we were born up to today. Illustrative examples include paying attention to our studies, displaying perseverance, associating with the wise, and having a clear and controlled mind since childhood. These good acts thus influence our thinking, speech, capacity to become more efficient, advanced by comparison to others of the same age, and development in life and the future."

"All the good deeds we have done bear the merits of good fruits for our lives. To easily correct these principles, the Lord Buddha concluded that there are three kinds of acts considered to be meritorious. These are: alms offering, observing the precepts, and practicing meditation. In brief, these are the ways by which merit can be performed, obtained, and accrued." (Dattajeevo, pp. 28-29) (The three `progressives`.)

Sharing Merit:

Rejoicing In Others' Merit (Saying Sadhu)

Buddhist Sutra

Lesson Title: **Rapture—Momentary Joy**

Lesson Number: **Twenty-three**

Key Vocabulary: emptiness, transcend, lightning (metaphorically), mudita, bliss, clarity, nonconceptuality, point of view, quenching, bodhichitta, nirodhanupassana, Nirodha, voidness

Assignment: Our meditation practice should be as often as possible and as long a time in each position in each session as possible. Caution: stop each practice before there is any muscle or tendon strain, this will not aid meditation. The important thing is that the body is stressed by pain and hunger to contribute to the production of natural chemicals that facilitate high levels of mental functioning. This will happen with repeated periods of mild stress rather than coming from self-inflicted injury.

Drink water beyond the point of thirst. This is an analogy to being quenched by dissolving of attachments, but it goes one step further. To contemplate the quenching of attachment is to contemplate Nibbana.

Define each of the Key Vocabulary in your own words.

After the Lesson, Samahito will choose a partner, who should be a different person each day, to accompany silently and safeguard during the day.

Review your journal and identify the learning gains and insights you most treasure.

To change your own nature you must first understand it. Do you agree?

Look for subtle signs—not bold or boisterous signs.

"We should not underestimate [the necessity to practice quenching and] this important realization." (Buddhadasa)

"Resting your mind between objectless meditation and object-based meditation gives you a chance to assimilate whatever you have experienced." Do you agree?

What are the adverse circumstances in our lives that can cause us to have the emotional reactions to "experience penetrating feeling like lightning?"

Recall (Lesson Seven) The progression of Precepts, concentration, Wisdom.

Give an example of how this sequence has been demonstrated in your progress.

Materials Required: fluid electrolytes, tea ceremony

Buddhist Sutra

Lesson Title: **Rapture—Showering Joy**

Lesson Number: **Twenty-four**

Rationale:

This "showering joy" is a feedback signal from meditation that can be very rewarding, and once one learns to "go there" it will become a very compelling part of meditation practice. But we must move on to obtain the third Jhana. Don't stop now.

"In the third jhana, the more subtle 'bliss' or 'happiness' intensifies. It fills you and floods every cell of your body. Confidence rises. Mindfulness and concentration strengthen. The external world may be gone but body feeling is still present and it is wonderful. The body is very still. The breath is very gentle." (Gunaratana, pg. 106) The third jhana comes without wishing it, without pride.

Proverb: When fate closes a door, come in through the window. (wellpage.com)

Discussion of Prior Lesson:

"The Buddha called the greatest happiness: to know peace unchanged by changing conditions." (Salzberg, pg. 132)

"Occasionally the meditator may make use of the mental power he has developed to make his body go rigid, with the result that he loses the awareness necessary for further introspection. This is a stubborn obstacle in the path to further progress, yet meditators usually approve of it, regarding it as a supernatural faculty, or even as the Fruit of the Path. Anyone who becomes so pleased with and infatuated by the attainment of deep concentration, this sitting with body rigid and devoid of all sensation, that he is unable to progress further in Vipassana, is in a most pitiable position." (Buddhadasa, 2005, pp. 118-119)

Proverb: Life is like riding a bicycle, you don't fall off until you stop. (wellpage.com)

Training Objective:

Gain a deep understanding of happiness and "merit." Wisdom and modesty are a source of long-term happiness—for both men and women. How to be bodhicitta. Step sixteen—no "I or mine" again.

Materials Required: fluid electrolytes, tea ceremony

Motivational Statement:

"Showering Rapture (Okkantika-piti): it is flood of joy. We feel it showering inside the body like waves breaking on the shore . . . The Third Jhana: mind has happiness and mental one-pointedness." (Wee, pp. 144-145)

"The third Noble Truth sets forth a state in which the cravings—the thirsts that hinder the attainment of the ideal—have been totally eliminated. In Buddhist terms, this state is called [and coincides with] nirvana . . . But it is not easy for the individual to reach the goal . . . and it is much more difficult to teach and lead others to it [which is also expected] . . . living a life of faith practiced according to [The Four Noble Truths] enables [us] to understand and provide limited experience with the state in which cravings have been completely extinguished . . . the third Noble Truth is a standard for the other three: [it is the positive side of Buddhist teachings] the deeper one's experience and knowledge of it, the deeper and more correct one's understanding of the others." (Mizumo, pg. 51) Each time a suffering is traced to its roots and eliminated for real, we have the right to celebrate, even if only within our own mental continuum [it is always okay to share this accomplishment,] and enjoy, if not the flood of joy, at least take a refreshing shower in it.

Proverb: Every great achievement was once impossible. (wellpage.com)

First Progressive:

"To view life *compassionately*, we have to look at what is happening and at the conditions that gave rise to it. Instead of only looking at the last point, or the end result, we need to see all of the constituent parts. The teachings of the Buddha can be distilled into an understanding that all things in the conditioned universe arise due to a cause. Have you ever had the experience of feeling resentful toward someone and then having an insight into what in their history might have caused them to behave in a certain way? Suddenly you can see the conditions that gave rise to that situation, not simply the end result of those conditions." (Salzberg, pg. 110) This is one way to understand the Buddhist concept of "compounded things," the suffering and resentments we might harbor are usually complex and often come in part from our own injured psyche. We can uncover these roots and contributing factors during insight meditation and break the chain of events and consequences.

". . . Whenever I blocked the compassion that is a natural quality of my mind, I inevitably found myself feeling small, vulnerable, and afraid. [This is the same feeling that accompanies most moral transgressions.] It's so easy to think that we're the only ones who suffer, while other people are somehow immune to pain, as though they'd been born with some kind of special knowledge about being happy that, through some cosmic accident, we never received. Thinking in this way, we make our own problems seem much bigger than they really are." (Mingyur, pg. 178) We must recognize suffering when it is such, and not exaggerate our symptoms.

"Why we should practice generosity or giving, with high priority?

1. Giving (dana) is a foundation and a basic virtue of doing good deeds. It can be compared to the first step on the stairway to heaven and is generally the easiest method of performing a good deed and gaining merit.
2. Dana is something we can carry with us like a provision to save us from danger. It will also provide comfort for those who still remain in the continuing round of rebirth (samsara), [and it creates happiness and joy.]
3. Dana is the direct path to Nirvana because it supports other perfections to be achieved more easily.
4. Dana is the noble means for escaping the round of rebirth . . . Therefore, we should study how to practice generosity." (Dattajeevo, pp. 63-64)

Thus charity and giving follows directly as a requisite for being at the level of Arahant.

Second Progressive:

Likewise, "Comparison or conceit is a gnawing, painful restlessness. It can never bring us to peace, because there is no end to the possibilities for comparison . . . In the classical tradition of Buddhism, the practice of 'sharing merit' counteracts the delusion and damage of such limited benefits [of comparison]. *We accrue merit through acting [modestly] in ways that are helpful and beneficial to others.* However, it is not as if we are piling up the benefits of our good deeds in a warehouse somewhere. Merit is a force that is far more dynamic and subtle than that. It is a power that is born in and grows through acts of goodness . . . The energy we feel; [by sustaining happiness] in this way we can dedicate to the well being of others. This is the sharing of merit [that we do after each lesson.] One traditional recitation in the practice is: '**May the**

merit of this action be shared by all beings everywhere, so that they may come to the end of suffering'." (Salzberg, pp.122-126) To be repeated.

In the third jhana, "Your mind turns toward bliss and one-pointedness in a way that is more delicate, refined, and stable . . . You gain a feeling of equanimity toward even the highest joy. It is just more material substance really. It is subtle, but it is still tying you to the hectic world of thought and the senses. You let it go and the joy fades away by itself." (Gunaratana, pg. 106) Equanimity is forgiveness of anyone who has transgressed against us. When we were violated by theft or abuse we throbbed with pain, and the opposite of that is to throb with forgiveness.

"In the preliminary stage, before attaining jhana, you had to make a strenuous effort to stay with the practice of moral principles. You disciplined yourself using the fourfold effort . . . you learned to pick up good habits and drop band ones. The mind was like a wild animal. It experienced the mundane enjoyment of sensual pleasures. Greed, hatred, delusion, and all those minor defilements were very strong. You needed a great deal of effort to overcome them, cultivate wholesome mental states, and maintain them. You have passed that stage. Holding off the defilements during meditation is much easier now." (Gunaratana, pg. 145) In this same way sustaining a life of moral rectitude becomes easier and a matter of course. You wonder how you could have ever been so inconsiderate or corrupted.

Third Progressive:

To recognize that life just is, thusness, and we must make (or accept) our own superior meaning, is perhaps a disturbing concept. "Reality cannot be described in terms of being and non-being. Being and non-being are notions created by you, exactly like the notions of birth and death, coming and going. If your beloved one can no longer be seen, it does not mean that from being she has become non-being. If you realize this truth about your beloved, you will suffer much less, and if you realize this truth about yourself, you will transcend your fear of dying, of non-being." (Hanh, pg. 295) This is another way to acknowledge *emptiness, because there is only being!*

What are the adverse circumstances in our lives that can cause us to have the emotional reaction to produce "waves breaking on the shore?" As we meditate we can take ourselves there, relive these experiences, nullify the causes and extinguish the suffering? If we have howled like a wolf with our sadness, we can turn that around and sing and whistle our joy. We know we have achieved this *turn around* when we have the same physical reaction during meditation as we had during the event itself. The convulsions, and internal gnawing of sadness can be exceeded by joy, the breath is involuntarily quickened, the waves of pleasant emotions can be revisited at any time like the pleasure of seeing the gift of a jeweled ring. We can smile uncontrollably, even when alone, from the sheer sense of relief and euphoria.

Proverb: The seeds of happiness are free, so plant them often. (wellpage.com)

"Mindfulness and concentration united in the first jhana and were struggling to appear clearly [and stabilize.] In the second jhana they became stronger, but still did not have enough strength to come out fully. In the third jhana they emerge completely and join hands: 'With the fading away of rapture, one dwells in equanimity [calmness,] mindful and discerning; and one experiences in one's own person that bliss [sukha] of which the noble ones say: 'Happily lives one who is equanimous and mindful'; thus one enters and dwells in the third jhana' . . . When the mind completely loses interest in joy [piti,] it glides into the third jhana without your wishing or thinking. The joy of the second jhana is like getting something. The happiness of the third jhana is like taking pleasure in it afterward." (Gunaratana, pg. 146) In this way the third jhana changes our lifestyles.

". . . When the mind loses interest in the first jhana and is ready to drop it completely, you don't have to make any volitional effort to move on to the second jhana. It just happens. It happens in the same sequential order for everyone. When the preparatory state is well established, what comes next will simply happen—naturally. That is the nature of Dhamma . . . After attaining the second jhana many times, you find it not giving you that same joy and happiness born of concentration that you experienced at the beginning of the second jhana. Joy becomes stale . . . Then the mind glides into the third jhana, where a more refined state of happiness is dominant." (Gunaratana, pg. 148)

Meditation Practicum:

"We suffer from hunger so much that we have to eat—and eat only a small amount of food just to survive. We have to practice by all postures and to the utmost of suffering [including lying posture before going to sleep.] Notice the mental states of hindrances [your mind trying to quit] consider hindrances thoroughly . . . and try to overcome them successfully. They are unwholesome mind state which prevents mind from succeeding in Concentration Meditation and Insight Meditation." (Wee, pg. 116)

"Gradually . . . you'll clearly distinguish the movements of thoughts, emotions, and sensations through your mind . . . [this is] the 'river' experience in which things are still moving, but more slowly and gently . . . You may feel that your body is becoming lighter and less tense. You may find that your perceptions are becoming clearer and, in a way, more 'transparent,' in that they don't seem so heavy or oppressive as they may have felt in the past . . . you're mind becomes calmer . . . you'll find yourself spontaneously experiencing a greater sense of confidence and openness . . . you will begin to sense the beauty of the world around you." (Mingyur, pg. 215)

"To the extent that you can acknowledge the true power of your mind, you can begin to exercise more control over your experience. Pain, sadness, fear, anxiety, and all other forms of suffering no longer disrupt your life as forcefully as they used to. Experiences that once seemed to be obstacles become opportunities for deepening your understanding of the mind's unimpeded nature." (Mingyur, pg. 102) Suffering can be extinguished by the activity of your mind and changing the way you live and respond to others.

When meditating ". . . If you think you can go on for another minute or two, by all means do so. You may be surprised by what you learn. You might discover a particular thought or feeling behind your resistance that you didn't want to acknowledge. Or you may simply find that you can actually rest your mind longer than you thought you could—and that discovery alone can give you greater confidence in yourself, while at the same time **reducing your level of cortisol,** increasing your level of dopamine, and generating more activity in the left pre-frontal lobe of your brain. And these biological changes can make a huge difference in your day, providing a physical reference point for calmness, steadiness, and confidence." (Mingyur, pg. 251)

In previous lessons we have suggested that looking at a Buddha icon is the equivalent of looking into a mirror. "The practice of bodhicitta—the mind of awakening—may seem almost magical, in the sense that when you choose to deal with other people as if they were already fully enlightened, they tend to respond in a more positive, confident, and peaceful manner than they otherwise might. But really there is nothing magical about the process. You're simply looking at, then acting toward people on the level of their full potential, and they respond to the best of their ability in the same way." This is particularly useful when you are dealing with a spouse or significant other. If you define your suffering as being caused by other people in your life, this practice of bodhicitta will disabuse you of this incorrect thinking.

"There are two aspects of bodichitta, absolute and relative. Absolute bodhicitta is the direct insight into the nature of mind . . . there is no distinction between subject and object, self and other; all sentient beings are spontaneously recognized as perfect manifestations of Buddha nature [as are you.] . . . relative bodhicitta shares the same goal: the direct experience of Buddha nature, or awakened mind . . . In the practice of relative bodhicitta, however, we're still working within the framework of a relationship between subject and object or self and other. Finally, according to many great teachers . . . development of absolute bodhicitta depends on developing relative bodhicitta." This is the refinement of the citta as Heart.

"Developing relative bodhicitta always involves two aspects: *aspiration* and *application*. *Aspiration bodhicitta* involves cultivating the heartfelt desire to raise all sentient beings to the level at which they recognize their Buddha nature . . . Aspiration bodhicitta focuses on the fruit, or the result, of practice . . . *Application bodhicitta*—often compared in classic texts to actually taking the steps to arrive at an intended destination—focuses on the path of attaining the goal of aspiration bodhicitta: the liberation of all sentient beings from all forms and causes of suffering through recognition of their Buddha nature . . ." (Buddhadasa) "When we generate the motivation to lift not only ourselves but all sentient beings to the level of complete recognition of Buddha nature, an odd thing happens: The dualistic perspective of 'self' and 'other' begins very gradually to dissolve, and we grow in wisdom and power to help others as well as ourselves." (Mingyur, pp. 189-190) To what level of relative bodhicitta have you arrived?

We have arrived at Step Sixteen: "*Patinissagganupassana*—Contemplating throwing back . . . returning, everything to which we were once attached . . . throughout our lives we have been thieves. All along, we have been stealing things that exist naturally, that belong to nature, namely, the sankhara. We have plundered them and taken them to be our selves and our possessions . . . for this we are being punished by dukkha. We suffer dukkha because of all our attachment and thieving. As soon as we observe the way things really are through the succession of steps in this tetrad, we let go. We cease being thieves. We return everything to its original owner—nature. Don't claim anything to be 'I' or 'mine' ever again! Our goal is made clear by this metaphor." (Buddhadasa, 1988, pg. 91) This is why initiates into the ranks of Bhikkhu, are only allowed to take a few items of traditional clothing, a tooth brush and one pair of sandals. In each of these cases we are talking about the development of our Hearts.

As we move wholesale into our pure Hearts, "This next jhana [third] is often called the 'base of nothingness.' The infinite awareness of the previous jhana has no object. It is empty, vacant, and void. [We] turn our awareness toward this emptiness. The [third] jhana is pure focus upon no-thing-ness. Our awareness dwells on the absence of any object." (Gunaratana, pg. 108) Words and ordinary language have difficulty distinguishing between the subtle levels of jhana, but the emotion of throbbing seems to give a useful clue. "Emptiness" for Buddhists never means worthless or nonsense, but open to expressions of awe and not having an absolute meaning given by a god or erstwhile prophet, for example.

Biographical Sketch:

"Understanding the nature of the mind in Mahamudra is conveyed by the term simultaneous mind. The term signifies that the mind's awareness and its manifest events literally 'arise together' in each moment of experience. Another way to say this is that the mind's awareness and the events of ordinary consciousness form an inseparable pair [like the image in a mirror,] and that the perception of duality is erroneous. Direct realization of the mind's non-duality is an essential prerequisite to awakening the mind . . . The observational perspective during Mahamudra meditation is not the ordinary sense of self. Ordinary special insight meditation on emptiness helps determine that there is no substantial, self-existing self that can serve as the point of observation during meditation [contrary to what is taught in yoga.]" Again, this realization happens in our Hearts.

There was a time, in fact for most of my adult life, when I was displeased or uncomfortable to receive praise, compliments and sympathetic comments. Not from modesty I think, but possibly from a false sense of privacy, or at times suspicion of the motivation behind them. And during that time I would often get uncomfortable when anyone gave me complaints, even advice, certainly I didn't like criticism. Then I noticed that these reactions rather limited the continuum of possible conversations, because I was taking away the high end where praise and genuine concern were involved, and eliminating the low end where complaints and helpful advice came from; what was left was a narrow middle range of permissible speech, from my perspective. This certainly created problems for me in my relationships, because my closest associates would naturally have difficulty knowing my proclivities and finding appropriate things to say that didn't make me uncomfortable. So I was restricting my world unintentionally and limiting my friendships. Once I made this realization, I began to accept compliments and concern, and became thankful for these offerings. It has been a larger stretch to accept complaints and negative comments without being defensive, but as I tried to see the constructive viewpoint with more equanimity, I practiced looking at the other person's point of view. Now I still edit myself, but I thank people for compliments and can even give thanks for both kinds of criticism without negative, defensive remarks as I challenge my own beliefs of what I saw and had perhaps concluded in each circumstance. All this growth, which might be normal for most people, was a huge gain in the potential for happiness for me. Being thankful for praise and advice comes from a place of confident happiness and equanimity.

Reading for the Day: Lotus Sutra

"At that time the nun Mahaprajapati, the nun Yashodhara, and their followers were all filled with great joy, having gained what they had never had before. Immediately in the presence of the Buddha they spoke in verse form, saying:

> World-Honored One, leader and teacher,
> You bring tranquility to heavenly and human beings.
> We have heard these prophecies
> And our minds are peaceful and satisfied.

The nuns, having recited these verses, said to the Buddha, 'World Honored One, we too will be able to go to lands in other regions and broadly propagate this sutra'."

Encouraging Devotion (Watson, pg. 192) The original Buddhism was more "politically correct" than most societies today.

There are still religions today where women are not on an equal footing with men; (as in Thailand) and this is a serious injustice, great loss of talent and huge tragedy in human terms, a loss of human potential, i.e. the Taliban. Any religion that does not actively share sacerdotal duties between women and men regardless, and this is more often the case than not, is unworthy of our respect. Can we love the misguided and abusive people and loath the *misogynist and chauvinist principle*, this separation is a difficult assignment and a test of enlightenment.

Protecting:

"This is what I heard," review by both Samahito and teacher.

Proverb: We cannot direct the wind, but we can adjust our sails. (wellpage.com)

Additional Teaching:

"In the past we went around foolishly picking up heavy objects, such as boulders. We lugged them along wherever we went. For this we constantly suffered dukkha. How many years has this gone on? Now, however, we realize how unwise we were in creating such problems for ourselves. We realize how burdensome these boulders are, and we just toss them away. Without these burdens we are light; all our problems disappear. Before, life itself seemed to be a burden because of our stupidity. We clung to those natural sankhara, carried them everywhere, and thus weighed ourselves down terribly. Now we throw them off. This is another metaphor that describes the final step of anapanasati—[giving back.]" (Buddhadasa, 1988, pp. 91-92)

"Another condition that may very easily come about is a blissful rapture the like of which the meditator has never encountered before. Once arisen it induces wonder and amazement and unjustified self satisfaction. While the rapture lasts, the body and the mind experience extreme bliss and all problems vanish. Things that formerly were liked or disliked are liked or disliked no longer when recalled to mind. Things the meditator had formerly feared and dreaded or worried and fretted over no longer induce those reactions, so that he gets the false idea that he has already attained liberation, freedom from all defilements; because for as long as he is in that condition he has all the characteristics of a genuinely perfected individual. Should satisfaction arise with respect to this condition, *it acts as an obstacle to further progress* in Vipassana. And in time [and once faced with the real world] the condition will fade away so that things formerly liked or disliked will be liked or disliked again just as before, or even more so." (Buddhadasa, 2005, pg. 119)

Preview: "In the fourth jhana, [next] nonverbal, non-conceptual realization begins to take place on a regular basis . . . Endowed with this powerful concentration, the fourth jhana penetrates the five aggregates and sees their impermanence, unsatisfactoriness, and selflessness at a nearly subatomic level. This is not inferential or theoretical knowledge. It is nonverbal, non-conceptual, and experiential, a direct seeing of the intrinsic nature of the aggregates." (Gunaratana, pp. 153-154)

Sharing Merit:

Rejoicing In Others' Merit (Saying Sadhu)

"May the merit of this action be shared by all beings everywhere, so that they may come to the end of suffering."

Buddhist Sutra

Lesson Title: **Rapture—Showering Joy**

Lesson Number: **Twenty-four**

Key Vocabulary: devotion, flood of joy, conceit, misogynist, chauvinist, bodhicitta, merit, aspiration, application, patinissagganupassana, absolute, relative

Assignment: Our meditation practice should be the same today as for the last few days—extended—as often as possible and for as long a time in each position in each session as possible. Caution: stop each practice before there is any muscle or tendon strain, this will not aid meditation. The important thing is that the body is stressed by pain, fatigue and hunger to contribute to the production of natural chemicals that facilitate high levels of mental functioning. This will happen with repeated periods of stress rather than coming from self-inflicted injury.

Visualize the concept of giving back. Each time we have a guest to our home, possibly identify something they might wish to take away with them. Give more to charity. Acquire fewer things. Contemplate how your life will change, and explain.

Seek to uncover the roots of long held resentments and negative emotions during insight meditation.

Define each of the Key Vocabulary in your own words.

After the Lesson, Samahito will choose a partner, who should be a different person each day, to accompany silently and safeguard during the day. Read the sixteen steps slowly to each other.

To what level of relative bodhicitta have you arrived?

Gaining wisdom and modesty is a source of long-term happiness. Do you agree? How deep is your happiness?

Distinguish between the law of cause and effect and the Law of Causation.

What are the adverse circumstances in our lives that can cause us to have the emotional reaction to produce "waves breaking on the shore?"

We share merit by this recitation in our practice: 'May the merit of this action be shared by all beings everywhere, so that they may come to the end of suffering.' (pg. 187)

Prepare a progress report on doing "incompletes" from Lesson Twenty.

Materials Required: hair cleansing ceremony, carry with you an electrolyte drink.

Buddhist Sutra

Lesson Title: **Rapture—Uplifting Joy**

Lesson Number: **Twenty-five**

Rationale:

"We are profoundly blessed when we have a mind that remains unshaken when it is touched by all the changes of the world—all of the joys and sorrows as they continually fluctuate." (Salzberg, pg. 131)

"Perception of no-thing-ness is still perception. Your mind gets bored even with that and swings away from any perception at all. Total absence of perception is sublime." (Gunaratana, pg. 108) Is this even possible? Does the mind disappear or go to sleep? Or find a different level?

Proverb: Nothing lasts forever . . . not even your troubles. (wellpage.com)

Discussion of Prior Lesson:

"The fundamental view of the mind in mahamudra is that the mind in its original state reflects its inherently awakened condition, what in earlier Buddhism was called Buddha-nature. In the mahamudra tradition it is called *the way the realized mind stays* (gnas lugs).

The ordinary individual, however, is blocked from realizing the mind's real nature by negative habits and *erroneous ideas* . . . Direct realization of the mind's *non-duality* is an essential prerequisite to *awakening* the mind." (Brown, pp. 13-14)

Share your progress on doing "incompletes."

"Throw away the burdens of life. Throw them away until no burdens remain. Before, we lived under their weight; their heaviness oppressed us. This is called 'living beneath the world' [*lokiya*] or 'drowning in the world.' Once we can toss away the burdens that hold us down, that trap us beneath the world, we ascend . . . We are 'lords of the world.' [*Lokuttara*] This is the true meaning of freedom and well-being." (Buddhadasa, 1988, pg. 92) Advertising, bargains, the proverbial "close-out sale," and promotions will have no affect on us.

Training Objective:

Responsibilities of an Arahant. The new role of equanimity in our lives. The three dimensional perspective of freedom. Turn-arounds to remain calm. "Orientation Association Area" and chanting Bud-dho.

Materials Required: hair cleansing ceremony, carry with you an electrolyte drink.

Motivational Statement:

"Uplifting Rapture (Ubbega-piti): [this means balance] during which we feel uplifted and express some feelings or do some actions unintentionally [yelling and cheering.] For example, we exclaim, or we feel the body is light and floats from the seat . . . The Forth Jhana: mind has equanimity (Upekkha) and mental one-pointedness (Ekaggata)." (Wee, pp. 144-145) Consider that sense of enthusiasm and *partisanship* when we cheer for our favorite team. This biased enthusiasm is called into service when we recognize life as a competition against our raw natures and—whether we win or lose—rooting for our own obtainment of nirvana.

Can we ". . . arrest the mind before it falls into extremes[?] Equanimity is a spacious stillness of the mind, a *radiant calm* that allows us to be present fully with all the different changing experiences that constitute our world and our lives . . . When we look at our own lives, we see extraordinary patterns of flow and movement [impermanence.] Think for a moment about what series of circumstances brought you to be sitting in the particular place where you are now . . . some of those experiences may have seemed very unfortunate, and yet in some way they had a role in this pattern that brought you here [where you can cleanse and heal] . . ." (Salzberg, pg. 139) Knowing how to make the best of the circumstances we confront is certainly a part of maturity that relates to any explanation of enlightenment.

First Progressive:

"To see things as they are, to see the changing nature, to see the impermanence, to see that constant flow of pleasant and painful events outside our control—that is freedom . . . Equanimity [gives us] all the warmth and love of [happiness and joy], but it also has balance, wisdom, and the understanding that things are as they are, and that we cannot ultimately control someone else's happiness and unhappiness." (Salzberg, pg. 146) Freedom gives us the effectiveness to act for our own *benefit and for the benefit of others.*

"Most of us don't live in isolation [nor would we want to.] We live in *an interdependent world.* If you want to improve the condition of your own life, then you need to depend on others to help you along the way. Without this kind of interdependent relationship you would not have food, a roof over your head, or a job to go to—you wouldn't even be able to buy coffee . . . So, if you *deal with others in a compassionate, empathetic way,* you can only improve the conditions of your own life. When you look at your relationship to the world and your own life in this way, you see that loving-kindness and compassion are very, very powerful."

"The other great benefit of developing compassion is that through understanding the needs, fears, and desires of others, you develop a deeper capacity to understand your own self—what you hope for, what you hope to avoid, and the truth about your own nature. And this, in turn, serves to dissolve whatever sense of loneliness or low self-esteem you may be feeling. As you begin to recognize that *everyone craves happiness* and is terrified of unhappiness, you start to realize that you're not alone in your fears, needs, or desires. And in realizing this, you lose your fear of others—everyone is a potential friend, a potential brother or sister—because you share the same fears, the same longings, and the same goals. And with this understanding, it becomes so much easier to really communicate with others on a heart—to—heart level." (Mingyur, pg. 231)

There is the possibility of being kind and compassionate to oneself, and this happens in private when we enter the fourth stage of jhana. "In the fourth jhana, you don't think conceptually about suffering, the cause of suffering, the end of suffering, or any of the rest. You just know, directly [that it is ended.] This is the level where the mind sees things through the eye of wisdom. Words, thinking, investigation, or even reflection have no place. They would just get in the way. They are too slow and everything is moving too fast. Every cell in the body undergoes change every moment. When body changes at this inconceivable rapidity, no mind without powerful concentration can keep up. You need steadiness, pliability, softness, and purity to notice that flashing, incessant change. This sharpness of the mind is present only in the concentrated mind." (Gunaratana, pg. 154)

Second Progressive:

"Because we often depend on intense pleasure and pain for a sense of feeling awake or alive, when the experience is neutral, we tend to react by falling asleep, either literally or by lapsing into inattention. In Buddhism this is considered falling into delusion . . . When we do not like the experience, when it is painful, we tend to react with aversion, by condemning or pushing away." (Salzberg, pg. 143) Because of this, sometimes when we read, we see what we want to comprehend, so we need to review the teachings, such as the Eight-fold Path from time to time, to each time gain something new from them.

"The fourth of the Four Noble Truths (The Eight-fold Path) sets forth the means of eliminating suffering step by step . . . it contains all the direct and indirect methods needed to remove suffering and to build a perfect personality in physical and spiritual terms. [Of course these ethical teachings need to be fleshed out a bit, as with *Buddhist Sutras*.] Developing such a personality—that of a Buddha or an arahant—resembles physical therapy aiming both to cure the present sickness and to create a sound, healthy body in which sickness does not occur. The comparison with the healing principle shows how rationally organized the doctrine of the Four Noble Truths is. It further shows the identity between these Truths and the research attitude of such fields of learning as modern natural science." (Mizuno, pg. 46) This recommends the benefit from simple teachings, such as Rational Buddhism, because the esoteric or Tantric practices are in effect optional (or divergent) to the goal of obtaining enlightenment.

What is necessary is to eliminate bad and destructive habits. "1. The source of all bad conduct comes from defilements hidden in our minds. 2. The extinction of defilements are hindered for these reasons: i) most people cannot see the defilements that reside in [their own] mind. ii) we take our defilements for granted; our mind is so used to being bathed in them as a fish is so used to water. iii) the way to remove defilements is elusive."

"The Lord Buddha taught an appropriate way of how to get rid of defilements that bear immediate and absolute results to the doer. The doer must hold fast to the following expression—'take a hair of the dog that bit you' or 'like cures like' . . . as our mind is burning and suffering due to defilements, we should in turn burn them back by practicing austerities. The Pali term is 'tapa,' which means to make something hot or to burn. In order to remove our bad habits and desires as aforementioned, the austere practice of self-control is a solution which is consisted of keeping the precepts, [and] meditation . . ." (Dattajeevo, pp. 123-124) One purpose of the meditation training of Anapanasati is to show the way to eliminate defilements and gain Jhana. We actually have to do something different rather than just talk the same old line of "bull shit."

"The defilements you eradicate at this level are deeply settled in the mind. Only this kind of nonverbal, non-conceptual mindfulness with clear comprehension and equanimity can reach the very root of those deeply embedded defects. You simply direct attention onto your own underlying tendencies. Jhana opens the door. Working together, mindfulness and concentration weaken the fetters, so that later, in the supra-mundane jhanas, you can destroy them altogether." (Gunaratana, pg. 155) Mindfulness can operate on many levels, and underlies our lives like a pleasant cushion if we allow this.

Third Progressive:

"In the fourth jhana you go deeper still. You turn away from all mental states that would counter total stillness, even happiness. The turning away happens by itself, no effort required. Equanimity and one-pointedness get even stronger. Feelings of pain went away at the first jhana. In the fourth jhana, feelings of bodily pleasure go away, too. There is not a single thought. You feel sensation that is neither pleasant nor unpleasant. You rest in one-pointedness and equanimity As your mind becomes progressively more still, [light and airy] your body and breath do the same. In the fourth jhana it feels like you have stopped breathing altogether. You cannot be roused. You emerge from the fourth jhana only at a predetermined time of your own choosing [so plan ahead.]" (Gunaratana, pg. 106)

What are the adverse circumstances in our lives that can cause us to have the emotional reaction of feeling depressed, heavy or slow, or just unwilling to engage actively in life (or at worst suicidal?) The opposite of this is to feel like exclaiming, or we feel the body is light and floats from the seat? As we meditate can we take ourselves to those negative places, relive these experiences safely, nullify the causes one by one and extinguish the suffering? We know we have achieved this turn around, when we have the positive physical reaction described by this level of rapture during meditation, the opposite of what we had during the event itself. The heaviness will become lightness; we may have the sensation of floating around the room (as if we were following the curser on a CAD program inspecting the features of the room in 3D.) After we can feel energized rather than depressed and anxiously look forward to the goal (and to the responsibilities) of enlightenment as an Arahant; we feel the sheer sense of ecstatic relief and euphoria and the subsequent sense of equanimity which gives us a stable balance from which to plan and live our lives.

"Equanimity's strength derives from a combination of understanding and trust. It is based on understanding that the conflict and frustration we feel when we can't control the world doesn't come from our inability to do so, but rather from the fact that we are trying to control the uncontrollable. We know better than to try to prevent the seasons from changing or the tide from coming in. Following autumn, winter comes. We may not prefer it, but we trust it because we understand and accept its rightful place in a larger cycle, a bigger picture. Can we apply the same wise balance to the cycles and tides of pleasant, unpleasant, and neutral experiences in our lives?" (Salzberg, pg. 145)

"At the stage of Forth Jhana, the mind can be free from the body . . . This part is the mind (Nama) and another part is the body (Rupa). When the mind develops concentration to the Forth Jhana, the mind experiences, with eyes closed, mental one-pointedness (Ekaggata). When we open our eyes, we see as if a small monk with red lips, holding a ceremonial fan, looking at us [this may be a ethnocentric signal—watch for any other entity as well] and smiling to us all the time. This is another state. When we change the posture and move, the small monk keeps appearing in front of us, smiling to us all the time like a shadow moving along with us . . . It is a natural phenomenon. When we experience such a natural phenomenon, bear in mind that it is feeling of the mind of the Forth Jhana. The mind is pure and is able to be free from the body . . . We have to know and understand the natural phenomenon in the Forth Jhana. If we do not study and do not know about it [in advance,] we will be frightened or we will not pay attention to what is happening. Consequently, we do not understand the state of the Forth Jhana and it will crumble easily because we have never known about it before and so we have no intention to maintain it." (Wee, pp. 145-146)

". . . Two American scientists have studied the relationship between religious experience and brain function for many years. (A. Newberg and E. d'Aquili) In their most elaborate experiment, they enlisted the help of an advance meditator [after an hour] . . . he had entered a deep state of meditation. A radioactive tracer was then injected into his veins via an IV drip. The dye entered his bloodstream, infused his brain cells, and a high-tech camera gave the scientists a freeze-frame snapshot of Robert's brain activities. The scientists saw something unusual: Robert's posterior superior parietal lobe, dubbed the 'orientation association area,' or OAA, showed markedly reduced activity at the height of his meditation."

"In our brains, the OAA acts as a gyroscope, radar, and GPS device all rolled into one. As we move about in our daily routines, the OAA functions like a supercomputer, continuously calculating the ever-shifting coordinates of our bodies in relation to everything around us. It allows us to negotiate our way safely through a crowded restaurant and to ride our bikes through traffic."

". . . Robert's OAA was blocked when he reached a transcendent state during his meditation. With no data to feed it, the supercomputer had a hard time delineating Robert's physical boundaries. It had no choice but to conclude that Robert had no boundaries, that he was one with everything around him: people, things, the whole works . . . Robert was asked later what he felt during this climactic moment in his meditation, he replied, 'It feels like I'm part of everyone and everything in existence. I'm connected to everything'." (Chan, pp. 121-122) This result is not exactly like the description of this forth jhana/rapture which can vary between different Buddhist texts, ". . . we feel the body is light and floats from the seat," but it is close enough to signal some reality for the potential of these sensations.

Clearly through meditation we change the moment to moment functioning of the brain, is this an aide to the achievement of our fundamental goal, reaching nirvana? Many people have dreams of falling, disorientation, dizziness as when partially drunk, and even my own youthful meditation on the "far-away" may be explained as the result of the disengagement of OAA. What is the status of your "posterior superior parietal lobe, dubbed the 'orientation association area"? When we feel deeply a connection to Universe, to humanity and to our ancient teachers, we are perhaps disengaging the activity of our OAA.

Meditation Practicum:

"Eat only when we suffer from hunger, before noon only. If you can resist hunger, no need to eat [just drink water and electrolytes every hour.] Practice by every posture to the utmost of suffering of each posture, be standing, walking or sitting except lying. We practice by lying only when we cannot stand [staying awake.] Notice mind state of hindrances. If we do not understand hindrances resulting from the practice, we cannot make progress in the practice because hindrances fetter mind from attaining wholesomeness. [This is an exercise in improving the self-discipline required to gain ethical purity as well.] We have to be mindful of hindrances when they occur and overcome them . . . Food consumption . . . is the most important destroyer for the practice. Please note that if we cannot stop worrying about food, it is hopeless for us to make progress in meditation practice. The body that we presume to be ourselves belongs to defilements in fact . . . we start the practice at dawn, eat small amounts before noon, and continue till dusk regularly. Even when we sleep, we lie down and practice till we fall asleep and when we wake up, we resume the practice." (Wee, pp. 116-117)

"Knowing what mind is and what matter is, at the time of practice we must mindfully note the mind and matter in time when clear feeling manifests. In the Vipassana Bhavana practice, meditators are required to remember by heart the state of the mind [aggregates] and matter." Thus to have a realistic awareness of their own status.

"Four Foundations of Mindfulness mean mindfulness of body, feelings, mind and mind-objects like seeing of eye, hearing of ear, etc., as the sense-objects throughout the time of the Insight Meditation . . . we chant at the same time as directing mindfulness on the mind and matter. The chanting words used are 'Bud—Dho:' the Buddha's [and our] sacred name." (Wee, pg. 157) Compare this to previous teachings which may be more elaborate, including 'feeling tone, and state of consciousness, etc." Notice how they relate to the four tetrads of the Sixteen Steps of Meditation.

"Metaphorically, an arrogant person or one without humility, is like one who cannot be united with others, like the rigidly cracked clod or deadwood." (Dattajeevo, pg. 94)

The fourth jhana is also the state in which mindfulness and concentration unite into an intense awareness that can penetrate deeply into the nature of existence. This is the ideal state in which to directly perceive the three primary qualities of all ordinary existence: annica, dukkha, and anatta. You passed through jhanas one through three, simply allowing them to develop and pass. You pause at the fourth jhana. You use the state to see deeply into impermanence, suffering [unsatisfactoriness,] and no-self." (Gunaratana, pg. 107)

Biographical Sketch:

"Svatthi, in the province of Uttar Pradesh, is located about thirteen and a half miles from Balrampur. In the days of the Buddha it was a thriving city, the capital of the kingdom of Kosala. Starting with the twentieth year of his Enlightenment, the Buddha spent every rainy season there except for the last one, twenty-four in all—i.e. Jeta's Grove, Anathapindika's Park . . . When Fa Hien came to the site in the early 400's, the city had become little more than a small town, although the monastery continued to prosper . . ."—900 years later.

The Buddha taught many lessons and discourses in Svatthi . . . One incident relates the conversion of Anguilmala, at the time a notorious murderer in the forest in the area. "Though warned three times by the country people of the danger posed by Anguliala, the Buddha journeyed along the road to where the killer was staying . . . he started after the Blessed One with the thought of killing him. However, despite the fact the murderer ran as fast as he could, he could not catch up with the Buddha, who was walking along at his regular pace. Angulimala, amazed, called out to the Buddha to stop. The Buddha replied: 'I have stopped, Angulimala, you stop too'. The latter, understanding that recluses speak the truth, asked for an explanation. The Buddha replied:

> 'Ahgulimala, I have stopped forever,
> I abstain from violence towards living beings;

But you have no restraint towards things that live:
That is why I have stopped and you have not'

The murderer, [understanding the koan] realizing that the Buddha had come to the forest for the very purpose of saving him from his wicked ways, had a complete change of heart and immediately requested to be ordained a monk. The Buddha, the 'Sage of Great compassion' made him a bhikkhu at once." The Buddha's words ". . . hold the key to an understanding of Enlightenment as emptiness, as putting a complete stop to the grasping and clinging of 'I' and 'mine.' (as opposed to Yoga teachings) 'so it is emptiness that is stopping and it is the only kind of stopping that could have made Angulimala an arahant . . . Cessation, the true stopping, is the emptiness where there is no self to dwell anywhere . . . If there is still a self then you can't stop' . . . The experience of the total emptiness of 'I' and 'mine' is the experience of Enlightenment: 'The truth-discerning awareness must be so impeccably clear that one has not the slightest feeling of 'self' or 'belonging to self' for it to be called supreme emptiness . . . this is Nibbana because it completely extinguishes the things that are on fire [tapa], the stream or whirlpool of flowing and changing phenomena . . . Enlightenment is the emptiness beyond opposing choices available to us in our daily lives. It is beyond even good and evil." (Inthisan, pp. 71-75) Self, in the Yoga sense, is understood as being characterized as the emptiness referred to here.

Reading for the Day: Lotus Sutra

"Medicine King, though there may be many persons, those still living in the household and those who have left it, who practice the way of the bodhisattva, if they are not willing to see, hear, read, recite, copy, embrace and offer alms to this Lotus Sutra, then you should know that such persons are not yet practicing the bodhisattva way in a fitting manner. But if there are those who will listen to this sutra, then they are capable of practicing the bodhisattva way in a fitting manner. If among the living beings who seek the Buddha way there are those who see or hear this Lotus Sutra, and who, having heard it, believe, understand and embrace it, then you should know that these persons can draw near to anuttara-samyak-sambodhi."

The Teacher of the Law (Watson, pg. 165) This is a *grace* associated with learning the Law and offering alms that is referred to several times in the Lotus Sutra.

Satipatthana is a technique of meditation that is complementary to Anapanasati, but not quite the same, so an Arahant will be proficient with both. "When the mind is well established in Samadhi it is not a matter of just the formal practice anymore; the mind should be in Samadhi while walking along the street and sitting in a car because the mind that is in Samadhi is the mind that is disciplined and obedient. It is the tamed mind, the mind that is orderly. There is not need to train it any further [but continued practice and use is essential.] To go and train the mind that is already tamed is not right. I accept other methods of practice if they give rise to sila, Samadhi and panya. Sila is the state of normality, Samadhi is the tamed mind that does not rebel, and panya is to thoroughly know all about proliferation. To know the body and mind as they really are and not be stuck in either of them."

"The method I teach is the most skillful one [satipatthana,] it is the way to develop the foundations of awareness. This type of practice doesn't make use of recitation and one shouldn't close one's eyes. We depend on movements in order to arouse sati . . . Having a lot of awareness is called mahasati . . . The mind undergoes a change from how it was before." (Suvanno, pp. 257-258)

Proverb: Life is the greatest bargain, we get it for nothing. (wellpage.com)

Protecting:

Hair ceremony: Take a cutting (snippet) of hair and place it in this alms bowl. We mix these together with crumbled incense to symbolize the oneness and beauty of our path. We place this on a tray and light a fire. Reach for the smoke, and as we breathe the smoke we sense a cleansing from all past mistakes and "sins." We smell the sweet incense, the pungent hair, the fragrance of equanimity by the body-door of nostrils. This is a mnemonic for protecting rapture and the insights from meditation, for solidifying our understanding of equanimity, and for awakening our nascent comprehension of emptiness leading to nirvana. We chant together softly as we meditate with each breath in unison "Bud-dho."

"This is what I heard," review by both Samahito and teacher.

Proverb: Happiness is like potato salad . . . when shared with others, it's a picnic. (wellpage.com)

The Seven Purifications:
  The Five Stages in Vipassana:
    The Nine Steps in the Perfection of Knowledge:

1. Moral purity
2. Mental purity
3. Freedom from false views (First stage in Vipassana)
4. Freedom from doubt (Second stage)
5. Knowledge and vision of what is the true Path (Third stage)
6. Knowledge and vision of the progress along the Path (Fourth Stage)
    a. Knowledge of arising and passing away
    b. Knowledge of passing away
    c. Awareness of fearsomeness
    d. Awareness of danger
    e. Disenchantment
    f. Desire for freedom
    g. Struggle to escape
    h. imperturbability
    i. Readiness to perceive the Four Noble Truths
7. Full Intuitive Insight (Fifth Stage in Vipassana)

(Buddhadasa, 2005, pg. 105f)

Sharing Merit:

Rejoicing In Others' Merit (Saying Sadhu)

Buddhist Sutra

Lesson Title: Rapture—Uplifting Joy

Lesson Number: Twenty-five

Key Vocabulary: erroneous ideas, non-duality, awakening, partisanship, radiant calm, delusion, lokiya, lokuttara, grace, satipatthana, mahasati, Orientation Association Area, Bud-dho

Assignment: Meditate on awakening factors: *mindfulness, investigation-of dhammas, energy, joy, tranquility, concentration, and equanimity*—for as long a time in each position in each session as possible. Caution: stop each practice before there is any muscle or tendon strain, this will not aid meditation. The important thing is that the body is stressed by pain (as well as hunger) to contribute to the production of natural chemicals that facilitate high levels of mental functioning. This will happen with repeated periods of mild stress rather than coming from self-inflicted injury.

Think about what series of circumstances that brought you here, and where you are now in your life.

Plan on having almost no solid food tomorrow, complete fasting except for electrolytes if this is possible. Define each of the Key Vocabulary in your own words.

After the Lesson, Samadhi will choose a partner, who should be a different person each day, to accompany silently during the day. Read out loud the sixteen steps slowly, as with a guided meditation, taking turns doing this.

Describe some of the new roles for equanimity in your life, new ways of acting and being. List some of the responsibilities of an Arahant.

Can you obtain the three dimensional perspective of enhanced freedom?

Identify one or more turn-arounds where you gained at least a sense of calm or a more peaceful emotional response.

What are the adverse circumstances in our lives that can cause us to have the emotional reaction of feeling depressed, heavy or slow, or just unwilling to engage actively in life?

Clearly through meditation we change the moment to moment functioning of the brain; is this an aide to achieving our fundamental goal, reaching nirvana?

After breakfast today fast the entire day—24 hours until noon tomorrow. Drink liquids.

Buddhist Sutra

Lesson Title: **Pervading Rapture (absorption)—Jhana**

Lesson Number: **Twenty-six**

Rationale:

This is the important fifth stage of rapture,—Rapture to Jhana. "The immaterial jhanas are four states that have very little relationship to our ordinary cognitive/sensory world. Normal words simply do not apply. These are called the 'formless' jhanas. The first four jhanas are attained by concentration on a material form [and we used past emotional events] or the feeling generated by certain concepts such as loving-friendliness. You attain the formless states of the immaterial jhanas by passing beyond all perception of form." (Gunaratana, pg. 107)

Proverb: The Constitution only guarantees citizens the right to pursue happiness; you have to catch it yourself. Benjamin Franklin

Discussion of Prior Lesson:

"If practicing until achieving the insight knowledge, we will experience the mental images by ourselves. We must seriously study and sharply remember the scriptures about the method of the meditation practice for comparison during the practice whether the practiced result is in line with theory [protection] and we can use theory as the map to tell us the right way. In the Dhamma practice, the level of concentration may happen from momentary concentration, [rise very quickly to one or the other level] access concentration to [the fourth] Jhanas which we can practice and attain. Therefore, we must know the Scripture very well to practice the dhamma [correctly]. It is not important whether or not the mind can cultivate concentration. The important point is that in whatever posture we are practicing, we must practice until the strongest painful feeling appears at the body[-door] and then change to a new practice posture. We must do the same every time of the practice." (Wee, pg. 187)

Training Objective:

The importance of the Lotus Sutra. The fifth level of pervading rapture is the gateway to achieving the state of liberation. Understanding perfect freedom when you feel it.

Materials Required: A prior day of fasting (only drinking water.)

Motivational Statement:

"Pervading Rapture (Pharana-piti): it is suffusing joy. We feel as if our body became bigger and bigger till it filled up the room where we sit. We may feel imbued with infused cold rising all over the body . . . There may be tingling and sensation of relief. It means that mind is so concentrated that it develops full concentration (Appanasamadhi)." From there we can move to the four levels of jhana of the formless sphere.

"There are two types of Jhana in Buddhism. They are Jhana of the fine-material sphere (Rupajhana) comprising the first-forth jhana and Jhana of formless sphere (Arupajhana) . . . We have to know and understand that the mental feelings rising during the first-forth Jhana are the feelings that rise during sitting meditating with eyes closed."(Wee, pg. 35-42) Thus we progress through the five stages of rapture to then again progress through the four stages of formless jhana which are somewhat parallel. This sequence is difficult to understand completely, and possibly it will be even more difficult to tell one sphere from another, but then I can't hear the key when music is played, and when it changes either; some people can.

First Progressive:

Having compassion for the entire world and the various ecosystems (i.e. the rain forest of Brazil) has become a popular trademark of Buddhist communities, and rightly so. For many, preserving the environment, recycling consumer packaging and household items, and such issues as stopping global warming are primary concerns for *"sharing merit" with the entire world's population,* albeit this becomes somewhat diffuse.

How do you prepare yourself to have *unlimited compassion*? "When you reach the next stage, which my teachers called the 'lake' experience, your mind begins to feel very smooth, wide, and open, like a lake without waves. You find yourself genuinely happy, without any ups and downs. You're full of confidence, stable, and you experience a more or less continuous state of meditative awareness, even while sleeping. [You are prepared to be part of the solution instead of part of the problem.] You may still experience problems in your life—negative thoughts, strong emotions, and so on—but instead of being obstacles, they become further opportunities to deepen your meditative awareness . . ."

"At the same time, your body begins to feel the lightness of bliss, and your clarity improves so that all your perceptions begin to take on a sharper, almost transparent quality, like reflections in a mirror . . . [like] A lotus begins to grow from the mud and sediment at the bottom of a lake or pond, but by the time the flower blooms at the surface, it bears no trace of mud; in fact, the petals actually appear to repel filth. In the same way, when your mind blossoms into the lake experience, you have no trace of clinging or grasping, [you are *ready to help others* because you have] none of the problems associated with samsara." (Mingyur, pg. 216)

"A different sort of equanimity develops in the fourth jhana, where consciousness is unified by concentration. In the fourth jhana and beyond, sensory impressions do not arise at all. Your equanimity is not based on any of the six senses. It arises based purely on concentration or one-pointedness of mind, along with mindfulness. There is no room for sensory experience and thus equanimity is smooth and continuous . . . The perfection of equanimity allows all the other factors to unite. This is where the *factors of enlightenment you have been cultivating all come together.* All the wholesome things you have been doing in your daily life—little by little, here and there—consolidate and produce results in the fourth jhana [as with making merit.] When the fourth jhana is attained, its equanimity is based on this unity of mind . . . because your senses are not responding to sensory stimuli." (Gunaratana, pg. 160)

Second Progressive:

"It is said that in the early part of the night of his enlightenment, Shakyamuni attained the first of the three types of superior wisdom: 1. remembrance of one's former existences, as well as those of others. 2. In the middle part of the night, he attained insight into the future and the eye capable of seeing everything. In the last part of the night he attained the most important wisdom: 3. perfect freedom enabling him to overcome all passions and thus to reach supreme enlightenment. These three types of superior wisdom constitute the last of the six supernatural powers of saving sentient beings attributed to Shakyamuni and to those of his disciples who attained ultimate enlightenment in the same manner as he. [The other three are:] 4. Perfect freedom of activity [walking on water, etc.] 5. Ears capable of hearing everything. 6. Insight into the minds of others." (Mizumo, pp. 164-165) These were traits pertaining to Buddha (violating the laws of physics) who had otherwise met all the requirements of moral perfection that he subsequently taught.

"In the Buddhist tradition, people don't talk much about their own experiences and realizations, mostly because such boasting tends to increase one's own sense of pride and can lead to misuse of the experiences to gain worldly power or influence over other people, which is harmful to oneself and to others. For this reason, training in meditation involves a vow or a commitment—known in Sanskrit as *samaya*—not to misuse the abilities gained through meditation practice . . ." (Mingyur, pp. 216-217)

This training through the stages of jhana is a very personal, solitary trek, one for which even finding the right words to explain it is considered virtually impossible. Whereas the development of skill in breathing-in-and-out, mindfulness, is preliminary, the progress through the fourth jhana is quite advanced. "According to the Buddha's teaching, when the mind is concentrated, you can see things as they really are . . . When we read about the way that the Buddha used his own fourth jhanic concentration, as given in many suttas, we have no reason to believe that he came out of jhana to develop the three kinds of knowledge that he used for seeing past lives, seeing beings dying and taking rebirth, and knowing that his own defilements had been destroyed . . . It is virtually impossible to find evidence in the suttas that one should come out of jhana to practice vipassana. If you come out of jhana to practice vipassana, you lose the jhanic qualities because your hindrances return. The jhanic state is a perfect state of mind to focus on the Four Noble Truths, impermanence, unsatisfactoriness, and selflessness and to attain liberation by eliminating the fetters." (Gunaratana, pg. 157) This is where the esoteric, intuitive, or non-rational nature of Buddhism finds expression.

Third Progressive:

The Lotus Sutra begins with a hyperbole that would make the most rhetorically gifted politician blush. "After several astounding [super-natural] events that impress upon us the truly cosmic scale of the drama that is unfolding, the Buddha begins to preach. The first important point he wishes to convey is that there is only one vehicle or one path to salvation, that which leads to the goal of Buddhahood. Earlier in his preaching career, he had described three paths for the believer, what he calls the three vehicles. One was that of shravaka or voice-hearer [Listener? Illiterate?] which leads to the realm of the arhat. Second was that of the *pratyekabuddha*, the being who gains enlightenment by himself and for himself alone, and the third was that of the bodhisattva [who lived for the purpose of sharing his enlightenment.] But now, the Buddha tells us, these lesser paths or goals are to be set aside and all beings are to aim for the single goal of Buddhahood, the one and only vehicle to true enlightenment or perfect understanding, a state designated in the Lotus Sutra by the rather daunting Sanskrit term *anuttara-samyak-sambodhi*."

"When asked why, if there is only the single vehicle or truth, the Buddha has earlier taught his followers the doctrine of the three vehicles, he replies that at that time they were not yet ready to comprehend or accept the highest truth . . . the Lotus Sutra [which was written as hindsight as much as 500 years after Buddha's life] . . . represents the highest level of truth, the summation of the Buddha's message, superseding his earlier pronouncements, which had only provisional validity." (Watson, pp. xvi-xvii) Some of the most important teachings of the Lotus Sutra have been included, where appropriate, throughout the *Buddhist Sutras*.

In addition to living a wholesome, compassionate life, for the Samahito to advance to the level of Arahant ". . . he/she has to be able to train mind to be concentrated, one-pointed to the level of the forth Jhana . . . To attain the highest level of the Teachings is called the final stage of holiness (*Arahattaphala*) or final freedom which is the ultimate goal of Buddhism. The person who attains this final stage of holiness is called the Holy One. The Holy One can give up all ten fetters; the three [1. false view of Self, 2. doubt, 3. adherence to mere rules] and seven more: 4. sensual lust 5. repulsion, irritation 6. attachment to realms of form 7. attachment to formless realms 8. conceit, pride 9. restlessness, distraction 10. ignorance. 'To attain' means to reach, to achieve, such as [to arrive.] . . . Therefore, 'to attain Dhamma' means to attain the Teachings of the Lord Buddha, that is, 'to attain the truth of all compounded things' . . . Another thing we should know is what the truth of all compounded things means. It means all compounded things are suffering because of: impermanence; suffering (physical and mental discomfort); non-self, soulless, subject to crumbling." (Wee, pp. 111-112) Each scenario of suffering is a complex mix of events, predilections, previous karma, psychological forces in ourselves, and bad luck at times, what else? thus these are "compounded things."

What are the adverse circumstances in our lives that can cause us to have the emotional reactions to feel bigger and bigger till we fill up the room where we sit? Pride, arrogance, success, or something positive such as wisdom? In this rapture we may feel imbued with infused cold rising all over the body? What are the adverse circumstances in our lives that can cause us to have the emotional reactions of cold? Nervousness, despair, stage fright, loss of a loved one? As we meditate we can take ourselves there, relive these experiences, nullify the causes and extinguish the suffering? We know we have achieved this turn-around when we have the same physical reaction during meditation as we had during the event itself, this is a kind of self-empathy with the past, then we see it for what it is, emptiness. The largeness will instead be expansiveness and generosity, the cold sensation will become a refreshing breeze like relaxation in an air conditioned room while it is hot outside, and there is possibly a tingling and sense of relief. The sense of sheer relief and euphoria from "pervading rapture" will nearly overwhelm us as we are able to make the turn-around.

Meditation Practicum:

"We practice the same as the previous day. Being able to absolutely control all the mentioned factors which affect meditation practice, we have to notice mental images appearing in mind. If we can control certainly all the mentioned factors since the first day till this day which is the sixth day, mind will be able to develop establishment [staying steady] which is concentration and cultivate insight. Mental images . . . [by the signs] we will then know how much progress in practice we make. They can confirm to us that we practice in a correct way." (Wee, pg. 117)

With the hunger you have achieved will come a heightened sense of taste. "Focusing on taste is an extremely practical technique that can be used to engage in meditation for a few moments at several points throughout the day . . . begin as usual by allowing [the] mind to rest naturally for a few moments, then allow [yourself] to focus attention lightly on the tastes [of the food you are given.] I didn't have to analyze a particular taste sensation, like bitterness, sweetness, or sourness. I just had to rest my attention lightly on all the tastes I perceived and then rest my mind naturally, alternating between bringing my attention to the sensation of taste and resting my mind naturally." (Mingyur, pg. 155) In this way we learn to appreciate what we receive and become in a special way acutely aware of our surroundings.

By the time Samahitos reach this point, they will be well equipped with mental strength to both avoid and eradicate their sufferings, and they will be ready to more frequently focus on offering help to others. The following prayer relies on this transitional potential. **"Meditation on Loving Kindness (*metta*) (Method I)" (Repeat each phrase together.)**

"May I be free from enmity, ill-will and grief, and may I take care of myself happily! As I am, so also may my teachers, preceptors, parents, and intimate, indifferent, and inimical beings, be free from enmity, ill-will and grief, and may they take care of themselves happily! May they be released from suffering! May they not be deprived of their fortune, duly acquired! All have [control of] kamma as their own."(Saddhatissa, pg. 55)

"Vipassana meditation is mental training aimed at raising the mind to such a level that it is no longer subject to suffering. The mind breaks free from suffering by virtue of the clear knowledge that nothing is worth grasping at or clinging to. This knowledge deprives worldly things of their ability to lead the mind into further thoughtless liking or disliking. Having this knowledge, the mind transcends the worldly condition and attains the level known as the Supra-mundane Plane (Lukuttara-bhujmi.) . . . The mundane plane comprises those levels at which the things of the world have control over the mind. Very briefly, three levels are recognized in the mundane plane, namely: 1) the sensual level or the level of a mind still content with pleasures of every kind; 2) the level of forms, the condition of a mind uninterested in sensual objects, but finding satisfaction in the various stages of concentration on forms as objects; 3) and lastly the formless level, the yet higher level of a mind finding satisfaction in the bliss and peace of concentration on objects other than forms . . . the human mind normally falls under the influence of the delightful in colours and shapes, sounds, odours, tastes, and tactile objects. Only on certain occasions is it able to escape from the influence of these seductive things and experience the tranquility and bliss which comes from practicing concentration on forms or other objects. It all depends on concentration . . . desire for change constitutes karma, so such a person has not yet transcended the worldly state. He is not yet in the supra-mundane plane . . . A mind dwelling in the supra-mundane plane has transcended the world. It views the worldly state as devoid of essence, self, or substance, and will have nothing of it . . . The ten fetters bind man and all beings to the world, keeping people in the mundane plane . . ." (Buddhadasa) Can you see that your character has changed gradually as you have caste off fetters?

1) "Self belief, the view that the body and mind is 'my self.' [self-illusion, sakkayaditthi]
2) Doubt, the cause of wavering and uncertainty . . . concerning the practice leading to liberation from suffering . . . [vicikiccha—questioning the truth of the Triple Gem.]
3) Superstition, or attachment to rules and rituals based on a misunderstanding of their real purpose, i.e. the belief in magic and magical practices . . . psychic powers . . . The objective [of taking the Five Precepts] is not rebirth in heaven . . . [this is] grasping and clinging, with false ideas. [silabbataparamasa]
4) The fourth fetter is sensual desire [grasping at form, sound, scent, taste, and touch—kamaraga]
5) the fifth is will . . . and ill will [irritability—patigha.] (Samahito is capable here)
6) next is the desire for the bliss associated with the various stages of concentration on forms. [Arahant begins here—ruparaga.]
7) The seventh subtle defilement is desire for [formless realms—aruparaga] the bliss associated with full concentration on objects other than forms.
8) The delusion of having this or that status relative to another . . . as good as . . . I am better or higher [conceipt—mana] . . . or not as good as . . . etc. one thinks along competitive lines.
9) Agitation, mental unrest, distraction, lack of peace and quiet . . . a desire to get, to be, not to get, or not to be, one thing

or another. [To be in someone special's presence, for example, ambition, carelessness, absent-mindedness—uddhacca]

10) The last is ignorance . . . [avijja] which covers every kind of defilement [of the 108] not mentioned . . . Ignorance causes people to misidentify suffering as pleasure, to such an extend that they just swim around in circles in a sea of suffering . . . and misidentify the causes of suffering." (Buddhadasa, 2005, pp. 133-148) (also Dattajeevo, pp. 157-160)

Biographical Sketch:

In his early days as an ascetic, "Siddhartha wandered through the Magadhan country until reaching the vicinity of Uruvela. Here he spent six years in extreme asceticism accompanied by five bhikkhus. He eventually realized that there was nothing wrong with eating a reasonable amount of food . . . Siddhartha went to meditate under a bodhi tree . . . While he was meditating he was tempted by Mara, death, the evil tempter, who tried to dissuade him from his efforts . . . In his meditation he passed through the first and second jhana to the 'third true knowledge' of enlightenment . . . The meaning of Enlightenment, i.e., Nibbana, is coolness—being cool and collected." Notice that it is no coincidence that the fifth rapture signal is "infused cold," and how that relates to nirvana.

"The shrine of Bodh Gaya is the place where the Buddha reached Enlightenment in 528 BC while meditating under a bodhi tree . . . After the Enlightenment the Buddha spent forty-nine days in the vicinity of Uruvela. Later the same year he returned to convert three famous ascetics . . . Thereafter, the Buddha apparently never came back to the place of his Enlightenment [and experienced no attachment.] Huien Tsiang, who visited the place in the early part of the seventh century, describes the monastery there as well as the Mahabodhi Temple, originally built probably in the early fourth century and appearing in the seventh much as it does today." (Inthisan, pg. 29-33)

The ordination of lay people in Thailand requires about three months of devotion and training, usually during the rainy season beginning in July also referred to as Thai lent. "The first part of the ordination that I will talk about today is the hair shaving. Preceding this, Nattawud paid respect to his dead ancestors and then bathed the feet of his elders. In the photo on the right are his grandparents (on his father's side), his grandmother (the one he calls mother) and his parents. Once he had finished, he prostrated himself at their feet." http://www.thaibuddhist.com/shaving_hair.html

Curiously, Buddha icons always have hair.

Reading for the Day: Lotus Sutra

"The Buddha said to the monks: "In future ages if there are good men or good women who, on hearing the Devadatta chapter of the Lotus Sutra of the Wonderful Law, believe and revere it with pure hearts and harbor no doubts or perplexities, they will never fall into hell or the realm of hungry spirits or of beasts, but will be born in the presence of the *Buddhas of the ten directions*, and in the place where they are born they will constantly hear this sutra. If they are born among human or heavenly beings, they will enjoy exceedingly wonderful delights, and if they are born in the presence of a Buddha, they will be born by transformation from lotus flowers. Devadatta" (Watson, pg. 185) Enlightenment is functionally a grace from the natural force of our Buddha nature that pervades our own innate buddhahood.

"Hence, in conclusion, are we not right in drawing the inference that the practice of Dhyana is the true gateway to Supreme Perfect Enlightenment? Is it not the Noble Path that all followers of Buddha must follow? Is not Dhyana the pole star of all goodness and the Supreme Perfect Enlightenment?"

"If anyone thoroughly understands what has been said here about Dhyana, he will appreciate that its practice is not an easy task. However, for the sake of aiding beginners to clear away their ignorance and hindrances and to guide them toward enlightenment, we will aid them all we can by explaining the practice of Dhyana in as simple words as possible, but at best, its practice will be difficult . . . Those who are really seeking Truth, but are more advanced, should not look upon this book with contempt because it is written simply and for beginners. They should be humble and prudent because of the difficulties they will encounter when they come to its practice. It is possible that some will be able to digest its teachings with great ease and, in the twinkle of an eye, their hindrances will be abolished and their intelligence will be boundlessly developed and so will be their supernormal understanding, also . . . The Ten Heads: 1. External conditions. 2. Control of sense desires. 3. Abolishment of inner hindrances. 4. Regulation and adjustment. 5. Expedient activities of mind. 6. Right practice. 7. The development and manifestation of good qualities. 8. Evil influences. 9. Cure of disease. 10. Realization of Supreme Perfect Enlightenment. These ten headings indicate the stages of correct Dhyana practice . . . [When] these ten stages are faithfully followed the mind will become tranquil, difficulties will be overcome, powers for concentrating the mind and for gaining insight and understanding will be developed, and in the future Supreme Perfect Enlightenment (*anuttara-samyak-sambodhi*) will be attained." (Goddard, pg. 441) There is a book here with these ten Heads as chapter titles.

Protecting:

"This is what I heard," review by both Samahito and teacher.

Proverb: Remember the darkest hour is only 60 minutes. (wellpage.com)

Additional Teaching:

"The Nature of Enlightenment:

Contrary to the slow ripening of meditative experience throughout the preliminary and essential stages of meditation, and even the gradual ripening of awakened wisdom during extraordinary meditation, crossing over to enlightenment is an immediate and compelling event, wherein the mental continuum undergoes a series of fundamental and enduring reorganizations. One implication of the term non-meditation is that the 'journey ends.' . . . First is the perfection of awakened wisdom . . . Second is perfect purification. The term 'liberation,' is derived from the same root as last. The practitioner becomes completely free of all defilements, false concepts, and negative emotional states . . . The enlightenment experience does not occur exactly as a momentary event, though it happens within a relatively short span of ordinary time. It is experienced as three very distinctive shifts in consciousness, which follow immediately upon each other. These are called: 1. basis, 2. path, and 3. fruition. . . . The first enlightenment is sometimes called samadhi-enlightenment because it typically occurs during continuous, uninterrupted mindfulness . . . The seeming reality of individual consciousness along with its functions and activities gives way, leaving only an infinite ocean of awareness-space."

"Path Enlightenment: puts in order the relative activity of the mental continuum. Awakened wisdom seems to shift its locus, now saturating every potential experience . . . The mind's manifest spontaneity is the very expression of awakened wisdom. The Tibetan word for buddha is the compound sang gye . . . the word literally means the blossoming of complete purity."

"Fruition Enlightenment: . . . The necessary condition by which fruition enlightenment comes forth is, once again, protecting practice, completely free of artificial activity . . . not artificially constructing this inconceivable attainment . . . being without effort and without making anything happen." (Brown, pp. 440-444)

Sharing Merit:

Rejoicing In Others' Merit (Saying Sadhu)

Buddhist Sutra

Lesson Title: **Pervading Rapture (absorption)—Jhana**

Lesson Number: **Twenty-six**

Key Vocabulary: fear, grace, formless sphere, Buddhas of the ten directions, voice hearer, samaya, perfect freedom, anuttara-samyak-sambodhi, pratyekabuddha, arahattaphala

After the Lesson, Samahito will choose a partner, who should be a different person each day, to accompany silently during the day.
Assignment: After the morning lesson, meditate for at least one hour before eating a normal lunch, then after eating rest your attention lightly on all the tastes you perceived and then rest your mind naturally, alternating between bringing attention to the sensation of taste and resting your mind naturally.

Meditate on each of the Ten Fetters.

1. false view of Self,
2. doubt,
3. adherence to mere rules, and seven more:
4. sensual lust
5. repulsion, irritation
6. attachment to realms of form
7. attachment to formless realms
8. conceit, pride

9. restlessness, distraction
10. ignorance.—as often as possible and for as long a time in each position in each session as possible.

Caution: stop each practice before there is any muscle or tendon strain, this will not aid meditation. The important thing is that the body is stressed by pain and hunger to contribute to the production of natural chemicals that facilitate high levels of mental functioning. This will happen with repeated periods of stress rather than coming from self-inflicted injury.

Define each of the Key Vocabulary in your own words.

Was the hair ceremony meaningful for you?
What are the accomplishments that mark our lives as successful?

How do you prepare yourself to have *unlimited compassion*?

What are the adverse circumstances in our lives that can cause us to have the emotional reactions to feel bigger and bigger till we fill up the room where we sit?

Recall from Lesson Seven and memorize:

> Monks chant to resonate consciousness (connecting to antiquity)
> Flowers are used to acknowledge impermanence (and soul-less-ness)
> Incense is used as sweet scent of moral virtue of the devout
> Candle flame symbolizes enlightenment and understanding (wisdom.)

What mental images, if any, have you experienced during meditation?

Materials Required: fluids, Existentialism, post-modernism, (orange sash)

Buddhist Sutra

Lesson Title: **Emptiness**

Lesson Number: **Twenty-seven**

Rationale:

This is considered a difficult and seemingly internally self-contradictory concept, even for the most adept Arahant. It tends to separate the intellectuals from the vast population that is content to accept the general principle without having a way to explain it in the glib (and sometimes apparently nonsensical) terms that characterize the many scholarly explanations. Understanding this immeasurable truth, however, is considered by some one of the final steps toward enlightenment.

Discussion of Prior Lesson:

"Our greatest fear is that when we die we will become nothing." (Hanh, pg. 213) This, instead, should be our greatest joy, we have arrived at enlightenment; yet most people are self-motivated by their instincts and training to conduct [karma] a life full of sensual satisfaction, void of self-meaning, with the meaning dependent on a vain hope for an even better afterlife.

Samahitos may share an image they have experienced during practice.

Review the prayer of compassion (pg. 239).

Training Objective:

Cessation of psychological angst. Identify emptiness where you can find it. The significance of Arahant. How will we know Nirvana when we see it? Review Hindrances. Logical Positivism.

Materials Required: fluids, Existentialism, post-modernism, orange sash

Motivational Statement:

"True love is a love without possessiveness. You love and still you are free, and the other person is also free. The kind of love that has no joy is not true love. If both parties cry every day, then that's not true love. There must be joy and freedom and understanding in love." (Hanh, pg. 291)

> One image of a person is their shadow
> except at noon it is emptiness
> then at night it is fullness. IHJ

"It is customary to speak of two paths to enlightenment—an instantaneous path, in which enlightenment seems to occur all at once, and a gradual path, in which progress toward enlightenment occurs in systematic, predictable stages [possibly throughout a lifetime.] Only the rare student becomes instantaneously enlightened when the mind's true nature is pointed out by the master. Most students can spend years in practice without achieving the end-state. How do we account for these remarkable differences in progress? . . . [There are] different ways to access the awareness capable of realizing *the mind's intrinsic nature*." (Brown, pp. 10-11) If we recall that nirvana is a point of view as well as a way of living, we can see that it is obtainable, it is not a mystical connection of constant or even frequent bliss—it is the mind's own intrinsic nature resting at peace.

First Progressive:

"The arahant lives out the remainder of his or her life [*helping others follow in his/her footsteps*] inwardly enjoying the bliss of Nibbana, secure at last from the possibility of any future rebirth. When the arahant's aeons-long trail of past kamma eventually unwinds to its end, the arahant dies and he or she enters into parinibbana—total Unbinding. Although language utterly fails at describing this extraordinary event, the Buddha likened it to what happens when a fire finally burns up all its fuel." (Bullitt, internet) In the religious tradition of Buddhism, such teachings make sense. For a Rational Buddhist who has achieved nirvana, this silent ending is all that is expected, no other incentive or punishment would change the motivation or course of their life.

There is joy in the realization of this kind of "voidness." "'According to Nagarjuna, emptiness means interdependency or interconnectedness,' the Dalai Lama said . . . 'Emptiness does not mean nothingness . . . *Emptiness is full, not empty* . . . it widens our view. It is very helpful to develop this holistic view'." (Chan, pg. 145) Realizing *interconnectedness* is what helps us understand how to implement the compassion we have developed. It is this very privately constructed, social contract that when implemented is a measure of the fullness of our enlightenment. The absolute ethical truth is a chimera, and the absence of this absolute requirement to care about others is what makes the caring we do, and the kindness we express by which we live, all the more virtuous and significant.

Proverb: We make a living by what we get; we make a life by what we give. (wellpage.com)

The Dalai Lama offers a further caution and puts enlightenment into perspective. "In the last step, the actual development of bodhicitta, the mind aspiring to achieve enlightenment for others, you should not be satisfied by seeing the importance of enlightenment for the sake of others alone. There is no way to fulfill that ultimate aim without your achievement of the omniscient state of Buddhahood, *from which you can best benefit others.* You should develop a very deep, heartfelt faith in the enlightened state, and that will lead to a genuine aspiration to achieve it. Generally speaking, there are many causes and conditions for the cultivation of bodhicitta, but chief among all of them is compassion." (Mehrotra, pg. 103)

"A person who repeatedly practices generosity develops the *energy of giving* and is therefore better prepared to give even more. The first act of giving may be difficult, if only because one is not used to it, but the first gift makes the second and subsequent ones easier, for it acts as the potential for a more advanced development of personal character . . . The law of kamma helps us to see the possibility of free choice and how we are truly responsible for our actions . . . it is always within our capacity to train ourselves . . ." (Plamintr, 2007, pg. 123)

Second Progressive:

The Lotus Sutra is a prime example of political rhetoric, not a clear exposition of the Law that was established by Buddhism, but justifying it and convincing people through emotional rhetoric to accept the control of the moral code advocated by the hierarchy of monks. Considering the context of the Indian/Nepalese societies when Siddhartha Buddha taught and immediately thereafter, such an attempt to unify and enunciate a moral based legal code was a potent political activity. Just as it is today (i.e. the Falun Gong in China), consider the "Moral Majority" in the USA. Buddha was the ultimate political wonk and quintessential lobbyist. Teaching kings and political leaders to have awareness (mindfulness) and compassion for all classes of people, espousing social/economic mobility (also among women) in this feudal/caste system was tantamount to a proposed overthrow of the existing political and social order. To motivate uneducated people, since the vast majority did not read and had no formal education, the category of "voice-hearer" (does this mean illiterate?) was a very non-exclusive invitation to all people to join the political juggernaut of Buddhism which would have overthrown the caste system in India.

"One writer has in fact been led to describe the Lotus Sutra as a text 'about a discourse that is never delivered . . . a lengthy preface without a book.' This is no doubt because Mahayana Buddhism has always insisted that its highest truth can never in the end be expressed in words, since words immediately create the kind of distinctions that violate the unity of Emptiness. All the sutra can do, therefore, is to talk around it, leaving a hole in the middle where truth can reside." (Watson, pg. xx) This sounds like a reference to infinity and the inability to understand that, and the limitations of language as an inadequate tool to express the meaning of abstract concepts. The teachings, however, do contain moral guides, Precepts etc., that are helpful and full of wisdom.

The Lotus Sutra is like the sheep dog who leads the flock into the corral, where they accept: [From Lesson Four] The essence of Buddhism is to follow a path inspired by ethical training. "In short, the real essence of Buddhism is to release mind from all defilements." (Wee, pg. 56) This involves following the teachings of Buddhism, not just the implications for an individual's personal life, but also following the political and cultural innovations, i.e. women's empowerment and suffrage.

It is instructive to consider Buddhist values according to the teachings about presumptive rewards in "future human rebirths." As much as this concept sounds like reincarnation, that is specifically denied in other teachings, it resurfaces frequently as an idealized concept. "The ten benefits of accumulating merit pertain to future human rebirths. They are as follows: 1. having a handsome face, 2. good complexion, 3. influential speech, 4. influence over associates, 5. the affection of gods and men, 6. the companionship of holy men, 7. robust health, 8. wealth, 9. higher rebirth, and 10. enlightenment. Additional benefits are sometimes described, such as being reborn in the blissful god realms [Pure Land teachings of China and Japan.] The benefit of accumulating wisdom is complete purification of all negative emotional states as an outgrowth of understanding the view of emptiness, and also potential attainment of mahamudra enlightenment in this lifetime." (Brown, pg. 119) If these are the rewards of "rebirths," then it stands to reason that this list can be used also as a template for identifying the values we should cherish in our present samsara, not the least of which is enlightenment. "Birth" and "rebirth" can be taken to mean the arising of the ego with each new experience, or the opposite—of shedding the pride and ego of craving and defilements, moving toward purification. This understanding is a significant departure from many Buddhist traditions where practitioners believe in what must be essentially considered as reincarnation.

Third Progressive:

"The concept [of Emptiness], often described in English as 'non-dualism,' is extremely hard for the mind to grasp or visualize, since the mind engages constantly in the making of distinctions and non-dualism represents the rejection or transcendence of all distinctions. The world perceived through the senses . . . was described in early Buddhism as 'empty' because it was taught that all such phenomena arise from causes and conditions, are in a constant state of flux, and are destined to change and pass away in time. They are also held to be 'empty' in the sense that they have no inherent [absolute] or permanent characteristics by which they can be described, changing as they do from instant to instant . . . It is this concept of Emptiness or non-duality that leads the Mahayana texts to assert that samsara, the ordinary world of suffering and cyclical birth and death, is in the end identical with the world of nirvana, and that earthly desires [for knowledge and wisdom] are enlightenment . . . This concept of Emptiness or Void is central to the whole Mahayana system of belief." (Watson, pg, xv) These technical terms are not entirely self-explanatory. Emptiness does not mean worthlessness, but that the specific context of the discussion and the details of our lives is what contributes to the development of meaning for the words we use to describe the claims that are made upon us, i.e. right vs. wrong.

"People are very afraid of nothingness. When they hear about emptiness, people are also very afraid, but emptiness just means the extinction of ideas [think of the post-modern idea of deconstruction.] Emptiness is not the opposite of existence. It is not nothingness or annihilation. The idea of existence has to be removed, and so does the idea of nonexistence." (Hanh, pg. 215) This is what ennobles and enables the human spirit to sore above the mundane aspects of every day life.

Take a piece of blank paper, and notice that there is nothing there, that is certainly a trivial kind of emptiness, really it is nothingness; but if that is the general case, we need to somehow become more specific. What is there about a concept or object that involves emptiness? I thought of trees, thinking of the trees that surround my life here and there, different species and shapes etc. So I drew a sketch of a tree (happened to be a fir tree). I saw this as a tree sketch and illustrative of the form of a tree, but certainly not all trees, and it was not any particular tree, so in a very real sense it was empty or devoid of any real tree-ness—but I had moved beyond the general case of trivial nothingness—to the case of the recognizable form of a tree. So I had created an example of emptiness as form, and if I hand the sketch to someone and say: "This is a tree?" they will say: "That is not a tree, it is simply the form of a tree." So I have illustrated how a "Form is emptiness, Emptiness is form." (Heart Sutra) The sketch of a tree or the general reference to a generic tree in ordinary conversation has this characteristic. The philosophy of Logical Positivism also introduced the argument about what is the most simple element of any object or concept (of a tree), the essential nature.

Certainly there was no essential tree-emptiness on the blank sheet of paper, so I had to rise to a description or sketch of the form before I could demonstrate the concept of tree-emptiness. And there is a parallel kind of emptiness in "[body,] feeling, perception, [mind] formation and consciousness"—"the five skandhas empty of nature". There are no common characteristics to all trees, but there is a "family resemblance" between the many different kinds of trees (Wittgenstein). It is our "transcendent wisdom" that allows us to go from the general form to any knowledgeable discussion of any particular tree. My apple tree changes with the seasons: in the winter just a bare form (body) or skeleton (although the buds are forming for leafs and fruit using the stored energy in the live trunk), then the flowers (feelings) emerge in the Spring, followed soon by leaves (perceptions), and in the Summer by nubs (mind formations) of fruit, then the fruit grows inside the protective canopy of leafs, ripens (consciousness) and drops, and the leaves fall off, returning to the winter emptiness. Even this emptiness has to have this minimum of form to exist. The life cycle of nature, the transcendent wisdom, is "the mantra of great insight" that contains this explanation of a dialectic that includes emptiness. This story repeats throughout our lives with such beautiful poetic (not occult) resonance.

Our minds operate by using *concepts* as part of our memory banks and thought process. (i.e. Many people have a concept of an afterlife because this has been such a ubiquitous teaching in both Western and Eastern cultures.) That is why, when we write, it is often so hard to find just the right words to express a concept that we can certainly feel or conceive as an idea. The Buddhist teaching—to learn concepts then move away from them—is not about erasing our memory, it is about knowing the subject in a way that we can explain it without necessarily committing the entire semantic map or taxonomy (there are so many in Buddhist literature) to memory. Each time we make an explanation we might choose different words and add to the meaning of a concept because that's how our minds naturally work. Theorizing and philosophizing about mysterious events or esoteric concepts (such as an afterlife) that are empty of any absolute reality, is what is to be avoided.

One form of suffering has been so well analyzed by Western philosophers that it has become part of pop culture. This not so subtle suffering is that associated with "Existential Angst." Although it is primarily associated with intellectuals who have theorized too much about life for their own good, it is also frequently the underlying psychology of morbid novels. This mental constipation is a frequent cause of depression, yet its basic form is a mental affliction that affects average people, and is essentially contagious. As a youth when I studied this extensively, I came to the conclusion that the best definition of existential angst was the thinker trying to live their entire life in just one sitting, and being overwhelmed by the daunting possibilities, all the choices presented, and the confusing philosophical quandaries such as: "Is there free will?" Subsequently I have learned about other sources of angst such as the elitism (snobbery) of only valuing the most excellent performance or achievement (Ayn Rand), thus denigrating the contribution of the average bloke who is just slogging it out the best he/she can. Schopenhauer (influenced indirectly by Buddhism) is thought to have contributed to some of the pessimism associated with these forms of angst, since his writings were popular at the inception of the Existential school of thought (see Kierkegaard, Sartre, Dostoyevsky et al.) Many intellectuals of the "Beat Generation" were essentially rescued from existential angst by Buddhism.

The quandary associated with finding meaning in life when one leaves, or is contemplating leaving, the religion of their birth, is something that confronts many teens as they move out of adolescence into young adulthood and try, with improper guidance and inadequate preparation, to make the most important decisions of their lives. They frequently suffer from identity crises, such as "Who am I, really?" They somehow "lose themselves" as if that were actually possible except in a linguistic game that confuses people. We too often think that there ought to be absolute meaning in words and life, and absolute truths—instead of the emptiness we find (which was presaged by Buddhism 2500 years earlier)—sometimes the meaning we put into life by our use of words seems so trivial or valueless. Instead we should have the patience to develop and uncover our own talents, and use these in service to others as a source of meaning.

Another source of modern angst is a result of the monstrous hydra of globalism that seems to be disenfranchising 95% of the world community (causing global warming as a consequence) who do not benefit directly from stock ownership in the mega-corporations which are controlling the world's resources, depleting the rain forests and monopolizing trade to the detriment of everybody else. The new imperialism, so the litany goes. The scale of the world's problems are so vast that we are frustrated and despair of every making a useful contribution, and we feel empty.

Rational Buddhism shows us the way out of all these sources of angst, as well as the angst identified by "post-modernism" with the compulsion to "deconstruct" the institutions and truisms of the modern world. For those who are largely unfamiliar with these various sources of intellectual angst, they are better off for not having waded into those squalid philosophical waters. Buddhist teachings warn that the failure to satisfy one's desires is suffering, and clinging to the five aggregates that compose the minds and bodies of all sentient beings is suffering—[part of the eight sufferings] these are associated sufficiently with existential angst to be informative, and the cure is the same, developing the mind to create and lead to achieving a positive goal. One can get an intuitive sense of "emptiness" without trying to understand the convoluted verses of Nagarjuna or the inchoate prose of Derrida. But you have to do the work and have patience in meditation practice; so is it worth it? What is the alternative solution?

Meditation Practicum:

"Disciplined meditation practice leads to a series of changes in consciousness that result in a transformation known as enlightenment. In early Buddhism, enlightenment meant the eradication of the mind's reactive tendency and its lapses in awareness. Such enlightenment does not change the content of our experience. Instead, whatever events we experience are experienced with full awareness and without any reactivity whatsoever. All life experiences—positive and negative—are embraced equally, with complete and continuous awareness, so that the quality of everyday experience is greatly enriched, moment-by-moment." (Brown, pg. 6) Is this enrichment or deadening of our senses?

"If we have followed all steps of the practice, our minds will be more concentrated on this day depending also on our will or perseverance each day . . . We can know the [level of] concentration from mental images appearing in the mind when it develops establishment [steadiness] and cultivates wisdom. We practice till mind develops the concentration to the Forth Jhana . . . If we manage to control internal mental states, we will produce a result eventually on the seventh day of the practice. We will be able to attain the *path of purity.* The most important point for the practice which is a must, is knowledge and understanding on the practice so that we can succeed eventually." (Wee, pp. 118-119) This is also the promise of the Satipatthana meditation scheme.

"When you try to hold on to an experience like bliss or clarity, the experience loses its living, spontaneous quality; it becomes a concept, a dead experience. No matter how hard you try to make it last, it gradually fades. If you try to reproduce it later, you may get a taste of what you felt, but it will only be a memory, not the direct experience itself. The most important lesson I learned was to avoid becoming attached to my positive experience if it was peaceful. As with every mental experience, bliss, clarity, and non-conceptuality spontaneously come and go. They are simply natural qualities of your mind." (Mingyur, pg. 219) In this same way, enlightenment is a natural state, not mysterious but a learned behavior (and expanded frame of reference.) Any experience that exists in memory has by nature an aspect of emptiness in it after it has transpired. In the sense that the raw circumstances or context becomes history, but we do not always remember accurately, nor do we remember all the details.

From the tradition of Satipatthana review each of the hindrances: "And how does he . . . abide contemplating dhammas in terms of the five hindrances? . . .

1. If sensual desire is present in him, he knows 'there is sensual desire in me' [if not] he knows how unarisen sensual desire can arise, how arisen sensual desire can be removed, and how a future arising of the removed sensual desire can be prevented."
2. "If aversion is present in him, he knows 'there is aversion in me' [if not] he knows how unarisen aversion can arise, how arisen aversion can be removed, and how a future arising of the removed aversion can be prevented."
3. "If sloth-and-torpor is present in him, he knows 'there is sloth-and-torpor in me' [if not] and he knows how unarisen sloth—and-torpor can arise, how arisen sloth-and-torpor can be removed, and how a future arising of the removed sloth-and-torpor can be prevented."
4. "If restlessness-and worry is present in him, he knows 'there is restlessness-and-worry in me' [if not] he knows how unarisen restlessness-and-worry can arise, and how arisen restlessness-and-worry can be removed, and how a future arising of the removed restlessness-and-worry can be prevented."

5. "If doubt is present in him, he knows 'there is doubt in me' [if not] he knows how unarisen doubt can arise, how arisen doubt can be removed, and how a future arising of the removed doubt can be prevented." (Analayo, pp. 8-9)

Biographical Sketch:

"Kusinara is the place where the Buddha passed away at the age of eighty . . . [thus entered parinirvana] Defending his choice of Kusinara as the place of his passing away in the face of Ananda's opposition, the Buddha says that Kusinara . . . was once a rich and populous capital that never slept . . . When Huien Tsiang came to Kusinara in the early part of the seventh century, the place was already in ruins . . . In 1876 Carlleyle, excavated the area around Kasia. He found the large reclining Buddha statue currently exhibited in the Nirvana Temple at Kusinara . . . The Buddha said his remains were to be treated like the remains of a 'wheel-turning monarch' . . . everything pleasant or unpleasant, is changeable, and that all things . . . decay . . . He told Ananda that he would have no successor: the only teacher after his death would be the Dhamma itself. To the assembly of the monks he spoke his last words: 'all conditioned things are of a nature to decay—strive on untiringly'." (Inthisan, pp. 55-60) The ultimate meaning of emptiness.

One experience from my youth was seminal in developing my understanding of "emptiness." "It wasn't long after he and Elder Simons arrived in their new accommodations when Jack began to suffer from a chronic and serious headache. He couldn't explain what the cause was; otherwise he didn't have any particular symptoms. He took aspirin and it didn't help. He rested and that only helped as long as he was perfectly still or asleep which was also difficult. His subconscious mind was churning profound ideas and confusing questions so rigorously that it kept him away from work without his knowing the reason."

"He didn't know what was happening now. He was looking at himself and saying, 'Why can't I believe? Why can't this religious life be simpler? Why can't I get answers to my repeated prayers?'

He was being defeated by mental confusion and deep searching. The headaches continued for three days."

"Just as suddenly as the pain began, it ended, and late at night on the third day he had what amounted to a revelation or realization. It didn't appear to come from any particular source. The answer was just there and the headaches were gone. It had to do with the recognition that the Universe is eternal and infinite; that there is no end or beginning. Man cannot comprehend infinity [the vastness nor the emptiness] in the same way we comprehend a long stretch of highway when we can't see the end, or even the imperceptible distance across the ocean. In these cases we know there is an end."

"No matter how hard we try there is no way to conceptualize infinity; no definition, because definition presumed some ending. Mathematics could deal with generalizations and manipulate symbols but there was no acceptable answer to the question: 'What is infinity?' It isn't something that corresponds to the interrogative pronoun 'what.' It's a fallacy of logic and language to attempt to give an explanation. Like dividing by zero, it leads to nonsense. Jack was not struggling with the same idea that plagued Rinaldo, about what it means 'to know, really.' Jack's confusion is ended by this new realization that nullified religion [the realization of emptiness.]"

". . . If we can live without the fundamental answer about infinity then we can live just fine without a whole sequence of answers. Just because we can't explain something, some mystery, it doesn't mean we should make up an answer or accept an answer that just happens to satisfy our psychic needs.' (Jacob, 1967)

"The Lord Buddha continued:—If any disciple were to say that the Tathagata, in his teachings, has constantly referred to himself, other selves, living beings, an Universal Self, what think you Subhuti? Would that disciple have understood the meaning of what I have been teaching?"

"Subhuti replied:—No, Blessed Lord. That disciple would not have understood the meaning of the Lord's teachings. For when the Lord has referred to them he has never referred to their actual existence; he has only used the words as figures and symbols. It is only in that sense that they can be used, for conceptions, and ideas, and limited thoughts, and Dharmas have no more reality than have matter and phenomena." The Diamond Sutra (Goddard, pg. 101)

Reading for the Day:

"The Buddha taught that there is no birth, there is no death; there is no coming, there is no going; there is no same, there is no different; there is no permanent self, there is no annihilation." (Hanh, pg. 211) Elimination of these dualisms are koans for contemplation.

Lotus Sutra: "Next, the bodhisattva or mahasattva should view all phenomena as empty, that being their true entity. They do not turn upside down, do not move, do not regress, do not revolve. They are like empty space, without innate nature, beyond the reach of all words. They are not torn, do not emerge, do not arise. They are without name, without form, without true being. They are without volume, without limits, without hindrance, without barriers. It is only through causes and conditions that they exist, and come to be turned upside down, to be born. Therefore I say that one should constantly delight in viewing the form of phenomena as this. This is what I call the second thing that the bodhisattva or mahasattva should associate himself with." Peaceful Practices (Watson, pg. 198)

"In many of his lectures and interviews, the Dalai Lama invariably brings up the subject of emptiness. He says over and over that everything that the Buddha taught can be reduced to the essential idea of fusing emptiness with compassion. This is the formula for happiness: Emptiness + Compassion = Happiness . . . we need to first achieve wisdom by seeing the world as it is . . . we could view everything around us clearly, without preconception . . . To do this, we have to develop real insight into emptiness . . . Emptiness is just another way of saying that things are devoid of individual, inherent existence . . . nothing can exist independently on its own . . . It highlights a subtle but ultimate truth: interdependence rather than independence defines our lives and everything around us." (Chan, pg. 134) Perhaps with a few more examples this would be easier to understand.

Protecting:

"The most important point for the practice which is a must, is knowledge and understanding on the practice so that we can succeed eventually." (Wee, pg. 119)

Once each Samahito reports the images they have experienced, they will be acknowledged accordingly. Our development is often subtle, so even if the Samahito cannot claim to have experienced the fourth Jana, they will be offered an orange sash to designate the status of—eventually being accomplished—as being an Arahant and to pay tribute to the buddha-inside their partially finished "Michelangelo statue." Each aspirant must accept on their own and acknowledge a commitment and understanding of their duties (given by the five precepts) and they must review daily the lessons from the Ten Fetters. Each is asked to offer an acceptable explanation about the concept of Emptiness. Now you will tell people when they ask, '***Yes, I am a Buddhist.***' Each repeats this as they receive the sash.

"This is what I heard," review by both Arahant and teacher.

Proverb: Answers that sound good are not necessarily good sound answers. (wellpage.com)

Additional Teachings:

"Nirvana is a condition not in any way comparable to any other. It is unlike any worldly condition. In fact, it is the very negation of the worldly condition. Given all the characteristics of the worldly condition, of phenomenal existence, the result of completely canceling out all those characteristics is Nirvana. That is to say, Nirvana is that which is in every respect precisely the opposite of the worldly condition. Nirvana neither creates nor is created, being the cessation of all creating. Speaking in terms of benefits, Nirvana . . . presupposes the complete elimination of the defilements, which are the cause of all unsatisfactory mental states. Nirvana lies beyond the limitations of space and time . . . Speaking metaphorically, the Buddha called it the realm where all conditional things [complications] cease to be. Hence it is the condition of freedom, of freedom from fetters. It is, as the end of torment and buffeting, stabbing and chafing, from any source whatsoever. This is the nature of the Supra-mundane, the ultimate. It is the Buddhist goal and destination. It is the final fruit of Buddhist practice. (Buddhadasa, 2005, pp. 151) Other explanations suggest that Nirvana is a point of view, the path rather than some end goal, a life-style that is rewarding and free of suffering—is it the diploma? or the attitude of basking in joy for the student who attends all his/her classes and blossoms in the process? How is this different (or the same) than living in a Poem?

From Lesson Seven—Buddhist training is in large part about unifying our mind, incorporating optimism, hopefulness and creativity; having integrity in our personality from day to day with a mind single pointed toward enlightenment. (Right Thought.)

The Buddha taught: "In comparison with Mind-Essence, all conditioned things are as empty as space. Existing as they do under conditions, they are false and fantastic; unconditioned things, having neither appearance nor disappearance, are as imaginary as blossoms seen in the air. As we are obliged to use false expressions to interpret the essence of things, so both the false expressions and the essence of things as thus interpreted by the false expressions become a pair of falsities. It is clear to see that the intrinsic Essence is neither the essence as interpreted, nor the non-essence of the interpretation. How can it be asserted that there is trueness in either the thing as perceived, or in the phenomena of perceiving?' The Surangama Sutra (Goddard, pg. 215) What kind of answer do we want? Ordinary language and perceptions work just fine.

"Viveka can be translated 'utmost aloneness, perfect singleness, complete solitude.' Consider that viveka has three levels: 1. Physical viveka (kaya-viveka) is when nothing disturbes the physical level of life . . . free of physical discomfort, noises, mosquitoes, etc . . . 2. Mental viveka (citta-viveka) is when no emotions disturb the mind . . . it isn't dependent on physical solitude. The third kind 3. spiritual viveka (upadhi-viveka) is when no feelings or thoughts of attachment to 'I" and 'mine,' 'soul' or 'myself' disturb the [heart] mind. When all three levels happen, you are truly alone and free." And this freedom can happen in and be perceived by our Hearts.

"If [you] bring emotional afflictions with [you] . . . true happiness will elude [you.] . . . there must be no feeling of 'I' or 'mine' interfering for it to be genuine, profound viveka. Then there will be no hunger [craving] of any kind disturbing and no hopes pestering. This is real solitude. The mind is perfectly alone. Just this is the happiness that is Buddhism's sole aim [and it can be, ironically, shared with others as peace.]"

"This solitude is vimutti (emancipation) on Buddhism's highest level. The final goal of Buddhism, the highest liberation, isn't a mind that is merely happy or quiet. The ultimate goal is total freedom from all attachment, from any clinging to 'I' or 'mine.' If you are able to practice mindfulness with breathing completely and correctly through all sixteen of its steps and stages, then you will discover these three kinds of viveka . . . Once you have, you will receive the genuine happiness born of the total absence of hunger [craving and clinging.]" (Buddhadasa, 2001, pp. 39-43) This teaching does not take us out of the world, it just means that we are no longer captive of and baffled by it.

Sharing Merit:

Rejoicing In Others' Merit (Saying Sadhu)

Buddhist Sutra

Lesson Title: **Emptiness**

Lesson Number: **Twenty-seven**

Key Vocabulary: possessiveness, angst, establishment, emptiness, interconnectedness, concepts, path of purity, viveka, vimutti

Assignment: "'According to Nagarjuna, emptiness means interdependency or interconnectedness,' the Dalai Lama said . . . 'Emptiness does not mean nothingness . . . Emptiness is full, not empty . . . it widens are view. It is very helpful to develop this holistic view'." (Chan, pg. 145) Consider this explanation, and memorize a written paraphrase (or haiku) of this.

Resume normal schedules, eat when you are hungry, throughout the day if you so choose.

Contemplate each of the Five Hindrances and see how they affect your life (sensual desire, aversion, sloth-and-torpor, restlessness-and-worry, and doubt.)

Define each of the Key Vocabulary in your own words.

Describe existential angst, and what are the alternative solutions to overcoming this suffering, if not Rational Buddhism?

Report on the “incompletes” you have completed and how it feels. What is the significance of Arahant?

How will we know Nirvana when we see it? Some explanations suggest that Nirvana is a point of view, the path rather than the end goal, a life-style that is rewarding and free of suffering—is it the diploma? How is this different (or the same) than living in a Poem?

Recall the ten fetters that prevent students from alleviating many different kinds of suffering they encounter “. . . that bind individuals to samsaric existence:

1. Belief in personality [some charismatic leader or Yoga Soul, Self]
2. Skepticism—lack of certainty about the Buddha’s teaching (doubt)
3. Attachment to rules and rituals—[strict vegetarianism, celibacy]
4. Sensuous craving—[inappropriate sexual conduct or stalking]
5. Ill will—[vengeance and hatred]
6. Craving for material existence—[luxury consumption]
7. Craving for non-material existence [afterlife in a heaven]
8. Conceit
9. Restlessness
10. Ignorance—[laziness toward studying dharma] (pg. 50, Lesson Five)

Evaluate your progress against this list, 10 points possible for each, 100 total possible.

Materials Required: Yoga Chakra chart, tea ceremony

Buddhist Sutra

Lesson Title: **Yoga Chakras—**

Lesson Number: **Twenty-eight**

Rationale:

Does the ancient teaching of chakras—force fields and useful energy in the body—have some relevance and a possible application to teach us how to intensify our concentration, and help us investigate the Four Foundations of Mindfulness? These teachings and related yoga practices predated Buddhism, in fact Shakyamuni was a yogi. Is there a "spiritual wind" that emanates from our core being?

Discussion of Prior Lesson:

"Next the prince asked what conditions were necessary to enable an ascetic to attain his goal. Shakyamuni replied by relating what he had to say to the art of riding an elephant . . . [have] faith, good health, honesty, perseverance in striving to improve, and wisdom . . . finally, the person must have deep and extensive experience and knowledge enabling him to view the total picture correctly . . . When all of these conditions are present, a person does not require long periods to attain eminence or to become enlightened. If he is instructed in the truth in the morning, he will be able to reach his goal by the evening." (Mizuno, pp. 146-147)

"Even if one is only half successful [achieving Nirvana,] some clear understanding will result. As the defilements are progressively eliminated, their place is taken by purity, insight, and peace." (Buddhadasa, 2005, pg. 153) Take a piece of paper and write (list) what prevents you from alleviating the many different kinds of suffering you encounter. (Answer: Ten Fetters)

Training Objective:

List and describe the chakras and potential influences. Identify the shared goal of Yoga and other teachings. The modesty of the Arahant. Five Aggregates

Materials Required: chakra chart, tea ceremony

Motivational Statement:

"The ascetic believes that human suffering is caused by the bondage of the spirit to the flesh. As long as this bondage continues, the spirit is unable to be free . . . death and the destruction of the body are the ultimate conclusions of such practices . . . Both Sankhya and Yoga, which teach meditation practices, hold that ultimate liberation can come only after death." (Mizuno, pg. 25) Buddhism does not subscribe to this teaching, and therefore we can utilize any resource of our [healthy] body to help us develop our minds and to develop the ". . . heart of benevolence . . . that is one of the four infinite virtues—**benevolence, compassion, giving happiness, and impartiality**—and means constant compassion and kindness for all beings, not just for those that are dear but also for unrelated beings and even enemies against whom one might otherwise entertain bitterness." (Mizuno, pg. 64) and this is to be achieved in this lifetime.

Furthermore, the idea that Buddhism is Truth, is a profound concept ". . . the deep hidden truth lying below the surface and invisible to the ordinary man. To see this truth is to know intellectually the emptiness of all things; the transience, unsatisfactoriness, and non-selfhood of all things; to know intellectually the nature of suffering, of the complete elimination of suffering and of the way to attain the complete elimination of suffering; to perceive these in terms of absolute truth, the kind that never changes and which everyone ought to know. This is Buddhism as Truth." (Buddhadasa, 2005, pg. 20) This is the foundation of the religion of Buddhism.

First Progressive:

We are all interconnected is the message of the Dalai Lama's interpretation of emptiness: Expressing a similar insight, the Vietnamese Buddhist master Thich Nhat Hanh once wrote: 'If you are a poet, you will see that there is a cloud in this sheet of paper. Without a cloud, there will be no rain; without rain, the trees cannot grow; and without trees, we cannot make paper'." (Chan, pg. 119)

> "Waking up this morning, I smile.
> Twenty-four brand new hours are before me.
> I vow to live fully in each moment
> And to look at all beings with eyes of compassion."
> (Hanh, pg. 102)

"The arhat is the ordinary hero of the Buddha's way as it was first enunciated. He/she is the person who has fully transcended all passion and desire to at last enjoy the cool bliss of nirvana. They do not manufacture any new karmic formation, but old ones still have to be worked out and through their momentum mundane life persists, though they put their remaining time in the world *to good effect by teaching dharma*." (Snelling, pg. 68) If we live in a difficult situation, our main students, beside ourselves, might be our family members and closest associates outside a Sangha. Teaching can proceed by example—Bodhicitta, compassionate orientation—and by the subtle pointing-out method of Buddha, or by incorporating the forces of ***chakra***, which is said to be a more rapid method to achieve enlightenment.

Yoga and Buddhism intersect in the teaching of compassion and thoughtfulness toward others. "With this conditioning [living in self-satisfaction, comfort, and everything going our way] in our background, we may find it hard to accept or appreciate why generosity is so important to our spiritual growth. The Buddha, on the other hand, deliberately put generosity first on the list of paramitas . . . [perfections] A traditional forest monk from Thailand came to this country to observe Buddhism in America firsthand. After a few months, he confided . . . 'In Asia,' he said, 'the classic sequence of the teachings and practice is first generosity, then morality, and then meditation or insight. But here in the United States, the sequence seems to be meditation first, then morality, and after some time, as a kind of appendix, there is some teaching about generosity. What's going on here?' . . . [When] we Americans do strive to break away from the materialistic, self-aggrandizing focus of our society, we still bring with us our cultural training as individualists. Many of us come to Buddhism [and yoga] in the first place as a means of self-improvement, and our initial focus tends to be on things we can do all by ourselves, and seemingly all for ourselves . . . [In contrast] We can begin right now, where we are, to be more compassionate and giving to others in our thoughts, words, and deeds . . . This makes generosity an excellent, viable, readily accessible starting point for practicing Buddhism in the day-to-day world at any age." (Surya Das, pp. 22-23) When we use our talents to succeed (optimize our talents in service) in business or academia, then use our expanded resources for the benefit of others, we are following the Buddha's path of generosity first.(Right Livelihood.)

Second Progressive:

"It is not necessary to burn out all one's karma in order to become enlightened . . . But if we are to be rigorous and apply basic Buddhist doctrine, who is the karmically-afflicted individual anyway? Haven't we already heard that the notion of an 'I,' an individual entity, is, in ultimate terms, a false view? As the Visuddhimagga ["Path of Purification"] asserts: "No doer of the deeds is found / No-one ever reaps their fruit; 'Empty phenomena roll on: / This view alone is right and true'." (Snelling, pg. 9) The effects of karma (actions) can disappear (consequences are not obligations) as we make virtuous choices, past mistakes need have no influence on our future lives; with the flick of a wrist, with our willingness to follow the Precepts and doing it, acknowledging our mortality as the source of our non-uniqueness (no I-ness), and fitting our lives into this worthy pattern we progress toward liberation and perfection.

So much of our lives is conducted by the sub-conscious mind, our desires and cravings grow there like so many mushrooms. Likewise, there is a lot of work being done there in our subconscious after meditation to foster the changes that we need in our personalities to avoid creating suffering and further complications in our lives. The Arahant set the sub-conscious part of the mental continuum to work to sculpt a new person, and it manifests as modesty and ethics to even the most casual observer.

The dream is the playground of our unconscious mind and its dictator our conscience where the drama of our past defilements plays out like some training video. What can we learn from this vague dreaming? The best way to regard emptiness is by comparing it to dreaming. "Buddha chose to describe the indescribable through metaphors and stories. In order to offer us a way to understand clarity in terms of everyday experience, he used the same analogy he used to describe emptiness, that of a dream . . . imagine the total darkness of sleep . . . descending into a state of total blankness. Yet within this darkness, he explained, forms and experiences begin to appear . . . We may find ourselves in places we've known or places freshly imagined [déjà vu, seeing into the future—can that happen?] In dreams, any and all experiences are possible [these are empty visions, yet this is] . . . an aspect of the pure clarity of mind." (Mingyur, pg. 99) Thus we must not get caught in our dreams, but measure the reality in front of us with a strict realism, thus we find fullness. Buddhism teaches it is not helpful or skillful to seek after para-normal powers, even if it were possible to suspend the laws of physics by the use of our mind power.

Third Progressive:

"The Tantric practices are twofold: 1) generation stage practice, which entails complex visualizations to stabilize the mind and manifest its essential nature, and 2) completion stage practice, which enhances these realizations at the subtle and very subtle levels of mind. Completion stage practices may involve manipulating the body's energy currents [in an active way] in order to make the very subtle mind more readily accessible." (Brown, pg. 8) We know that when we are in pain for example from a headache, this interferes with the normal functioning of our mind for such activities as concentration, reading and simple conversations. Conversely, when our minds are elevated to a positive state, beyond normal, this ought to enhance our ability to focus and develop absorption, if that is our goal; or at least carry on an intelligent conversation.

The Taoists took a different tack, "They advocated a return to simplicity and harmony with nature, and their ideal was wu wei, a kind of uncontrived mode of being that flowed with all the effortless suppleness of water out of the darkness of the ultimate unknowable mystery and adapted itself to whatever it encountered . . . Buddhism was able to penetrate their culture . . . as 'a sort of foreign Taoism'." (Snelling, pg.122) Being in touch with these subtle, unseen, tranquil energies was the key to Taoism, as it is with the study of chakras. What relationship do these have to Buddhism? Perhaps conceptualizing these forces can help us develop a "positive state", a tranquil mind?

Again: "At the level of Highest Yoga Tantra, there are two main stages: the Generation Stage and the Completion Stage . . . Generation is preparatory . . . the practitioner learns to conjure the deity [metaphorically for ones own mind] out of the primal emptiness of his mind or out of a [mantra], to visualize the deity in fine detail and to dissolve him/her back into emptiness."

"The Completion Stage is about actualization—specifically the achievement of full buddhahood by special yogic means . . . the gross human body is containing two other bodies of increasing subtlety . . . The most subtle body consists of fine channels called nadi along which a number of plexus points of chakras are disposed. A so-called 'wind energy' circulates through this system, which is basically inseparable from consciousness, but in its most gross forms manifests as passions like anger and lust. In the unregenerate individual, the nadi are knotted up, so the movement of the wind energy is vitiated. [clogged] Using the virtuoso powers of concentration perfected by means of intensive practice at the Generation Stage, the Tantric yogi seeks to direct and dissolve the wind energy into the minute bindu or 'droplets' situated in the heart chakra. If this is achieved, conceptual thought automatically and instantaneously ceases, and what remains is nothing less than the primordial state itself: Mahamudra." (Snelling, pg. 101) The Arahant can pick and choose from the various Yoga teachings to identify which for him/her are effective. That is after all well within the capacity of a rational Buddhist, let alone an Arahant, to apply insight meditation to evaluate and identify the suitability of any proposed training ritual.

Yoga practice can be useful. "The yoga asanas or postures work primarily on the muscles, since these are virtually the only parts of the body over which we have conscious control. We can make the muscles move as we like, subject only to our physical limitations . . . So a well-instructed yoga practice is designed to move our body, in co-ordination with the breath, into a variety of positions that will undo the body by stretching, exercising and strengthening all our muscles. Allowing the breath to soften the muscles lets us release them, and this in turn creates *space in the spine and in the joints*, [presumably for the finer forces to flow] allowing us to breathe into them. This freeing of muscles and skeletal connections rids the entire body of tension and permits the body's natural intelligence to function. Since the spine protects the central nervous system, and improvement in the spine's flexibility immediately improves the working of the nervous system itself." Beware of unusual exertions which can result in strained muscles that manifest several days after the offending movement of the body.

"This internal process [opening the path of chakras] works from the outside in, from the gross or heavy to the subtle. So although we begin our yoga practice working with the body (and breath) . . . we then focus more exclusively on the breath, which is finer, and end up in a state of meditation in which we work directly with the mind, which is finer and more subtle still. This gradual focusing inwards eventually leads to a state of samadhi, when all thoughts are stilled, the mind quietens, the senses withdraw from the busy noisy outside world and we find ourselves absorbed in a blissful and peaceful awareness of primal consciousness." (Forstater, pg. 31) There is too much detail involved to explain each chakra, to identify the exercises that can be targeted toward each and how to develop the *kundalini forces* in more particular detail. This information is available to the Arahant with a simple search of the internet.

"In Tai Chi we locate the *ci energy*—the life energy—somewhere below the navel in a place called the Tan Tien, and in yoga this same life energy is the prana which travels in channels all around the spine and eventually up and down it when the kundalini energy is released . . . the solar plexus, identified with the heart . . . is the first place in our body where we are aware of feelings—'aware' being too subtle a word for what is a basic and direct visceral reaction [often very forceful] a wrenching of the guts . . . this is the home of our intuition . . ." (Forstater, pg. 56) This ancient *noetic science* is, perhaps for some people, worth investigating in more detail, but it is more likely to be a diversion.

"What he [the Dalai Lama] was trying to explain was this: most of us attach meaning and significance to everything as a way of understanding and interpreting our world. But our experiences influence how we see the world [circular perceptions.] To apprehend things without distortion, we need to investigate them with scientific rigor . . . Now let's look at ultimate reality . . . What exactly is it? [looking at a tea mug] . . . We're seeing color, shape. But if we take away shape, color, material, what is mug? Where is the mug? This mug is a combination of particles: atoms, electrons, quarks. But each particle not 'mug.' The same can be said about the four elements, the world, everything. The Buddha. We cannot find the Buddha. So that's the ultimate reality. If we're not satisfied with conventional reality, if we go deep down and try to find the real thing, we ultimately won't find it." (Chan, pp. 148-149) We find emptiness in this case, which is a clear expression of a philosophical conundrum, similar to the discussions of Logical Positivists i.e. Bertrand Russell.

Meditation Practicum:

When we look at the icon of a buddha it is useful to notice the position and character of the hands which often display a mudra, or mystic pose of the hands. "The dhyana [jhana] mudra, representing [Buddha's] meditation (samadhi) under the Bodhi-tree . . . both hands lie on the lap, the right on top of the left, with the palms turned upward, and the figure, with the legs closely locked, formed a perfect triangle . . . As buddha, 'Liberator of the Nagas' he may have a special pose of the hands, held at the breast with all fingers locked except the indexes, which are raised and touch at the tips . . . Buddha, [may invoke] the earth to witness his resistance of the temptations of the Spirit of Evil, Mara,. the bhmisparsa mudra. The right arm is stretched downward, all the fingers are extended, the tips touching the earth, the palm turned underneath." (Getty, pg. 19) The importance of this is for teaching, and when we meditate we may choose a mudra to aid our concentration if we come to the understanding that it is effective.

There is some virtue in being able to grasp the essence of a situation or teaching. "The essence viewpoint asserts three levels of mind: *coarse, subtle, and very subtle*. The coarse level pertains to mental content, such as thoughts, sense perceptions, and emotions. The subtle level is the fleeting mental activity surrounding sensory experience before that activity becomes full-blown mental content. The very subtle, or extraordinary, level is the level where impressions due to past actions are accumulated before these ripen in fresh experience. This very subtle mind is sometimes called the storehouse consciousness. The point of observation of this storehouse consciousness transcends our ordinary sense of self and individual consciousness. Like a vast ocean of awareness, this vantage point for the extraordinary meditation is typically referred to as the always-here mind or as awareness in and of itself. When the mind operates primarily at this very subtle level, [sub-conscious] the individual is significantly more prepared to realize the mind's primordial nature, which is always there [buddha nature], unaffected by all the mental activity at the coarse and subtle levels. Thus the essence perspective cuts right to the **heart** of the mind's natural state, and invites the practitioner to awaken to it in direct experience, the result of which is enlightenment." (Brown, pg. 9) Is this where we get the idea of a fleeting thought, an inspiration, and does distinguishing "*coarse, subtle, and very subtle*" take us to the origin of the ***higher truth*** that is so often referred to even in Buddhist teachings?

Recall from some of the earlier lessons about breathing: "Many people breathe shallowly and only from the chest, not realizing that the whole body [in Yoga] is itself a respiratory organ and that failure to breathe properly inhibits the body from its proper physiological function." (Forstater, pg. 39) Thus we wear loose fitting clothing to encourage the oxygen of breath to flow to all our extremities, and especially to our brain. This permits our mind to develop its full capacity, and possibly send out stronger signals from the more subtle realms of cognitive activity if we are patient and receptive.

From the **Satipatthana** tradition meditate on the five aggregates. "Again, monks, in regard to dhammas he abides contemplating dhammas in terms of the five aggregates of clinging. And how does he in regard to . . . the five aggregates of clinging? Here he knows, 'such is material form [physical body,] such its arising, such its passing away;

Such is feeling, such its arising, such its passing away;

Such is cognition, such its arising, such its passing away;

Such are volitions, such their arising, such their passing away;

Such is consciousness, such its arising, such its passing away'." (Analayo, pp. 9-10) How does this compare to the life cycle of a tree? Thus we answer the question, what part of our behavior and life's work is to simply satisfy one or more of the five aggregates, and what has a higher purpose? Is there a dialectic at each stage?

Biographical Sketch:

"The influence of the Madhyamika philosophy as taught in the Three Treatises school [in Japan], The Way of Emptiness . . . [taught] Emptiness as the ultimate character of all things. Things are empty of any enduring selfhood or identity, because they are transitory and subject to change. Only Emptiness endures, is final and absolute. [like a platonic form] From the emphasis on universal change we may see how directly the Madhyamika stands in opposition to the Han Confucian view of the universe as stable and orderly . . . The Way of Emptiness insisted on the need to free oneself from anything external, including such concepts as Heaven, in order to seek the ultimate, undifferentiated reality within. Externals are so changeable that they can only deceive. They must therefore be negated exhaustively until all the distinctions and concepts which arise from incomplete knowledge are destroyed and ultimate truth is intuitively realized . . . the answer must lie on the side of intuitive truth rather than in the domain of the demonstrable." (de Bary, pg. 262) This is parallel to the ability to appreciate poetry.

"What think you, Subhuti? Suppose a disciple has attained the degree of Arahant (Fully enlightened,) could he entertain within his mind any such arbitrary conception as, 'I have become an Arahant'?"

"No, Honored of the worlds! Because speaking truly, there is no such thing as a fully enlightened one. Should a disciple who has attained such a degree of enlightenment, cherish within his mind such an arbitrary conception as, 'I have become an Arahant,' he would soon be grasping after such things as his own selfhood, other selves, living beings and a universal self . . . delight [yourself] in the practice of silence and tranquility'." The Diamond Sutra (Goddard, pg. 93)

Reading for the Day:

A question for the Dalai Lama: "How did you develop your understanding of interdependence?"

"With time, with time," he replied. "Spiritual progress takes time. It's not like switching on a light. More like kindling a fire: start from small spark, then becomes bigger and bigger, more light, more light, like that. All mental transformations like that . . . At beginning, not noticeable. Often I tell people: spiritual development—we cannot see results within weeks or months. Even years. But if we make comparison, today's experience compared to ten years ago, or twenty years ago, then you feel some change. That I always tell other people. My own case also like that." (Chan, pg. 120)

The goal of Yoga is the same for Buddhism, to bring us to the answer of the question: "What is Nirvana?" This is usually explained as a non-sensible experience, not nonsense but not physical. "And it certainly cannot be described in words. To do so would be like trying to describe the color red to a blind person . . . we can and must come to it through direct insight, and this indeed is basically what the Buddha's way is all about . . . The word nirvana itself possess connotations of blowing out or extinguishing [coolness], as a flame [or cravings] may be blown out or extinguished once the fuel that feeds it has been exhausted. It is cool and peaceful. Dukkha doesn't touch it, nor the passions of greed, hatred, and ignorance . . . it is nevertheless lavishly praised in the Buddhist scriptures as amounting to supreme bliss, no less." (Snelling, pg. 45)

Proverb: Stress is like an ice cream cone, you have to learn to lick it. (wellpage.com)

Protecting:

"This is what I heard," review by both Arahant and teacher.

Additional Teaching:

"Be well aware that this [sixteen steps of Anapanasati Bhavana] is the way to emancipation. Anapanasati successfully practiced through this final step brings emancipation, or liberation. When we are liberated from all bonds, we either let go of all burdens or release ourselves out from under those burdens. Whether we say 'letting go of ourselves' or 'letting go of the burdens,' the meaning of the realization is the same. There is 'letting go,' and the result is emancipation. Or it might be called 'salvation,' 'deliverance,' 'release,' or 'liberation.' They all signify that we have obtained the best thing possible for human beings. We have not wasted our lives and the opportunity of having found the Dhamma, which is the best thing that human beings can obtain. This is the end of the story." (Buddhadasa, 1988, pp. 92-93)

"When the 'I' wants to get something, there is greed; when it doesn't get that something, there is anger; when it hesitates and doesn't know what it wants, there is confusion, involvement in hopes and possibilities. Greed, anger, and delusion of whatever kind are simply forms of the 'I'—idea, and when they are present in the mind, that is everlasting Samsara, total absence of Nirvana. A person in this condition does not live long . . . to reduce the periods of suffering, or Samsara, by preventing as far as possible the birth of 'I' and 'mine' . . . practice right living . . . namely the Noble Eightfold Path." (Buddhadasa, 2005, pg. 216)

Sharing Merit:

Rejoicing In Others' Merit (Saying Sadhu)

Buddhist Sutra

Lesson Title: **Yoga Chakras—**

Lesson Number: **Twenty-eight**

Key Vocabulary: kundalini, ci energy, noetic science, bindu, chakra, bodhicitta, generating stage, completion stage, nadi, wu wei, letting go, higher truth

Assignment: Meditation on liberation, Tantric power and freedom as an Arahant.

Practice all sixteen steps of Anapanasati Bhavana.

Define each of the Key Vocabulary in your own words.

Use insight meditation on the mental concept of emptiness, during your regular practice.

Identify emptiness where you can find it, give an example.

Review the description of Yoga Charkas from the internet.

List and describe the chakras and the potential influence of each.

Identify the shared goal of Yoga and other teachings.

What can you gain/if anything from Yoga practice?

Contemplate and comment on each of the four "Infinite Virtues."

Benevolence
Compassion
Giving Happiness
Impartiality

What is peculiar about the Yoga approach to religion that makes it special?

Review this Prayer again. "May I be free from enmity, ill-will and grief, and may I take care of myself happily! As I am, so also may my teachers, preceptors, parents, and intimate, indifferent, and inimical beings, be free from enmity, ill-will and grief, and may they take care of themselves happily! May they be released from suffering! May they not be deprived of their fortune, duly acquired! All have [control of] kamma as their own."(Saddhatissa, pg. 55)

Taoism, and the study of chakras: What relationship do these have with Buddhism?

Materials Required: Tea ceremony, incense

Buddhist Sutra

Lesson Title: **Super-Natural**

Lesson Number: **Twenty-nine**

Rationale:

For Rational Buddhists, there is very little of the super-natural that has any reality for one's life. Very little? More likely nothing; this is another place where emptiness can be found. However there is something to be said for the collective consciousness of humanity, and for the Buddha nature of grace that pervades us like moisture in the air, which is relative to temperature, pressure, and so many other conditions that are not visible. We can sometimes feel the oppressive humidity without seeing it, especially in Thailand. Therefore, it is worth at least being aware of super-natural teachings, unless one is otherwise equipped with all the answers. It would be super-natural or at least more-than-enough to know all the questions.

Discussion of Prior Lesson:

What can we learn from the teachings of Yoga? Possibly the operation and development of the chakras through physical postures and breathing has some merit? Certainly the physical exercise is useful. Can the chakra power help us hold the mind in awareness, can it help us understand emptiness by giving object lessons?

If there is no afterlife, no god, no external source of meaning in our lives, in what way is that a form of emptiness?

Training Objective:

The main concepts beyond the purview of the mind. Earth, air, water and fire. Using the Buddha icon. Self-realization, Tathagata meditation.

Materials Required: tea ceremony

Motivational Statement:

"For about an hour, the Dali Lama had patiently explained . . . how he himself was transformed in baby steps, over the years, by using a sensible, logical approach to his spiritual practice. He underscored the importance of reason. He was emphatic that anyone could achieve genuine happiness by focusing on two fundamental precepts of Buddhism: compassion and emptiness [not the super-natural tradition]." (Chan, pg. 151)

"The [Arahant] is empowered with the 'wisdom of omniscience' [having a broad frame of reference,] the subtlest degree of emptiness. Even though the effects may not at all be obvious at first . . . if you practice diligently following empowerment, 'You will become enlightened even though you don't think about enlightenment.' These are the propensities of empowered awakened wisdom [these] progressively gain force and eventually ripen. The necessary groundwork has been laid. The subsequent [methods] are simply manifestations of the progressive ripening of this same wisdom. Furthermore, the three stages of enlightenment—basis [dharma], path [practice], and fruition [enlightenment]—are also manifestations of this same deepening wisdom. With the four influences [see below] the practitioner develops the potential to understand that 'the body, speech, and mind of the lama and your own body, speech, and mind are indistinguishable . . . You quickly become like the Ancient Ones."

(Brown, pg. 129) Remember, being enlightened—being in a state of nirvana—is a state of mind, like a point of view!

First Progressive:

"Love relieves suffering." (Hanh, pg. 275)

"'Compassion is something like a sense of caring, a sense of concern for others' difficulties and pain,' the Dali Lama said. 'Not only family and friends, but all other people. Enemies also. Now, if we really analyze our feelings, one thing becomes clear. If we think only of ourselves, forget about other people, then our minds occupy very small area. Inside that small area, even tiny problem appears very big. But the moment you develop a sense of concern for others, you realize that, just like ourselves, they also want happiness; they also want satisfaction. When you have this sense of concern, your mind automatically widens. At this point, your own problems, even big problems, will not be so significant. The result? Big increase in peace of mind. So, *if you think only of yourself*, only of your own happiness, the result is actually less happiness. You get more anxiety, more fear'." (Chan, pg. 166) Can you confirm this from your own experiences?

"Supernatural powers are never a major goal in Buddhism. The three types of superior wisdom [last of the three following] and six powers of saving sentient beings manifested by Shakyamuni and his arahant followers were always merely expedient byproducts intended for use in teaching and conversion but never for personal fame or fortune . . . [recall 1. Perfect freedom of activity, 2. ears capable of hearing everything, 3) insight into the minds of others, 4.) remembrance of one's former existences, 5. eyes capable of seeing everything, and 6. perfect freedom] . . . Even Yoga teaches that one must not make supernatural powers a primary aim and that sources of evil will vanish and profound enlightenment be attained when a person has ceased being interested in such things. From the Buddhist standpoint, the most important thing is to attain the sixth power [rapture] perfect freedom—and, after thus reaching perfect enlightenment, to *work selflessly and compassionately for the good of all members of society*." (Mizuno, pp. 169-172) These stories and powers were somewhat embellished after some five hundred years of telling, like fish stories, each time getting bigger.

"The four *elements* is an analytical system to help [us] develop mindfulness. It works very well with the practice of mindfulness of breathing meditation. This is an ancient categorization scheme [found in many disparate cultures] for looking at the nature of our own experience. It analyzes every experience we have in terms of symbolic qualities that are like some of the primary things we see in the normal world: earth, water, air and fire. Please keep in mind that these are not mere words, nor are they some highly philosophical or mystical qualities only available to deep thinkers and spiritual supermen. These are things [we] are experiencing right now. It is just a different way of analyzing the experience [we] are having at this very moment. Each of the four elements manifests in the single practice of mindfulness of breathing." (Gunaratana, pg. 62) This frame of reference helps us practice both rational and spiritual sensitivity to everything around us. The four foundations of meditation are found in many traditions by other names.

Second Progressive:

"Shakyamuni used supernatural powers not as an end in themselves but *for the sake of teaching sentient beings*, and he forbade his followers to employ them willfully for their own glory or profit . . ." (Mizuno, pg. 169) People who believe in supernatural powers are those for whom the natural laws of physics and chemistry are not sufficiently mysterious and wondrous.

"The references to 'the three times' and to 'whatever has arisen' [frequently found phrases in Buddha's teachings] pertain to an acute awareness of the *process* of unfolding of events (not the content) in the mental continuum. The practitioner more and more experiences the mental continuum as an orderly flow of successive mental events. Though these events may vary in their respective content, each successive event is experienced as a discrete unit. One event occurs and ceases before another comes forth. Instead of the previous chaos of many conflicting trains of thought at once, events now unfold one at a time, moment by moment, in a regular succession.

The phrase whatever has arisen signifies the shift from the disorder of the ordinary mind to the orderly stream of the contemplative mind . . . The phrase indicates that attachment to specific mental content becomes less important. The content is simply 'whatever.' The *process* of how mental events come forth over time becomes much more important. At this point the mental continuum begins to rearrange itself in the form of an orderly temporal flow of discrete events." (Brown, pg. 174) Understanding this process will help us avoid making ethical and moral mistakes. There is the saying that "the third time is the charm" and it would not surprise me if its origin came from this teaching.

"In Buddhism, the wholesome action that is considered best virtue is the one in mind by concentrating mind to be one-pointed and develop wisdom to get rid of all defilements completely. It is called mind development." This is the advanced stage of meditation, although it is suggested as being the foundation stone of enlightenment and thus, as a worthwhile goal, the beginning point of every practice.

"If somebody can practice [to develop] mind till it is concentrated and develops wisdom . . . to eradicate all defilements, achieves the ultimate goal in Buddhism, that means he accomplishes the Fruit of the Worthy One (Arahant). This is the highest level of making merit. Only the Holy One/ Worthy One (the one who has attained Nibbana—extinction of all defilements and suffering) can extinguish perfectly all defilements. [This] . . . means being able to extinguish all suffering because all defilements are the causes of all suffering." (Wee, pg. 22) This is an ideal state of mind. So? We keep trying!

"The earth element represents the property of solidity, heaviness, solidness, compactness. Its characteristics are hardness or softness." Thus the concepts of fortitude and steadfastness can be associated with "earth". "Just feel yourself sitting. Place your attention on that solid feeling where your body touches whatever you are sitting on. Feel your feet pressing against the floor. Those are hard sensations. Feel the light touch of the air against your skin. That is a soft sensation. This is the earth element." (Gunaratana, pg. 63) Let this direct awareness of the constituents of our bodies stabilize our emotional tone and guide us into consistent, virtuous action. We can make similar associations with water, air and fire in subsequent teachings, turning the mundane into elements of inspiration and comfort.

Third Progressive:

The "mystery" and vastness of Universe is confusing and a cause of angst (thus suffering) for some people, especially those who have not had the fortune to study astronomy, astrophysics or modern, general science. "This universe already exists, even if we don't realize it at present [ontological.] The aim of Buddhist teachings is to develop the capacity to recognize that this universe—which is really nothing more or less than the infinite possibility within our own being—exists in the here and now. In order to recognize it, however, it is necessary to learn how to rest the mind. Only through resting the mind in its natural awareness can we begin to recognize that we are not our thoughts, not our feelings, and not our perceptions . . . And everything I've learned as a Buddhist and everything I've learned about modern science tells me that human beings are more than just their bodies." (Mingyur, pp. 244-245) Is this a useful perspective?

"We use this term, [transmigration] which is the most usual one, with reference to the general Indian doctrine of reincarnation and rebirth; but it must be remembered that it is misleading when applied to Buddhism, which maintains that no entity of any kind migrates from one body to another." (de Bary, pg. 5) Materialism? Rational Buddhism!

But there is a lingering and substantial belief in the supernatural, according to the Dalai Lama, "Past and future lives certainly exist, for the following reasons: Certain ways of thinking from last year, the year before that and even from childhood can be recollected now. This clearly establishes that there existed awareness previous to the present continuity of awareness of an adult. Likewise, the first instant of consciousness of this life is not produced without cause, nor is it born from something permanent; neither is it produced from a solid, inanimate, incongruent substantial cause—therefore it must surely be produced from a congruent substantial cause. In what way are they congruent? Since a moment of mind is an awareness which is clear and knowing, it is preceded by a similar moment of mind which was clear and knowing. It is not feasible [or could there be another explanation?] that such a preceding awareness be produced by a similar moment of mind which was clear and knowing. It is not feasible that such a preceding awareness be produced other than on the basis of a previous birth. Otherwise, if the physical body alone were the substantial cause of mind, then the absurd consequences of a dead body having a mind and a change in the body necessitating a change in consciousness would also ensue." (Mehrotra, pg. 174) What kind of logic (or fallacy) is at play here? How much of our DNA, instincts, etc. dictate the thoughts and personality we have?

Most people need help organizing the information of the world into coherent patterns of lessons for life. "How does one go about creating a meaningful life in the absence of any of these structures [of organized religion and super-natural beliefs,] unconstrained by doctrine or myth? It's reasonably simple to look around and find out what works in society [i.e. lines on the street to organize traffic.] Those actions that lead toward a better functioning society ought to be given strong consideration. An enlightened, thoughtful society creates its own morality [by identifying what works well.]"

"Religious belief is fearful and desperate if it is based on the fire and brimstone Evangelism or emotional blackmail [or the promise of a Pure Land blessed afterlife.] This belief is simpleminded if it is only a convenient reaction to the need to have answers, any answers. It is more profound if it is consciously based on an appreciation of the mystery that [naturally] engulfs the world. Man can be forgiven for surrendering to a realization of his insignificance in the face of infinite Nature. When we acknowledge the limitations of our own perceptions as the roots of religious belief, we begin to acknowledge the possibility for life as art . . ."

"Those who captured this mystery and incorporated it into their ritual came closer to giving proper homage to the vastness of Universe and to the conspicuously limited role of humanity. Ritual is metaphor for reality when it engenders connection to infinity . . . It is more honest to say 'I don't know,' then proceed to solve the puzzle of life." (IJ, Jack and Lucky, 1993)

On a more personal level for Buddhists, when we look around the sky at night and see our corner of Universe, we see so many different formations of galaxies (in the abstract as stars), nebulae, double and triple suns, black holes, and radiation and waves that we can't see . . . all formed by the same laws of nature based on the rule of proximate association—the law of causation in this broader context, each element obeying its properties—and combining into molecules and crystals—building all we see and touch. Is there a pattern or a reason behind all this? If we think so, how is our concept different than astrology?

". . . There really is no difference between the mind that thinks and thoughts that come and go in the mind. The mind itself and the thoughts, emotions, and sensations that arise, abide, and disappear in the mind are equal expressions of emptiness—that is, the open-ended possibility for anything to occur. If the mind is not a 'thing' but an event, then all the thoughts, feelings, and sensations that occur in what we think of as the mind are likewise events. As we begin to rest in the experience of mind and thoughts as inseparable, like two sides of the same coin, we begin to grasp the true meaning of clarity as an infinitely expansive state of awareness." (Mingyur, pg. 96) What is spirituality anyway? if the mind is the same as its thoughts, and there is no duality of body and spirit? Is enlightenment when we realize that we are alone in Universe (yet connected with our Sangha,) and we are able to cope with this reality effectively with calmness, coolness, i.e. nirvana?

Meditation Practicum:

"A lot of people think that meditation means achieving some unusually vivid state, completely unlike anything they've experienced before. They mentally squeeze themselves, thinking, I've got to attain a higher level of consciousness . . . I should be seeing something wonderful, like rainbow lights or images of pure realms . . . I should be glowing in the dark. That's called trying too hard . . ." (Mingyur, pg. 96) This is not believing in supernatural but expecting the non-existent.

"Consider, on the other hand, the case of Buddhologists who accept the propositions of transpersonal psychology, for example the assertion that embedded in the potentials of each person's *unconscious* are the keys for achieving *self-realization*. *Mental blocks*, symbolized in myth by subterraneous dragon-like creatures such as nagas, guard and keep them submerged. The methods for self-realization remain concealed in the unconscious until an individual reaches a sufficient level of *spiritual development* and "the times are ripe" for their revelation. Because such Buddhologists consider the unconscious as an equivalent for the clear light continuum, they can accept a shared level of meaning with tantra practitioners concerning the statement that Buddha taught the tantras, although they soundly reject its literal meaning. They could accept that Buddha is the source of tantra teachings only in the sense that Buddha represents [and explains] the unconscious. In other words, the tantra teachings come from the unconscious of the various masters in whose minds they spontaneously arise." (Berzin) These kind of mystical teachings must, as all others, be examined with a grain of salt.

"Meditations with virtuous mental factors align the mind with a perfect template during the *Tathagata meditation*. Through intense concentration the practitioner's unfolding mental continuum more and more approximates that of the perfect Tathagata image—all of the good qualities. Because the meditator's mind progressively takes the form of the Tathagata image as visualized, the outcome is called *great virtue*. 'Since you are able to concentrate on an *intended object* like the Tathagata's body [or Buddhist icon,] you should attain great accumulation of merit from that. Such activity is to be praised'!" (Brown, as JP, pg. 30a) This is like learning how to play tennis by watching a video, then practicing and doing it again, and each time you learn something new. Will you ever be a great tennis player? Probably not, but you can certainly have a good time.

"Any object visualized repeatedly for a long time becomes more and more part of the practitioner's field of mental and perceptual experience. One interesting sign of the visualization's ripening, is that the Buddha is experienced by the meditator as being actually present and is felt to be deeply connected with him or her . . ." (repeat Bud—dho.)

"This icon is first visualized in front as a substance. Then the practitioner visualizes the same image as an internal reflected image. Repeated practice using this reflected image leads to staying with respect to the image [as well as awakening the virtue of buddhahood for the Arahant.]" (Brown, pg. 199) Remember how the human physiology of sight explains retina fatigue, which can create a reciprocal or complementary image in color. Thus, whenever we stare at any light, our retina tires and sends a signal that is the complement, the opposite color in the spectrum to our brain; this is not a mystical aura. And since our eyes are constantly moving when we stare, this retina fatigue appears to us as a hazy halo of color surrounding the visual object.

"The air element is experienced primarily as motion or stillnes. The moving quality of anything [consider the breath] is the air element expressed through that thing . . . The breath itself [combines] the earth [and air] elements. The breathing can be hard or soft. [We] would not feel anything unless there were solid flesh doing the feeling and [we] can feel that solidity. [We] feel whatever part of the body the air contacts as hard. You feel the solidness of the abdomen as it rises and falls. [We] feel the solidity of the nostrils as the air passes over them. Sometimes the breath has a rougnness to it. Sometimes a gentle breath is so soft you can scarcely feel it . . . Mindfulness of breathhing shows us the hard, soft, and solid qualities of our experience." (Gunaratana, pp. 63-64) This is how we develop a sensitive association with the breath.

"The fire element manifests as heat or cold or any sense of temperature in between. It also manifest as the dry sensation that goes with heat. When [we] feel hot and want to be cooler, the pure feeling that precedes the thought is the fire element manifesting. The temperature in the room drops and [we] feel cold. [There is less heat and perhaps you chill and sneeze.] That is the fire element manifesting [the coolness of Nirvana.] The temperature feels neutral and you have to really seek to feel any temperature at all. That is the fire element too . . . The air often feels cool against the nostrils on the in-breath, warmer on the out-breath. That is the fire element . . . Mindfulness of breathing shows us the hot-cold or energetic qualities of our experience . . . We contemplate the four elements of the breath body as a meditation exercise to examine our own experience with precision . . . the whole purpose is to push us, almost against our will, into contact with the pure, experiential essence of sensory reality. Training the mind to see the impingements of material experience as simply elemental vibrations helps to break down our usual mental habits. It frees us from the concepts that usually arise and the mental reactions to those concepts." (Gunaratana, pp. 64-65) And as with the fourth jhana, we see with direct awareness without words, without mystery, the elements of nature that surround us and are the constituents of our bodies, minds and will. We see impermanence in the way we are connected to Universe and this is manifest through the changing nature of the four elements.

Biographical Sketch:

"Then for Pukkusati's sake [a potter living in Magadha] Shakyamuni preached a sophisticated sermon, probably because he perceived that this man was of intellectual capacity sufficient for him to understand difficult Buddhist theories. The sermon was a detailed, logical presentation showing that human beings have six senses—sight, hearing, smell, taste, touch, and thought—for perceiving six objects: earth, water, fire, wind, air, and knowledge. From this operation of perception are born the sixteen kinds of emotions and sensations, including pain and pleasure and joy and sorrow. Knowledge of nature [not the super-natural] and sources of these emotions leads to understanding of the truth that there is no permanent self and that there should be no attachments [craving for] conditioned phenomena. This in turn leads to paramount wisdom and the realization that nirvana is the ultimate Noble Truth. The person realizing this can attain the highest realm of tranquility by abandoning all things that cause delusions and by breaking with the three poisons of covetousness, anger, and delusion . . ." Is it possible to gain relief from these poisons? or 108 defilements as listed earlier? Chapter 20.

"In our teaching, a mistake is forgiven if it is sincerely repented. You repent from your heart and are therefore forgiven." (Mizuno, pp. 113-114) This is where cleansing ceremony can help protect this kind of sincere repentance, and let us begin our lives clean, revitalized and refreshed. Water is often used as a symbolic element for cleansing. "The water element has a moist or flowing quality . . . And most of the time [we] ignore [the water that makes up our body.] . . . Any sensation that is damp, humid, or clammy in nature [humidity in the air] is in this category too . . . Mindfulness of breathing shows us the liquid, moist, and flowing qualities of our experience . . . The flow of blood, [as experienced in the pulse, is one] sensation that reveals the liquid factor . . ." (Gunaratana, pp. 63-64) This connects us to our living, vital consciousness. The fluids of our body carry the solid particles that are delivered by our food and breath. Monks use water droplets to transfer merit to those who practice rituals in temples, but this water is only made holy in the minds of recipients.

Likewise, many Buddhists honor and transfer merit to their ancestors and teachers on every occasion of merit making and sharing. Japanese Buddhists give special honor and merit to their ancestors three times each year: on the spring and autumn equinoxes in March and September and during the month July 15-August 15. The equinox festivals, called Higan, "Other Shore," mark times of transition in nature and therefore are occasions to reflect on the passage of time and the progress of being toward enlightenment—the other shore.

One of the most famous legends about Buddha relates to his maturity and forcefulness just after birth. "The infant stood firmly on the ground and took seven strides to the north . . . he stopped to look around and gave out a fearless utterance known as the 'lion's roar.' His proclamation has been imagined as follows:

> Supreme am I in the world;
> Greatest am I in the world;
> Noblest am I in the world.
> This is my last birth;
> Never shall I be reborn." (Plamintr, 2007, pg. 46)

This accounts for the origin of the lion figures that often guard the entrance to temples. But from a scientific perspective, how is it possible that one person—and not all the rest of us—is a non-returner? A Koan.

Reading for the Day:

"Emptiness and compassion. Wisdom and method. These are the twin pillars of the Dalai Lama's practice—everything we need to know about spiritual practice." (Chan, pg. 169)

> Lotus Sutra: "You who seek the three vehicles,
> If you have doubts and regrets,
> The Buddha will resolve them for you,
> Bringing them to an end so that nothing remains."

". . . There is no other vehicle. There is only the one Buddha vehicle." (Watson, pp. 22, 33)

"The essence of the Buddha's teachings was that while formal practice can help us to develop direct experience of emptiness, wisdom, and compassion, such experiences are meaningless unless we can bring them to bear on every aspect of our daily lives. For it's in facing the challenges of daily life that we can really measure our development of calmness, insight, and compassion."

"Even so, the Buddha invited us to try the practices for ourselves. In one of the sutras, he urged his students to test his teachings through practice, rather than accepting them simply at face value:

> As you would burn, cut, and rub gold,
> Likewise, the wise monk examines my teachings.
> Examine my teachings well,
> But don't take them on faith." (Mingyur, pg. 205)

Protecting:

"This is what I heard," review by both Arahant and teacher.

Additional Teaching:

"We ought always to train ourselves this way, that is, 'mouth is one and mind another.' The mouth says one thing, but the heart knows otherwise . . . it can be applied to a person who really practices Dhamma, that is, whose external behavior conforms with worldly conventions but whose internal reality is another story . . . [this apparent] dishonesty and crookedness becomes the most noble and excellent form of speech . . . when it comes to the Dhamma language of the Buddha . . . the outside appears one way, while the inside is the opposite. Outwardly, in our speech and actions, we may possess all the things that others possess, but in the mind we possess nothing . . . When practicing austerities, don't let others see. If we wish to give alms or make a donation to charity, do so secretly ' . . . sticking gold on the image's back.' . . . wise people take the words to mean something good, because one doesn't receive any recognition, praise, status, or honor from the act . . . one makes more merit than if one were to stick the gold [conspicuously] on the front of the image" (Buddhadasa, 1993, pp. 26-28) an Arahant will not make claims about his/her enlightened mind.

Sharing Merit:

Rejoicing In Others' Merit (Saying Sadhu)

Buddhist Sutra

Lesson Title: **Super-Natural**

Lesson Number: **Twenty-nine**

Key Vocabulary: mental blocks, unconscious, self-realization, great virtue, intended object, spiritual development, non-returning, art of living

Assignment:
Choose a Buddha icon and use that to visualize in meditation.

How is your reaction and process different than in the beginning lesson?

Meditate on compassion and emptiness as being two sides of a single coin.

Review your journal and prepare questions and results for discussion.

"It's so easy to think that we're the only ones who suffer . . ." Has this feeling every surfaced in your consciousness?

"The power . . . other people held over me became a terrible threat to my own well-being." (Mingyur, pg. 179) Is this a problem in your life?

How do "ignorance, attachments and aversion" factor into your life? (from Lesson Six)

How does "mindfulness" influence our interpretation of super-natural explanations?

Greed, possessiveness, scared, insecure, misuse of money, excess possessions, weak sense of identity, feeling separate, alienated, isolated from others, and acting selfishly: How many times, and in what ways have these kinds (or causes) of suffering affected you?

"So, *if you think only of yourself*, only your own happiness, the result is actually less happiness. You get more anxiety, more fear'."

Can you confirm this from your own experiences? Discuss

Sharing Merit: Rejoicing In Others' Merit (Saying Sadhu)

Materials Required: tea ceremony, incense, flowers, two candles

Buddhist Sutra

Lesson Title: Commencement—Cautions

Lesson Number: Thirty

Rationale:

"Buddha says: You can change your life . . . beliefs are not needed. In fact, these beliefs are the barriers for real change. Start with no belief, start with no metaphysics, start with no dogma. Start absolutely naked and nude, with no theology, no ideology. Start empty! That is the only way to come to the truth." (Foreman, pg. 113) In this lesson we review some of the meditation techniques discussed in earlier lessons. This is a new beginning for the newly inspired and accomplished Arahants.

Discussion of Prior Lesson:

"Buddhism has a rational foundation enabling it to withstand any criticism on the theoretical plane. Its rationalism is not concerned solely with abstract truth for its own sake, but is a basis for actual practice of religious faith. This means that Buddhist faith is not merely unfounded enthusiasm, but practical faith with a firm rational and ethical basis. Buddhist theory and practice are one. In Buddhism there is no theory that does not take practice into consideration, and there is no practice lacking theoretical substantiation." (Mizuno, pg. 159)

"The Buddha . . . warned his disciples not to be attached to miracles. He even forbade his monks from performing them to attract attention. There is a grave penalty imposed on monks who boast of having higher supernatural powers that they do not [or could not] have . . . miracles are irrelevant in a spiritual pursuit although quite a few students of the Dhamma may find it rather intriguing . . . investigation for the sake of academic understanding is another matter." (Plamintr, pg. 47) What about the ecstatic effects of Hindu spirituality that is taught by "Life Bliss"?

Training Objective:

Adjusting to change in our lives. To summarize and prepare for return to civilization—we take compassion, love and a capable meditation practice. Seven **Elements of Enlightenment.** Be ready to teach others.'Three Lustres,'

Materials Required: tea ceremony, incense, flowers, two candles

Motivational Statement:

"Allow yourself to be a torch, and allow the flame of your torch to be transmitted to other torches. Practicing like that, you can help peace and joy grow in the entire world." (Hanh, pg. 277)

Buddha cautioned that he did not want to create attachment to his place of death. "Ananda then complained that after the death of the Tathagata the Order would be deprived of the opportunities its members had enjoyed of meeting with and paying respect to the many enlightened monks who had gathered around him during his lifetime. Shakyamuni told Ananda that after his death believers would revere four places: the place of his birth (Lumbini), the place where he attained enlightenment (Bodh Gaya), the place where he preached the first sermon (Deer Park in Benares), and the place of his death Kushinagara). Good, faithful believers would gather in these places, he said, and if any one of them should die while making such a pilgrimage, he would be reborn in a blessed state." (Mizuno, pg. 186) Having been introduced to Buddhism, making such a pilgrimage seems like an attractive tourism prospect.

First Progressive:

How do we set out to find happiness? (Let each person answer.)

"When compassion begins to awaken in your own heart, you're able to be more honest with yourself. If you make a mistake, you can acknowledge it and take steps to correct it. At the same time, you're less likely to look for flaws in other people. If people do something offensive, if they start screaming at you or treating you badly, you'll notice (probably with some surprise) that you don't react in the same way you once might have . . . Meditating on compassion involves more than trying to invoke a sense of warmth or kindness for someone we find irritating or frustrating. It actually requires a bit of analytical investigation into the other person's motivations, as well as an attempt to develop some sense of **understanding** of the other person's feelings—an understanding that, just like ourselves, everyone shares the same basic desire to be happy and to avoid unhappiness." (Mingyur, pp. 229-230) This kind of analysis is also how we learn step by step to apply a Rational Buddhist's moral code in our lives.

"True love is made of understanding—understanding the other person, the object of your love; understanding their suffering, their difficulties, and their true aspiration. Out of understanding there will be kindness, there will be compassion, there will be an offering of joy." (Hanh, pg. 287)

Meditate on each of the four insights.

1. The world is transient,
2. The body is impure
3. To produce good, and
4. to increase good when produced.

These teachings are essential to the development of compassion. Combine with that something of what it means to find emptiness, then fill it with goodness and offer it to others.

"When I began to practice meditation on compassion, however, I found that my sense of isolation began to diminish, while at the same time my personal sense of empowerment began to grow. Where once I saw only problems, I started to see solutions. Where once I viewed my own happiness as more important than the happiness of others, I began to see the well-being of others as the foundation of my own peace of mind." (Mingyur, pp. 178-179)

This "how to"—developing this kind of pure compassion needs to be followed in our practical, everyday lives. "Helpfulness is the prime product of Bodhicitta, the awakened heart-mind. Even at the simplest level, we can intentionally manifest it—for example, by giving up our seat on a crowded bus to an elderly person or helping an insecure child cross the street. To uncover this enlightened form of consciousness in our own lives, we simply need to rid ourselves gradually of our negative conditioning. Living in a world where there's so much suffering and violence, we tend to become cynical. We're trained to protect ourselves by suspecting the worst from people. We need to open up our hearts more, as fearful as we may have become about doing that, retraining ourselves according to wisdom and compassion." (Surya, pp. 16-17) We need not be naïve, but looking first on the positive side of each person we meet, seeing the glass half full, won't hurt our priorities.

Proverb: The best thing to do behind a person's back is to pat it. (wellpage.com)

Second Progressive:

"Charity is a moral obligation. Stealing of any kind is obviously a potent form of harm and violence [such as cheating on your taxes,] and if at the same time we deny the reality of our actions to ourselves, we add lying to the mix . . . The yogi sees that there is an abundance in the world, not a lack, and that to take something that is not freely given shows an imbalance, a distortion of the human personality.

Because he has no desires and feels no envy, he is content with what he has and counts on his Self to provide him with everything he will need, at just the right time. Because he lives in abundance, he is able to give freely and unconditionally of everything he has, and the world rewards him in return." The most valuable gift is the gift of knowledge.

"Non-greed, non-possessiveness points out what these teachings are aiming at. We are greedy because we are scared and insecure, and we use money and possessions to shore up our weak sense of [identity] . . . I feel separate, alienated and isolated from others, and in that isolation I act selfishly." (Forstater, pg. 66) How many times have these kinds of suffering affected us? To what extent is this about having unreasonable expectations?

If we live our own truth, would that help? "Mahatma Gandhi thought so highly of these first two yamas—**non-violence and truth**—that he modeled his life and political program on them. Although it is easy to think of them as too idealistic to put into practice, Gandhi's example, and his achievement in gaining Indian Independence in 1948, proved that these are realistic as well as idealistic methods. Gandhi believed that the truth was God, and that if a person lived his or her own truth with absolute integrity and honesty, this truth would bring them into the closest possible connection with the God they respected and worshiped." (Forstater, pg. 65) The force of his personality was fueled by his humility.

If life is but an illusion, why should we bother concerning ourselves about ethical and moral codes? "Thus, although individual dreams are marked off from real life by the fact that they do not fit into the continuity of experience that runs constantly through life, and waking up indicates this difference, yet that very continuity of experience belongs to real life as its form, and the dream can likewise point to a continuity in itself. Now if we assume a standpoint of judgment external to both, we find no distinct difference in their nature, and are forced to concede to the poets that life is a long dream." (Schopenhauer, pg. 18) Meditation is when we "assume a standpoint of judgment external to both," and we exam our dreams with the same objective measures (mindfulness) and moral scrutiny as we apply to our lives, but we know the difference. For it is in our lives where we engage karma—as will—, and in our dreams where we merely see the consequences or witness the results of our imagination.

Imagine a dangerous situation when you are unable to control the circumstances that are irresolutely headed for some tragic outcome, as in a bad dream, or being at a party where the participants are getting progressively more rowdy and out of control. Recognize that meditation is just the opposite, where there is no danger but relaxation, you are in complete control, you are alone, your mind is thinking serenely and resolving a koan in your life, you feel satisfied (the root word *sati*) and increasingly pleased, and you can make plans for a positive resolve for your future about which you have increasing confidence! This is how we incorporate morality into our choices for our life.

Buddhism is all about teaching us to think before we act (kamma). "A need to distinguish clearly between a first stage of observation and a second stage of taking action [as in meditation] is, according to The Buddha, and essential feature of his way of teaching. The simple reason for this approach is that only the preliminary step of calmly assessing a situation without immediately reacting enables one to undertake the appropriate action." (Analayo, pg. 57) For this reason, when a monk is asked a question they often pause for what seems like a rather long time before proffering the answer. This thoughtful consideration is a moral imperative.

Proverb: Tact is the art of recognizing when to be big and when not to be little. (welpage.com)

Third Progressive:

How will your life be in the future? "Most relationships are based upon the craving to be loved . . . This is a quest for approval and validation in the eyes of another, and no matter how much we receive, usually it is never enough . . . as the individuals caught in these webs begin to battle for power, control, or constant affirmation [complications,] as love turns to hate and then rejection . . . From the Zen point of view, this kind of love is a trap . . . An important core of Zen practice is to dislodge us from addiction to counterfeit forms of love . . . Most feel they have lost something precious in their lives. They have no idea where it has gone or how to retrieve it. Many believe they will find it when they find that one special person or relationship that will take their loneliness away and fill their hungry hearts. But a temporary respite from loneliness cannot give them what they truly crave . . . The further they search for love outside themselves, and the more they think they've found it, *the deeper essential loneliness can grow.*" (Shoshanna, pg. 76) A rational approach to Buddhism can help people apply this useful advice and put their lives into a better perspective. A practicing Buddhist may become more independent, certainly less likely to actively search for superficial, sensually active relationships.

One of the motivations behind the Tantric practice is to be "on the fast track" to enlightenment. This kind of selfish inclination also leads to a distortion of meditation practices and goals. "[These] four influences pertain to a specific level of meditation within the Tantric tradition that corresponds to one of the various levels of attainment in the mahamudra tradition. For example, the Tantric

1. generation stage develops deep concentration using an *extraordinary deity* [what would this be?] as the meditation object. The mahamudra concentration practices use a different meditation object, but the result is the same.
2. The base empowerment potentiates[?] the development of each, respectively.
3. The Tantric perfection stage consists of meditations utilizing subtle [imaginary physical] energy currents. (We must be taught to sense these currents.)
4. Equalization and direct realignment are extraordinary.

Tantric practices potentiated by the insight and wisdom empowerments, respectively." (Brown, pg. 128) Confusing terminology. This is probably not the most skillful way to meditate, since it borders on forcing the outcome, which we now know to be counterproductive. Some of these words are veiled references to the secret, esoteric and sexual practices that are part of Tantra, but first one must love oneself in order to return the blessing to someone else.

If we leave these Buddhist lessons and lapse back into old patterns, or chase new adventures before we apply thoroughly what we know, it may be because . . . "Reflection is a cognitive process, and therefore subject to possible error . . . the 'five faults of not grasping the basis' . . . The potential errors are as follows: 1. not grasping the words, 2. not grasping their meaning, 3. not grasping their subsequent explanation, 4. grasping the meaning incorrectly, and 5. grasping only part of the meaning. These errors must be guarded against, and abandoned when discovered." (Brown, pg. 57) This is an iterative process and when applied in the inverse, invites each Arahant to change, grow, examine and continue their practice and advance their study of dharma.

"From the Zen point of view change is release, it is inevitable [positive not negative.] We are change. Change is not failure. When something changes in a person's life that they haven't initiated they may feel like they've failed, that there's something wrong with them. As people get older they can become encrusted, calling the change they've experienced disappointment. Their lives become smaller and narrower. They meet fewer people, walk fewer blocks, take the same vacations with the same friends every year. They do not want to experience any more change. The life force in this person becomes diminished. Living an encrusted life causes both physical and mental illness. In these cases it's the psychological self causing difficulties, by demanding life to go its way and refusing to look more deeply at the nature of life as it is. Healing is opening up to the power and also to the beauty of change, letting go of our fear of it." (Shoshanna, pp. 120-121) If we fear change, impermanence, we set ourselves up for an unsatisfactory life. This also points to the value of living in the reciprocal care of a Sangha.

We have discussed many different schools of thought relating to Buddhism during these Thirty Lessons, but an ecumenical idea is: ". . . everyone ought to consider Buddhism as Art, as the Art of Living—in other words, as skill and competence in being a human being, living in a way that is exemplary and praiseworthy, which so impresses others that they automatically wish to emulate it. What we have to do is to cultivate the 'Three Lustres,'

1. firstly developing moral purity,
2. then training the mind to be tranquil and steady and fit to do its job,
3. and finally developing such an abundance of wisdom and clear insight into the nature of all things that those things are no longer able to give rise to suffering.

When anyone's life has these Three Lustres, he can be considered to have fully mastered the **art of living** . . . Penetrating so far into the real essence of Buddhism that we are able to take it as our guide to living induces spiritual good cheer and joy, dispersing depression and disillusionment. It also dispels fears, such as the fear that the complete giving up of spiritual defilements would make life dry and dreary and utterly devoid of flavour, or the fear that complete freedom from craving would make all thought and action impossible, whereas in reality a person who organizes his life in accordance with the Buddhist Art of Living is the victor over all the things about him. Regardless of whether these things be animals, people, possessions, or anything else, and regardless of whether they enter that person's consciousness by way of the eye, ear, nose, tongue, body, or mind, they will enter as losers, unable to becloud, defile, or perturb him. The victory over all these things is genuine bliss." (Buddhadasa, 2005, pg. 23)

Meditation Practicum:

"The four syllables [a-ma-na-si] school of mahamudra originated with Maitripa . . . The four points to this teaching on mahamudra include:

1. cutting off the root of ignorance by realizing emptiness,
2. settling the mind in samadhi on the correct view of the natural mind,
3. protecting against errors, and
4. taking the natural mind and its manifestations as the path." (Brown pg. 24)

This relates to a holistic approach, a sequence to follow during each meditation session, then doing it again and again. This is another useful choice in our repertoire.

Here is advice that can become a goal for practice. "There are several ways of applying full awareness during a given meditation session—the episodic method and the continuous method. Less experienced meditators episodically disengage from the meditation object, quickly assess the quality of the body posture and the quality of the meditation (degree of staying, ease of recognizing distraction, amount of effort needed to make the necessary correction and direct the mind back to the intended object, presence or absence of faults such as dullness, etc.), and then redirect the mind back to the intended meditation object. More experienced meditators *reserve a small part of the mind* to practice full awareness continually while the larger part of the mind remains bound to the intended meditation object. It is important to apply full awareness in a balanced way. Trying too hard will only increase thought elaboration. In addition to these standard strategies, the mahamudra tradition recommends utilizing a form of protecting practice at the end of each meditation session." (Brown, pp. 156-157) We have set this as a pattern for our lessons, along with sharing merit. Both of these elements of practice can be carried on even if "protecting" is merely writing in a personal journal.

This following is an admonition in favor of Anapanasati from a different source: "Watching over in-and-out-breathing, thus practiced and developed, brings the four fundamentals of attentiveness to perfection." (Goddard) Use the sixteen step meditation over and over, close your eyes and follow this brief synopsis. Perhaps alternating the structured program of Anapanasati with a more free association is a good practice. Now each Arahat can evaluate this summary.

(Body) "1. Whenever the disciple (a) is conscious in making a long inhalation or exhalation, or (b) in making a short inhalation or exhalation, or (c) is training himself to inhale or exhale whilst feeling the whole (breath-) body, or (d) whilst calming down this bodily function (i.e. the breath)—at such a time the disciple is dwelling in contemplation of the body, full of energy, clearly conscious, attentive, after subduing worldly greed and grief. For, inhalation and exhalation I call one amongst the bodily things." This is our preparation for receptivity to jhanas.

(Feelings) "2. Whenever the disciple is training himself to inhale or exhale (a) whilst feeling the mind [piti,] or, (b) [sukha] joy, or (c) the mental functions, or (d) whilst calming down the mental functions—at such a time he is dwelling in contemplation of the feelings, full of energy, clearly conscious, attentive after subduing worldly greed and grief. For, the full awareness of in-and-out-breathing I call one amongst the feelings."

(Mind) "3. Whenever the disciple is training himself to inhale or exhale (a) whilst feeling the mind, or, (b) whilst gladdening the mind, or (c) whilst concentrating the mind, or (d) whilst setting the mind free—at such a time he is dwelling in contemplation of the mind, full of energy . . . For, without attentiveness and clear consciousness, I say, there is no Watching over In-and-Out-breathing."

(Dharma) "4. Whenever the disciple is training himself to inhale or exhale, whilst contemplating (a) impermanency, or (b) the fading away of passion, or (c) extinction [of defilements,] or (d) detachment—at such a time he is dwelling in contemplation of the phenomena, full of energy, clearly conscious, attentive, after subduing worldly greed and grief."

"Watching over in-and-out-breathing, thus practiced and developed, brings the four fundamentals of attentiveness to perfection." (Goddard, pp. 54-55)

There is more good advice that can be applied in our every day lives that comes from the advice of Buddha. "A close examination of the instructions in the Satipatthana Sutta reveals that the meditator is never instructed to interfere actively with what happens in the mind. If a mental hindrance arises, for example, the task of satipatthana contemplation is to know that the hindrance is present, to know what has led to its arising, and to know what will lead to its disappearance. A more active intervention is no longer the domain of satipatthana, but belongs rather to the province of right effort." Meditation is successful . . . In summary, ". . . satipatthana is [also] the 'direct path' . . . to the realization of Nibbana. This way of understanding also fits well with the final passage of the Satipatthana Sutta. Having stated that satipatthana practice can lead to the two higher stages of realization within a maximum of seven years, [. . . *and reduces its invitation to seven days!!*] the discourse closes with the declaration: 'because of this, it has been said—this is the direct path' . . . in the sense of its potential to lead to the highest stages of realization within a limited period of time." (Analayo, pp. 28-29) This is the theme of *Bodhicitta: Higher Truth.*

"But how do the four fundamentals of attentiveness [mindfulness], practiced and developed [in both Anapanasati and Satipatthana,] bring the seven **Elements of Enlightenment** to full perfection?" These are a restatement of the awakening factors in the Satipatthana teaching. (Review Chapter 25.) Contemplate this as a koan.

"1. Whenever the disciple is dwelling in contemplation on the body, feelings, mind and phenomena, strenuous, clearly conscious, attentive, after subduing worldly greed and grief—at such time his attentiveness [mindfulness] is undisturbed . . . he has gained . . . the Element of Enlightenment **Attentiveness** . . ."

"2. And whenever, whilst dwelling with attentive mind, he wisely investigates, examines and thinks over the Law (Dhamma)—at such a time he has gained and is developing the element of Enlightenment [called] **Investigation** of the Law; and thus this element of enlightenment reaches fullest perfection.

"3. And whenever, whilst wisely investigating, examining and thinking [with enthusiasm] over the law, his energy is firm and unshaken—at such a time he has gained and is developing the Element of Enlightenment **Energy** . . ."

"4. And whenever in him, whilst firm in energy, arises super-sensuous rapture at such a time he has gained and is developing the Element of Enlightenment **Rapture** . . ."

"5. And whenever, whilst enraptured in mind, his body and mind becomes tranquil at such a time he has gained and is developing the element of Enlightenment **Tranquility** . . ."

"6. And whenever, whilst tranquillized in body and happy, his mind becomes concentrated—at such a time he has gained and is developing the Element of Enlightenment **Concentration**; and thus this element of enlightenment reaches fullest perfection."

"7. And whenever he thoroughly looks with indifference to his mind thus concentrated—at such a time he has gained and is developing the Element of Enlightenment **Equanimity**."

"The Seven Elements of Enlightenment, practiced and developed, bring Wisdom and Deliverance to perfection . . . bent on detachment, absence of desire, extinction and renunciation . . . so that he may drive out of himself[/herself] his[/her] wonted worldly ways and wishes, his wonted worldly unruliness, obstinacy, and violence, and win to the True and realize Nibbana." (Goddard, pp. 54-55) This is a difficult sequence to follow in one gulp, that is why we learned each of the sixteen contemplations of Anapanasati one at a time, and it is a good thing that we have the rest of our lives to unravel Satipatthana (see *Bodhicitta: Higher Truth*) as well.

Biographical Sketch:

"Though a formal distinction is actually made in Japan between the clergy and the laity, Southern Buddhists, who still attempt to preserve the organization and strict precepts of the time of Shakyamuni, recognize nothing like either Order or monks in Japanese Buddhism today. Nothing resembling the rules and way of life of the ancient Sangha is in effect, and many Japanese *priests have wives and children and live very much like ordinary lay believers.* The use of the Japanese term [Vimalakirti] for the Order to indicate the whole body of believers, lay and clergy alike, results from this set of circumstances." What changes would this make in the actual practice or efficacy of Buddhism? Is this a more rational approach?

"One may give up the world physically and become a nun or a monk, or one may remain in the world while devoting oneself to religious development. In Japan, where the characteristic Mahayana flexibility finds wide application, actual physical separation from the world—which is still practiced by Theravada Buddhists—is much rarer than spiritual devotion to the religious life while remaining part of ordinary society. This attitude has long been preferred in Japan and is symbolized by the life of the ancient wealthy Indian lay householder named Vimalakirti, who remained a layman yet attained great heights of enlightenment. Vimalakirti became popular among Japanese Buddhists at an early time." (Mizuno, pp. 107-108) Is this *a more compassionate Buddhism*?

Buddha told Ananda and the assembly of Monks (on the eve of his death) that he would have no successor: the only teacher after his death would be the Dhamma (the teachings) itself. To the assembly of the monks he spoke his last words: "all conditioned things are of a nature to decay—strive on untiringly." (Inthisan, pg. 61) There are, however, numerous teachers and bodhisattvas who have contributed to the development of Buddhism including such luminaries as, Ananda, Nagarjuna, Osho, Boowa, Chah, Man(Mun), Buddhadasa Bikkhu, and the Dalai Lama in various incarnations . . . can you name any more?

Reading for the Day:

"When you're trained as a Buddhist, you don't think of Buddhism as a religion. You think of it as a type of science, a method of exploring your own experience through techniques that enable you to examine your actions and reactions in a nonjudgmental way, with the view toward recognizing, 'Oh, this is how my mind works. This is what I need to do to experience happiness. This is what I should avoid to avoid unhappiness.' At its heart, Buddhism is very practical." (Mingyur, pg. 11) Yet if we miss the benefits of associating with Buddhism as a religion, we have missed a great deal that we could experience without creating attachments to it.

"Thus . . . enlightenment is both liberation and also a manifestation of omniscience—the awakened wisdom of the Buddha. The awakened mind of the Buddha manifests as **infinite wisdom and inexhaustible compassion** [the significance of the two lit candles in many rituals.] Thus while early Buddhism emphasizes the eradication of negative qualities, Mahayana enlightenment entails the full manifestation of all positive qualities of mind, the quintessence of our human potential." (Brown, pg. 7) And when we combine these two approaches [science and compassion] with the ritual of Taking Refuge, we have an even better chance at success!

Protecting:

"This is what I heard," review by both Arahant and teacher.

Additional Teaching:

". . . In adapting and developing suitable rituals as an integral part of our practice, we come to realize the inestimable role they play in strengthening our resolve and motivation, offering as they do, a tangible form by which we can express our commitment and devotion." (Cittaviveka, pg. 8) Participation in appropriate rituals can help us develop the capacity of our Hearts.

"The ideal student of Buddhism would be one who, whether scientifically trained or not, was prepared to admit the possibility of a spiritual experience which would transcend the physical senses and the rational mind, and who would be willing to give unprejudiced consideration to the Buddha's claim that he had achieved this experience himself and that by following his Teaching others might achieve it for themselves too. Such a person would not commit the mistake of thinking that the intellect, though capable of performing useful preliminary work, was able to penetrate the inner meaning of Buddhism, or that Truth would reveal itself to any faculty save to *intuition awakened by spiritual practice*. He or she would be free from beliefs which, though they pass for religious doctrines in the world, are in fact born of fear, craving and other egocentric emotions. Resolved fearlessly to pursue, frankly to examine and faithfully to accept and follow, whatever the truth about Buddhism might turn out to be, such an ideal student could be said to be fairly well equipped for the study of Buddhism, and to approach the Dharma with at least an approximation to Right Motive [Mindfulness] in the specifically Buddhist sense." (Sangharakshita, 1957, pg. 38.) We suspend our rational thinking long enough and in the same way we might when reading, feeling or writing poetry with the intention of being inspired and moved emotionally. Return to Chapter Six, and reread the predictions that were made about Right View, and see how your understanding has changed after all this work.

"Even now, we must know nibbana [be cool and ready] to some extent in order to be able to sit here and discuss Dhamma like this . . . Therefore, we should understand that Nibbana is related to us at all times, with every inhalation and exhalation . . . when lust, hatred, and delusion aren't present in our minds, we experience a small degree of Nibbana, a brief taste or free sample of Nibbana . . . Keep calming and cooling things, that is, destroy 'I' and 'mine'." (Buddhadasa, 1993, pp. 34-35) by developing the Heart.

Sharing Merit:

Rejoicing In Others' Merit (Saying Sadhu)

Buddhist Sutra

Lesson Title: **Commencement—Cautions**

Lesson Number: **Thirty**

Assignment:
Meditate on each of the four insights.

1. The world is transient,
2. The body is impure
3. To produce good, and
4. to increase good when produced.

What changes in the actual practice or efficacy of Buddhism would it make to have monks living in their married households?

Is this a more rational approach?

Review "refuge" as explained in Lesson Eighteen.

How is the teaching of the middle way so unique? (Lesson Three)

"No matter how long you meditate, or what technique you use, every technique of Buddhist meditation ultimately generates compassion . . ." (Mingyur, pg. 251) discuss

How has reflection become part of your Spiritual Practice?

Recall from Lesson Eleven on Right Effort (pg. 107) ". . . the six defilements:

1. pride, that is, looking without really listening, or listening disrespectfully;
2. lack of faith;
3. lack of effort toward the truth;
4. distraction toward external things, so as not to mirror the teaching in thought;
5. shutting down the mind, that is, falling asleep; and
6. fatigue, that is, listening with a wandering mind and failing to intellectually understand the meaning of the teachings.

Such defilements must be abandoned, and the [Practitioner] must 'listen without defilements day and night.' Otherwise . . . 'you will cast aside the teachings'."

Measure your character against these six standards.

If we recall that nirvana is a point of view as well as a way of living, we can see that it is obtainable, it is not a mystical connection of constant or even frequent bliss—it is the mind's intrinsic nature when it is accessible and able to be shared.

Bibliography

Access: http://www.accesstoinsight.org/lib/authors/gunaratana/wheel351.html#ch1.3

Active Meditation: *http://www.activemeditation.com/ActiveMeditations/FiveStages.html*

Aitken, Robert, 1982. Taking the Path of Zen. New York: North Point Press.

Analayo, PhD. (ne Steffens), 2003. Satipatthana, The Direct Path to Realization. Cambridge: Windhorse Publications Ltd.

Armstrong, Karen, 2006. The Great Transformation, The beginning of our Religious Traditions. Alfred A. Knopf: New York.

Baba, Meher, 1967. Discourses. Sheriar Press, Inc. USA.

Berzin. http://www.berzinarchives.com/web/en/archives/e-books/unpublished_manuscripts/ making_sense_tantra . . .

Bloom, Alfred, 2007. Translated by Ruben Habito. The Essential Shinran, A Buddhist path of true entrusting. Bloomington, IN: World Wisdom, Inc.

Brown, Daniel P., PhD., 2006. Pointing Out The Great Way, The stages of meditation in the Mahamudra tradition. Boston: Wisdom Publications.

Boowa, Venerable Acayiya Maha Boowa Nanasampanno, 1998. Free Book, A Life of Inner Quality, A comprehensive guide to Buddhist practice. Udorn Thani: Wat Pa Baan Taad, c/o Songserm Service. 41000 Thailand.

Boowa, http://www.what-buddha-taught.net/Books4/Maha_Boowa_Amata_Dhamma.pdf

Buddhadasa Bhikkhu, May18-20, 2548/2005. Handbook for Mankind, International Buddhist Conference on the United Nations Day of Vesak, UNESCO, Bangkok: Thammasapa Press.

1. 2006. The Truth of Nature. The Master Buddhadasa Explains the Buddha's Teachings. Bangkok: Amarin Publishing.
2. 2003. A Handbook for a perfect form of Anapanasati-Bhavana. Condensed by: Chien Nurn Eng. Translated by James RtanaNantho Bhikku. Bangkok: Mental Health Publishing House.
3. 2001. Happiness and Hunger, brochure by Atammayata for Wisdom and Perfection Project.
4. 1999. Keys to Natural Truth, translated by Santikaro Bhikkhu, Rod Bucknell and others. Bangkok: The Dhamma Study & Practice Group. Third printing: Mental Health Publishing.
5. 1993. No Religion, brochure by buddhadharma Meditaton Center, Hinsdale, Il. The Dhammadana Foundation.
6. 1988. Mindfulness with Breathing, A manual for Serious Beginners. Translated by Santikaro Bhikkhu, Chaing Mai: Silkworm Books.

Buddhaghosa, Bhadantacariya, 400 abt. The path of purification, **Visuddhimagga.** Translated from the Pali by Bhikkhu Nanamoli. Singapore: Singapore Buddhist Meditation Centre.

Bullitt, John, 2005. What is Theravada Buddhism? http://www.accesstoinsight.org/lib/authors/bullitt/ theravada.html

Carrithers, Michael, 1983. The Buddha. Oxford: Oxford University Press (Past Masters).

Chan, Victor, and His Holiness the Dalai Lama, 2004. The Wisdom of Forgiveness. Intimate Conversations and Journeys. New York: Riverhead Books—Penguin Group (USA) Inc.

Chapman, Gary, 1992. The Five Love Languages, How to Express Heartfelt Commitment to Your Mate. Chicago: Northfield Publishing.

Chittaviveka, 2001. Buddhist Rituals & Observances, by Ajahns Sucitto and Candasiri, Amaravati Publications, from the internet.

Dalai Lama, 2005. The Essential Dalai Lama, His important teachings. Edited by Rajiv Mehrotra, New York: Viking.

Dattajeevo, Phra Phadet, 2007. Dhamma Talk by Phrabhavanaviriyakhun, Bangkok: Rung Silp Printing Co. Ltd.

de Bary, Theodore, et. al. 1969. The Buddhist Tradition, in India, China, and Japan. New York: Random House, Inc.

de Bary, Wm. Theodore, (ed) 1960. Sources of Chinese Tradition. Columbia University Press.

Edwards, Paul. Editor in Chief, 1967. The Encyclopedia of Philosophy. New York: Macmillan Publishing Co., Inc. & The Free Press.

Erricker, Clive, 1995. Buddhism, world faiths. London: Hodder Headline Plc.

Forstater, Mark, and Jo Manuel, 2002. Yoga Masters, How Yoga theory can deepen your practice and meditation. Cambridge University Press.

Frost, Gavin and Yvonne Frost, 1989. Tantric Yoga, The Royal Path to Raising Kundalini Power. York Beach, Main: Samuel Weiser, Inc.

Forman, Judith, 1987. Bhagwan: The Buddha for the Future. Poona, India: The Rebel Publishing House.

Garfield, Jay L., 1995. The Fundamental Wisdom of the Middle Way; Nagarjuna's Mulamadhyamakakarika. Oxford: Oxford University Press.

Getty, Alice, 1988. The gods of northern Buddhism. New York, Dover Publications, Inc.

Goddard, Dwight, 1938. A Buddhist Bible. Boston: Beacon Press.

Gunaratana, Bhante Henepola, 2009. Beyond Mindfulness, in plain English. Somerville, MA: Wisdom Publications.

Inthisan, Phramaha Thanat, 2007. Walking on the Path of The Buddha, edited by Duwayne Engelhart. Samutprakarn, Thailand: Pimpinit Printing Ltd., Part.

Hanh, Thich Nhat, 2004. Taming the Tiger Within, Meditations on Transforming Difficult Emotions. Eddited by Pritam Singh. New York, Riverhead Books (Peguin Group).

~1998. The Heart of the Buddha's Teaching, Transforming Suffering into Peace, Joy, and Liberation. New York: Broadway Books.

~2012. Awakening of the Heart—essential Buddhist sutras and commentaries. Berekely, CA: Parallax Press—Unified Buddhist Church, Inc.

Holymtn: http://www.holymtn.com/teapots/sutra.htm

Jacob, Irvin H. 1967-91. Jack and Lucky. Internet Book

-Frame of Reference, 2003, internet Book

Kagyu Thubten Choling, 1999. Karmapa: The Sacred Prophecy. Eds. Willa Baker et al. Wappinger Falls, NY: Kagyu Thubten Choling Publications Committee.

Khantipalo: http://www.accesstoinsight.org/lib/authors/khantipalo/wheel206.html#meditation

Kokusai: http://www.sotozen-net.or.jp/kokusai/sotozenschool.htm

Kornfield, Jack and Paul Breiter, eds. 1985. A still forest Pool: The Insight Meditation of Achaan Chah. Weaton, IL: Theosophical Publishing House.

McLeod, Melvin, 2009. The best Buddhist writing. Edited. Boston: Shambhala Publications, Inc.

Mehrotra, Rajiv editor,—and Dalai Lama. 2005. The Essential Dalai Lama, His Important Teachings. New Delhi: The Foundation for Universal Responsibility of His Holiness the Dalai Lama.

Mingyur, Yongey Rinpoche, 2007. The Joy of Living. Unlocking the secret and science of happiness. New York, Harmony Books. (written with Eric Swanson.)

Mizuno, Kogen, 1980. The beginnings of Buddhism. (Bukkyo no Genten) Translated by Richard L. Gage. Tokyo: Kosei Publishihng Co.

Mondo: http://goliath.ecnext.com/coms2/gi_0199-1543776/The-Zen-Mondo-an-analytical.html

Moore, W. Edgar. 1955. Creative and Critical Thinking.

Nyanatiloka, Mahathera, 2004. Buddhist Dictionary, A Manual of Buddhist terms and Doctrines. Chaing Mai: Silkworm Books.

Pannapadipo, Pra Peter, 1998. One Step at a Time, Buddhist meditation for absolute beginners. Bangkok: The Post Publishing Plc.

Payutto, P.A., 1994. Dependent Origination, The Buddhist law of conditionality, translated from the Thai by Burce Evans. Bangkok: Buddhadhamma Foundation.

Plamintr, Sunthorn, Ph. D. 2007. The discovery of Buddhism. splamintr01@yahoo.com. Nueng, Nonthaburi: Write & Read Publishing Co., Ltd.

Radhakrishnan, Sarvepalli; and Charles A. Moore, 1957. A Source Book In Indian Philosophy. Princeton, NJ: Princeton University Press.

Sacred texts: http://www.sacred-texts.com/bud/cob/cob07.html

Saddhatissa, Ven. Dr. H., 2007. An Introduction to Buddhism. The Council of Thai Bhikkhus in U.S.A. Wat Mongkolratanaram of Florida.

Salzberg, Sharon, 2002. Lovingkindness, The Revolutionary Art of Happiness. Boston & London: Shambhala.

Sangharakshita, 1997. The rainbow road. Melksham, Wiltshire: The Cromwell Press.

Schettini, Stephen, 2009. The Novice, why I became a Buddhist monk, why I quit and what I learned. Austin TX: Greenleaf Book Group Press

Shoshanna, Brenda, Ph.D., 2002. Zen Miracles, Finding Peace in an Insane World. New York: John Wiley & Sons, Inc.

Smith, Huston; and Philip Novak, 2003. Buddhism: A Concise Introduction. San Francisco: Harper Collins. http://www.harpercollins.com

Snelling, John, 1991. The Buddhist Handbook, A complete guide to Buddhist schools, teaching, practice, and History. Rochester, VT: Inner Traditions International.

Stanford Encyclopedia of Philosophy (Schopenhauer) 2003. http://plato.stanford.edu/entries/schopenhauer/

Sunnahonline: http://www.sunnahonline.com/ilm/dawah/0020.html

Surya Das, Lama, 2007. Buddha is as Buddha does. San Francisco: HarperCollins.

Suvanno, Loo-Ang Por Kamkee-an, 2006. Watching: Not 'Being', following the Satipatthana Sutta. Translanted by Venerable Tone Jinavamao (A.G.J. van der Bom). Bangkok: Kled Thai, Ltd.

Suzuki, D. T., 1956. Zen Buddhism, selected writings of d.t.suzuki. William Barrett, Ed. New York, Doubleday, Image Books, 1996.

ukonline: http://web.ukonline.co.uk/buddhism/merits.htm

Ussivakul, Archan Vinai, 2003 (2546). An introduction to Buddhist Meditation for results. Bangkok: Tipitaka Study Center, Tippayawisuit Ltd., Partnership. (Courtesy of Sally and Ian Timm.)

Virtue: http://www.virtuescience.com/defilements.html

Vishvapani, 2001. Introducing the Friends of the Western Buddhist Order. Birmingham: Windhorse Publications.

Walpola Sri Rahula, 1959. What the Buddha Taught. Oxford, England: Oneworld Publications.

Watson, Burton, 1993. The Lotus Sutra. New York: Columbia University Press.

Watts, Alan W., 1957. The Way of Zen. New York: Vintage Books, Alfred A. Knopf, Inc., Random House, Inc., Pantheon books Inc.

Wee, Handyman, 2007. Techniques and Tips on Concentration Meditation and Insight Meditation in Buddhism. Translated from Thai by Saichol Chuncharoephol. Bangkok: National Office of Buddhist Printing.

Wellpage.com; Oregon Health Foundation, Seaside, OR. (expired page)

Wittgenstein, Ludwig,1953. Philosophical Investigations, translated by G.E.M. Anscombe. New York: The Macmillan Company.

Zimmer, Heinrich, 1951. Philosophies of India. Edited by Joseph Campbell. Bollingen Foundation Inc., New York: Meridian Books, Inc.

Glossary

Abhidharma—last part of the Tipitaka, it has been described as philosophy, psychology, Metaphysics. Detailed and systematic analyses of Buddha's teachings.

Abhijjha—covetousness, desires—

Abhijjhadomanassa—desires and discontent

abhinivesa—clinging to life or to a process that should go on without end. Hindrance.

absolute bodhicitta—direct insight into the nature of mind, all people are perfect buddhas

absorption—Jhana

abyakatapanha—questions which the Buddha would not answer—not skillful.

Acariya—Teacher, term of respect for a senior Bhikkhu.

Acinteyya—the unthinkable, incomprehensible

Action potential—Karma (Kamma) is frequently described as action, or potential or wrongly as accumulated destiny or inheritance.

Addictions—to chase bliss in meditation instead of growth

Adinava—the unsound or noxious quality of a thing desired, that creates suffering.

Admiration—intensified interest, as for a cherished possession

Adrenaline—a chemical produced by the body to enhance awareness and defenses

advanced preliminaries—developed mind when signs indicate success in meditation—special insight

aesthetic—the artistic side of life, also in virtue and human conduct

Afterlife—a belief, or figment of our historical imagination, often attributed to Buddhism

Affirmation—slogan, verse, used as a ritual or oath

Aggregates (five)—(Sanskrit skandha, Pali khandha, (group") The five aspects that make up human appearance and being, 1. material composition, 2. sensations, 3. perceptions, 4. mental formations, 5. and consciousness. These are impermanent, constantly, changing, and do not constitute a "self." Or our soulless nature.

Ahamkara—the creation of the 'I' ego consciousness

akaraparivitakkena—question common sense, doubt intuitions or snap judgments

Akusala—unwholesome

Amida—(Japanese; Sanskrit Amitabha, "infinite light") Celestial Buddha who, while a bodhisattva, vowed to lead all beings to the Pure Land. Amida is the focus of devotion in Pure Land Buddhism and one of several revered Buddhas of the Mahayana tradition whose name is often repeated in chanting.

Anagami—non-returner, next to Arahat in transcendent insight

analytical methods—meditation that involves dissolving sources of suffering

Anapanasati (-bhavana)—the cultivation of mindfulness (to recall anything at all as an object while breathing in and breathing out) with attention to breathing. Meditation scheme that is based on the Four Foundations of Mindfulness.

Anatman—no soul, no Higher Self as taught in yoga.

Anatta—(Pali: anatta) The understanding that there is no "Soul" that resides in the body nor a living essence that persists after this life. One of three universal characteristics of all phenomena (with annica and dukkha.)

Androgynous—incorporating features of both genders

Angst—as in existential angst, to be perplexed by your entire future at once

Anicca—Impermanence—aniccam, inconstancy, a universal characteristic which is a source of suffering.

aniccanupassana—contemplating impermanence completely—step thirteen

anjali—hands together, respect, single-pointed

Anupassana—contemplation: method of training cognition, wise reflection as a basis for sustained practice.

Anusaya—latent tendency, mental habits, proclivities
anussavena—questioning, healthy skepticism
anuttara-samyak-sambodhi—buddhahood, ultimate wisdom and serenity, perfect
Application—bodhicitta focuses on the path or practice to obtain fruits of meditation
Arahant—(Arhant) (Sanskrit, "foe-destroyer") (Arhat—Pali) One who is free from craving and has attained nirvana, the goal of Theravada Buddhism.
arahathaphala—final freedom, final stage of holiness or final freedom which is the ultimate goal of Buddhism.
Arising—samudaya
Ariya—Noble, enlightened, prefix (ariyan—noble one)
ariya-dhana—Noble wealth; inner riches: qualities which serve as capital in the quest for liberation—conviction, virtue, conscience, scrupulousness, breadth of learning, generosity and wisdom.
Ariya-sacca—Noble truth; The Four Noble Truths: and all four stages.
Ariya puggala—A Noble One; a supreme person; one who has attained to any of the four transcendent paths: Stream-enterer, Once-returner, Non-returner, or Arahant.
Arupa—Immaterial, formless, non substantial, incorporeal.
Arupa-jhana—meditative absorption in a formless mental notion or state.
Asava—the ingrained seedbeds of defilements, outflow (effluents) from conditioned origination, 'flow out' from the Heart into thoughts, speech, and action. (4)Sensual desire, desire for existence, views and opinions, and fundamental ignorance.
Ashoka—ruler about 200 years after Buddha who established Buddhism, built columns
Ashrana—set back, failing to practice; anashara, no setback
asmita—the crude sense of I am, that can be overcome in the Heart. Self-identity that is an Hindrance.
Aspiration—bodhicitta that focuses on result of practice
Assada—the attractive, satisfying, lovely, infatuating quality of charm of something—which creates emotions, craving and desires that lead to suffering.
Atapi—diligence, "tapas", ascetic practices

Attachments—is like an addiction or compulsion to an external source for happiness

Aversion—fear of losing what makes us happy, generates feelings of fear or vulnerability

Avidya—(Sanskrit, "Ignorance," Pali: avijja) Fundamental ignorance, which is the root of suffering. Delusion about the nature of the mind, lack of insight. Ignorance so profound that it is self-obscuring, turning everything upside down, it makes us believe that what is wrong is right, what is unimportant is important, what is bad is good. An Hindrance.

awakening—(bojjhanga) the emergence of suddha, faith, Buddha's enlightenment.
Mudra: right hand touching ground "repelling of Mara" meeting reality, dispelling delusion

Awareness—sati, carefulness

Avijja—ignorance, nescience, delusion; ignorance to the Four Noble Truths.

Ayatana—sense bases; often distinguished as internal or external

bad mental state—

Barter—an exchange of effort to be virtuous, to receive peace and happiness

Basis—condensed visions of the "right view" of the enlightened mind

Believer—(belief—yid chas pa, Tibetan) beginning practitioner

bhabbarupataya—question authorities, avoid dogma and indoctrination

Bhava—becoming, state of existence, precondition for birth;

Bhavana—mental growth, cultivation, meditation, training to cultivate concentration

Bhavatanha—craving for being, craving for states of becoming.

Bhikkhu—Buddhist monk who depends on the generosity, begging for basic necessities.

Bijaniyama—the natural law of cause and effect pertaining to heredity, or biological lawa; one of five niyama or natural laws

Bikkhuni—A female monastic.

Bindu—droplets of wind energy—mystical relating to chakras.

Birth—arising of the idea of "I am." in a figurative sense in the Buddhist language game.

bliss—mental state of calm, pleasurable perceptive peace, everything is made of love.

Blurting—speaking out suddenly with out thinking

Bodh Gaya—Buddha's place of enlightenment

Bodhicitta—(Sanskrit, "thought of enlightenment") An important concept in Mahayana

Buddhism. Personal resolve to strive for enlightenment. In a cosmic sense it is the reality that makes enlightenment possible. (wise-mind/heart) In Tantric

Buddhism, it is the fusion of wisdom with compassion in the bliss of perfect enlightenment for the benefit of others.

Bodhisattva—(Sanskrit, "one whose essence is wisdom") In Mahayana Buddhism, future buddhas who postpone nirvana (out of compassion) in order to help free others from suffering. Goal of Mahayana Buddhism—to be an Awakening-being.

Bodhi tree—(Bodhi—wisdom of enlightenment—"awakened" Buddhahood; state of full enlightenment, in which things are seen as they really are.) Tree under which Buddha first received enlightenment. Distinctive pointed leaf. Ficus religiosa

Brahma—supreme Hindu God, non corporeal, mystical

Brahmacariya—the Higher Life, the Divine Life; life of celibacy and religious training

bramaloka—"heaven" where there are no objects of sensuality.

Brahman—Hindu holy lineage, keeper of the tradition.

Brahmin—caste in India; to denote a religious man worthy of respect

brightness—Quality of mind un-obscured by elaborated thoughts, generating concentration.

Buddhahood—(Sanskrit and Pali: Buddha—"Awakened One" A fully enlightened being.) That which in each of us resides as the potential to become enlightened as a buddha, and live in nirvana. As: the Buddha icons are a mirror of our own buddhahood. Buddha-nature (Sanskrit; buddhata; Japanese bussho)—anuttara-samyak-sambodhi

Buddhas of the ten directions—metaphorical place of rejuvenation

buddho—awake; one who has attained enlightenment.

Butsu—(Japanese) Buddha
Byapada—aversion

calming—advanced stage of meditation; stay for long time. (Samatha)
carelessness—cause and effect dealing with the individual, past, present and future. serious fault
Celibacy—giving up sexual stimulation in favor of ascetic ways—to preserve power
Cessation—nirodha
Cetana—intention, choice, volition
Chado—(Japanese "tea-way") Tea ceremony in Zen Buddhism. Intended to overcome ordinary consciousness and subject-object distinctions, dualism.
chakra—force, energy centers in the body
Chant—syllables that connect to ancient traditions and pacify our turbulent minds
chanda—desire
Ch'an—(also Chan, Chinese) Zen (from jhana, dhyana)
chauvinist—forceful personality, i.e. that dominates the opposite gender
ci energy—Tai Chi, Chinese martial dance form
citta—feeling aspect of the mind; loving open space of the "Heart," state of mind.
Underlying essence (abstraction) of mind that manifests as feeling, memory, thought, and consciousness. It is that fundamental quality of knowing in the Heart, because the experience of those who are skilled in meditation is that the incoming sensations appear to 'gravitate' to the Heart, so it is from here that the manifestations of the citta appear to spring forth.
cittanapassana—contemplation of the mind / Heart when breathing
cittaniyama—the natural law of cause and effect pertaining to the workings of the mind, psychic laws; on of five niyama or natural laws
Clarity—understanding right view, "figuring it out," creative aspect. (alokasanna)
cleansing—rituals or ceremonies, i.e. that allow us to forgive ourselves
clinging—upadana

clearly knowing—sampajanna
cognition—sanna
cognitive restructuring—developing new neuronal pathways in the brain.
Confidence—saddha
Compassion—karuna
Compounded things—Complications in one's life. consequences of action that may be changed
completion stage—enhances manifestations of essential nature in tantra
conceit—unwillingness to listen or learn (mana)
Concentration Meditation—of eighth step of the Four Noble Truths (samadhi)
Concepts—theories, beliefs based on intuition, logic or solutions to mysteries, even memories—proliferataion (papanca)
condition a new birth—epiphany for new beginnings, changing one's life, attaching "I am" or "mine" to an even or thing.
conditioning factors—what we have been taught since birth
Conditional co-arising—The operation of dependent co-arising stems from ". . . the conditional interrelation of phenomena, constituting a web of interwoven events, (like twelve links in a chain) where each event is related to other events by way of both cause and effect. Each conditioning factor is at the same time itself conditioned . . . which thereby excludes the possibility of a transcendent, independent cause." (Analayo, pg. 110)
conflictual emotional states—cognitive dissonance, causing indecision
consciousness—vinnana
Contemplation—to focus on an object or concept—(anupassana)
Craving—tanha
cynicism—a negative approach, critical to a fault

Dana—most often refers to a gift to the monastic order. To give selflessly brings lasting happiness to the giver, thus it is central to Buddhist practice. also generosity
Defilements—bad habits that create suffering, non-skilful behaviors—pg. 214

delusion—falling asleep, lapsing into inattention, aversion to painful experience—(moha)
delight—pamojja
dependent co-arising—paticca samuppada
desire—abhijjha
Despair—unresolved sadness
Destroyers—perceptions or experience acting as raw human nature, aggregates
Devotion—exercise of pure faith
Dhammaniyama—the universal natural law of cause and effect.
Dharma (dhamma)—Buddha-dharma—Teachings of the Buddha, another name for Buddhism. 1) The way nature is. 2) the laws of nature, 3) the duties 4) the truth. In the plural means: objects of mind, concepts, theories.
dialectic—theories that expose two contrasting points of view
Diligence—repeated practice, routine meditation—(atapi)
directing—steering the mind to stay on the intended object
Discipline—ability to do what one knows is appropriate
Discontent—domanassa
Disenchantment—anabhirati
Dispassion—viraga
Dissatisfaction—arati
Ditthasava—the outflow of views (attachment to or delusion in views)
Ditthi—views, beliefs, preferences, ideals either good or bad. Right or wrong.
Ditthinijjhanakkhantiya—question proofs and empirical methods, avoid finding facts to fit and support argument
Ditthupadana—clinging to views and opinions, one of four bases of clinging
Dojo—(Japanese) place of enlightenment, under the dodhi tree; the training center
Domanassa—grief
Doors of perception—five faculties of sense perception (plus mental concousness)
dopamine—chemical produced by the brain that simulates happiness
Dorje Chang Tungma—

Dosa—anger, hatred, aversion, even self recrimination, lack of self-esteem, failure to forgive oneself, oppressed, irritated, offended, or resentful.

Doubt—vicikiccha

Dreamscape—mental screen, visualization, dream theatre

dualistic ignorance—distinguishing between self and other, and seeing others as a source for happiness.

Dukkha—(Pali) (-Sanskrit: duhkha) Suffering—the first of the Four Noble Truths. The unsatisfactory nature of all phenomena. One of three universal characteristics of existence. That which is difficult to endure.

Dukkham—it is painful and unbearable

dullness—unable to focus or unwilling to think seriously. lacking spirituality

dvesa—hatred, repugnance, disinclination

Dzinpa—(Tibetan) craving, grasping

ecstatic meditation—a goal of Tantric practice, or a physical activity to change focus

effort—vayama

Ekaggata—Means 'to have a single peak, focus, or apex.' Single minded.

Ekayano—direct path

ego—Freudian concept of the personality

Elaborated—a mind that is lost in constructing content and images, wandering

emotional blackmail—a teaching that employs guilt or release from suffering as a ploy

Emotional response—feeling that results from a perception

Empathy—understand the feelings of others in a visceral way

empowerment—respect for ancient teachings is prerequisite, through extreme admiration we gain power.

emptiness—is full, an essence, abstract concept, soullessness—necessitates interdependence—(sunnata)

Enlightenment—owning wisdom, dharma is your life

epinephrine—a chemical that stimulates the body and heart

Epiphany—sudden realization or understanding

Equanimity—in the fourth jhana, absorption, aware of object only, beyond feelings of pain or pleasure. Follow teachings fairly, even-handily, consistently—upekkha
erroneous ideas—negative habits block our minds from realizing our real nature
Esoteric Buddhism—mystical concepts, i.e. the benefit of chanting ancient sounds.
esoteric power—the possibility of paranormal experiences
Essence—the central theme or concept, the thread that connects different aspects
establishment—(create habits?)
eternal life—mysterious religious concept relating to continued existence in afterlife
ethical conduct—sila
ethno centric—a bias toward one's own cultural conditioning
Euphoria—our sense of ecstatic happiness in lesser jhana
Eye of the Law—understanding Right View, status of Arahant
Existence—bhava
External life—avocation, vocations; relationships with family, friends—bhiddha, bahira
Extinction—the ideal condition in which suffering has been totally extinguished

faculty—indriya
fading away—viraga—dispassion
falling away—in the ritual of dojo, zazen, the bells and clappers, the order of eating a meal, the sutras and the bows, all encourage the experience of . . .
false speech—musavada
Fear—source of restriction on our personality and ability to follow the path
Feeling—vedana
fetters—obstacles to developing one pointedness, pg. 122—(samyojana)
Figure of speech—a way of speaking, such as a poetic device or colloquial phrase
five-point prostration—preparation for meditation, to convey a sense of calm composure

Five Precepts—(sila) Customarily the oaths repeated at the time of ordination into Buddhism. Obligations that both monks and laypersons undertake. They are to 1. abstain from harming any living being; 2. taking anything not given; 3. sensual misconduct; 4. false speech; and 5. losing control through intoxication.
flood of joy—accomplishment in obtaining Jhana
fondling—taking precepts repeatedly and interrupting practices over and over
form—rupa
formation—sankhara
formless sphere—mental influences
four quadrants—*scanning of the four quadrants,* unobstructed knowledge, mudra
freedom by wisdom—pannavimutti
freedom of the mind—cetovimutti
Fruition—achieving signs during meditation, and developed meditation skill
full awareness—Right Understanding, View, wisdom, nirvana

gacchami—(Pali) going to, will undertake
gassho—(Japanese) to join the palms in reverence, greeting or respect
Gautama—The given name of the historical Buddha.
generating stage—complex visualizations to stabilize the mind—Tantric
giving and taking—Tonglen
good—punna/ kusala
goose bumps—sign of jhana, at the lesser thrill first stage
great—mahaggata
grace—to hear Lotus Sutra, believe, understand and embrace it; our ontological existence
Great Faith—does not need an external object for meditation, concentration
Greed—lobha
Guru—(Sanskrit)—Spiritual teacher in Yoga and Hinduism; venerable, a preceptor.

haiku form—Japanese poetic form in 17 syllables, 5—7—5
Hanh—Vietnamese monk who writes inspirational books and leads a Buddhist movement
Happiness—our goal, yet in Buddhism it is raised to an esoteric level—(sukha)
harsh words—obstacle to enlightenment, karma that creates complications in our lives
heaviness—a feeling unsuitable for meditation
higher Self—a yoga concept, for which Buddha lead an empty, and pointless search
Hinayana—(Sanskrit) Lesser Vehicle, Southern Buddhism, as in fundamentalists
Hindrances—(nivarana) Mental and emotional obstacles to be removed to attain Knowledge, enlightenment: 1. desire, 2. anger, 3. sloth, 4. worry, 5. and doubt.
Home—an abstract concept relating to be present in the moment and true to oneself
Honest—asatha
humility—feeling of receptivity to the teachings of Buddhism, and pleasure in Sangha

Icon (vs. idol)—an image that operates as metaphor or reminder, vs. an holy object
idappaccayata—conditionality, the law of cause and effect—sources of suffering
identity—How we picture ourselves (compare to how others see us?)
Iddhis—(rishis) magician, mysticism, supernatural
ignorance—failure to recognize the potential of our own minds, lack of study—(avijja)
Impermanence—everything changes; this fact is often a cause of suffering—(anicca)
Immaterial—arupa—not physical
inborn trait—buddhahood, the personality associated with DNA or inheritance
incompletes—activities or duties that have been procrastinated
incubation—using the unconscious mind (in the frame of reference) to solve problems

infinite virtues—benevolence, compassion, giving happiness, impartiality

in front—parimukham

insight meditation—using mental objects (i.e. emotions or fears), sensations in the body as a focus for meditation—literally looking inside oneself—(vipassana)

Integrity—having a consistent personality and character all the time

Intended object—focus of meditation, either real or mental

intensity—when concentration is pleasurable and uplifting, feature of meditation

Interest—(dum pa Tibetan) first step in changing your life, pg 14

internal wholesome deeds—intentions

Intentions—what leads our decisions, our goals, sometimes subconscious—(sankappa)

Interconnectedness—Dalai Lama considers this an essential characteristic of humanity

Internal—ajjhatta

isometrics—metaphor relating to mental exercise and development

itikiraya—second guessing, questioning rumors

Jainism—religion contemporaneous with Buddha that is strictly atheist and ascetic

Jaramarana—aging and death; loss of identification with ego or self

jati—rebirth; arising of the sense of self

Jhana—(Sanskrit: Dhyana) States of concentration in meditation. The Buddha passed through successive jhanas before he reached enlightenment. Absorption

Joy—piti, somanassa

Kamacchanda—sensual desire

Kama—sensuality—relates to possessions, necessities, gems, jewelry, gold, and money, all sensations and thoughts including cravings for sexuality.

Kamma—volitional action, Intentional acts of body, speech and mind which result in becoming and birth. Also

Kammabhava—actions which condition rebirth; pattern of behavior, actions which condition life states or situations.

Kammaniya—or kammaniyo (activeness, readiness) Meaning 'fit for work'—associated with mental concentration—samadhi.

Kamasava—the outflow of sensual desire

Kamatanha—sensual craving

Kamupadana—clinging to the sense world, or sights, sounds, tastes, smells and bodily sensations.

Karate—(Japanese) empty hand; one of the Japanese martial arts

Karma—(Pali: kamma) action. Moral law of cause and effect in which good actions have good effects and bad actions have bad effects. A Hindu concept that was absorbed, largely unchanged into Buddhism (some don't teach previous lives.)

Karuna—(Sanskrit and Pali "compassion") An important virtue in all Buddhism, but especially emphasized in Mahayana.

Kaya—(Pali: group) the body, one of four proper objects of contemplation, made up of all five aggregates.

Kaya-sankhara—is using breathing or breath conditioning. (synonym: temporizing)

Kayanupassana—The first of the four objects of meditation, the body group, the kaya tetrad—contemplation of the body—kayagatasati

Kendo—(Japanese) the way of the swordsman; Japanese fencing

Kensho—(Japanese) to see into essential nature; Gnostic experience in Zen practice.

Khandha—Component or aggregate. Buddha taught that sentient beings do not have an eternal soul or self, but are the composite of five khandhas or aggregates: form, feeling, perception, volitional impulses, and consciousness.

Khanti—patient endurance

Ki—(Japanese) has source in, breath; spirit; spiritual strength

Kilesa—defilements—greed, anger, delusion, mental impurities, spoilants (staining)These are what soil, stain or defile the Heart making it impure and dirty.

Kinkin—(Japanese) sutra walking, right hand thumb enclosed against stomach by left; everyday actions are themselves sutras.

Knowledge—nana

koan—word puzzles used to teach and assess students progress; (Japanese) relative/absolute; an expression of harmony of empty oneness with the world of particulars; a theme of zazen to be made clear.

Ku—(Japanese) sky, sunyata, emptiness, the void

Kuan-yin—Chinese feminine bodhisattva of mercy and compassion. Derived from Avalokiteshvara, compassionate bodhisattva who is described in the Land of Bliss sutras as standing by the side of Amida to welcome the deceased to the afterlife. Source of many beautiful images. She is a popular object of devotion who plays a role similar to that of the Virgin Mary in Catholic Christianity.

Kundalini—yoga practice, to use mystical energies

Kusala—wholesome, skillful, good

kusali—much emphasis on meditation, no reflection on quality of experience or wisdom

Kushinagara—the place where Buddha died. Kushinagara is described as the place where Buddha attained nirvana.

Kwan Yin—a Bodhisattva who has the capacity to listen with great compassion.

Kyosaku—(Japanese) the flat stick carried by the Zen monitor during zazen.

Lama—Tibetan spiritual leader.

language game—concept popularized by Wittgenstein to describe jargon or sources of meaning out of the ordinary, i.e. the use of slang, and Dhamma language.

lantent tendency—anusaya

Law of Causation—Dependent arising. Also "dependent origination," "conditioned genesis," Key Buddhist doctrine that all appearances are interdependent and are based on decisions we make based on craving and desires that have consequences. Also paticca-samuppada. Deals with spatial and temporal issues among individuals and their environment

law of the world—how the world operates

Law of the Universe—dharma

liberation—is a generalized idea of enlightenment, elimination of suffering—(vimokkha)

life as an art form—the diligent exercise of life choices based on Buddhist teachings

lightning (metaphorically)—a sudden realization or inspiration

Limbic resonance—being in tune with others

lineage tradition—one of many formal teachings of Buddhism (i.e. Zen)

lobha—greed

logical reasoning—akaraparivitakka

Lo-han—Chinese term for arhant.

lokiya—living beneath the world, mundane, not transcendent

lokuttara—living above the world, being a lord of the world, transcendent, beyond defilements and attachment

longing—abhijappa

Lotus buds—Central symbol of Buddhism. Because the lotus grows in the mud but blooms untainted above the surface—it symbolizes those who overcome ignorance and attain enlightenment. It is used to signify the beauty of Dharma, and given as an offering as a metaphor for the impermanence of all things.

Lotus Sutra—An early and important Mahayana Sutra. Composed between the 1st century BCE and 2nd century CE. It presents itself as teachings of the historical Buddha but provides new interpretations of traditional beliefs. For instance, the Buddha is represented not as a mere mortal but a celestial being who teaches myriads of followers in a mythological paradise. Mystical poetry and restated in prose.

Loving kindness—metta

Lumbini—location of The Buddha's birth

Lust—raga

Magga—Fourth of the Four Noble Truths: The Noble Eightfold Path is the way to end suffering. Path or the four transcendent paths.

Mahaggata—great

Mahayana—(Sanskrit; "greater vehicle") School of Buddhism emphasizing a path to enlightenment that does not require monasticism and so is open to all. The Mahayana ideal is the bodhisattva, who, out of compassion, helps others—as opposed to the Arhat of Theravada Buddhism. The Mahayana school incorporates a variety of traditions, lifestyles, mysticism, and rituals, including the meditation-focused Zen and the devotional Pure Land Buddhism. also Tibetan

Mahamudra—means a total orgasm with the universe. The two are no more two.
Maitri—loving kindness for the world's populations
making merit—conducting rituals and compassion to cleanse and generate a better future
mamamkara—the notion of mine, selfish attachment
manasikara—attention
Mandalas—In Tibetan Buddhism, a symbolic and sacred representation of the universe. It most commonly features the five jhanas or Dhynani Buddhas.
Mantra—(Sanskrit, "mind protection") Syllables recited during meditation, chanting. Used in common language to suggest a slogan or motto; a spell.
Mara—personification of the temptations, and mental defilements
ma samano no garu ti—don't believe just because of charismatic teachers. Intellectual freedom. Even question the Buddha's teachings.
Matter—physical composition of Universe, solid stuff—material form—rupa
Maya—illusion
Mental afflictions—mental blocks—factors that limit our progress on the path
Mental application, initial—vitakka; sustained—vicara
Mental continuum—thinking patterns, but also our inherited tendencies
Mental object—dhamma
Merit—make merit by performing a good or charitable deed, engage the law of cause and effect in a good and positive way. (punna)
Meta-cognition—thinking about thinking, self-reflection about meditation
Metaphor—poetic or literary device that uses an image to substitute for the reality.
Method—naya
Metta—(Pali) Buddhist virtue, loving kindness, goodwill toward all beings. Friendliness
Miccha sati—wrong mindfulness
Middha—torpor—heat induced laziness

Middle Way—Monastic lifestyle advocated by the Buddha, which is midway between asceticism and the pursuit of pleasure. Characterization of Buddhism and dharma teaching of moderation in all things.

Mind—mano

Mindfulness—awareness, attentiveness, be present to what is happening. Central

teaching of many Buddhist schools in West. (sati)—to the body—(kayagatasati)

Misogynist—for example men who hate or despise women by refusing equality

Moha—is feeling infatuated because of not knowing an object as it really is. Doubtful, having hope, expectations, 'astray or lost' 'dark or dim' delusion.

mudita—sympathy, joy or to have a sense of gladness

mudra—(Sandskrit) seal, hand position that is symbolic

mudu—gentle and supple

muni—a silent one, a sage

mystical—a concept or belief that is not based on the scientific method

nadi—channels in the body along which the chakras are disposed, path of esoteric forces

Nagarjuna—philosophical monk (cir. 150 A.D.) who elaborated many teachings (koans)

Nagas—serpent kings, protectors, mythical instructors

nama—mind comes along with rupa (i.e. forms, things)—namarupa; the essence of form, invisible thing, mental formations based on perceptions

Namaste—blessing exchanged or given with hands together, Thai style

Namadhamma—mental properties or phenomena

Narrative representation—story that explains a presumed or exaggerated historical event

Naya—method, (deductive and inductive reasoning)

nayahetu—reasoning based on assumptions or hypotheses

neocortex—part of the brain

Neuronal pattern—connections in the brain that can be developed by habit

Neurons—nerves in the brain
Neurotransmitter—chemicals that travel in the brain as messengers
Nibbana—the state of liberation (Pali: nirvana) extinction of geed, hatred and delusion.The unbinding of the mind from mental effluents, the 10 fetters which bind it to rebirths. Cooling, ultimate peace.
Nimitta—A mental image—an imaginary object used in calming the mind. sign, cause
Nirodha—Cessation of suffering upon attainment of nirvana (third of Four Noble Truths.)
nirodhanupassana—quenching (not masking) of attachments, using breath to eliminate defilements and suffering
Nirvana—(Sanskrit, "to snuff out" extinguish))(Pali: Nibbana) Cool. Unbound. Liberation from suffering and samsara, in which all desire, passion, craving, hatred, and delusion is extinguished. In Thailand an icon of Buddha is washed with water containing flower pedals to symbolically cool the image and acknowledge enlightenment.
nivarana—Hinderances: five—1) feelings of sensuality, 2) aversion, 3) depression and drowsiness, 4) agitation and distraction, 5) doubt and uncertainty.
Noble—ariya; noble truth—ariyasacca
noetic science—new age teachings relating to esoteric or mystical aspect of Universe
"no immortal, immutable self or soul"—anatta
Nonconceptuality—pg. 17, not theorizing or making intuitive explanations, i.e. afterlives
Non-duality—mind is unified, not spirit and body, no bias no limitations
Non-returner—anagami
Not-self—anatta
numinous—greater than the sum of parts, mystical force or attribute
nutriment—ahara
Nying-jay—tibetan

object—idea or icon used for meditation
Objectification—cultural conditioning to turn people into objects, i.e. prostitution

Object meditation—using any concept image or icon as subject matter for meditation
Once returner—sakadagami
One-pointed—effortless transition into meditation or an intended object—(Ekaggata)
Ontology—the study or realization that life is a given, existence is evident not mystical
optical illusions—illustrations that can give more than one interpretation
Optimal—the very best procedure, skillful
Oral tradition—anussava
Osho—(Japanese) father, the priest's title
ovadapatimokkha—the summary of all exhortations: "Avoid evil, do good, purify the mind."

Paccayakara—inter-dependence—theme of the Dali Lama
Pali—The language thought to have been spoken by Gotama Buddha and his contemporaries. No longer in use except as preserved in the Buddhist doctrines. Taught to monks in Thailand and used as a measure of advancement.
Pamojjha—joy
Pandit—scholar too much in the head, learning, not enough practice
Panna—wisdom or spiritual knowledge
Pannavimutti—freedom by wisdom
Pantanjali—compiled Yoga Sutras, most ancient text on yoga philosophy
Papa—evil
paramasa—Fondling; touching; handling; adherence; contagion.
Paramita—(Sanskrit) perfection, buddhahood;
paramparaya—wariness, questioning traditions
Parideva—lamentation
Parinirvana—(Sanskrit) The death of one who is enlightened, never to be reborn again.
Parisuddho—(purity) a mind empty of defilements.
Paritta—Buddhist healing and blessing rite.
Partisanship—bias for a team, or devotion, sense of worth through association
Path of purity—following and showing the Buddhist teachings

Paticcasamuppada—the principle of Dependent Origination
patighanusaya—latent tendency to aversion; built into a habit of character trait
patimokkha—The code of monastic rules; the 227 rules for Buddhist monks that are usually recited every fortnight.
Passaddhi—tranquility
Passing away—atthagama, vaya
Pasture—gocara
Path—magga
Paticca samuppada—dependent co-arising
Patience—khanti
Patinissagganupassana—returning everything to which we were once attached
Patinissagga—letting go
Patthana—foundation, cause
Pattidana kusala—Sharing one's merit with others
Perfection—an unrealistic goal, often associated with nirvana
perfect freedom—choice, liberation
perfections, six: 1. giving [the basis for compassion], 2. ethical behavior, 3. patience, 4. diligence, 5. contemplation and 6. special insight. These comprise the standard training of a bodhisattva . . ." (Brown, pg. 484)
personal power—gained by having confidence and knowledge
phala—Fruition. Specifically, reaching any of the four transcendent paths (magga)
phassa—sense contact—ignorant sense experience
Phenomenology—ways of knowing observable phenomena, and the mind inside
pitakasampadamena—questioning writings, powers of discrimination
Piti—Contentment, excitement or disturbance at a conscious level, joy, pride
Pliability—state of mind that is amenable to change and control through meditation
Pleasant—sukha
Pliancy—mental capacity, factor that removes bad mental states and makes the mind an obstacle to meditation
Pointing-out—teaching style, as with koans, offering a lesson and having students determine the significance, relevance or truth

point of view—bias or preconceived idea, or simply a perspective
poisons—negative thoughts of others taken too seriously
positive mental factors—progress in meditation requires cultivation of . . .
possessiveness—inculcating the "I or mine" into objects
power—gala
Practitioner—someone who acts decisively toward Dharma, to stop doing bad
prajna-paramita—perfection of wisdom
Pratyekabuddha—the being who gains enlightenment by himself and for himself alone
Precepts—ideas and teachings of a doctrine, as in the Five Precepts, rules of conduct
Presence—upatthana
pride—being overly proud of oneself and one's own accomplishments, an hindrance
Protecting—internalizing, reviewing the learning gains made in meditation and comparing this to Dharma
proximate concentration
puggala—an individual; a person
punjas—is an Indian word for formal worship.
punna—good, meritorious
Pure Land Buddhism—Devotional form of Mahayana Buddhism holding that by faith in the grace of Amida, one will be reborn in the Pure Land realm. The Pure Land is a paradise (literally an afterlife state) that is so conducive to enlightenment—one can easily gain nirvana from there. Practice centers on devotion to Amida Buddha and the chanting of his name (nembutsu). The movement began in India, then spread to China and Japan. It is now the most popular form of Buddhism in Japan.
Purification—to eliminate and cleanse defilements or bad habits—(visuddhi)
'purified on the path'—improving step by step, overcoming defilements
put in order—looking at seemingly external appearances introspectively, such that one's perspective is transformed or rearranged
puthujjana—the unenlightened being, a worldling with defilements

radiant calm—be present fully with all the different changing experiences, equanimity

raga—(raja) lust for sexual pleasures or wealth, jewelry, gold, food, housing, or possessions that are considered attachments. Passion, Hindrance.

Raganusaya—latent raga, or lust until it has become a habit or character trait.

Rainbow body—The penultimate transitional state of meditation in which matter begins to be transformed into pure light. It is said to be the highest state of attainable in the realm of samsara before the "clear light' of Nirvana.

Rakan—Japanese word for arhat.

Ranto—Japanese egg-shaped tower on the tomb of a Zen monk.

Re-birth—each time we attach "I am . . ." and begin again during our daily lives.

Recollection—anussati

Reflection—introspection, self-evaluation

refuge—Traditional prayer, three refuges: Buddha, Dharma, Sangha. changes our state of consciousness

relative bodhicitta—working in a relationship of subject and object, comparison, involving aspiration and applications.

Remanifesting—recalling events as objects during meditation

residual basis nirvana—accomplishment during ones lifetime

right—samma

Right Action—samma kammanta

Right Concentration—samma Samadhi

Right Effort—samma vayama

Right Livelihood—samma ajiva

Right Mindfulness—samma sati (motivation)

Right Speech—samma vaca

Right Thought—samma sankappa

Right View—samma ditthi (understanding)

Rolling the Wheel of the Law—the Buddha's beginning of his teaching journey

Roshi—(Japanese) Zen spiritual, venerable teacher.

Rupa—corporeality, one of five aggregates, body form or condition both mental and physical, which make up existence, both gross and subtle.

rupadhamma—physical properties or phenomena
rupa-jhana—Meditative absorption in a single mental form or image.

Sabbai—Thai word for happiness, I was told that was what giving alms meant, making merit, early morning worship in Thailand; that is what it meant to this person.
Sacca—Truth; true, real.
Sacred—a numinous relationship with some icon
saddha—faith, "this is right" confidence born out of conviction. It signifies devotion to the Buddha, the Dhamma (Teaching) and the Sangha (The Order).
Sadhu—Well-done! a Sanskrit and Pali term used as an exclamation for something (i.e. dharma lesson) well done.
saha—world
Sakadagami—once-returner, second level of transcendent insight
Sakyamuni—"Sage of the Sakya tribe." Another name for the historical Buddha.
Sala—multipurpose room in a wat used for both teaching or meditation
Salayatana—the six sense bases
sasana—Buddha-sasana; Buddha-discipline, another name for Buddhism.
Samadhi—(Sanskrit. Pali; samatha) State of deep meditation and concentration. mental collectedness, and stability, one pointedness, absorption.
Samaditthi—Samahito (stability, collectedness) A mind that is firm, steady, undistracted, and focused on a single object. Right View
Samanas—recluse or mendicant, left home to pursue the Higher Life (brahmacariya)
Samara (samsara:Sanskrit, Pali "wandering") The cycle of death and rebirth, suffering.
struggle to get what we want to make us happy, in our lives of delusion.
Samasati—Right Mindfulness seventh step of the Eight
samatha—tranquility, calm
samisa—worldly
Samaya—vow to not abuse psychic power

sammatta—state of rightness

Sampajanna—Wisdom-in-action or ready comprehension, clarity of consciousness, clear comprehension, mindfulness. (clearly knowing—sampajana)

samsara—round of rebirth, perpetual wandering, reborn with 'I,' wheel of suffering

samsaravatta—the cycle of wandering, the round of rebirth

Samudaya—Second of Four Noble Truths: Suffering caused by desire; craving—arising.

Samudaya-sacca—is the truth of the cause of suffering

samyojana—fetter (ten) pg. 168

Sangha—(Sanskrit) The social or cultural community of Buddhist members. Harmony of Buddha and Dharma. Congregation, aggregate, fellowship; the Buddhist monastic order.

Sankhara—The single word sankhara can mean 'conditioning," or the subject of the conditioning, 'the concocter' as well as 'the concoction.' Kaya-sankhara is body conditioner. (synonym: temporizing) mental formations, one of five aggregates when referring to the thought and imagination in the mind.

sanna—perceptions, or sometimes for consciousness in its entirety, awareness of object's distinctive marks, ideas, objects of meditation. One of five aggregates—cognition when it is associated with the function of memory. Gives meaning and significance which colours all of ones personal perceptions.

sappurisa—worthy person

sarana—(Pali) shelter, home, refuge; freedom from conditioning

saranam gacchami—(Pali) undertake to find abode in; find freedom from conditioning

sarada—(Sanskrit) fresh, clever, skillful, proficient, cunning, learned, wise.

Sasana—meaning the teachings

Sassataditthi—belief in an (eternal) self

Sati—mindfulness or reflective awareness, recollection; that which facilitates and enables memories. Perhaps as much as 1/100 part of Buddhism.

Sati-panna—mindfulness and wisdom

Satipatthana—based on four foundations of meditation, pg. 112 This is a path of meditation that is intended to prepare the individual for enlightenment, similar to anapansati, but incorporating different techniques and sequence for contemplation. Presence of mindfulness.

Satori—Experience of enlightenment in Japanese or for Zen Buddhists.

Sawatdee—Thai greeting.

scanning practice—Looking over the body with the mind in meditation.

Seclusion—viveka

Seiza—(Japanese) quiet sitting; alternative posture sitting on ones folded legs

Sekha—learner, initiate: one who has attained any of the three lower levels of transcendent insight (sotapanna, sakadagami, anagami)

Self—Yoga concept of personal identity with a spiritual essence.

self-realization—fulfilling your own potential, or self-awareness

sem—mind in Tibetan, that which knows

Semantic field—a taxonomy or rendering of meaning as in a translation, synonyms.

Sense-bases—The objects and sources of perceptive stimuli. Sense sphere—ayatana

Sensei—(Japanese) teacher

Sensual desire—kamacchanda

Serenity—peacefulness and equanimity

Serotonin—chemical in the brain often associated with happiness, anti-depressant.

Sesshin—(Japanese) to touch, receive, convey the mind; Zen retreat, usually seven days

seven-points—cross legged meditation posture

Shakyamuni—The Buddha

Shinay (shamata)—meditation on nothingness, or calm-abiding, being at peace or tranquility (Tibetan)

Siddhartha—The Buddha's juvenile or given name.

Sign—nimitta—signless—animitta

Sila—"precepts," Basic obligations and pledge for Buddhists. Observance of morality, virtue of the Eightfold Path. Keep body and speech wholesome. Ethical conduct.

Silabbata—Rules and ceremonial observances.

Silabbataparamasa—clinging to particular rules and observances—hindrance

simultaneous mind meta-cognition, thinking and thinking about thinking.

skandha—(Sanskrit) group, see five aggregates.

skillful means—adept at following the Path, useful learning activities. (Kusala)

soka—sorrow

Solipsism—to confuse cause for effect, source for consequence.

sotopanna—Stream Enterer—into the Dharma, first stage of holiness

soul—abstract concept of the human character, personality, memory and self.

Soul-lessness—condition of humanity which often results in suffering.

spiritual practice—the development of a routine of meditation and self-improvement.

spiritual development—an abstract concept relating to knowledge of Dharma

spiteful scolding—nindarosa

splendid mind—receptive and wise person developing along the Path with equanimity.

spontaneity—Receptive to new ideas and willing to act at times without regard to others.

Sri Lanka—One of the original countries where Buddhism took root and persisted.

Standpoint—sdhitthana

State of mind—citta

straw-man argument Creating a false generalization in order to defeat the idea in debate.

Stream Enterer—mid-stage development of meditation and belief—(sotapanna)

Stupa—(Sanskrit) Monument containing relics, usually of the Buddha. A certain style or architectural shape, compare to chedi and pagoda.

Suan Mokkh—Monastery and retreat center located on the southern peninsula near Chaiya (Surat Thani) Thailand. Ten day retreats the first of each month.

Suffering—the consequence of living, impermanence, unsatisfactoriness, and

soullessness

Sukha—higher joy, tranquil, in step six of Anapanasati meditation, the essence of joy

sunnata—void of self-hood (see anatta, in opposition to the yoga "self") emptiness

Supernatural—beyond the realm of science, mythological or superstitious.

Sutra—(Sanskrit) Pali: Sutta; Discourse (sermons) of The Buddha or section of teachings.

Synapses—nerve connections in the brain, physiologically.

Takkahetu—challenge logics, takka, and be a freethinker

Tanha—craving or Desire as the cause of suffering

Tanha-upadana—craving and clinging

Tantra—Tantric Buddhism is derived from Indian thought. Tantrism is generally characterized by an emphasis on male-female polarity and sensuality. Vajrayana (Tibetan) is the Tantric form of Mahayana Buddhism.

Tantra Yoga—Source of extreme involvement in sensuality to teach djhana and loss of attachments.

Tamas—basis of all lack of feeling, dullness, ruthlessness, insensibility and inertia.

Taoism—Chinese teaching, which posits the emptiness, and essences of nature.

Tapa—to make hot or to burn, as in the practice of austerities to remove defilements.

Tathata—thusness, just like that; Tathagata (Sanskrit)—'Perfect One,' one who has come the full way.

tautology—absolutely true logically, or the same as.

Taxonomies—dividing a topic into categories, aspects to better explain or learn.

tears—crying, sign in meditation of compassion and/ or jhana

Technology—Man's mechanical, ideological, and sociological developments.

Tevijja—threefold higher knowledge

Teleology—The study of the why things happen, or the study of karma.
Theravada—"Tradition of the elders." Southern or Lesser Vehicle of Buddhism (also Hinayana.)
Theory—concept, hypothesis based on evidence, deduction
Thina—sloth, lazy
Thought—vitakka
Tilakkhana—Three Characteristics of existence: impermanence, suffering and not-self
time-space matrix of the ordinary mental continuum
Tipitaka—(Pali. Sanskrit; tripitaka "three baskets") The collection of Buddha's teachings, in three sections: sutra, vinaya (disciplines), and Abhidharma.
Ti Sarana Gamana—(Pali) Taking the Three Refuges; the ceremony of making one's home in Buddha, Dharma, and Sangha
Tonglen practice—Tibetan meditation to destroy defilements or negative emotions. Sending and taking, cleansing.
Torpor—laziness, or lackadaisical
tranquility—peace, impermanent, temporary resting place (seventh step) (passaddhi)
transcend—rise above defilements
Trishna—(Pali: tanha) a gnawing dissatisfaction, or 'thirst'
Truth—sacca

Ucchedaditthi—annihilationist view: vs. sassataditthi the eternalist view
Uddhacca—restlessness
Unattractive—asubha
unconscious—Fruedian concept, latent ideas or potentialities for action, plied by Tantric rituals.
Unification of the mind—cittassekaggata
Unity—ekatta
universal values—an idealized concept of absolute correctness or virtue
unpleasant—dukkha, unsatisfactory
unsurpassable—anuttara
unwholesome—akusala

unworldly—niramisa
upadana—relating to attachments—the source of suffering (raga), clinging, grasping
upapattibhava—state of rebirth in physical realm
upatthana—presence
upaya—(Sanskrit) appropriate, skillful means, elements of compassionate teaching
upayasa—despair
upekkha—equanimity, ethical quality belonging to sankhara-group. Indifferent feeling
uposatta days—were times when monks met on the full moon and new moon to confess
Utilitarianism Philsophical idea of "The most good for greatest number.'
utopia The ideal society or experiment with living in a wholesome group.
Utuniyama—natural law of cause and effect pertaining to the physical world, one of five niyama,

Vacisucarita vaci-sankhara—'verbal karma-formation' or verbal function. Right Speech, good conduct.
Vaisakha—the full moon of May, Death of Buddha commemorated
Vairochana—physical alignment in meditation posture known as Seven Points
Vajra—(Sanskrit; Tibetan rdo-rje, "diamond" or 'thunderbolt') Double-headed ritual instrument in Tibetan Buddhism used along with a ritual bell. The vajra is held in the right hand and represents skillful means, compassion, samsara, and the masculine principle.
Vajrayana—(Sanskrit "diamond vehicle") Esoteric form of Buddhism focused on attaining enlightenment more quickly (in one lifetime), combining Nahayana Buddhism and Hindu practices. Also know as Tantric Buddhism. Closely related to, but not synonymous with Tibetan Buddhism.
Vatta—cycle, related to mental formations
Vaya—passing away
Vayama—effort

Vedana—The complex of emotions and feelings that motivate and disturb us, or relax, sensation, one of five aggregates. Appreciation of sense data as pleasant, etc.
Vibhavatanha—craving for annihilation, to be rid of unpleasant situations.
Vicara—sustained mental application
Vicikiccha—doubt
Vikkhitta—distracted
Vimutta—liberated
Vinaya (Sanskrit and Pali) The Buddha's teachings, monastic rules, ethics, disciplines.
vinnana—fifth aggregate, consciousness
vipaka—Result, fruition, consequence of one's action.
Vipassana—insight meditation, clear seeing, deep and effective in curing the defilements. Insight which arises from wisdom and is based on a clear and quiet mind.
Vipassana Bhavana—mental development, penetrative seeing using the breath
Vipaka—results of kamma (vipakavatta—relating to cycle of rebirth)
viraga—without attachment, or the elimination of suffering. Fading away
viriya—energy
vision—dassana
vitakka—initial mental application
Viveka—Detachment, seclusion, bodily; mental or inner isolation from sensuous thing; and the absence of the five hindrances—utmost aloneness, perfect singleness, complete solitude
voice hearer—A person who hears the truth of the Wheel of the Law (illiterate?)
Volition—Will or citana. by free will; eliminating negative karma. (sankhara)
vow—A personal pledge that is often made to oneself for self improvement.

Wandering—The mind that is not focused or one pointed.
Wat—Buddhist temple in Thailand.
Well established—supatitthita

Wheel of Life Dhamma-cakka
Wholesome—kusala
Will—cetana, "turning of the Will" possibly testosterone, stubbornness
Wisdom—what we learn about the truth of living, the art of living—(panna)
Wordly—samisa
Worry—kukkucca
Wrong mindfulness—miccha sati
wu wei—natural flow of nature, Taoism, uncontrived, effortless flow of being.

Yama—Yama-deva are a kind of heavenly beings of the sensuous world.
Yoga—unify, to control and still the swirling currents of thought.
Yoga's God—Lord, similar to Hindu gods
'yokes, bonds'—is another name for the four cankers or cravings
Yoniso manasikara—wise attention, careful consideration, intellectual reflection.

zafu—(Japanese) sitting cushion; the cushion for zazen
Zazen—(Japanese) "sitting" "absorption" Sitting meditation, which is the basic meditation practice of Zen Buddhism.
Zen—(Japanese, "meditation") Branch of Mahayana Buddhism that focuses on meditation instead of doctrines or scriptures, developed in China as Ch'an Buddhism before spreading to Japan (and around the world.) dhyana; the harmony of empty oneness and the world of particulars
Zen sickness—ordinary life seems meaningless, people chase enlightenment, bliss, self-righteousness to distraction.
Zendo—(Japanese) Large hall in Zen monasteries in which zazen is practiced.

' ' ' '

Sixteen Steps for Contemplation

A Spiritual Practice by Achun Buddhadasa Bhikkhu—
Based on the *Four Foundations or supports of Mindfulness*

Anapanasati—Giving attention to in and out breathing as an object of meditation.
Vipassana-bhavana—The cultivation of insight or direct realization.

I. Relating to the body.

One Learning and using Long Breaths (the Breath-body—Pranayama)
Two Understanding how short breathing affects us.
Three To understand sankhara, the condition of the body by the breath, which replaces any consideration of a "soul." We see the conditioner, the condition, and the process of conditioning. [The breath being the cause of life.]
Four 1) Calming the body-conditioner—the breath-body.

1. Guard an image and
2) manipulate it.
3) The fourth technique is controlling the mental images as we wish.
4) Concentrating everything on this one point is the fifth of our skillful means.

You should practice [the four initial steps] until these steps require no effort and you have become well-versed in these activities." These should be repeated at the beginning of each practice session.

II. Feeling Tone / Emotions

Five "Step one of the second tetrad, 'experiencing piti' consists of contemplating piti (contentment) every time we breathe in and breath out . . . Find what this feeling is like.
Fully experience it. Is it heavy? Is it light? How coarse is it? How subtle? This is called "knowing its flavor." (Buddhadasa, 1988, pg. 59)

Six Focus on sukha (joy) as arising out of piti (contentment)... sukha does not simulate or excite; sukha is the agent that makes the citta tranquil . . . Usually piti obscures sukha, but when piti fades away, sukha remains. The coarse feeling gives way to calm. Taste the tranquil flavor of sukha with every inhalation and exhalation."

Seven Vedana—feelings: condition coarse thoughts and subtle thoughts. It is an art; practice the spiritual art of controlling piti and sukha so that they benefit our lives.

Eight Calming the mind conditioner while breathing in and breathing out—either by samadhi—a higher level of concentration; or by the wisdom—panna—method. We aim at the one pinnacled mind that has santi or Nibbana as its object. Panna (wisdom) realizes the true nature (characteristics, qualities, conditions) of all things to understand how piti arises and what will cause it to cease. Learning to control emotions, and dissipate negative emotions that cause or would create suffering.

III. Consciousness—Perceptions

Nine Examine mind (citta)—A feeling of *wanting, grasping is 1)raga.*
2) *Dosa* does not like, does not want, it is negative, pushing away (aversion).

3) *Moha* is ignorant. It does not know wrong and right, good and evil, running in circles. Get to know your mind: Is it superior—sharper or common? supreme—exalted or lacking yet to develop? Are we concentrated—samadhi?—or lacking focus? Is the mind liberated or grasping and clinging in attachment? Begin to understand our own minds.

Ten Allow the mind to rest in joy, delighted and content, supported by Dharma. Bask in joyfulness free of defilement (kilesa)."

Eleven To concentrate the mind—Samadhi. Having three distinct qualities.

Samahito—firm, steady, undistracted—focused on a single object. Stability, collectedness.
Parisuddho—purity A mind empty of defilements.
Kammaniyo—fit and supremely prepared to perform the duties of the mind. (not sleepy or tired.)

Twelve Liberation: not letting the mind become attached to anything 1) e.g. Sensuality, possessions, necessities, gems, jewelry, gold, or money etc. 2) Let go of opinions, beliefs, views, and theories (because of ignorance avijja). 3) Dismiss traditions, habits, obsessions, superstitions. 4) Release possessions as 'I' or 'mine.' *Let go* with in and out breaths. Identify hindrances and apply the breaths to these five: 1 feelings of sensuality, 2) aversion, 3) depression and drowsiness, 4) agitation and distraction, and 5) doubt and uncertainty. Further, eliminate greed, anger, delusions and defilements.

This is huge, to be reviewed every time one practices meditation.

IV: Objects of the Mind—Ideas about Dhamma

(Extraordinary Meditation)

Thirteen Contemplating *impermanence*—Realize the impermanence of each of the twelve preceding steps. There is the simultaneous realization of when impermanence is truly seen. It also has the characteristic of dukkham, namely: it is painful and unbearable (unsatisfactoriness.) We can also find the characteristic of not-self (*anatta*) in it. As these things are always changing, impermanent, unsatisfactory [thus sources of suffering,] and beyond our control, we realize anatta as well . . . We see they are void of self-hood, which is sunnata . . . Impermanence is just thus, just like that, thusness [a fact of all nature.]
And so, tathata is seen as well. The short phrase aniccanupassana (contemplating impermanence) includes the realization of unsatisfactoriness, not-self, voidness, thusness, and conditionality as well. (ontology)

Fourteen Dissolving, or viraga. Vi, in this case, means 'not' or 'not having.' Raga is another name for attachment [also upadana.] Watching attachment dissolve is like watching the stains in a cloth slowly fade away.

Fifteen Quench the fear of birth, aging, illness, and death. Quench the symptoms of dukkha, such as pain, sorrow, sadness, and despair. Quench the wants and desires of agreeable and disagreeable things. Finally, quench the view of any of the five khandha [aggregates] as 'self.'

Sixteen Contemplating throwing back . . . returning, everything to which we were once attached.

Lokiya living beneath the world—
lokuttara living above the world.